• • • • • • • • • • • • • • • • • • • •

NATIONAL TRUST GUIDE
MEETING PLANNER'S GUIDE
TO HISTORIC PLACES

NATIONAL TRUST GUIDE MEETING PLANNER'S GUIDE TO HISTORIC PLACES

Susan Reyburn

PRESERVATION
PRESS

JOHN WILEY & SONS, INC

New York • Chichester • Weinheim • Brisbane • Singapore • Toronto

This text is printed on acid-free paper.

Copyright © 1997 National Trust for Historic Preservation

Published by John Wiley & Sons, Inc.

Book design by Tenth Avenue Editions, Inc.
for John Wiley & Sons, Inc.

This publication is designed to provide accurate and authoritative information in regard to the subject matter covered. It is sold with the understanding that the publisher is not engaged in rendering legal, accounting, or other professional services. If legal advice or other expert assistance is required, the services of a competent professional person should be sought.

Library of Congress Cataloging in Publication Data:
Reyburn, Susan.
     National Trust guide meeting planner's guide to historic
  places / Susan Reyburn.
         p. cm.
     Includes index.
     ISBN 0-471-17891-8 (cloth: alk. paper)
     1. Convention facilities--United States--Guidebooks. 2. Historic
buildings--United States--Guidebooks. 3. Meetings--United States-
-Planning. I. National Trust for Historic Preservation in the
United States. II. Title.
TX907.2.R49   1997
647.9473--dc21   97-7478

Printed in the United States of America.

10 9 8 7 6 5 4 3 2 1

CONTENTS

Introduction

People have always needed places to gather for special occasions and business affairs, but in recent years there has been a significant increase in the number of corporate retreats, strategy sessions, workshops, and similar gatherings that are held off-site, with the expectation that a change of scenery will bring a freshness and vitality to the proceedings. More than ever, corporations, government agencies, associations, community and civic organizations, and other groups are looking for out-of-the-ordinary settings to conduct business activities that were once held in-house. Managers and planners have come to realize the value in gathering with employees and colleagues outside the office—even outside the city or state. Consequently, as more and more meetings occur off-site and groups look for interesting venues, meeting planners will have to increase their options and become more creative in their site selection. To assist planners and to further awareness of some of the notable treasures from America's past, the National Trust for Historic Preservation is pleased offer this first edition of the *Meeting Planner's Guide to Historic Places*.

Is This Book for You?

This is the first national guidebook to provide meeting planners, travel agents, party planners, and others with basic information on historic properties that are available for business meetings, social events, or both. Although this book is primarily aimed at professional meeting planners, caterers, party planners, and anyone interested in holding a group event—from a convention to a family reunion—at a historic property will find this guide valuable.

WHY GO TO A HISTORIC MEETING PLACE?

Groups looking for something unusual or special to add to their events will find that historic meeting places, with their old-fashioned charm, colorful stories, and links to the past can be the perfect gathering places. And while there may be a fax and a modem amid the antique furnishings, or modern conference facilities within an authentic colonial mansion, there is also a vivid acknowledgment of, and respect for, that which has shaped our cultural heritage. For many groups, meeting in a major city with its convenient transportation and cultural or recreational institutions at hand is sufficient, but add to that mix a historic setting and the event gains another valuable perspective. Likewise, meeting in a smaller historic town or out-of-the-way place can provide a welcome change of pace, as well as focus attention on some of the most inspiring celebrations of history the country has to offer. So whether you are looking for the ideal spot to conduct a memorable business meeting or to host a special reception, flip through these pages and let some of the mansions and mills, castles and cathedrals, ships and farms, hotels and opera houses from America's past offer you an invitation to meet with them.

SITES INCLUDED IN THIS GUIDE

The places listed in this guide were selected for their preservation of the past. More than 400 historic meeting places from across the country are included, from large resorts to small bed and breakfasts, from landmark hotels in busy downtown metropolitan centers to ranches and farms far removed from urban life. In many cases, well-known historical figures lived at or visited these places, and a number of the sites are associated with significant historic events. To be included, a property must be a least 50 years old and have maintained its architectural integrity and historical flavor. Many of the sites presented here have received specific designations testifying to their historical value, and many others are located in recognized historic districts, where they contribute to the area's valuable historical, architectural, and cultural settings. The entries are diverse in age as well, ranging from colonial taverns dating back to the seventeenth century to chic Art Deco hotels from the 1930s. What they have in common is their commitment to preserving—as much as possible in today's world—the architecture, the fashion, the furnishings, the atmosphere, the names, and the stories that make these places tangible connections to America's past.

ABOUT THIS GUIDE

Entries are listed alphabetically, by state and then by city. For each historic meeting place, there is a site description and table of information based on material provided to the National Trust by that site. The descriptive section highlights the history and architectural features of the site and generally provides information on the types of meeting space available or the functions that can be accommodated. There is also an overview of the types of guest rooms, dining options, and recreational facilities that are available, as well as nearby attractions. If your event or meeting requirements are unusual, however, do not hesitate to call a site that interests you—many places will be happy to make additional arrangements that will help to make your function a success, even if the site does not appear to be a perfect match at first glance. If a property has a particular historic designation, that information is also given following each description. Such designations include those listed here:

National Historic Landmark: The Secretary of the Interior grants landmark designation to those sites that are significant in a given field, are associated with notable figures and events, and whose original and intangible elements that contribute to its national significance are still intact. As of 1996 there were more than 2,200 National Historic Landmarks.

National Register of Historic Places: The National Historic Preservation Act of 1966 authorized the National Register of Historic Places as the nation's official list of historic places worth preserving. Sites in the National Register may be listed independently or as part of a designated historic district. As of 1996, more than 65,000 sites were listed.

Historic Hotels of America: The National Trust hotel marketing association comprises and promotes a select group of historic properties that are at least 50 years old, have maintained their historic integrity, architecture, and ambiance, and are listed in, or eligible for, the National Register of Historic Places, or are recognized locally as having historic significance.

National Trust for Historic Preservation Historic Sites: These sites are house museums and architecturally significant properties owned by the National Trust.

Listing in state and local historic registers, landmark, and historic marker programs.

Awards for historic preservation, restoration, and similar achievements.

The final section provides general information on the site's location, capacity, food service, limitations, and other features. But please note the following:

> **General information on location/directions** includes nearby airports, major travel routes, and distances to major cities in the area. Travel times are based on car travel unless otherwise noted.

> **Meeting space identified** is based on the maximum capacity per room style (such as conference or banquet style); total guest capacity may exceed that given if an event uses more than one room.

> **"Breakfast with room"** indicates that breakfast is included in the rates for overnight accommodations. "Modified American Plan" refers to breakfast and dinner included with room; "Full American Plan" refers to breakfast, lunch, and dinner with room.

> **Facilities open year-round** may not be open on a particular holiday, and the prices of meeting rooms and, particularly, guest rooms (although not listed here), may vary, depending on the season.

> **"Restrictions on smoking"** may mean that smoking is permitted only out-doors, or only in some areas indoors.

There may be a number of other limitations and restrictions on the use of meeting space, including details on decorations, music, contractual matters, and other items not included here. Those policies should be spelled out further by each site when you are booking an event.

Available on-site parking may be limited or difficult for large groups; we have made note of it where possible, but be sure to check when making plans.

Abbreviations for credit cards are as follows:

AmEx = American Express; DC = Diners Club; MC = Master Card.

ACKNOWLEDGMENTS

Many thanks go to Tracy Steeneck for her skillful management
of this project, and to Mary Billingsley, Sarah Cooke,
Michael Di Rienzo, Beth Kenny, and Scott Gerloff
for their assistance on this book.

ALABAMA

EUFAULA

KENDALL MANOR BED AND BREAKFAST INN

534 W. Broad Street, Eufaula, AL 36027
Phone: 334/687-8847   Fax: 334/616-0678

CONSTRUCTION of Kendall Manor began in 1860, but with the onset of the Civil War building came to a halt and it was not completed until 1872. Plantation owner James Turner Kendall, a successful dry goods merchant, hired local architect George Whipple to design the mansion and supervise construction. The Italian Renaissance style house has traces of several other architectural styles, perhaps as a result of the extended time needed for its completion. The majestic belvedere, with its rounded arch windows that opened to ventilate the house, also served as Kendall's observation tower, where he could watch boats carrying his business cargo arrive on the Chattahoochee River. Also of note are the mansion's 16-foot ceilings, gold leaf cornices, marble mantelpieces, and the etched ruby glass around the entrance doors. The manor is furnished with antiques and period furniture, including pieces original to the house. Group meeting space is available in the parlor, dining room, and breakfast room. A wraparound verandah and deck overlook the gardens, and an upstairs sitting porch allows visitors to relax and enjoy the elegance of this antebellum home. Lake Eufala, created in 1973 when the river was dammed, is just seven blocks away.

Kendall Manor

Listed in the National Register of Historic Places

Location: Kendall Manor is located two blocks from the intersection of Route 431 and US 82 and is on the Alabama-Georgia border, 52 miles southwest of Columbus, Georgia. Air service is a 1 hour drive away in Columbus and Dothan, Alabama, and 1.5 hours from Montgomery.
Function Space: 1,320 square feet; 3 rooms
Capacity—Conference: 40; Reception: 125; Banquet: 60
Equipment On-site: Slide projector and screen, overhead projector, fax, copier
Food Service: Breakfast with room; either in-house or outside catering available
Overnight Accommodations: 6 rooms
Limitations/Restrictions: No smoking; no children under 14; no pets
Access: On-site parking, open year-round
Payment: Check, credit card

MOBILE

RADISSON ADMIRAL SEMMES HOTEL
251 Government Street, Mobile, AL 36602
Phone: 334/432-8000   Fax: 334/405-5942
E-mail: Roominfo@adadmSemmes

ADMIRAL Raphael Semmes, for whom the hotel was named, is one of Alabama's most distinguished figures, a lawyer, writer, and editor who served as the only commander of the Confederate ship *Alabama*. Under his leadership the *Alabama* destroyed or captured 82 Union vessels before it sank in battle in 1864. Semmes survived and later became Admiral of the James River Fleet. In 1940, Mobile celebrated the opening of the Admiral Semmes Hotel, but with the 12-story building's construction occur-

ring toward the end of the Great Depression, its symmetrical brick facade was simple and restrained. However, the hotel's grand interiors—from the marble staircase and floors to the Art Deco brass elevator doors—made for a vivid contrast. Hurricane Frederick caused considerable damage to the building in 1979, but six years later the beautifully renovated and restored luxury hotel reopened. Meeting space includes a variety of function rooms, ranging from the splendid Crystal Ballroom to the handsomely appointed Directors Room. Located in the Conde Historic District, the Admiral Semmes Hotel is just two blocks from Mobile's civic center and is convenient to a number of museums. Other area attractions include Bellingrath Gardens and the USS *Alabama* Battleship Memorial Park.

Member of Historic Hotels of America

Location: The Radisson Admiral Semmes Hotel is accessible via I-10 and I-65, and is just 11 miles from the Mobile Regional Airport. Limousine, bus, and taxi service available.
Function Space: 5,850 square feet; 7 rooms
Capacity—Conference: 80; Reception: 450; Banquet: 300; Theater: 450
Equipment On-site: Audiovisual equipment available
Food Service: Catering/food service available; restaurant and lounge
Overnight Accommodations: 170 rooms
Limitations/Restrictions: Restrictions on smoking; all food and beverage service must be provided by hotel
Access: Handicapped accessible; on-site parking; open year-round
Payment: Cashier's check or major credit card

The Woman's Club

1200 Government Street, Mobile, AL 36606
Phone: 334/432-4452 Fax: 334/476-8484

ARCHITECT George B. Rogers, known for a number beautiful buildings in the area, designed this stately 1905 Greek Revival mansion in Mobile's Old Dauphin Way Historic District, one of the largest historic districts in the country. The house remained a private residence until 1929, when the Woman's Club purchased it for their clubhouse. Four hundred members strong, the group sought to promote the advancement of education, civic duty, art and literature, and community service, and among its founders was Bessie Bellingrath, owner of the famous Bellingrath Gardens. Today the house, with its Victorian decor, is available for meetings, banquets, weddings, receptions, and other gatherings. Groups may use the entire first floor, with its Great Hall (originally a ballroom), parlor and dining room, or individual rooms as needed. An upstairs sitting room is also available for meetings, and groups may tent the front yard as well. The club also provides lists of recommended vendors for all occasions and has plenty of tables and chairs on hand. The Woman's Club has been recognized by the Mobile Historic Development Commission for excellence in preservation and maintenance of a building.

Listed in the National Register of Historic Places

Location: Mobile is 2.5 hours east of New Orleans and 6 hours south of Atlanta and is accessible via I-10, I-65, Highway 90 and Highway 98. The Mobile Municipal Airport is 6 miles from the Woman's Club.
Function Space: In 3 rooms; or entire floor first can be rented
Capacity—Conference: 300; Reception: 300; Banquet: 160
Equipment On-site: Microphones, lectern, speakers, CD player
Food Service: Catering through the Woman's Club available, or client may use outside caterer; full kitchen available
Limitations/Restrictions: Restrictions on smoking
Access: On-site parking; open year-round
Payment: Cash, check

ALASKA

PALMER

COLONY INN

(Mailing address)
P.O. Box 118
(Street address)
325 E. Elmwood, Palmer, AK 99645
Phone: 907/745-3330   Fax: 907/746-3330

Location: Palmer is located 45 minutes northeast of Anchorage and is accessible via AK 1.
Function Space: 2 rooms
Capacity—Conference: 30; Reception: 100
Banquet: 30
Food Service: Catering/food service available; restaurant
Overnight Accommodations: 12 rooms
Limitations/Restrictions: No smoking
Access: Handicapped accessible; on-site parking; open year-round
Payment: Cash, check, credit card

IN 1935 more than 200 families from the drought-stricken Midwest arrived in Palmer to establish a farming community. The Matanuska Colony project was part of President Roosevelt's New Deal; not only did it prove a success, but farmers in the area are still known for producing huge vegetables. By 1936 a dormitory was built to house traveling teachers brought in to instruct local children, and a number of other facilities had sprung up as well, including a trading post, barber shop, bakery, and hospital. Today the restored Teachers' Dormitory is the Colony Inn, whose wooded, lodge-like exterior hints at the cozy rooms found inside. The individually decorated guest rooms are furnished with antiques, and most have whirlpool tubs as well. The great room and the dining room, with their original, beautiful wood paneling, are available for group meetings. The Colony Inn is located in the Matanuska Maid historic district, where it enjoys mountain views in the scenic Matanuska Valley. A self-guided walking tour of the town reveals both Palmer's Midwestern roots and its frontier character, as many of the original buildings remain.

Listed in the National Register of Historic Places

ARIZONA

PHOENIX

PUEBLO GRANDE MUSEUM
4619 E. Washington Street, Phoenix, AZ 85034-1909
Phone: 602/495-0901   Fax: 602/495-5645

PERHAPS one of the more unusual settings for a business meeting or social event is the Pueblo Grande Museum, a complex that encompasses the ruins of a Hohokam town dating back to A.D. 500–1450. The Hohokam people lived in southern and central Arizona beginning at about A.D. 1, building prosperous communities that often featured platform mounds and ballcourts. Excellent farmers, the Hohokam built hundreds of miles of irrigation canals to grow corn, beans, squash, and cotton. They also created beautiful red-on-buff pottery, textiles, and jewelry, as seen on display in the museum. Whether as a result of natural disasters or because of internal conflict, the Hohokam left the area around the mid-fifteenth century, and the town was in ruins when Spanish explorers arrived in the sixteenth century. At one time the town covered about 500 acres, and today 100 acres have been preserved. The Pueblo Grande Museum, adjacent to a platform mound, is the repository for materials and artifacts found during archeological projects conducted in Phoenix. Meetings, receptions, and other functions are held in the museum's community room, and groups can arrange in advance for site presentations and museum visits as part of their events.

Listed in the National Register of Historic Places

Location: The Pueblo Grande Museum is located in downtown Phoenix and is accessible via I-10 and Route 143. The museum is just minutes from Sky Harbor International Airport.
Function Space: 2,300 square feet; 1 room
Capacity—Conference: 100; Reception: 300; Banquet: 100; Theater: 200
Equipment On-site: Projection TV, slide and overhead projectors, public address system
Food Service: Food service must be provided by a licensed caterer; museum has caterers list available
Limitations/Restrictions: No smoking
Access: Handicapped accessible; on-site parking; open year-round
Payment: Check

PRESCOTT

HASSAYAMPA INN
122 East Gurley, Prescott, AZ 86301
Phone: 520/778-9434   Fax: 520/445-8590

THE Hassayampa Inn, named with an Indian word meaning "river that loses itself," was built in 1927 as "Prescott's Grand Hotel." Improved highways and the increase in automobile travel made the inn and Prescott a popular destination. Architect Harry Trost's Pueblo Art Deco facade was toned down to a simpler brick design in the early stages of construction at the request of local citizens to better suit their Midwestern sense of style, and the elegant lobby is known for its painted ceiling of Southwestern motifs. Cozy guest rooms are furnished with lace curtains and oak period furniture, and room rates include breakfast and a welcoming cocktail. The conference center with state-of-the-art equipment comprises six handsome meeting rooms available for both business and social events. All-day dining is available in the Hassayampa's acclaimed Peacock Room, known for its innovative entrées. Prescott enjoys cool, "mile-high" temperatures and beautiful pine-shaded scenery while offering a number of attractions and activities, including pioneer and Indian museums, golf, horseback riding, and hiking, and the world's oldest rodeo.

Listed in the National Register of Historic Places; member of Historic Hotels of America

Location: Prescott is less than two hours north of Phoenix and is accessible via I-17, Route 69, and Route 89.
Function Space: 3,000 square feet; 6 rooms
Capacity—Conference: 70; Reception: 120; Banquet: 110; Theater: 150
Equipment On-site: TV, VCR, slide and overhead projectors, flip chart, dataports available
Food Service: Breakfast with room; catering /food service available; restaurant
Overnight Accommodations: 68 rooms

Limitations/Restrictions: Restrictions on smoking; all catering provided by hotel; all alcoholic beverages must be purchased on-site
Access: Handicapped accessible; on-site parking; open year-round
Payment: Cash, check, credit card

SCOTTSDALE

MARRIOTT'S CAMELBACK INN RESORT, GOLF CLUB & SPA

5402 E. Lincoln Drive, Scottsdale, AZ 85253
Phone: 602/948-1700 or 800-24-CAMEL
Fax: 602/951-8469

WITH its distinctive Pueblo-style architecture, the Camelback Inn Resort is set on 125 acres of naturally landscaped desert. Surrounded by the Camelback and Mummy mountains, the resort was an immediate success when it opened in 1936 and became a popular destination for many

Hassayampa Inn

Marriott's Camelback Inn

of Hollywood's Golden Age celebrities. A wide variety of rooms are available for a full range of social and business events, including conventions, conferences, receptions, and exhibitions. The unique Board Room features a ceiling of hand-carved kiva logs, Native American artwork, and exceptional audiovisual facilities. Guests stay in Pueblo-style casitas with private patios or balconies; some suites even have private pools. A variety restaurants and lounges are available, including the Chaparral, which serves fine continental fare. A full-service resort, the Camelback offers a world-class European health spa, fitness and exercise facilities, two acclaimed 18-hole USGA championship golf courses, and numerous facilities for a variety of other sports. Other activities available nearby include desert jeep tours, hot air ballooning, river float trips, and horseback riding. The resort can also help meeting planners arrange special group activities and themed events.

Location: The Camelback Inn is 10 miles northeast of Phoenix Sky Harbor Airport in Paradise Valley, minutes from downtown Scottsdale and Phoenix, and is accessible via Squaw Peak Parkway (Route 51), I-10, and Loop 202.

Function Space: 40,000+ square feet; 24 rooms

Capacity—Conference: 750; Reception: 2,500; Banquet: 1,000; Theater: 1,500

Equipment On-site: Audiovisual equipment and business services

Food Service: Catering/food service available; six restaurants, lounge

Overnight Accommodations: 427 rooms

Limitations/Restrictions: Restrictions on smoking

Access: Handicapped accessible; on-site parking; open year-round

Payment: Cash, check, credit card (AmEx, Diners Club, MC, Visa)

TUCSON

THE LODGE ON THE DESERT

306 N. Alvernon Way, Tucson, AZ 85721
Phone: 520/325-3366   Fax: 520/327-5834

IN 1936, Cornelia and Homer Lininger converted this Spanish hacienda-style home, which had
been built five years earlier, into a lodge. The
facility has been a resort ever since, except during
World War II when it served as an apartment
hotel. Over the years the lodge has grown to
include dining rooms, patios, and lounges. The
spacious guest rooms—some actually made of
adobe—are decorated with hand-painted
Mexican tiles and authentic Monterey furniture,
and many even have mesquite-log-burning fireplaces. The lodge is a quiet oasis in the center of
Tucson, surrounded by palm trees and sprawling
lawns, with the Santa Catalina Mountains as its
backdrop. Rates include a continental breakfast,
and arrangements can be made for a memorable
Western barbecue dining experience. Its secluded
atmosphere and tranquil setting make the lodge a
quiet place for retreats and meetings, as well as for
receptions and other social gatherings. Two 18-hole
golf courses and 25 tennis courts are located nearby, and various Indian sites, historic Tombstone,
Arizona, and Mexico are convenient for day-trip
excursions.

Location: The Lodge on the Desert is located in
downtown Tuscon and is accessible via I-10.
Function Space: 2,200 square feet; 4 rooms
Capacity—Conference: 50; Reception: 150;
Banquet:100; Theater: 65
Equipment On-site: Slide projector and VCR
Food Service: Breakfast with room; catering/
food service available; restaurant
and lounge
Overnight Accommodations: 40 rooms
Limitations/Restrictions: Food and beverages
must be provided by the lodge
Access: Handicapped accessible; on-site
parking; open year-round
Payment: Direct billing to company, credit card

ARKANSAS

EUREKA SPRINGS

DAIRY HOLLOW HOUSE, COUNTRY INN AND RESTAURANT

515 Spring Street, Eureka Springs, AR 72632
Phone: 501/253-7444 or 800-562-8650
Fax: 501/253-7223

RENOWNED in the late nineteenth century for its natural springs, Eureka Springs today is a well-preserved community boasting both the beauty of the Ozarks and the Victorian era's charming architecture. And just a mile from historic downtown Eureka Springs is the award-winning Dairy Hollow House, which comprises two homes on either side of a wooded valley. The 1889 Farmhouse in the Hollow, tucked away from the road, and the lively Main House, a 1949 bungalow, have been carefully restored. Guest rooms feature Victorian or country furnishings, and each morning large breakfast baskets are delivered to the bedroom doors. With check-in comes a beverage and homemade cookies; other amenities include a hot tub above the garden and a porch lined with rockers. A meeting room is available for business and social functions, and the country setting makes for a peaceful getaway to do business or celebrate. The inn's Restaurant at Dairy Hollow specializes in "Noveau 'Zarks" cuisine, a combination of classic French and regional ingredients. Silver Dollar City, the Passion Play of the Ozarks, and outdoor activities are all nearby, and guests can peruse the inn's clever Moos-Letter for details on other events as well.

Location: Eureka Springs is located 50 miles northeast of Fayetteville and is accessible via Highway 62 and Highway 23.
Function Space: 740 square feet; 1 room
Capacity—Conference: 40; Reception: 50; Banquet: 45
Equipment On-site: Fax and photocopier available
Food Service: Breakfast with room; catering/food service available
Overnight Accommodations: 6 rooms
Limitations/Restrictions: No smoking
Access: Handicapped accessible (meeting room only); on-site parking; open February–December
Payment: Check or major credit card

LITTLE ROCK

THE CAPITAL HOTEL

111 W. Markham Street, Little Rock, AR 72201
Phone: 501/374-7474   Fax: 501/370-7091

AFTER a fire destroyed the Metropolitan, Little Rock's most prominent hotel, the downtown Denckla building was converted into a first class hotel in 1876. The Capital Hotel's ornamental cast-iron facade was preassembled and bolted to the building, giving the plain original structure a strikingly handsome appearance. Located a block from the historic Old State House building, the Capital Hotel was soon the scene for many a political deal, and it became a favorite with political officials and international journalists during Bill Clinton's 1992 presidential campaign. The award-winning hotel was beautifully restored during the 1980s, and the lobby features a lovely stained glass ceiling, colonnaded mezzanine, mosaic tile floor, and grand marble staircase. Elegant meeting facilities, ranging from a small private meeting room for

10 to the mezzanine foyer and balcony area, are available for business and social events, and guest rooms are comfortably furnished with an old Southern touch. Also on-site is Ashley's Restaurant, highly regarded for its hearty regional specialties and continental cuisine, and the Capital Bar.

Listed in the National Register of Historic Places

Location: The Capital Hotel is located in downtown Little Rock and is accessible via I-30, I-40, and Highway 10.
Function Space: 3,860 square feet; 5 rooms
Capacity—Conference: 36; Reception: 225; Banquet: 100; Theater: 90
Equipment On-site: Audiovisual equipment, fax and photocopying available
Food Service: Catering/food service available; restaurant and bar
Overnight Accommodations: 123 rooms
Limitations/Restrictions: Alcohol must be purchased on site and cannot be taken off premises; no pets except for handicapped assistance
Access: Handicapped accessible; on-site parking; open year-round
Payment: Cash, credit card, or billing on approval

VILLA MARRE

Quapaw Quarter Association
(Mailing address)
P.O. Box 165023
(Street address)
1321 S. Scott Street, Little Rock, AR 72202
Phone: 501/374-9979 Fax: 501/374-8142

LOCATED in the MacArthur Park Historic District, Villa Marre is a gracious Victorian mansion whose exterior has been seen by millions in the television series *Designing Women*. The mansion, which combines Italianate and Second Empire architectural styles, was built in 1881 for saloon keeper Angelo Marre, an Italian immigrant, and his wife, Jennie. After Marre's death in 1889, the Villa was rented to Governor Jeff Davis, and from 1905 until the early 1930s the Edgar Burton Kinsworthy family owned the house. Preservationists rescued the house from demolition in 1964, and Villa Marre was restored to its original splendor. Today the mansion is a lovely house museum offering visitors a look at late nineteenth-century life. The first floor of the house, including the elegant dining room and parlor, is available for meetings and special events. During the Christmas season the house features Victorian decorations. The mansion is located in downtown Little Rock near the Governor's Mansion Historic District in the Quapaw Quarter.

Listed in the National Register of Historic Places; Quapaw Quarter Historic Structure

Location: The Villa Marre is accessible via I-40 and I-30 and is within six blocks of interstate access; the house is also within 10 minutes of Little Rock National Airport.

Function Space: 1,500 square feet; 4 rooms

Capacity—Conference: 40; Reception: 150 (using four main rooms of house); Banquet: 40; Theater: 50

Equipment On-site: Slide projector and screen

Food Service: Catering/food service available

Limitations/Restrictions: No smoking

Access: Handicapped accessible (first floor only); on-site parking; open year-round

Payment: Cash, check

Villa Marre

CALIFORNIA

BELMONT

RALSTON HALL

1500 Ralston Avenue, Belmont, CA 94002
Phone: 415/508-3501   Fax: 415/637-0493

A magnificent Italianate villa on the College of Notre Dame campus, Ralston Hall was built in 1868 as a summer showplace for Bank of America founder William Chapman Ralston. San Francisco's mid-nineteenth-century boom followed the discovery of gold, and many of the city's wealthy entrepreneurs engaged in lavish building projects. In 1864 Ralston purchased the Cipriani estate in the southern San Francisco Peninsula and set about improving the original structure. He hired architect John P. Gaynor to create a palatial mansion for entertaining. Many of the villa's original features remain today, including crystal chandeliers hanging from molded ceilings, period furniture, skylights, and mirrors. The bright, spacious rooms feature inlaid wood floors and tall windows, some with etched, frosted panes, creating an airy and refined atmosphere. The entire first floor or separate wings are available for business meetings, luncheons, workshops, and seminars. Weddings, receptions, and other events can be held either indoors or out, and the formal grounds and terraced gardens can be tented for events as well.

National Historic Landmark; listed in the National Register of Historic Places

Location: Belmont is 25 miles south of San Francisco on US 101 and 15 miles south of San Francisco International Airport; direct rail and bus service to Belmont available.
Function Space: 4,530 square feet; 3 rooms
Capacity—Conference: 175; Reception: 150; Banquet: 110 Theater: 210
Equipment On-site: TV, VCR, overhead projector, podium with microphone
Food Service: Renter selects from approved list of caterers
Limitations/Restrictions: No smoking; no balloons, no lighted candles; insurance by the renter is required
Access: Handicapped accessible (first floor); on-site parking (limited); open year-round
Payment: Check

Ralston Hall *(Michael Collopy)*

BURLINGAME

KOHL MANSION—"THE OAKS"

2750 Adeline Drive, Burlingame, CA 94010
Phone: 415/992-4668   Fax: 415/342-1704

SET on 40 oak-filled acres not far from San Francisco Bay, the Kohl Mansion was built in 1914, but its owners, Frederick and Bessie Kohl, lived there only until 1916, when they separated. The mansion was the setting for the 1921 film classic *Little Lord Fauntleroy*, starring Mary Pickford. The Sisters of Mercy purchased the estate in 1924 for use as a convent, and since 1931 it has been the campus of Mercy High School. The impressive 63-room Tudor-style mansion, built of rose bricks shipped from England and around Cape Horn, features a Great Hall with a 40-foot-high arched ceiling and a walnut floor. When it was built, the house was also outfitted with an elevator and a chapel for Bessie. The grounds included a tennis court, a sunken garden, a large carriage house, and a 150,000-gallon reservoir. Today the mansion hosts corporate events, weddings, parties, and filming. The Great Hall, the spacious and airy dining room, the morning room overlooking the rose garden, and the library, with its richly paneled walls and marble fireplace, are all available for rent, as are the grounds.

National Historic Landmark; listed in the National Register of Historic Places

Location: The Kohl Mansion is eight minutes south of San Francisco International Airport and five minutes north of San Mateo. The mansion is accessible via US 101, Highway 280, and Route 92.

Function Space: 4,000 square feet; 5 rooms
Capacity—250 seated guests inside; 450 seated guests outside
Food Service: Catering/food service available
Limitations/Restrictions: No smoking indoors
Access: Handicapped accessible; on-site parking, open year-round
Payment: Check

CARMEL

LA PLAYA HOTEL

(Mailing address)
P.O. Box 900
(Street address)
Eighth Avenue and Camino Real
Carmel, CA 93921
Phone: 408/624-6476   Fax: 408/624-7966

IN 1904, Norwegian artist Christopher Jorgensen, known for his paintings of California missions and landscapes, completed his luxurious stone mansion—partly inspired by mission architecture, but also equipped with Carmel's first swimming pool. The Jorgensens later sold the property to Agnes Signor, who turned the mansion into a hotel. During the 1920s the mansion was connected to a new building, which comprises most of La Playa's guest rooms today. As the grande dame of Carmel-by-the-Sea, the hotel continued to expand over the years, taking on a Mediterranean appearance. In 1984, La Playa was restored and refurbished, and today the hotel's decor is an elegant mix of European antiques and California memorabilia. The comfortable guest rooms feature hand-carved furnishings with a mermaid motif and boast views of the ocean, residential Carmel, and La Playa's extensive, lush gardens and landscaped patios. Five private, beautifully appointed function rooms, each with an ocean or garden view, are available for business or social events. La Playa is just two blocks from the beach, four blocks from Carmel's boutiques, and just minutes from world-famous Seventeen Mile Drive.

Member of Historic Hotels of America

Location: La Playa is located in the heart of Carmel, accessible via Highway 1 and US 101. Monterey Airport is just minutes away, and San Francisco International Airport is two hours away.
Function Space: 5,000 square feet; 5 rooms
Capacity—Conference: 60; Reception: 100; Banquet: 100; Theater: 120
Equipment On-site: Audiovisual equipment available through outside source
Food Service: Catering/food service available; restaurant, lounge, room service
Overnight Accommodations: 80 rooms
Limitations/Restrictions: Restrictions on smoking; no outside food and beverage service; approved music vendors only
Access: Handicapped accessible; on-site parking; open year-round
Payment: Credit card, direct billing

La Playa Hotel

COLUMBIA

COLUMBIA CITY HOTEL

(Mailing address)
P.O. Box 1870
(Street address)
Main Street
Columbia State Historic Park
Columbia, CA 95310
Phone: 209/532-1479
Fax: 209/532-7027
E-Mail: Info@cityhotel.com
http://www.cityhotel.com

ONE of the largest mining towns in Gold Rush California, Columbia is one of the best preserved as well. The Columbia State Historic Park encompasses a 12-block district featuring a number of mid-nineteenth-century buildings, including the City Hotel, which was built in 1856. The two-story hotel on tree-lined Main Street is furnished with antiques, and an award-winning restoration has enhanced its Gold Rush atmosphere. Rates include a generous buffet breakfast, and the hotel's acclaimed restaurant serves a seasonally changing menu emphasizing local ingredients cooked with a French flair. Wines from the Sierra Foothills wine-growing region are featured on the wine list. The What Cheer Saloon, with its original cherry wood bar shipped around the Horn from New England, is named for the hotel's original moniker. Throughout the year the City Hotel hosts a number of special events and welcomes groups meeting for business or social functions. Wonderful sightseeing opportunities are available in the park, as well as a chance to pan for gold or to take a stagecoach ride. Visitors can also tour nearby caverns, vineyards, and the scenic Gold Country.

Listed in the National Register of Historic Places

Location: Columbia State Park is 140 miles east of San Francisco, one hour east of Stockton, five minutes north of Sonora, and 2 miles off Highway 49. Columbia's airport is 1 mile west of town, and Oakland International Airport is two hours west via Highways 580, 205, and 120.
Function Space: 2,500 square feet; 3 rooms
Capacity—Conference: 75; Reception: 75; Banquet: 60; Theater: 200+ (in nearby historic hall)
Equipment On-site: TV, video, screen; fax, copier, computer, e-mail access available
Food Service: Breakfast with room; catering/food service available; restaurant and bar
Overnight Accommodations: 24 rooms
Limitations/Restrictions: No smoking
Access: On-site parking; open year-round
Payment: Business check

CORONADO

HOTEL DEL CORONADO
1500 Orange Avenue, Coronado, CA 92118
Phone: 619/522-8000 or 800-HOTEL DEL (Reservations); 619/522-8011 or 800-758-4333 (Sales Department) Fax: 619/522-8239

ONE of the world's largest wooden structures, the Hotel del Coronado opened in 1888, fulfilling railroad tycoon Elisha Babcock's dream of building a resort that would become "the talk of the Western World." The Del, as this dazzling Victorian masterpiece is also known, was built on the islandlike Coronado peninsula, across the bay from San Diego, and Thomas Edison is reported to have personally supervised the electric light installation. The hotel's distinctive white facade, red conical roofs, and spectacular seaside surroundings have made it one of the most famous hotels in the nation, as well as a popular film location, most notably as seen in the 1959 classic *Some Like It Hot*, starring Marilyn

Columbia City Hotel

Carter House Victorians *(John Swain)*

Monroe. Over the years, the Del has welcomed 14 U.S. presidents and numerous celebrities, including the Prince of Wales—later Edward VIII—who may very well have met Wallace Simpson for the first time in the hotel's ballroom. Extensive function space is available for a variety of business and social events, including the oceanfront ballroom and a range of meeting and banquet rooms. A full-service destination resort, the Del offers a variety of dining options, recreational facilities, shops and boutiques; a championship golf course, boat house, and marina are nearby as well.

National Historic Landmark; listed in the National Register of Historic Places; member of Historic Hotels of America; California Historic Landmark

Location: Coronado is a 5.3-square-mile peninsula connected to the city of San Diego by a 2.3-mile bridge. The island is 14 miles from San Diego International Airport, 120 miles south of Los Angeles, and 16 miles north of Tijuana, Mexico.
Function Space: 62,000 square feet; 45 rooms
Capacity—Conference: 125; Reception: 1,200; Banquet: 1,200; Theater: 1,200
Equipment On-site: Audiovisual equipment available, business center
Food Service: Catering/food service; nine restaurants and lounges, room service
Overnight Accommodations: 691 rooms
Limitations/Restrictions: Restrictions on smoking; no outside food or beverage service permitted
Access: Handicapped accessible; on-site parking; open year-round
Payment: Cash, check, credit card

EUREKA

THE CARTER HOUSE VICTORIANS

301 L Street, Eureka, CA 95501
Phone: 707/444-8062   Fax: 707/444-8067

KNOWN for its lumber and fishing industries, Eureka overlooks the deep blue Pacific and is bounded by ancient redwood forests. This Northern California city is also known for its rich Victorian heritage, and perfect examples can be found at the award-winning inn known as the Carter House Victorians. The complex comprises three structures, Belle Cottage (1889) and two others built from nineteenth-century plans, the Hotel Carter (1986) and Carter House (1982), each situated a short walk from Humboldt Bay. The interiors are richly furnished and accentuated with fresh flowers and original local art; the guest rooms feature luxurious appointments as well—marble fireplaces, four-poster beds, and whirlpools with views of the marina. Rates include complimentary wine and hors d'oeuvres in the evening, a late night snack, and a full breakfast. Space is available in each of the three facilities for business meetings and social functions. The Carter House's Restaurant 301 offers a wide-ranging menu including seasonal seafood and ingredients from the inn's garden, which grows more than 300 varieties of herbs, greens, fruits, and vegetables. A stroll into Old Town Eureka leads to quaint boutiques, museums, antique shops, restaurants, and more.

Location: Eureka is five hours north of San Francisco and two hours south of the Oregon border off US Highway 101. Arcata Airport is 15 miles north.
Function Space: 1,000 square feet; 3 rooms
Capacity—Conference: 60; Reception: 75; Banquet: 80; Theater: 60

Equipment On-site: Audiovisual equipment and business services available
Food Service: Breakfast with room; restaurant
Overnight Accommodations: 31 rooms
Limitations/Restrictions: No smoking; outside food and beverages may not be brought in
Access: Handicapped accessible; on-site parking; open year-round
Payment: Cash, check, credit card

THE EUREKA INN

518 Seventh Street, Eureka, CA 95501
Phone: 707/442-6441   Fax: 707/442-0637

SINCE 1922, the Eureka Inn has been a North Coast landmark in this center of industrial and agricultural commerce, surrounded by towering redwood forests and ruggedly beautiful beaches. The inn is a distinctive blend of English Tudor and contemporary design, and its builders made generous use of the local redwood in its construction. The Grand Lobby exhibits an Old World style

The Eureka Inn

with its high ceiling of polished redwood beams and baronial half-timbering, crystal chandeliers, and massive brick fireplace. Four function rooms, including the stylish Colonnade Room, are well suited for business meetings, conferences, receptions, and banquets. Guest accommodations are spacious and comfortably furnished, and amenities include VIP and business services, saunas and a pool, and a complimentary morning newspaper. A variety of dining options are available at the inn, ranging from fine dining in the Rib Room to the lively atmosphere of the Rathskeller pub. Through the years the inn has hosted a number of dignitaries, including Winston Churchill, Presidents Hoover, Ford, and Reagan, and celebrities such as Stan Laurel and Oliver Hardy, Bill Cosby, and Mickey Mantle.

Listed in the National Register of Historic Places; member of Historic Hotels of America

Location: Eureka is five hours north of San Francisco and two hours south of the Oregon border off US Highway 101. Arcata Airport is 15 miles north.
Function Space: 6,011 square feet; 4 rooms
Capacity—Conference: 80; Reception: 500; Banquet: 300; Theater: 400
Equipment On-site: Audiovisual equipment and basic business services available
Food Service: Catering/food service available; two restaurants, pub, lounge, room service
Overnight Accommodations: 105 rooms
Access: Handicapped accessible; on-site parking; open year-round
Payment: Cash, check, credit card

GEORGETOWN

HISTORIC AMERICAN RIVER INN

(Mailing address)
P.O. Box 43
(Street address)
Orleans and Main, Georgetown, CA 95634
Phone: 800-245-6566   Fax: 916/333-9253

SET in the stunning foothills of the Sierra Nevada in El Dorado County, the American River Inn was a stagecoach stop that served the area's mid-nineteenth-century mining camps. By 1853, when the inn was built, $2 million in gold had been mined in historic Georgetown, and the most famous find of all was a 126-ounce nugget from the nearby Woodside Mine. Fire damaged the inn in 1899, but by popular demand it was rebuilt, and it continues to welcome visitors with their own exploring to do. The inn features country Victorian and turn-of-the-century decor, and the grounds include a Victorian garden and dove aviary. Guests can take a dip in the mountain stream pool or relax in the gardens playing bocce ball, croquet, horseshoes, and other games; the inn also provides bicycles for rides through the scenic Gold Country, and the innkeepers can arrange white-water rafting and hot air balloon trips. Rates include a full breakfast, and hors d'oeuvres and local El Dorado wines are served in the parlor in the afternoon. Banquet and meeting facilities are available for weddings, retreats, and other gatherings.

Location: Georgetown is 50 miles northeast of Sacramento, between I-80 and Highway 50 via Highway 49.
Function Space: 980 square feet; 1 room
Capacity—Conference: 40; Reception: 50; Banquet: 35; Theater: 50

Equipment On-site: VCR, overhead projector, fax, flip charts, computer/phone line
Food Service: Breakfast with room; catering and food service available
Overnight Accommodations: 25 rooms
Access: On-site parking, open year-round
Payment: Corporate check or credit card

HEALDSBURG

CAMELLIA INN
211 North Street, Healdsburg, CA 95448
Phone: 707/433-8182 or 800-727-8182
Fax: 707/433-8130
E-mail: info@camelliainn.com
http://www.camelliainn.com

Many of the more than 50 varieties of camellias surrounding the Camellia Inn and its villa-style swimming pool are between 50 and 100 years old. The Italianate house was built in 1869 by Ransome Powell, and the arched windows and round-arched doorway and porch enhance its redwood facade. Dr. J. Walter Seawell purchased the house in 1892 for use as his home, office, and, later, the town's first hospital. The elegant inn, with its heavily carved crown molding, double parlors with twin marble fireplaces, and inlaid hardwood floors, is available for meetings and retreats, and guests may also use the solarium, which overlooks the courtyard. Guest rooms are individually furnished with antiques, and rates include a hearty breakfast and afternoon refreshments. The inn, located within walking distance of many fine restaurants and shops, is also convenient to the Russian River and its many recreational opportunities. Sixty wineries, Lake Sonoma, redwood forests, and the coast are just a short drive away. The Healdsburg Historical Society has recognized

the Camellia Inn as an excellent example of historic preservation and maintenance.

Location: Healdsburg is 70 miles north of San Francisco on US Highway 101.
Function Space: 900 square feet; 3 rooms
Capacity—Conference: 25; Reception: 50; Banquet: 25
Equipment On-site: Tables and chairs included in rental; easel, overhead projector additional; fax, jacks in meeting room
Food Service: Breakfast with room; renter selects caterer; beverages included in rental; refrigerator available
Overnight Accommodations: 9 rooms
Limitations/Restrictions: Smoking outside only; food and beverage service must be arranged through inn in advance
Access: Handicapped accessible (limited); on-site parking; open year-round
Payment: Check, credit card (MC, Visa)

HOLLYWOOD

HOLLYWOOD ROOSEVELT HOTEL
7000 Hollywood Boulevard, Hollywood, CA 90028
Phone: 213/466-7000 or 800-950-7667 (reservations)
Fax: 213/462-8056

FEW establishments can rival the glamorous past of the Hollywood Roosevelt Hotel, a favorite gathering place for stars of the silver screen during Hollywood's Golden Age. In 1927 real estate magnate Charles E. Toberman, hoping to draw together the leading members of the film industry in a fashionable setting, opened this classic Spanish revival hotel named for President Theodore Roosevelt. Two years later, Douglas Fairbanks hosted the first Academy Awards ceremony in the now-famous Blossom Room, and the Cinegrill lounge continues to be popular with celebrities. The hotel's luxurious interior is particularly well expressed in the beautiful lobby, with its hand-painted ceiling, classical archways, and large potted palms. Hotel facilities can easily accommodate groups of 6 to 800 for meetings, receptions, and other occasions. Surrounded by Hollywood landmarks, the hotel is just a short walk away from historic Mann's Chinese Theatre, and the "Walk of Fame," a strip of granite stars honoring film and music legends, passes right outside the hotel's front entrance.

Location: The Hollywood Roosevelt Hotel is 6 miles from downtown Los Angeles, 13 miles from Los Angeles International Airport, and is accessible via I-10, US 101, I-5, and the San Diego Freeway (405).
Function Space: 12,200 square feet; 9 rooms
Capacity—Conference: 200; Reception: 800; Banquet: 300; Theater: 400
Equipment On-site: Audiovisual equipment available through outside vendor (hotel will arrange); fax and photocopiers available through front office
Food Service: Catering, restaurant, lounge, room service

Overnight Accommodations: 320 rooms
Access: Handicapped accessible; on-site parking; open year-round
Payment: Credit card (MC, Visa)

JAMESTOWN

HISTORIC NATIONAL HOTEL—BED AND BREAKFAST
(Mailing address)
P.O. Box 502
(Street address)
77 Main Street, Jamestown, CA 95327
Phone: 209/984-3446   Fax: 209/984-5620

SET in the heart of historic Jamestown, the National Hotel offers a charming return to the glory days of California's gold-mining past. Established in 1859, the National is one of the oldest continuously operated hotels in the country. Restored guest rooms feature brass beds, patchwork quilts, and lace curtains, and most of the furnishings are original. Visitors can enjoy gourmet restaurant dining or belly up to the Gold Rush Saloon's original nineteenth-century bar. Guest room rates include a hearty continental breakfast, and guests can also order a picnic basket to take along while exploring the area's historic Gold Rush towns, caverns, and parks. The National's award-winning Gold Country wine list offers excellent selections, including many produced at nearby wineries. On Jamestown's Main Street, guests can pick up tips on gold panning and prospecting, or visit the many local antique shops. The hotel is especially well suited for luncheons, banquets, small meetings, seminars, and receptions, and all 11 rooms may be booked for private parties.

Little River Inn

Listed in the National Register of Historic Places

Location: Jamestown is located just south of Sonora at Routes 108 and 49, one hour northeast of Modesto and an hour and 15 minutes from Stockton, which provides commercial airline service. Small plane service available at Columbia Airport, 10 minutes away. Taxi service available.
Function Space: 500 square feet; 1 room
Capacity—Conference: 30; Reception: 75; Banquet: 45
Equipment On-site: Tables and chairs included in rental
Food Service: Breakfast with room; restaurant, bar
Overnight Accommodations: 11 rooms
Limitations/Restrictions: Restrictions on smoking
Access: Open year-round
Payment: Cash, credit card (Discover, MC, Visa)

LITTLE RIVER

LITTLE RIVER INN

(Mailing address)
P.O. Box B
(Street address)
7751 N. Highway One, Little River, CA 95456
Phone: 707/937-5942   Fax: 707/937-3944

OVERLOOKING the rocky shore and the Pacific Ocean, the Little River Inn is a beautiful coastal resort on world-famous scenic Highway 1. The seaside inn was built as a family home in 1853, and today the fourth and fifth generations are active in the resort's operation. Set on 225 acres, the inn lies nestled between a thick forest of trees and the deep blue Pacific. All guest rooms feature spectacular ocean views, and visi-

tors enjoy country dining in the garden-view dining room. The Whale Watch Lounge has a cozy, old-fashioned atmosphere that hails the area's rugged pioneer past. Meeting space is available in ocean-view rooms for retreats, seminars, receptions, and other gatherings. A regulation nine-hole golf course and two tennis courts are available, and the surroundings make for excellent hiking and quiet beachcombing. The inn is just two miles south of the historic village of Mendocino, which boasts art galleries, antique shops, and fine examples of nineteenth-century New England-style architecture. Chartered fishing boats and a train ride through the redwoods are also available not far from the resort.

Listed in the National Register of Historic Places

Location: The Little River Inn is accessible via Highway 1 (Coastal Highway) and is two miles south of the historic village of Mendocino and 3.5 hours from San Francisco.
Function Space: 2,000 square feet; 3 rooms
Capacity—Conference: 50; Reception: 100; Banquet: 80; Theater: 80
Equipment On-site: Public address system, VCR, screen, blackboards, easels; modem hookups, copier, fax available
Food Service: Catering/food service available; restaurant and bar
Overnight Accommodations: 65 rooms
Limitations/Restrictions: Restrictions on smoking (permitted in some guest rooms)
Access: Handicapped accessible; on-site parking; open year-round
Payment: Cash, check, credit card (MC, Visa)

LONG BEACH

LORD MAYOR'S BED & BREAKFAST INN

435 Cedar Avenue, Long Beach, CA 90802
Phone: 310/436-0324   Fax: 310/436-0324

BEAUTIFULLY restored by owners Laura and Reuben Brasser, the Lord Mayor's Inn was home to Charles H. Windham, the first mayor of Long Beach. Windham was dubbed "Lord Mayor" by a group of visiting British beauty contestants, and the 1904 Edwardian house retains the elegant style its name suggests. Guest rooms have 10-foot-high ceilings and access to a sun deck; each is furnished with antiques, such as a French armoire and eighteenth-century Austrian beds. Overnight visitors enjoy a full breakfast in the dining room or on the deck overlooking the garden, and tea and homemade goodies are served in the evening. The inn is set in the heart of Long Beach, close to beaches and the marina, and is within walking distance of the Promenade, a farmer's market, and the World Trade Center. The Shoreline Village features specialty shops, restaurants, and a sea full of sailboats. Also nearby are state and local government offices and the Long Beach Convention Center.

Recipient of the 1992 Great American Home Award from the National Trust for Historic Preservation

Location: The Lord Mayor's Inn is two blocks north of the Civic Center and five blocks from the 710 Freeway. Blue Line rapid transit to Los Angeles is one block away; local bus service is available. Thirty minutes to Los Angeles by three major freeways; Long Beach Airport 4 miles away; Los Angeles International Airport 21 miles away.
Function Space: 500 square feet; 2 rooms
Capacity—Conference: 20; Reception: 20; Banquet: 20 (one room); Theater: 20

Food Service: Breakfast with room
Overnight Accommodations: 5 rooms
Limitations/Restrictions: Smoking limited to patio and porches; no alcoholic beverages
Access: On-site parking; open year-round
Payment: Cash, check, credit card (AmEx, Discover, MC, Visa)

LOS ANGELES

HOTEL BEL-AIR

701 Stone Canyon Road, Los Angeles, CA 90077
Phone: 310/472-1211   Fax: 310/476-5890

ITS secluded location deep in the canyons of Bel-Air Estates makes the Hotel Bel-Air an idyllic hideaway for those seeking privacy. Built in 1946, the award-winning hotel comprises a series of Mission-style villas spread over 11.5 enchanting acres of palm-shaded gardens and a grove of rare coast redwoods. Tranquil courtyards, a winding stream, and a waterfall cascading into Swan Lake contribute to the atmosphere of this present-day Shangri-la. The bright, airy guest rooms are individually appointed and mirror the rich outdoor landscaping with their floral-pattern furnishings, potted palms, and colorful flower arrangements. Three function rooms, including a newly renovated boardroom, are available for meetings, and the hotel's expansive lawn is a popular site for weddings. Recreational facilities include a unique oval-shaped pool and a state-of-the art fitness center located in what was once known as the Marilyn Monroe Cottage. Also on site is the renowned Hotel Bel-Air Restaurant, which serves seasonal French-California cuisine, and year-round alfresco dining is available on the terrace under a canopy of brilliant bougainvillea. Adjacent to Beverly Hills, the hotel is convenient to Rodeo Drive shopping, Westwood Village and UCLA, Century City and Malibu.

Location: Hotel Bel-Air is located just off Sunset Boulevard in Bel-Air Estates, 20 minutes from Los Angeles International Airport, and is accessible via the San Diego Freeway (405).
Function Space: 1,370 square feet; 3 rooms
Capacity—Conference: 60; Reception: 325; Banquet: 200; Theater: 200
Equipment On-site: Overhead projector, VCR, and monitor
Food Service: Catering/food service available; restaurant and bar
Overnight Accommodations: 91 rooms
Limitations/Restrictions: No outside food and beverage service; one hour cash bar
Access: Handicapped accessible; on-site parking; open year-round
Payment: Credit card (AmEx, DC, MC, Visa)

THE REGAL BILTMORE

506 S. Grand Avenue
Los Angeles, CA 90071-2607
Phone: 213/624-1011   Fax: 213/612-1546
http://www.thebiltmore.com

OPULENT in decor and palatial in scale, the Regal Biltmore takes its architectural cue from Spanish and Italian Renaissance styles. Soaring classical columns rise to vaulted, coffered, muraled, and sky-lighted ceilings that extend above ornate carvings, crystal chandeliers, and hand-oiled wood paneling. With such a grand setting to offer, the Biltmore hosted the founding banquet for the Academy of Motion Picture Arts and Sciences in 1927, and the concept and design for the "Oscar" statuette was sketched there on a linen dinner napkin. Several Academy Award ceremonies were held at the Biltmore during the 1930s and 1940s, and over the years the hotel has welcomed international dignitaries, royalty, and celebrities. The hotel's extensive meeting facilities accommodate conventions, lavish social events, and business meetings, and its function spaces include a conference suite and meeting rooms, exhibit rooms, and spectacular ballrooms. A variety of dining options are available on-site, including award-winning Bernard's, whose tables are set with 1920s silver, and the Rendevous Court, renowned for its rococo decor. The hotel is located in the city's financial and cultural districts, in close proximity to the Music Center, the Civic Center, shopping, and entertainment.

City of Los Angeles Historic Landmark; member of Historic Hotels of America

Location: The Regal Biltmore is located downtown, 35 minutes from Los Angeles International Airport and accessible via I-5, I-10, I-110, and I-710. The hotel is within walking distance of bus, train, and metrolink access. Complimentary morning weekday transportation to downtown office buildings; weekend shuttle service to downtown attractions and shopping.
Function Space: 76,000 square feet; 17 rooms
Capacity—Conference: 1,000; Reception: 1,000; Banquet: 1,000; Theater: 1,000
Equipment On-site: On-site audiovisual department; all business services available
Food Service: Catering/food service available; five restaurants, lounge, deli/bakery, room service
Overnight Accommodations: 683 rooms (non smoking rooms available)
Access: Handicapped accessible; on-site parking; open year-round
Payment: Cash, check, major credit card

MURPHYS

MURPHYS HISTORIC HOTEL AND LODGE

457 Main Street, Murphys, CA 95247
Phone: 209/728-3444   Fax: 209/728-1590

ORIGINALLY known as the Sperry & Perry, James Sperry and John Perry's picturesque hotel first opened in 1856. The supposedly fireproof building burned down in 1859, but rebuilding began later that year; this time the walls were constructed entirely of stone. Iron shutters covered the doors and windows, and by 1861 visitors to the Gold Country were once again staying at the Sperry & Perry. Visitors to the hotel's saloon included Ulysses S. Grant, Black Bart, and Mark Twain, whose stay in the area inspired his classic short tale, "The Celebrated Jumping Frog of Calaveras County." In 1961 the hotel's name was changed, but the owners have retained its remarkable historic character. Meeting facilities, banquet rooms, and a lawn garden are available for meetings, receptions, and special events. Not far away are the spectacular Calaveras Big Trees, a gold mining camp at Angel's Camp, and world-famous wineries.

Listed in the National Register of Historic Places

Location: Murphys is located in California's Gold Country on Highway 4.
Function Space: 900 square feet
Capacity—Conference: 60; Reception: 155; Banquet: 85; Theater: 115
Equipment On-site: Overhead projector, TV/VCR, flip chart, public address system
Food Service: Catering/food service available; restaurant and saloon
Overnight Accommodations: 29 rooms

Limitations/Restrictions: Smoking permitted in saloon and some lodge rooms, not in meeting rooms; no pets
Access: Some handicapped accessibility (to lodge rooms); on-site parking; open year-round
Payment: Balance due on departure unless advance approved credit

PACIFIC GROVE

THE MARTINE INN

255 Oceanview Boulevard
Pacific Grove, CA 93950
Phone: 408/373-3388 or 800-852-5588 (reservations)
Fax: 408/373-3896

PERCHED on a cliff overlooking Monterey Bay, the Martine Inn enjoys a spectacular view of the rocky Pacific coastline. Originally a Victorian-style house when it was built in 1899, the inn's exterior was later converted to a Mediterranean design. The grounds feature a courtyard pond and oriental fountain, a carriage house, and a display area for several vintage MGs. Owners Don and Marion Martine have fully renovated the mansion, whose exquisite Victorian interiors are filled with nineteenth-century American antiques and authentic fixtures such as claw-foot tubs and marble sinks. The interior's wall coverings, paint colors, fabrics, and furniture reflect the Martines' extensive research into Victorian decor and design. Among the home's treasures are an outstanding collection of bedroom suites, including the Malaren Estate's Mahogany suite exhibited at the 1893 Chicago World's Fair. Guests can further sample the tastes of another era when they sit down to a 12-course Victorian dinner featuring recipes taken from 1880 White House cookbooks.

Location: Pacific Grove is 90 minutes southwest of San Jose in the Monterey Peninusla and is accessible via Highway 1 and Highway 68. Monterey Airport is 5 miles away; San Jose Airport, 70 miles; San Francisco International Airport, 90 miles.

Function Space: 6 rooms

Capacity—Conference: 20; Reception: 120; Banquet: 40

Equipment On-site: Audiovisual equipment available

Food Service: Breakfast with room; catering/ food service available

Limitations/Restrictions: Licensed for beer and wine only

Overnight Accommodations: 20 rooms

Limitations/Restrictions: Restrictions on smoking

Access: Handicap access; on-site parking; open year-round

Payment: Discover, MC, Visa

PASADENA

THE CASTLE GREEN

99 South Raymond Avenue, Pasadena, CA 91105
Phone: 818/793-0359   Fax: 818/793-6314

CONSIDERED one of the finest surviving examples of Pasadena's grand resort architecture, Castle Green is located in the heart of historic Old Pasadena. The castle was first known as the Central Annex when it was built in 1898 as part of the spectacular Hotel Green complex. At that time, the annex was connected to the main hotel (razed in 1934) by a second-story covered bridge, which was used by a miniature trolley car to transport guests and their luggage. A stylish mix of Moorish, Spanish, and Victorian elements, the annex was Pasadena's first fireproof building. The Central Annex became Castle Green in 1924 when the building was divided into 50 apartment units, which today remain private residences. The castle's public rooms and gardens, however, are available for parties, weddings, receptions, corporate meetings, and filming. Many of the original Victorian and Moorish furnishings remain, and other features, such as the marble staircase and original wrought-iron cage elevator in the lobby, and the coffered ceilings and antique furniture in the Main Salon, remind guests of the castle's grand history.

Listed in the National Register of Historic Places, the State Historic Register, and the City of Pasadena's list of Historic Places

Location: Castle Green is 15 minutes from the Burbank Airport via Highway 134 and 45 minutes from Los Angeles International Airport via the 405 or 110 freeway. Castle Green is accessible via the 110, 134, and 210 freeways, and is 15 minutes from downtown Los Angeles. Area bus service is one block away; Pasadena also has a local free transit system that passes near most of the local major hotels.

Function Space: 5,000+ square feet; 5 rooms

Capacity—Conference: 250; Reception: 400; Banquet: 225 (sit-down in ballroom); Theater: 300

Equipment On-site: Audiovisual equipment can be rented

Food Service: Three catering companies to choose from

Overnight Accommodations: Available nearby

Limitations/Restrictions: No smoking; no red wine

Access: Parking available across the street; open year-round

Payment: Cash, check, money order

The Inn at Rancho Santa Fe

RANCHO SANTA FE

THE INN AT RANCHO SANTA FE

(Mailing address)
P.O. Box 869
(Street address)
5951 Linea del Cielo, Rancho Santa Fe, CA 92067
Phone: 619/756-1131   Fax: 619/756-1604

THE Inn at Rancho Santa Fe is an elegant small hotel, surrounded by gentle hills, citrus groves, and eucalyptus trees. In 1845 the last Mexican governor of California granted Juan Maria Osuna, mayor of the Pueblo of San Diego, 8,825 acres of land. The Santa Fe Railway purchased Osuna's ranch in 1906 and set about planting three million eucalyptus tree seedlings as a future source of wood railway ties. The plan failed, but the trees prospered and some of them now shade the inn's 20 acres of landscaped grounds. In 1924, Lillian Rice, one of the first female architects in California, designed the red tile-roofed inn as a guest house for the railroad, and though it has

grown over the years, the inn remains a small resort. Most of the guest accommodations are located in cottages, many with secluded patios. Fully equipped conference rooms and hospitality suites are available for meetings, retreats, receptions, and other gatherings. Tennis, swimming, croquet, and miles of scenic trails are available for recreation, and guests may use the inn's beach cottage at Del Mar during the day. The inn is also within 45 minutes of the San Diego Zoo, Sea World, and the San Diego Harbor.

Rancho Santa Fe Historical Society Landmark

Location: The Inn at Rancho Santa Fe is located in the Village of Santa Fe, between I-5 and I-15, 25 miles north of San Diego's Lindbergh Field International Airport and 15 miles south of Palomar Airport (private and commuter flights). Amtrak and airport shuttle service is available. *Function Space:* 5,232 square feet; 4 rooms *Capacity*—Conference: 60; Reception: 200; Banquet: 150; Theater: 200

Equipment On-site: Audiovisual equipment available through outside source; copier and fax available
Food Service: Catering/food service available; restaurant, room service
Overnight Accommodations: 89 rooms
Limitations/Restrictions: Restrictions on smoking (not permitted in public areas); pets allowed
Access: Handicapped accessible; on-site parking; open year-round
Payment: Cash, traveler's checks, credit card

REEDLEY

REEDLEY OPERA HOUSE

1708 10th Street, Reedley, CA 93654
Phone: 209/638-1900   Fax: 209/683-8479

DANISH sea captain Jesse Jansen built the Reedley Opera House in 1903, but it was always more than a stage for the performing arts. The house hosted grand balls, square dances, town meetings, graduations, and numerous other local events, and even housed the Catholic church for several years, with the priest hearing confessions in the same booth used for Saturday night ticket sales. In 1974 the opera house faced demolition, but local citizens created a Turn-of-the-Century partnership to save the theater and surrounding buildings. The opera house was remodeled in 1983, and visitors again enjoy the beautiful Victorian lobby furnished with antiques and boasting a tin-type ceiling. Today the Reedley Opera House continues to present theater productions, but it also serves Central California as a historic meeting center. A horseshoe balcony overlooks the stage and dance floor, and the two-level atrium hospitality area includes both indoor and outdoor spaces. Groups may use the conference rooms, dining room, and theater for receptions, meetings, and other social and business events.

Listed in the National Register of Historic Places

Location: Reedley Opera House is 22 miles southeast of Fresno and is accessible via Highway 99.
Function Space: 9,000+ square feet; 4 rooms
Capacity—Conference: 200; Reception: 300; Banquet: 200; Theater: 140
Equipment On-site: TV, VCR, lighting/sound system
Food Service: Jon's Bear Club is exclusive caterer
Access: Handicapped accessible; open year-round
Payment: Check

RIVERSIDE

MISSION INN

3649 Mission Inn Avenue, Riverside, CA 92501
Phone: 909/784-0300   Fax: 909/784-5525

REMINISCENT of both a Mediterannean palace and a Spanish alcazar while defying traditional architectural labels, the distinctive Mission Inn occupies an entire city block. Construction began in 1876 and continued through 1931 as Frank Miller, the original owner, filled his hotel with art and antiques from his overseas journeys. The inn showcases multiple design elements, including flying buttresses, original redwood beamed ceilings, archways, domes, a five-story open-air rotunda, a circular wrought-iron staircase, and richly textured courtyards and patios. Under the sway of palm trees, guests can relax in the gardens, on the sun deck, or in the pool. Guests can also take a docent-guided tour of the inn and its museum, noting the seventeenth-century gilt altar in the

Mission Inn

National Historic Landmark; listed in the National Register of Historic Places; member of Historic Hotels of America

Location: The Mission Inn is 55 minutes east of Los Angeles and 20 minutes from Ontario International Airport.
Function Space: 10,000 square feet; 12 rooms
Capacity—Conference: 40; Reception: 275; Banquet: 210; Theater: 280
Equipment On-site: Audiovisual equipment and business services available
Food Service: Catering/food service available; two restaurants, lounge, room service
Overnight Accommodations: 234 rooms
Access: Handicapped accessible; on-site parking; open year-round
Payment: Credit card

SAN DIEGO

U. S. GRANT—A GRAND HERITAGE HOTEL
326 Broadway, San Diego, CA 92101
Phone: 619/232-3121   Fax: 619/232-3626

St. Francis Chapel and the multimillion dollar, 6,000-piece art collection on display throughout the hotel. A variety of indoor function rooms, as well as outdoor meeting space, are available for business and social events, and the Riverside Convention Center is right next door. The hotel has hosted U.S. presidents and numerous film stars, and it was here that Richard and Pat Nixon married and Nancy and Ronald Reagan honeymooned. Golf, tennis, horseback riding, the Temecula Valley wine country, and California's desert resort region are all nearby.

AS an admirer of Ulysses S. Grant, the developer of this classic 1910 luxury building named his grand hotel for the Civil War Union general and eighteenth president of the United States. Among the hotel's guests have been Charles Lindbergh, Albert Einstein, Henry Ford, Franklin D. Roosevelt, and numerous Hollywood celebrities. Noted for its superb craftsmanship, the U. S. Grant boasts travertine colonades, crystal chandeliers, and Dutch and Venetian paintings in its stunning lobby; guest rooms are stylishly furnished with Queen Anne reproductions. Extensive meeting space is available for nearly any type of business or social event, and facilities include handsome boardrooms and exquisite salons. Dining options include the cozy and intimate Grant Grill, an award-winning restaurant, and the Grant Lounge is a popular gathering place offering live jazz. From its downtown location in the city's business and cultural district, the U. S. Grant is within walking distance of convention centers, exclusive shopping, restaurants, theaters, and the harbor. Also nearby is the historic Gaslamp District, Balboa Park, Seaworld, and the world-famous San Diego Zoo.

Listed in the National Register of Historic Places

Location: The U. S. Grant Hotel is in downtown San Diego, across from Horton Plaza and 5 minutes from San Diego International Airport (complimentary airport van service available).
Function Space: 33,000 square feet; 23 rooms
Capacity—Conference: 500; Reception: 900; Banquet: 700; Theater: 800
Equipment On-site: Audiovisual equipment, fax, photocopier available
Food Service: Catering/food service available; two restaurants, bar/lounge
Overnight Accommodations: 280 rooms
Access: Handicapped accessible; on-site parking; open year-round
Payment: Credit card

SAN FRANCISCO

1409 SUTTER
1409 Sutter Street, San Francisco, CA 94109
Phone: 415/561-0869   Fax: 415/561-0833

WILLIAM CURLETT, a famed California architect, built this Victorian mansion in 1881 for Theodore and Pauline Payne, whose family fortune came flowing with the Gold Rush. Curlett

U. S. Grant

integrated the Eastlake, Stick, and Queen Anne styles into his design, and he included such modern conveniences as bathrooms and central heating. Oak-paneled walls, a great oak stairway, and wide oak pocket doors grace the house, which also features stained glass windows. Since the Paynes' day, 1409 Sutter has seen many uses, having housed a restaurant, commercial businesses, a Japanese-American YMCA, and a private club. Today the mansion, one of the few remaining large homes of the many once located between Franklin and Gough Streets in outer Pacific Heights, is available for a variety of gatherings, including receptions, weddings, business luncheons, cocktail parties, dinners, seminars, and all-day conferences.

Listed in the National Register of Historic Places

Location: 1409 Sutter is 5 to 10 minutes from downtown and is accessible via US 1, Highway 101 and 280, 580, and 680. San Francisco International and Oakland Airports are 20 minutes away. Cable car, subway, and bus service available.
Function Space: 1,600 square feet; 4 rooms
Capacity—Conference: 50; Reception: 250; Banquet: 120; Theater: 60
Equipment On-site: Podium, overhead projector, screen; other equipment can be rented from A/V company
Food Service: In-house catering or select from preferred caterers list
Limitations/Restrictions: No smoking
Access: Handicapped accessible; arrangements can be made for preferred garage parking, valet parking, limousine service, or shuttle buses; open year-round
Payment: Check, no credit cards

CHANCELLOR HOTEL

433 Powell Street, San Francisco, CA 94102
Phone: 415/362-2004   Fax: 415/362-1403
E-mail: Chnclrhtl@aol.com

THE Edwardian-style Chancellor Hotel opened in 1914 to accommodate visitors arriving in San Francisco the following year for the Pan Pacific International Exposition. When it opened, the hotel was the tallest building in the city, but with the reverberations of the 1906 earthquake still in mind, the Chancellor's builders hailed it as both fireproof and indestructible. Almost since its opening the hotel has been family owned and operated, and in the late 1970s the decor was returned to its original Edwardian appearance. While guest rooms have all the modern conveniences, old-fashioned touches remain, including the original deep,

claw-foot-style bathtubs. In 1937 the hotel's Clipper Ship Lounge opened in honor of the inaugural Pan Am Flights to the Orient. Today the lounge is the Clipper Ship Room, one of the city's most distinctive meeting rooms. The interior is reminiscent of an airplane, and a large photographic mural on each wall gives a panoramic aerial view of the Bay Area in 1935. The room is available for meetings and small banquets and receptions. Located on the Powell Street Cable Car line at historic Union Square, the hotel is convenient to Chinatown, the theater district, and world class shopping and dining.

Location: The Chancellor Hotel is located in the center of San Francisco at Union Square and is easily accessible to the BART subway system and cable car service.
Function Space: 400 square feet; 1 room
Capacity—Conference: 40; Reception: 40; Banquet: 30; Theater: 40
Equipment On-site: Audiovisual equipment and fax available
Food Service: Catering/food service available; restaurant and bar, room service
Overnight Accommodations: 137 rooms
Limitations/Restrictions: Restrictions on smoking
Access: Open year-round
Payment: Cash, check, credit card

SIR FRANCIS DRAKE HOTEL

450 Powell Street, San Francisco, CA 94102
Phone: 415/392-7755   Fax: 415/677-9341

SINCE its opening in 1928, the Sir Francis Drake Hotel has remained an impressive structure, designed to reflect the Renaissance era of its namesake. Sir Francis Drake, the English explorer, arrived in the area in 1579, just missing San Francisco Bay and sailing instead into Drake's Bay, 28 miles north. The Grand Lobby and mezzanine boast marble walls, recessed mirrors, and murals depicting Drake's life, and crystal chandeliers hang from the vaulted gold-leafed bas relief ceilings. The renovated guest rooms are a blend of Spanish, Moorish, and European classical design. Large receptions, banquets, and other events are accommodated in the Empire Room and the Franciscan Room, and smaller meeting rooms are available for groups of 15 to 140. Also on-site are Harry Denton's Starlight Room, offering breathtaking city views in a luxurious 1930s-style nightclub setting; Scala's Bistro, featuring regional country Italian/country French cuisine; and Caffe Espresso, a casual sidewalk cafe. The theater district, Yerba Buena Gardens, Chinatown, and numerous fine shops, restaurants, and boutiques are within walking distance, and historic Union Square is just a block away.

Location: The Sir Francis Drake Hotel is located in downtown San Francisco, one block from Union Square and on the famed Powell Street cable car line.

Function Space: 20,000+ square feet; 15 rooms

Capacity—Conference: 225; Reception: 400; Banquet: 300; Theater: 350

Equipment On-site: Full audiovisual department

Food Service: Catering/food service available; three restaurants

Overnight Accommodations: 417 rooms

Access: Handicapped accessible; on-site parking by valet; open year-round

Payment: Cash, check, credit card

THE WESTIN ST. FRANCIS

(Mailing address)
335 Powell Street
(Street address)
Union Square
335 Geary Street (between Post and Powell)
San Francisco, CA 94102
Phone: 415/397-7000   Fax: 415/774-0124
http://www.westin.com

A San Francisco landmark since it opened to great fanfare in 1904, the Westin St. Francis has witnessed significant history as an anchor of the city's cultural life. Modeled after the finest hotels of Europe, the St. Francis was designed to offer guests a full range of services and amenities, just as it does today. Fire following the great San Francisco earthquake of 1906 damaged the hotel, but it remained structurally sound and reopened the following year. Ten U.S. presidents, European royalty, and numerous other prominent figures have visited the luxury hotel at Union Square, including delegates during the formation of the United Nations in 1945. The beautifully furnished hotel features the great Magneta clock in the lobby. Made in Saxony, it was the first master clock introduced in the West, and meeting friends "under the clock" remains a local custom. Thirty meeting rooms, including the Grand Ballroom, which accommodates up to 1,500, are available for a full range of convention, business, and social events. On-site facilities also include shops, boutiques, a fitness center, a nightclub, and several dining options, such as the St. Francis Cafe, Dewey's (sports bar), and the Compass Rose (luncheon and tea).

The Westin St. Francis

Location: The Westin St. Francis is located between Post and Geary Streets on Powell Street at Union Square. San Francisco International Airport is 15 miles away.

Function Space: 45,000+ square feet; 30 rooms

Capacity—Conference: 1,200; Reception: 1,500; Banquet: 1,100; Theater: 1,100

Equipment On-site: All audiovisual equipment and business services available

Food Service: Catering/food service available, including kosher catering; three restaurants; 24-hour room service

Overnight Accommodations: 1,192 rooms

Limitations/Restrictions: Restrictions on smoking (smoking and nonsmoking rooms available)

Access: Handicapped accessible; on-site valet parking; open year-round

Payment: Major credit card

SAN JOSE

HYATT SAINTE CLAIRE

302 S. Market Street, San Jose, CA 95113
Phone: 408/295-2000, 800/824-6835, or 408/885-1234 (Sales Department)   Fax: 408/977-0403

A prominent San Jose historic landmark in the heart of the Silicon Valley today, the Hotel Sainte Claire was the centerpiece of real estate mogul T. S. Montgomery's plan for the city's downtown. Weeks and Down designed the hotel, which opened in 1926 and was restored in 1992, with a combination of Spanish and Italian Renaissance Revival elements. The handsome lobby features antique furnishings from Czechoslavakia, elaborate gilt scroll-work and hand-carved and painted ceiling panels. The Grande Ballroom, one of the largest in California, opens to an ornate Spanish courtyard and garden. Extensive meeting facilities are also available in the hotel's conference wing, with executive business suites, boardroom and private deck, and breakout rooms. Catering and banquet service are provided by Sainte Claire's on-site restaurant, Il Fornaio, which specializes in traditional northern Italian cuisine and uses authentic Tuscan recipes. The deluxe guest rooms come with feather-down mattresses, in-room safes, mini-bars, and multiple phone- and data-line hookups. The hotel enjoys a convenient downtown location next to the San Jose McEnery Convention Center, and nearby attractions include museums, numerous wineries, and the puzzling Winchester Mystery House.

Listed in the National Register of Historic Places; member of Historic Hotels of America

Location: The Hyatt Sainte Clare is located in downtown San Jose, 15 minutes from San Jose International Airport, 45 minutes to 1 hour from

San Francisco International Airport, and 15 minutes from both Amtrak and CalTrain stops; the hotel is also on the San Jose Light Rail system.

Function Space: 10,000 square feet; 10 rooms

Capacity—Conference: 35; Reception: 400; Banquet: 280; Theater: 300

Equipment On-site: Complete audiovisual equipment available; the Grande Ballroom and the Sainte Claire Room are equipped for teleconferencing and remote projection of computer images, video, and slides; fax and photocopier available

Food Service: Catering/food service available; restaurant, lounge, 24-hour room service

Overnight Accommodations: 170 rooms

Limitations/Restrictions: No smoking; no outside food or beverages allowed

Access: Handicapped accessible; on-site parking (fee); open year-round

Payment: Major credit card

The Huntington Library

SAN MARINO

THE HUNTINGTON LIBRARY, ART COLLECTIONS AND BOTANICAL GARDENS

1151 Oxford Road, San Marino, CA 91108
Phone: 818/405-2135   Fax: 818/449-5656

HENRY Edwards Huntington's brilliant legacy is centered on his 200-acre estate, renowned for its world-famous research library, art collection, and botanical gardens. Huntington acquired his fortune in railroads and real estate, and after retiring he set about acquiring rare books, maps, and illuminated manuscripts, including the famous Ellsmere manuscript of the *Canterbury Tales*. Huntington also collected American, French, and British masterpieces, such as Thomas Gainsborough's *The Blue Boy*, as well as the necessary elements to create spectacular landscapes, which today have blossomed into the Rose, Japanese, Shakespeare, Camellia, Jungle, Palm, Australian, and Desert Gardens. The San Gabriel Mountains form an enchanting backdrop for Huntington's 1909 Beaux Arts mansion and for the North Vista, a classical garden with seventeenth-century stone statues depicting mythological subjects under a colonade of palm trees. Today the Huntington is a nonprofit educational trust, welcoming scholars and visitors from around the world. Library members may hold events in Friends' Hall, its walls showcasing fine European art, or in the smaller wood-paneled Overseers' Room, featuring a beautiful tapestry and a fireplace. Outdoor terraces and loggias accommodate small gatherings as well as large events.

El Encanto Hotel and Garden Villas

Location: The Huntington Library is located in San Marino, adjacent to Pasadena and part of greater Los Angeles. It is accessible via I-10, US 101, the Pasadena Freeway (110), and the Foothill Freeway (210). Los Angeles International and Burbank Airports are 60 and 30 minutes away, respectively.

Function Space: 4,664 square feet; 2 rooms

Capacity—Conference: 30/200; Reception: 50/300; Banquet: 48/325; Theater: 60/400; 200 acres of gardens available for special events

Equipment On-site: Slide projectors, screen, podium microphones

Food Service: Catering/food service available (818/405-2249)

Limitations/Restrictions: Restrictions on smoking; no food or beverages in gallery areas; preapproved vendors only; no fund-raisers, weddings, or wedding receptions; use of facilities is a privilege of membership; call for membership information

Access: Handicapped accessible; on-site parking; indoor facilities open year-round, garden use recommended May–October

Payment: Check

SANTA BARBARA

EL ENCANTO HOTEL AND GARDEN VILLAS
1900 Lasuen Road, Santa Barbara, CA 93103
Phone: 805/687-5000   Fax: 805/687-3903

LONG known as an ideal place for a romantic getaway, the El Encanto ("The Enchanted") occupies 10 acres overlooking Santa Barbara, the Pacific Ocean, and the Channel Islands. The California Craftsman Cottage and Spanish Colonial Revival architecture testify to this landmark's coastal location and the city's colorful and historic Spanish associations. Built in 1915, the hotel and villas, set

in rolling hills and lush gardens, have been pro-
gressively restored to their original appearance. In
the dining room, judged by some as the most beautiful in Santa Barbara, guests order from a menu
that changes weekly and offers fresh fare from local
fishermen and farmers. Private meeting rooms with
spectacular ocean views, accommodating groups of
5 to 50, are ideal for workshops, seminars, executive board meetings, retreats, and planning conferences; larger groups can be accommodated for banquets and receptions as well. Swimming and tennis
are available on-site, and Santa Barbara's famous
cultural and recreational activities, including museums, beachside art shows, biking, and roller-blad-
ing, are just minutes away.

Member of Historic Hotels of America
Location: The El Encanto is accessible from
US 101 and is 10 minutes from Santa Barbara
Airport and 90 miles north of Los Angeles.
Amtrak, taxi, and bus service available.
Function Space: 1,641 square feet; 3 rooms
Capacity—Conference: 35; Reception: 100;
Banquet: 70; Theater: 50
Equipment On-site: Lectern, blackboards,
and easels, supplied at no charge; audiovisual
equipment, overhead projector, screens, and
microphones, supplied at charge; fax,
computer, and printer available
Food Service: Catering/food service
available; restaurant
Overnight Accommodations: 84 rooms
Limitations/Restrictions: No smoking; no
outside catering; corkage fee $15;
no amplified music
Access: Handicapped accessible; on-site
parking; open year-round
Payment: Credit card

THE UPHAM HOTEL & GARDEN COTTAGES

1404 De la Vina Street, Santa Barbara, CA 93101
Phone: 805/962-0058   Fax: 805/963-2825

BOSTON banker Amasa Lincoln built this lovely Italianate hotel in 1871, and, as the oldest continuously operating hostelry in Southern
California, the Upham itself is a landmark in historic Santa Barbara. Filled with antiques and
period furnishings, the hotel has been completely restored and refurbished. The timbered structure, topped by a cupola, is set on an acre of gardens and is one of the city's quaint Victorian
gems in a local mosaic of white-washed, red-tiled
Spanish architecture. Groups may meet in three
executive boardrooms (complimentary with a
pickup of 10 guest rooms) or in the delightful
garden room (complimentary with a pickup of 20
guest rooms). Guest room rates include a continental buffet breakfast and afternoon wine and
cheese. Louie's Restaurant, next to the main
lobby, provides catering and food service, special-
izing in fresh seafood, pasta, and California cuisine. The Upham is a short walk from art galleries, museums, parks, and waterfront shuttle
service, and just two blocks from State Street,
famous for its arcades, shops, and outdoor cafes.

Santa Barbara Historic Landmark

Location: The Upham is four blocks from
US 101 and 15 minutes from the Santa Barbara
Airport; Santa Barbara is 90 miles north of
Los Angeles.
Function Space: 1,845 square feet; 4 rooms
Capacity—Conference: 28; Reception: 100;
Banquet: 70; Theater: 100

Equipment On-site: Overhead projector, screen, 35mm projector, TV/VCR; fax and photocopy machines
Food Service: Breakfast with room; catering/ food service available; restaurant
Overnight Accommodations: 50 rooms
Limitations/Restrictions: No pets
Access: On-site parking; open year-round
Payment: Check

SANTA ROSA

HOTEL LA ROSE

308 Wilson Street, Santa Rosa, CA 95401
Phone: 707/579-3200   Fax: 707/579-3247

BUILT in 1907 of locally quarried stone, the four-story Hotel La Rose is part of the historic Old Railroad Square, an area that bustled with train activity in the late nineteenth century but is now a shopping and dining district. In 1985,

Sonoma County honored Hotel La Rose for its excellent building restoration, and the hotel is adjacent to a thriving redeveloped area of business and government offices. The hotel's English country interior and gracious guest rooms reflect a turn-of-the-century decor, and the corridors are lit with simulated gaslights. Twenty-nine nonsmoking guest rooms are available in the main building, and the Carriage House, built in 1985, accommodates an additional 20 guest rooms, each with its own balcony or patio, around a garden courtyard. Meeting and banquet facilities are available for small business gatherings, executive retreats, receptions, and other events. French continental cuisine is served at Josef's Restaurant, and the cocktail lounge features a fine selection of Sonoma County wines. A continental breakfast is included in the rates, and special packages are available to include balloon rides, golf, and wine country tours.

Listed in the National Register of Historic Places; member of Historic Hotels of America

Upham Hotel & Garden Cottages

Location: Hotel La Rose is one block from both US 101 and Highway 12, and 45 minutes from Oakland, 50 minutes from San Francisco, and 2 hours from Sacramento. Airport shuttles available to Sonoma County Airport; taxi and local bus service available.
Function Space: 1,864 square feet; 4 rooms
Capacity—Classroom: 40; Reception: 75; Banquet: 63; Theater: 63
Equipment On-site: Audiovisual equipment, fax, photocopier, modem hookups available

Food Service: Breakfast with room; catering/food service available; restaurant; room service
Overnight Accommodations: 49 rooms
Limitations/Restrictions: No smoking in main building; no pets other than guide animals
Access: Handicapped accessible; on-site parking; open year-round
Payment: Cash, credit card (AmEx, MC, Visa)

SONOMA

Hotel La Rose

BUENA VISTA WINERY
(Mailing address)
P.O. Box 1842
(Street address)
18000 Old Winery Road, Sonoma, CA 95476
Phone: 707/938-1266   Fax: 707/939-0916

HUNGARIAN Count Agoston Haraszthy founded California's oldest premium winery in 1857, earning his title as the "father of California viticulture." During his European travels he collected cuttings of *vitis vinifera* grapevines for use at Buena Vista; such vines were the source of many of France's great wines. Located in beautiful Sonoma Valley, the winery was already one of California's leading wineries when Haraszthy died in 1868. Today the historic stone winery is owned by the Moller-Racke family of Germany, whose investment in Carneros vineyard land has made Buena Vista the largest estate winery in the area. In addition to hosting weddings, banquets, and other gatherings, the winery offers visitors a taste of current wines and rare vintages, site tours, creekside picnic areas, and a selection of local gourmet picnic items. The works of local artists-in-residence are showcased in the winery's gallery.

California Registered Historic Landmark

Location: The Buena Vista Winery is located just south of Santa Rosa and is accessible via US 101 and Highway 12.
Function Space: 2,000 square feet; 1 room
Capacity—Reception: 200; Banquet: 100
Equipment On-site: Tables and chairs
Food Service: Preferred caterers list provided
Limitations/Restrictions: Restrictions on smoking; only Buena Vista wines allowed
Access: On-site parking
Payment: Cash, check, credit card

YOSEMITE

THE AHWAHNEE HOTEL

(Reservations)

5410 E. Home Avenue, Fresno, CA 93727

Phone: 209/252-4848   Fax: 209/456-0542

(Group sales)

Yosemite Concession Services

Yosemite National Park, CA 95389

Phone: 209/372-1122   Fax: 209/372-1220

CONSIDERED one of the most dazzling jewels in the National Park Service's crown, Yosemite National Park is a place of remarkable beauty and geological wonder. Domes and pinnacles carved by glaciers, spectacular waterfalls, including Yosemite Falls, among the tallest in the world, and restful meadows characterize the grand scenery. And in a landscape of natural landmarks, the historic Ahwahnee Hotel has become a landmark itself, with views of Half Dome, Royal Arches, and Yosemite Falls. Built in 1927, the six-story luxury hotel has a rustic exterior, while Indian motifs, hand-woven Indian baskets, mosaics, murals, stained glass, and other original artwork grace the Ahwahnee's interior. Numerous recreational activities are available nearby, and the Ahwahnee is linked to other locations in Yosemite Valley via free shuttle bus service. Long a favorite with backpackers and hikers, Yosemite offers seemingly endless areas of interest, including Glacier Point, Happy Isles, Mirror Lake, and Tuolomne Meadows. Many of the sites are within walking distance or a short hike or drive away from the hotel and Yosemite Village.

National Historic Landmark; listed in the National Register of Historic Places; located in Yosemite National Park Historic District

Location: The Ahwahnee Hotel is in the Yosemite Valley, 1 mile east of Yosemite Village, and 36 miles from the park entrance. The park entrance is two hours (89 miles) north of Fresno.

Function Space: 3,975 square feet; 5 rooms

Capacity—Conference: 60; Reception: 200; Banquet: 75; Theater: 100

Equipment On-site: Audiovisual equipment included in rental

Food Service: Catering/food service available; dining room

Overnight Accommodations: 123 rooms

Limitations/Restrictions: Restrictions on smoking; meetings can be booked mid-October through mid-April

Access: Handicapped accessible; on-site parking; open year-round

Payment: First night lodging due 90 days in advance, balance due 30 days prior to arrival

COLORADO

ASPEN

HOTEL JEROME

330 E. Main Street, Aspen, CO 81611
Phone: 970/920-1000 Fax: 970/544-0260

IN 1889, at the peak of the Colorado silver boom, Jerome B. Wheeler, president of Macy's department store, opened his grand Victorian hotel in downtown Aspen to rival the Ritz in Paris. With the Rocky Mountains forming a dramatic backdrop, the restored three-story luxury hotel is built of red brick and sandstone and retains its rich Eastlake-Gothic decor and Western atmosphere. Meeting space for business and social events includes the Antler Bar, with its unique antler chandelier, the Grand Ballroom, and the handsome boardroom; private dining and conference rooms are also available. Fine dining is available at the stately Century Room, while the J-Bar, with its original cherry wood bar, remains a popular Aspen gathering spot, just as it was when folks spent their newly acquired mining fortunes here more than a century ago. The spacious guest rooms are individually decorated with period antiques and include oversized beds and luxurious marble baths. A private fitness center, a pool and jacuzzis, and a ski shop are all on-site, and the hotel is just steps away from numerous recreational activities, boutiques, restaurants, and nightlife. Shuttle buses provide frequent service to Aspen's world-renowned ski areas.

Listed in the National Register of Historic Places; member of Historic Hotels of America

Location: The Hotel Jerome in downtown Aspen is just minutes from the base of Aspen Mountain and a 10-minute drive to Aspen Airport. Denver is 4 hours east, or 45 minutes by air.
Function Space: 7,500 square feet; 7 rooms
Capacity—Conference: 200; Reception: 500; Banquet: 300; Theater: 400
Equipment On-site: Video monitors, VCR, screens, podium, microphone, cascl; fax, photocopier, computer, portable phone available
Food Service: Catering/food service available; two restaurants, bar, 24-hour room service
Overnight Accommodations: 93 rooms
Limitations/Restrictions: Restrictions on smoking; food and beverage service must be supplied by hotel
Access: Handicapped accessible; on-site parking; open year-round
Payment: Cash, credit card

SARDY HOUSE HOTEL

128 E. Main Street, Aspen, CO 81611
Phone: 970/920-2525 Fax: 970/920-4478

NESTLED under towering 72-foot Colorado blue spruce trees, this charming Victorian hotel, with its reddish facade, balustraded porches, and fairy-tale turret, remains delightfully picturesque no matter what the season. Built in 1892, the Sardy House is within easy walking distance of historic Aspen's fine shops, restaurants, and ski shuttles. The guest rooms and suites are decorated in the Victorian style, with cherry wood armoires and feather comforters, and overnight guests are treated to a full complimentary breakfast. The candlelit dining room and Jack's Bar each offer a pleasant ambiance, and an excellent wine list and such entrées as the Colorado Rack of Lamb make for a memorable dining experience. The Sardy House is available for private parties, weddings, and receptions, and the third-floor meeting room, with its beaded paneling, black walnut table, and deep green tufted leather chairs, is a comfortable place for business gatherings or cocktail parties.

Location: The Sardy House is in downtown Aspen, approximately 10 minutes from Aspen Airport and 4 hours from Denver.
Function Space: 600 square feet; 1 room

Capacity—Conference: 15; Reception: 15; Banquet: 15; Theater: 24
Equipment On-site: TV/VCR, slide and overhead projectors; fax and phone service available
Food Service: Breakfast with room; food service available; restaurant, bar
Overnight Accommodations: 20 rooms
Limitations/Restrictions: Restrictions on smoking
Access: Limited on-site parking; open year-round
Payment: Cash, check, credit card (AmEx, DC, MC, Visa)

DENVER

THE BROWN PALACE HOTEL
321 17th Street, Denver, CO 80202
Phone: 303/297-3111   Fax: 303/293-9204

IN the late nineteenth century, businessman Henry Cordes Brown, owner of a triangular lot at the intersection of Seventeenth and Broadway, hired architect Frank E. Edbrooke to design a hotel that would be both luxurious and unprecedented. Following four years of construction and a $1.6 million expenditure—considered remarkable in its day—the Italian Renaissance-style Brown Palace opened in 1892. Built of Colorado granite and Arizona sandstone, the triangle-shaped hotel with its white onyx walls features a stunning eight-story stained glass atrium lobby where afternoon tea is served. Rocky Mountain spring water flows from the original 720-foot-deep well to faucets in every room, including the warmly furnished guest rooms. A wide variety of meeting rooms are available for business and social functions, whether week-long conferences or grand banquets. Dining options include the elegant main dining room, Ellyngton's, as well as the Palace Arms and the

The Brown Palace

Ship Tavern, both of which offer a cozy, intimate atmosphere. The Brown Palace Hotel, a historic landmark anchoring downtown Denver, is within walking distance of the state capitol, the central financial district, the convention center, and other well-known attractions, including the Museum of Western Art and the U.S. Mint.

Listed in the National Register of Historic Places; member of Historic Hotels of America

Location: The Brown Palace Hotel is located at Seventeenth and Tremont Place in downtown Denver. Denver International Airport is within 45 minutes by car, 24 miles from the hotel. Downtown shuttle bus service is one block away
Function Space: 13,000 square feet; 15 rooms
Capacity—Conference: 50; Reception: 1,000; Banquet: 460; Theater: 600
Equipment On-site: Audiovisual equipment rentals available and full-service business center on-site
Food Service: Catering/food service available; three restaurants, lounge
Overnight Accommodations: 205 rooms, 25 suites
Limitations/Restrictions: Smoking in designated areas only; no outside food and beverage service
Access: Handicapped accessible; on-site parking; open year-round
Payment: Credit card, direct billing

DURANGO

THE ROCHESTER HOTEL

(Mailing address)
721 E. Second Avenue
(Street address)
726 E. Second Avenue, Durango, CO 81301
Phone: 970/385-1920 or 800-664-1920
Fax: 970/385-1967
http://www.creativelinks.com/rochester

ORIGINALLY known as the Peeples Hotel when it was built in 1892, this two-story brick hotel embodies the flavor and atmosphere of the Old West. Renamed the Rochester in the early twentieth century, the hotel underwent extensive renovation and restoration during the 1990s. The many Western movies filmed in the Four-Corners area have provided inspiration for the Rochester's spirited decor—original movie posters line the hallways outside the guest rooms, named for classics such as *Butch Cassidy and the Sundance Kid* and *How the West*

The Rochester Hotel

Was Won. Guests stay in luxurious rooms with 15-foot ceilings decorated in an Old West motif, and softly playing cowboy music fills the lobby while old Westerns are shown on the large-screen TV. The Western theme continues in the meeting rooms; of particular interest is the Denver and Rio Grande Room, a train car facility built around the original windows of a Denver-Rio Grande Western Railroad car. Rates include a gourmet breakfast served in the lobby and courtyard, and guests can partake of complimentary refreshments in the late afternoon. Additional accommodations are available across the street at the Leland House bed and breakfast, which is also under hotel ownership.

Location: Durango is in southwestern Colorado, 50 miles north of Farmington, New Mexico, and 300 miles from Denver. The Rochester Hotel is accessible via Highways 160 and 550; La Plata Airport is 15 miles away.
Function Space: 3,000 square feet; 6 rooms
Capacity—Conference: 40; Reception: 150; Banquet: 100 (including garden and patio)
Equipment On-site: VCR and large-screen TV; fax and photocopier available
Food Service: Breakfast with room; catering/food service available; restaurant
Overnight Accommodations: 26 rooms
Limitations/Restrictions: No smoking
Access: Handicapped accessible; on-site parking; open year-round
Payment: Cash, check, credit card; payment due 30 days prior to arrival for group event

ESTES PARK

THE STANLEY HOTEL AND CONFERENCE CENTER—A GRAND HERITAGE HOTEL
(Mailing address)
P.O. Box 1767
(Street address)
333 Wonderview Drive, Estes Park, CO 80517
Phone: 800-976-1377   Fax: 970/586-4964

F. O. STANLEY, co-inventor of the Stanley Steamer automobile, opened his magnificent Georgian-style hotel in 1909, and, in the process, he helped open the western United States to automobile tourism as well. In his day, Stanley welcomed international celebrities to his Rocky Mountain retreat, and it was here that author Stephen King drew inspiration for his thriller *The Shining.* The Stanley is located less than six miles from Rocky Mountain National Park in the Stanley Historic District, and many of the hotel's guest rooms provide stunning mountain views, as does the MacGregor Ballroom and the dining room. Banquet and conference rooms accommodate groups of 20 to 300; the Manor House and Concert Hall offer exhibit space and additional meeting rooms. Fine dining, entertainment, and dancing can be found at the Dunraven Grille and Bar, while the Front Veranda offers summer dining and picturesque views. A heated outdoor pool, volleyball courts, and picnic area also are located on the hotel's 35 acres. Downtown Estes Park, with its shops and restaurants, is within walking distance of the Stanley, and the area abounds in recreational activities, including boating, horseback riding, golf, skiing, and, of course, mountain climbing.

Listed in the National Register of Historic Places

The Stanley Hotel

Location: The Stanley Hotel sits above the village of Estes Park on Highway 36, 78 miles northwest of Denver and an hour from Boulder.
Function Space: 18,000 square feet; 6 rooms
Capacity—Conference: 200; Reception: 200; Banquet: 300; Theater: 200
Equipment On-site: Audiovisual equipment available
Food Service: Catering/food service available; restaurant and bar
Overnight Accommodations: 92 rooms
Limitations/Restrictions: Restrictions on smoking; nonsmoking guest rooms available
Access: Handicapped accessible; on-site parking; open year-round
Payment: Cash, credit card

SPRINGFIELD

PLUM BEAR RANCH

(Mailing address)
P.O. Box 241
(Street address)
29461 County Road 21, Springfield, CO 81073
Phone: 719/523-4344   Fax: 719/523-4324

THE Plum Bear Ranch, named after the two creeks that run through the property, occupies 300 acres in a peaceful, rural setting. A working cattle ranch, the Plum Bear Ranch was homesteaded by the Waugh family in the early 1900s, and the old stone homestead dates back to about 1910. It has been restored and is now a living museum; there are also restored barns, built in the 1940s, near the house. Guests stay in a new two-story guest house with spacious rooms and have access to several common areas equipped with a fireplace and TV/VCR. Rates include a full, family-style breakfast in the morning, and a continental breakfast is also available. The meeting hall accommodates up to 35 and is ideal for business meetings and retreats. The ranch is a good base for exploring the area's many nearby natural wonders, including Picture Canyon, with its Natural Arch, Balanced Rock, and Indian petroglyphs; and Capulin Volcano, an early national monument.

Location: The Plum Bear Ranch is 4 miles west of Springfield (where Highways 160 and 287 intersect), and 52 miles south of Lamar in southeastern Colorado; airport service in Lamar and Pueblo is one and three hours away, respectively, by car.

Function Space: 720 square feet; 1 room

Capacity—Conference: 35; Reception: 35; Banquet: 30; Theater: 35

Equipment On-site: TV, VCR, fax, copier, personal computer

Food Service: Breakfast with room; catering service provides lunch and dinner

Overnight Accommodations: 5 guest rooms and 2 bunkhouse rooms

Limitations/Restrictions: No smoking; alcohol consumption not permitted

Access: On-site parking, open year-round

Payment: Cash, check, credit card (MC, Visa)

CONNECTICUT

HARTFORD

THE GOODWIN HOTEL

One Haynes Street, Hartford, CT 06103
Phone: 860/246-7500   Fax: 860/247-4576

FORMERLY the residence of financier J. P. Morgan, this handsome four-story Queen Anne building opened as the Goodwin Hotel in 1989. A small, European-style luxury hotel, the Goodwin is beautifully decorated with both classic and modern furnishings and nineteenth-century art. The hotel's elegant meeting facilities are especially suited for high-level meetings, conferences, and business retreats for groups as small as 5 to more than 100, and comprehensive conference services include all catering and business needs. Small social gatherings and large formal receptions are also easily accommodated on the mezzanine and in the atrium, impressive with its monumental columns. Stylish guest rooms feature antique sleigh beds, built-in armoires, and large marble baths. The JP Morgan Suite, with its spacious parlor, is ideal for private dining, corporate functions, and cocktail parties. Dining options include the casually elegant Pierpont's and the America's Cup Lounge, which offers light fare and a library of literary classics. The Goodwin Hotel is located in downtown Hartford across from the Civic Center and is within walking distance of theaters and other attractions.

Listed in the National Register of Historic Places

Location: The Goodwin Hotel is located in downtown Hartford, accessible via I-91 and I-84; 13 miles to Bradley International Airport.
Function Space: 3,500 square feet; 8 rooms
Capacity—Conference: 40; Reception: 400; Banquet: 300; Theater: 120; Classroom: 70
Equipment On-site: Audiovisual equipment and business services available
Food Service: Catering/food service available; restaurant, lounge
Overnight Accommodations: 124 rooms
Limitations/Restrictions: Restrictions on smoking
Access: Handicapped accessible; on-site parking; open year-round
Payment: Cash, credit card (AmEx, Discover, MC, Visa)

THE MARK TWAIN CARRIAGE HOUSE

351 Farmington Avenue, Hartford, CT 06105
Phone: 860/247-0998   Fax: 860/278-8148

SEVEN of Mark Twain's major works, including *The Adventures of Tom Sawyer* and *The Adventures of Huckleberry Finn*, were written while Twain (Samuel Clemens) lived in his Victorian Hartford home between 1874 and 1891. The 19-room house has been restored and is now a museum and research center, offering a wide range of cultural and educational programs. On display in the house is an excellent collection of fine and decorative arts and the only remaining domestic interiors by Louis Comfort Tiffany. The nearby Carriage House, where Twain's coachman lived and where two carriages, a sleigh, and four horses were kept, is on the grounds of the main house and is available for meetings and special events. Filled with Twain photographs and memorabilia that capture the spirit of one of America's favorite authors, the Carriage House is also rich in Victorian charm. Private tours of the Mark Twain House are available with evening rentals of the Carriage House, and guided group tours of the house can be arranged for Carriage House daytime rentals.

National Historic Landmark; listed in the National Register of Historic Places

Location: The Mark Twain House and Carriage House are located in the west end of Hartford, 10 minutes from downtown and 100 miles from New York and Boston, with easy access to I-91 and I-84. Bradley International Airport is within 30 minutes, and Union Station, served by major bus lines and Amtrak, is 2 miles away.
Function Space: 1,000 square feet; 1 room
Capacity—Conference: 30; Reception: 80; Banquet: 50; Theater: 70; May to October the covered porch of the Mark Twain House is available for receptions
Equipment On-site: Screen, slide projector, VCR and monitor, speaker's podium and microphone available

Old State House

Food Service: Renters select caterer; kitchenette available
Limitations/Restrictions: Restrictions on smoking
Access: Handicapped accessible; on-site parking; open year-round
Payment: Check

OLD STATE HOUSE

800 Main Street, Hartford, CT 06103
Phone: 860/522-6766   Fax: 860/522-2812

BUILT on the site of Thomas Hooker's small 1636 meeting house, the three-story neoclassical Old State House designed by renowned architect Charles Bulfinch was completed in 1796 and was once the tallest building in Hartford. Even with the addition of the handsome cupola in the nineteenth century, the Old State House is surrounded by considerably taller structures today, but it remains a powerful link to Connecticut's early national past. Talk of demolishing the building galvanized citizens during the 1970s, and preservation of this landmark was secured. An extensive, award-winning renovation and restoration effort followed, and the historic building was formally reopened on its 200th anniversary. The Senate Chamber was restored to its early nineteenth-century appearance, the City Council Chamber now looks as it did in the 1890s, and the court room is once again in the Colonial Revival style of the early 1900s. Today the building is both a vibrant living history museum and a meeting center for business, civic, and social functions.

National Historic Landmark; listed in the National Register of Historic Places

Location: The Old State House is located at the intersection of Central Row and Main Street and is within a 10-minute walk of Hartford train and bus stations. The Old State House is accessible via Route 84 and Route 91; Bradley International Airport is within 30 minutes; Boston is 2 hours away, and New York City 2.5 hours away.
Function Space: 1,600 square feet; 1 room
Capacity—Conference: 100; Reception: 150; Banquet: 100; Theater: 75
Food Service: Caterers list available
Limitations/Restrictions: No smoking; legal liquor liability coverage required for alcohol service
Access: Handicapped accessible; open year-round
Payment: Check, credit card (MC, Visa)

MYSTIC

THE INN AT MYSTIC

(Mailing address)
P.O. Box 216
(Street address)
Junction of Route 1 and Route 27, Mystic, CT 06355
Phone: 860/536-9604   Fax: 860/536-7563

NESTLED in the picturesque, sheltered coves of Mystic Harbor, the Inn at Mystic has been providing warm hospitality in a turn-of-the-century setting since 1963. The Colonial Revival-style mansion built in 1904 was once the home of Katherine Haley, widow of a late nineteenth-century owner of the Fulton Fish Market. The luxurious mansion, where Humphrey Bogart and Lauren Bacall honeymooned, offers a gorgeous view of the harbor and Long Island Sound from its Victorian verandah. The Inn's complex comprises both elegant and modest accommodations,

all with a colonial flavor, on 13 wooded acres overlooking Pequotsepos Cove. Recreational activities include tennis, sailing, and canoeing. A waterfront walking trail and pool and hot spa are also available. Beautiful English gardens, an orchard, recreational facilities, and the acclaimed Flood Tide Restaurant round out the hillside retreat. Nearby attractions include Mystic Seaport, the country's largest maritime museum, Mystic Marinelife Aquarium, and the U.S. Coast Guard Academy.

Listed in the National Register of Historic Places

Location: The Inn at Mystic is on the coast in southeastern Connecticut, 90 miles from Boston and 130 miles from New York City.
Function Space: 2,000 square feet; 2 rooms
Capacity—Conference: 30–40; Reception: 100; Banquet: 100
Equipment On-site: Overhead and slide projectors, screens, VCR
Food Service: Full-service restaurant, lounge
Overnight Accommodations: 5 rooms in the mansion, 68 total guest rooms on-site
Access: Handicapped accessible; on-site parking; open year-round
Payment: Cash, check, credit card

WHALER'S INN

20 E. Main Street, Mystic, CT 06355
Phone: 860/536-1506   Fax: 860/572-1250

LOCATED in the Mystic historic district and only steps away from the water's edge, the sparkling white Whaler's Inn was built in 1901 on the site of several renowned nineteenth-century inns. Mystic was originally settled in 1654, but in the mid-nineteenth century it was a booming shipbuilding center, and much of the town's historic architecture dates back to the Victorian era. Today the renovated inn, honored by both the area's historical society and the local garden club for its beautiful restoration, offers comfortable accommodations, and guest rooms are traditionally furnished and decorated with canopy beds and wingback chairs. On-site is Bravo Bravo, a gourmet restaurant, the seasonal Cafe Bravo, offering alfresco dining, and a bagel shop, CC Bagel. The inn's charming 1865 House, with its white ballustraded verandah, has a meeting room furnished with antiques available for meetings and receptions. With its downtown location, the inn is conveniently placed for walking tours of historic Mystic and its colorful Main Street.

Location: Mystic is 90 miles south of Boston, and the Whaler's Inn is accessible via I-95 to Route 27.
Function Space: 800 square feet; 1 room
Capacity—Conference: 25; Reception: 35; Banquet: 35; Theater: 35
Equipment On-site: VCR, overhead projector, podium, fax, typing service
Food Service: Full-service restaurant
Overnight Accommodations: 41 rooms
Limitations/Restrictions: Restrictions on smoking; food and beverages must be purchased on-site
Access: On-site parking; open year-round
Payment: Credit card

NEW HAVEN

THREE CHIMNEYS INN

1201 Chapel, New Haven, CT 06511
Phone: 203/789-1201   Fax: 203/776-7363
E-mail: chimneys.nh@aol.com

FORMERLY the Inn at Chapel West, the refurbished Three Chimneys Inn is New Haven's first urban inn. The 1870 mansion, with its charming Victorian exterior touches and verandah, is beautifully furnished in the Georgian and Federal styles. Overnight guests enjoy a complimentary breakfast, and tea is available as an afternoon refreshment. The 10 distinctive guest rooms, with oriental rugs and four-poster and canopied beds, combine Old World comfort with modern conveniences. Two conference rooms and the library are available for meetings, and the Inn offers complete meeting packages, which include catered meals, refreshments, and audiovisual equipment. Located in the Chapel Street Historic District, Three Chimneys is just one block from the Yale University campus and within easy walking distance of New Haven's "College and Chapel" area, known for its fine shopping, dining, and entertainment.

Location: Three Chimneys Inn is located one block from Yale University at the intersection of I-95 and I-91, and is served by Tweed Airport.
Function Space: 952 square feet; 3 rooms
Capacity—Conference: 24; Reception: 36; Banquet: 24; Theater: 36
Equipment On-site: VCR, overhead projector, in-room modem jacks, fax, copier
Food Service: Breakfast with room; catering/food service available
Overnight Accommodations: 10 rooms
Limitations/Restrictions: No smoking

Access: On-site parking, open year-round
Payment: Credit card (AmEx, Visa)

NORWALK

LOCKWOOD-MATHEWS MANSION MUSEUM

295 West Avenue, Norwalk, CT 06850
Phone: 203/838-9799   Fax: 203/838-1434

THE striking Lockwood-Mathews Mansion, completed in 1868, is considered one of the nation's earliest and finest surviving Second Empire-style country houses. In selecting Norwalk as a site for his palatial mansion, LeGrand Lockwood, a New York investment banker and self-made millionaire, returned to the tranquil town of his childhood. European architect Detlef Lienau designed the 52-room mansion to suit both American tastes and the physical climate, and his sophisticated plans for the mansion required both exotic materials and the skill and artistry of Italian stonecutters, carvers, painters, and other European craftsmen. Prominent New York designers Leon Marcotte and Gustav and Christian Herter were responsible for the exquisite interiors and the integral furnishings that grace the mansion. Meeting space is available in the 42-foot-high octagonal rotunda gallery, with its double-skylighted ceiling, that once housed Lockwood's notable art collection, including Albert Bierstadt's *The Domes of Yosemite*. Functions are also held in the ornate Billiards Rooms, and guests are welcome to view the marble entrance hall, foyer, and adjacent museum galleries. The Mathews family acquired the mansion in 1876, and it was purchased by the City of Norwalk in 1941. Since 1968 it has served as a museum dedicated to the study and preservation of Victorian art and culture.

National Historic Landmark; listed in the National Register of Historic Places

Location: The Lockwood-Mathews Mansion Museum is at the intersection of US Route 7 and I-95, and is approximately 40 miles northeast of New York City and a 10-minute drive

Lockwood-Mathews Mansion Museum
*(Courtesy of Lockwood-Mathews
Mansion Museum, Inc., of Norwalk)*

from the South Norwalk MetroNorth rail station; 1 hour from LaGuardia Airport and 1.25 hours from JFK International Airport (New York City) and Bradley International Airport (Hartford, Connecticut).

Function Space: 2,300 square feet; 2 rooms
Capacity—Conference: 150; Reception: 250; Banquet: 200
Equipment On-site: Speaker's podium, tables and folding chairs (100) included in use arrangement
Food Service: Large serving kitchen (no food preparation on site) included in use arrangement; caterer must be approved by the museum
Limitations/Restrictions: Use of the museum is restricted to government agencies, nonprofits, educational institutions, and member corporations; insurance, provided by the user, is required; no open flame (i.e., candles, sterno),

smoking, or propane tanks permitted
Access: Handicapped accessible; limited on-site parking available; open March to December
Payment: Cash, check, credit card

OLD LYME

OLD LYME INN

(Mailing address)
P.O. Box 787
(Street address)
85 Lyme Street, Old Lyme, CT 06371
Phone: 860/434-2600 or 800-434-5352
Fax: 860/434-5352
E-mail: oli@aol.com

FAMED for its impressionist art colony at the turn of the twentieth century, the small village of Old Lyme boasts a small fine arts college, an art museum, and an art association, all within walking distance of the Old Lyme Inn. The inn's farmhouse, (c. 1850), once part of a 300-acre farm, has been restored, renovated, and furnished as a nineteenth-century country home. Adorning the walls are murals of local scenes and works of art by famous local artists, including examples of impressionist painting from the Old Lyme School. Other features of note are the chestnut paneling in the dining room and the curly maple ballisters on the staircase. Guest rooms are furnished in the Empire and Victorian styles, and rates include a continental-plus breakfast. Both casual and formal dining and meeting rooms are available for retreats, small conferences, seminars, and celebrations, and the inn's restaurant has been consistently noted for its creativity and fine food. Located on historic Lyme Street, the inn is convenient to antique shops, casinos, and outdoor

Old Lyme Inn

recreational activities, and the maritime ports of Essex and Mystic are just a short drive away.

Location: Old Lyme is off I-95, Exit 70, two hours from New York City and Boston; Amtrak service is available to nearby Old Saybrook. The Groton-New London Airport is 20 minutes away, and the Bradley (Hartford/Springfield) and Warwick (Providence, Rhode Island) airports are 55 minutes away.
Function Space: 1,500 square feet; 4 rooms
Capacity—Conference: 70; Reception: 100+; Banquet: 70; Theater: 70
Equipment On-site: Audiovisual equipment, photocopier, and fax available
Food Service: Breakfast with room; catering/food service available, can accommodate all dietary limitations; restaurant
Overnight Accommodations: 13 rooms
Limitations/Restrictions: Restrictions on smoking
Access: Handicapped accessible; on-site parking; open year-round
Payment: Cash, check, credit card

RIDGEFIELD

THE CASS GILBERT GARDEN HOUSE AT THE KEELER TAVERN MUSEUM

(Mailing address)
P.O. Box 204
(Street address)
132 Main Street, Ridgefield, CT 06877
Phone: 203/431-0815 or 203/438-5485

ARCHITECT Cass Gilbert, who, like many other wealthy New Yorkers, summered in Ridgefield, purchased the eighteenth-century Keeler Tavern in 1907 and shortly thereafter designed the lovely Garden House. Best known for designing the U.S. Supreme Court building, Gilbert also has New York's Woolworth Building and several state capitols and university libraries to his credit, but this simple yet classic Garden House was intended for his own use as a bright and elegant place to entertain guests. Opening onto a beautifully manicured lawn and landscaped gardens, the Garden House continues to be an elegant gathering place for receptions, concerts, teas, weddings, and other social functions. The house has been restored and has an attached support facility with a catering kitchen, restrooms, and storage space. The Keeler Tavern was built as a private residence prior to 1730, but in 1769 Timothy and Esther Keeler turned it into a tavern. It is now a museum and open for tours conducted by costumed guides on Wednesdays and weekends.

Listed in the National Register of Historic Places

Location: Ridgefield is in southwestern Connecticut, 15 minutes from Danbury, 1 hour from Hartford, and 1.5 hours from New York City, and is accessible via I-84 and Route 7, I-684 and Route 35, and the Merritt Parkway to Route 7 and Route 33. Airport service is available at Weschester Airport, White Plains, New York; LaGuardia and JFK in New York City; and Bradley International Airport in Hartford.
Function Space: 1,250 square feet; 1 room
Capacity—Conference: 100; Reception: 100; Banquet: 100
Equipment On-site: 100 chairs available
Food Service: Catering kitchen on site
Limitations/Restrictions: Restrictions on smoking; only food and beverages supplied by caterer permitted; no amplification or loud music; rental

available daily for 8-hour periods, 9:00 A.M. to 10:00 P.M.
Access: Handicapped accessible; on-site parking; open year-round
Payment: Check

WATERBURY

SEVENTY HILLSIDE

70 Hillside Avenue, Waterbury, CT 06710
Phone: 203/596-7070   Fax: 203/754-5515

WATERBURY'S Hillside Historic District, where many turn-of-the-century industrialists built grand homes, comprises a number of houses listed in the National Register of Historic Places. Among them is Seventy Hillside, a handsome brick and wood-trim mansion atop a gentle hill in a parklike setting. Built in 1901, the house remains in the family that built it, and it continues to be a gathering place for weddings, receptions, and other social events. But today it is also used for corporate meetings, seminars, retreats, and other business functions. Restored to its early Victorian appearance, Seventy Hillside features elaborately carved interiors, leaded glass windows, marble fireplaces, oriental rugs, and original antique furnishings. Events may be held in the library, the dining room, the "brick room," and the large central hall, with its sweeping staircase and fireplace. The enclosed formal rose garden is also available for outdoor events. Room rates include a continental breakfast, and a bed and breakfast affiliated with the mansion is just a block away.

Listed in the National Register of Historic Places

Location: Seventy Hillside is located a half-mile from the intersection of I-84 and Route 8, approximately 1.5 hours from New York City and 45 minutes from Bradley International Airport. Train and bus stations are a half-mile away.
Function Space: 2,500 square feet; 4 rooms
Capacity—Conference: 50; Reception: 120
Equipment On-site: Audiovisual equipment and other services arranged through outside vendors
Food Service: Breakfast with room; renter selects caterer; kitchen available
Overnight Accommodations: 3 rooms
Limitations/Restrictions: No smoking
Access: On-site parking; open year-round
Payment: Check

WESTPORT

THE INN AT NATIONAL HALL

2 Post Road West, Westport, CT 06880
Phone: 203/221-1351   Fax: 203/221-0276

BUILT in 1873, this stately Italianate structure housed Westport's First National Bank as well as the town meeting hall—thus its name, National Hall. The inn is the cornerstone of Westport's National Hall Historic District, which includes three acres of waterfront overlooking the Saugatuck River. Modeled after Europe's elite manor houses, the inn and its individually designed guest rooms are graced with stenciled works of art inspired by nature and fairy tale. Selected chambers boast soaring two-story ceilings with loft bedrooms, expansive windows, and splendid river views as well as VCRs and refrigerators, and room rates include continental or full breakfasts. Among the inn's unique touches are whimsical map murals and other trompe l'oeil features, such as the custom-designed elevator that appears lined with book-filled shelves. The boardroom comfortably accommodates 14 around the conference table, and breakfast and lunch can be catered for meetings. Contemporary French and Italian cuisines are on the menu at the inn's renowned Restaurant Zanghi, which serves lunch and dinner daily. Guests can enjoy local beaches, theater, shopping, art, and antiquing, as well as many fine restaurants—all within walking distance of the inn.

Listed in the National Register of Historic Places

Location: The Inn at National Hall is between I-95 (Exit 17) and Route 15 (Exit 41), 25 miles from Westchester Airport and 48 miles from LaGuardia Airport. New York City is one hour away.
Function Space: 500 square feet; 1 room
Capacity—Conference: 14

Equipment On-site: TV/VCR, overhead projectors, 35mm slide projector
Food Service: Breakfast with room; catering/food service available; restaurant
Overnight Accommodations: 15 rooms
Limitations/Restrictions: No smoking; no pets
Access: On-site parking; open year-round
Payment: Major credit card

WOODSTOCK

BOWEN HOUSE, ROSELAND COTTAGE
(Mailing address)
P.O. Box 186
(Street address)
556 Route 169, Woodstock, CT 06281
Phone: 860/928-4074   Fax: 860/963-2208

THE Heritage Trail that stretches from Old Sturbride Village in Massachusetts down to Mystic Seaport passes through the quiet country town of

The Inn at National Hall

Woodstock, a charming cluster of colonial New England villages. A striking contrast to the area's traditional architecture is found at the bright pink Gothic Revival-style Bowen House. From its intricate barge boards and rich exterior ornamentation to its stained glass windows and medieval interior atmosphere, its details help to make Bowen House one of the finest examples of its style in the country. Henry Chandler Bowen built the house as a summer residence in 1846, throwing lavish parties and his famed Fourth of July festivities, which even had U.S. presidents in attendance. Today the carriage house welcomes guests for weddings, receptions, meetings, and other events. The grounds can also be tented for outdoor functions, and the shaded lawns and impressive parterre garden, first laid out in 1850, make for a lovely setting. Newspaper readers have cited Bowen House as the best museum in northeast Connecticut, and arrangements may be made for function guests to take full tours. There are several other historic structures on the property as well, including a barn with one of the country's oldest surviving bowling alleys.

National Historic Landmark; listed in the National Register of Historic Places

Location: Bowen House, Roseland Cottage, is located on Route 169 in northeastern Connecticut. The house is 1.5 hours from Boston, 45 minutes from Providence, Rhode Island, and 1 hour from Hartford, Connecticut, and is accessible via I-84, Route 44, and I-90 to I-395.

Function Space: 1,440 square feet; 1 room

Capacity—Conference: 125; Reception: 80-100; Banquet: 100; Theater: 100; tented grounds accommodate 300

Equipment On-site: Slide projector and screen; fax and copier available

Food Service: Catering kitchen available

Limitations/Restrictions: Restrictions on smoking; insurance and permit required for alcohol by renter

Access: Handicapped accessible; on-site parking; open May–October

Payment: Check

DELAWARE

WILMINGTON

HOTEL DU PONT

Eleventh and Market Streets
Wilmington, DE 19801
Phone: 302/594-3100   Fax: 302/656-2145

THE regal Hotel du Pont has been a Wilmington landmark since it open in 1913, and in its first week 25,000 visitors poured in to see the new luxurious facilities. Then, as now, visitors marveled at the rich interior spaces, whose carved woodwork, gilded ceilings, and intricate marble and mosaic floors required the labors of 18 French and Italian craftsman for more than two years. In addition to its architectural splendors, the hotel's interiors feature more than 700 original paintings showcasing the work of some 250 artists, including three generations of Wyeths. Each of the spacious, renovated guest rooms has its own sitting room. A full range of business and social events can be accommodated, and facilities include the French neoclassic Gold Ballroom, a state-of-art conference center, and the multipurpose Playhouse Theater. The conference center blends modern, high-tech features with polished elegance, making it ideal for training meetings, seminars, and other business functions. Located in downtown Wilmington in the city's historic and financial district, the Hotel du Pont is close to a number of museums and historic sites, including Longwood Gardens, the du Pont family's country residence.

Member of Historic Hotels of America

Location: Wilmington is 25 minutes from Philadelphia International Airport, less than an hour from Baltimore, and two hours from Washington, D.C., and New York City. The hotel is 4 blocks from I-95 and 10 blocks from the Amtrak train station.

Function Space: 30,000 square feet; 30 rooms
Capacity—Conference: 44 ; Reception: 450; Banquet: 400; Theater: 120 (meeting room); Playhouse Theater seats 1,239

Equipment On-site: VCR, overhead and slide projectors, screen, flip chart, easel; basic business services available, extensive services require advance notice

Food Service: Catering/food service available; two on-site dining rooms, lounge, 24-hour room service

Hotel du Pont *(Tom Crane)*

Overnight Accommodations: 216 rooms
Limitations/Restrictions: Restrictions on smoking (nonsmoking rooms available); no outside catering
Access: Handicapped accessible; on-site parking; open year-round
Payment: Major credit card

WINTERTHUR

WINTERTHUR MUSEUM GARDEN AND LIBRARY

(Mailing address)
Winterthur, DE 19735
(Street address)
Route 52, Winterthur, DE 19732
Phone: 302/888-4804   Fax: 302/888-4820

LOCATED in the Brandywine Valley, Winterthur was the magnificent estate of Henry Francis du Pont (1880–1969), collector and horticulturalist. James Antoine Bidermann, son-in-law of E. I. du Pont de Nemours, founder of the DuPont Company, built the original residence on the estate in 1839. Many years later Henry Francis set about creating an unrivaled collection of early American decorative arts (1640–1860) displayed in 175 period rooms and 2 galleries. Among the more than 89,000 examples of these artworks are 6 silver tankards by Paul Revere and a 66-piece dinner service made for George Washington. Winterthur's spectacular 200-acre garden, showcasing native and exotic plants, is colorful throughout the year, and the renowned Winterthur Library is famous for its 80,000-volume collection relating to American arts from 1640–1914. In 1951, Winterthur opened to the public, and programming includes a number of educational, cultural, and social activities, as well as guided and self-guided tours. Meeting space is available in the Visitor Pavilion, which opens to the gardens, and in the Copeland Lecture Hall. Corporate members of Winterthur may also use additional meeting facilities and rooms, including several with elegant Early American decor.

Listed in the National Register of Historic Places

Location: Winterthur is six miles north of Wilmington, Delaware, less than an hour from Philadelphia, and halfway between New York City and Washington, D.C.
Function Space: 9 rooms
Capacity—Conference: 22; Reception: 400 (with tents, 1,000); Banquet: 300; Theater: 348
Equipment On-site: Slide and overhead projectors, screens; other equipment can be arranged
Food Service: Exclusive caterer available; restaurant, cafeteria, cafe
Limitations/Restrictions: No smoking; no outside catering; food and beverages not permitted in some areas; corporations that are members of the Winterthur Business Associates may host events at all available facilities; nonmember groups have access to the Pavilion and Copeland Lecture Hall
Access: Handicapped accessible; on-site parking; open year-round (except Thanksgiving, Christmas, New Year's)
Payment: Invoice

DISTRICT OF COLUMBIA

ARTS CLUB OF WASHINGTON

2017 I Street NW, Washington, DC 20006
Phone: 202/331-7282   Fax: 202/857-3678

TIMOTHY Caldwell began building his Federal-style mansion in 1802, adding the front portion in 1805. But the Caldwell-Abbe House, as it is listed in the National Register of Historic Places, is generally known as the Monroe House. It was here that President James Monroe's inaugural reception was held and where he lived for the first six months of his presidency while the White House was repaired following the War of 1812. In 1877, Professor Cleveland Abbe, founder of the U.S. Weather Service, became the home's owner, and he added a third story. Today the house at 2017 "Eye" Street and an adjoining structure, the Macfeely House, are the home of the Arts Club of Washington, an organization founded in 1916 to promote and support local artistic and cultural endeavors. There are art exhibitions in both houses and in the garden, and the club welcomes groups meeting here for formal dinners, business sessions, weddings, receptions, recitals, lectures, and other events. The facades of both houses have been restored, and the interiors are decorated with antiques and period furnishings.

National Historic Landmark; listed in the National Register of Historic Places

Location: The Arts Club of Washington is in the Foggy Bottom district, five blocks west of the White House and three blocks from both the Foggy Bottom and Farragut West metrorail stations.
Function Space: 3,600 square feet; 6 rooms
Capacity—Conference: 50; Reception: 200; Banquet: 102; Theater: 115
Equipment On-site: Sound system, screens, piano
Food Service: Catering/food service available
Overnight Accommodations: 2 rooms (members only)
Limitations/Restrictions: No smoking; customer supplies own alcohol
Access: Open September through July
Payment: Check

THE CARLTON HOTEL

923 16th and K Streets NW, Washington, DC 20006
Phone: 202/638-2626   Fax: 202/638-4231

A traditional grand hotel, the eight-story Carlton was built in 1926, modeled after an Italian Renaissance palazzo. Since its opening, this restored luxury hotel has hosted presidents, prime ministers, and other dignitaries. The stunning lobby features an intricately detailed beamed ceiling, crystal chandeliers, and rich furnishings. Meeting space ranges from the Crystal Ballroom, which accommodates up to 400 guests, to smaller rooms for groups of as few as 10, and a garden terrace. Complete business and other services are available through the 24-hour concierge. The Allegro Restaurant serves breakfast, lunch, and dinner and features continental cuisine, while the

Allegro bar offers evening entertainment. Guest rooms boast all the modern conveniences, and the Presidential Suite is arranged to accommodate the needs of traveling dignitaries and their staffs. On-site recreational facilities include a fitness center, and exercise equipment can be delivered to guest rooms on request. The Carlton Hotel is just two blocks from the White House, and the Smithsonian's Renwick Gallery, the National Mall, and numerous fine shops and restaurants are just a short walk away.

Listed in the National Register of Historic Places

Location: The Carlton Hotel is in downtown Washington, D.C., at Sixteenth and K streets, 1.5 miles from Union Station, 7 miles from National Airport, and 30 miles from Dulles International Airport.
Function Space: 10,000 square feet; 9 rooms
Capacity—Conference: 150; Reception: 400; Banquet: 300; Theater: 350
Equipment On-site: Audiovisual equipment available; complete business services arranged through concierge

Food Service: Catering/food service available; restaurant and bar; 24-hour room service
Overnight Accommodations: 193 rooms
Access: Handicapped accessible; on-site parking; open year-round
Payment: Cash, check, credit card

THE CORCORAN GALLERY OF ART

500 17th Street NW, Washington, DC 20006-4804
Phone: 202/639-1780   Fax: 202/639-1785

HOUSED in a curving 1897 Beaux Arts building between the White House and the National Mall is Washington's largest privately supported art museum, one of the three oldest art museums in the country. William Wilson Corcoran, in his day a leading patron of the arts, founded the museum in 1869. The Corcoran's permanent collection of nineteenth-century American art is considered among the finest in the world, and the museum maintains an outstanding collection of American prints and drawings. In addition to its ongoing exhibitions of contemporary art and its surveys of historic and modern photography, the Corcoran also has on display an excellent collection of seventeenth-century Dutch and nineteenth-century French paintings, tapestries and textiles, and ancient and modern sculpture. Among the museum's most stunning displays is the restored Salon Doré (gilded room), originally part of the hôtel de Clermont, an aristocratic private residence in eighteenth-century Paris. Receptions and gatherings in the atrium and on the upstairs bridge allow guests to meet in a classical setting amid beautiful works of art.

The Corcoran Gallery of Art
(Courtesy of the Corcoran Gallery of Art)

National Historic Landmark; listed in the National Register of Historic Places

Location: The Corcoran Gallery of Art is one block southwest of the White House; five and six blocks from metrorail stations Farragut West (Blue/Orange Lines) and Farragut North (Red Line).
Function Space: 14,012 square feet; atrium and bridge available
Capacity—Reception: 1,000; Banquet: 400 (seated dinner)
Food Service: Caterer's guidelines available
Limitations/Restrictions: No smoking; no red wine may be served for a standing reception
Access: Handicapped accessible; five blocks to metrorail station; open year-round
Payment: Check only

Decatur House
(Ron Blunt. Courtesy of the National Trust for Historic Preservation)

DECATUR HOUSE

748 Jackson Place NW, Washington, DC 20006
Phone: 202/842-0917   Fax: 202/842-0030

DECATUR House has a long and lively history as a place for social gatherings and remains a favorite meeting spot for the city's social and political elite. Designed by architect Benjamin Henry Latrobe and built in 1818 for Commodore Stephen Decatur and his wife, Susan, the Federal-style townhome on Lafayette Square is just one block from the White House. After Decatur's untimely death in 1820 following a duel with a fellow naval officer, the house was occupied by a series of distinguished diplomats and politicians, including Henry Clay and Martin Van Buren. Diplomat Edward F. Beale purchased Decatur House in 1871, and he and his descendants hosted lavish parties in the second-floor formal parlors. Today the home is a house museum; the

ground-floor rooms are decorated in the Federal style of Decatur's time, while the upstairs reflects the Victorian-era decor of the Beales' occupancy. The Carriage House and courtyard, adjacent to Decatur House, are available for groups of 10 to 500, and the rental fee includes walk-through tours of the house museum. The house museum itself is available for use on a limited basis.

National Historic Landmark; listed in the National Register of Historic Places; National Trust for Historic Preservation Historic Site

Location: Decatur House is on Lafayette Square, one block from the White House; one block from the Farragut West metrorail station (Orange/Blue Lines) and two blocks from the McPherson Square (Orange/Blue Lines) and Farragut North (Red Line) stations.

Function Space: 2,100 square feet; 2 rooms
Capacity—Reception: 250 (with a tented court-yard, 500); Seated: 120 (with a tented courtyard, 220); Theater: 175
Equipment On-site: Podium/microphone rental available
Food Service: List of approved caterers provided
Limitations/Restrictions: Restrictions on smoking; no throwing birdseed, rice, rose petals at wedding receptions; no cash bars; functions must end by midnight; after 11:30 P.M. dancing and amplified music not permitted; insurance is required
Access: Open year-round
Payment: Check

DUMBARTON HOUSE

2715 Q Street NW, Washington, DC 20007
Phone: 202/337-2288   Fax: 202/337-0348

AN excellent example of Federal-period architec-ture, Dumbarton House was built in about 1800 on land granted to Indian fighter and Scotsman Ninian Beall by the General Assembly of Maryland in 1703. Samuel Jackson of Philadelphia built the mansion, which has had a number of owners, including Joseph Nourse, first register of the U.S. Treasury, from 1805 to 1813. For years local lore held that Dolley Madison sought refuge here after fleeing the White House during the War of 1812, but it was not until the 1995 discovery of a mili-tary secretary's letter that the tale was confirmed. The Colonial Dames of America purchased the property in 1928 and restored the house shortly thereafter. Today, Dumbarton House is their head-quarters, as well as a house museum featuring late eighteenth- and early nineteenth-century furnish-ings, decorative arts, Chinese export porcelain, and

historic documents signed by George Washington and Thomas Jefferson. Both business and social functions are accommodated in Dumbarton's ele-gant reception room, which features 13-foot ceil-ings, hardwood floors, and French doors that open onto an enclosed courtyard.

Location: Dumbarton House is located in historic Georgetown, in northwest Washington, DC, 10 minutes from Washington National Airport.
Function Space: 1,350 square feet; 1 room
Capacity—Conference: 120; Reception: 180; Banquet: 180; Theater: 120
Equipment On-site: Microphone, podium, screen
Food Service: Preferred caterer's list provided
Limitations/Restrictions: No smoking; no red wine; no rice thrown
Access: Handicapped accessible; on-site parking; open year-round except December 24–January 2
Payment: Check

THE HAY-ADAMS HOTEL

800 Sixteenth Street NW, Washington, DC 20006
Phone: 202/638-6600 or 800-424-5054
Fax: 202/638-2716

OVERLOOKING the White House and Lafayette Square is the Hay-Adams Hotel, a 1928 Italian Renaissance-style building named for two promi-nent Washingtonians. John Hay, President Lincoln's private secretary, who later served as sec-retary of state, and Henry Adams, great-grandson of John Adams, owned adjoining townhomes where the hotel now stands, which were for years an elite social center before being demolished in 1927. The historic Hay-Adams Hotel continues to make the site a distinguished meeting place with its five elegantly appointed private meeting and function rooms available for business and social events. Both the Federal Suite and the John Hay Suite enjoy White House views, and the Concorde Room faces St. John's Church. The John Hay Room, with the hotel's most elaborately molded ceiling, dark wood accents, and Persian carpets, offers the largest meeting space, and the handsome Windsor Room boasts an authentic Windsor coat of arms over the fireplace. A semiprivate room, separated by French glass doors from the renowned Lafayette restaurant, accommodates 24 guests, and under special circumstances the seasonal roof deck is available for receptions. The hotel is within walking distance of the National Mall, the convention center, and fine shopping.

Member of Historic Hotels of America

Location: The Hay Adams Hotel is located at Lafayette Square across from the White House and is just a block from the McPherson Square and Farragut West metrorail stations.
Function Space: 4,400 square feet; 6 rooms
Capacity—Conference: 40; Reception: 200; Banquet: 140; Theater: 100; the seasonal roof deck of the hotel may be available for private functions (150 for standing reception) under special circumstances
Equipment On-site: Audiovisual equipment and 24-hour business services available
Food Service: Catering/food service available; restaurant, lounge, 24-hour room service
Overnight Accommodations: 143 rooms
Access: Limited handicapped accessibility; on-site parking; open year-round
Payment: Credit card

HENLEY PARK HOTEL
926 Massachusetts Avenue NW
Washington, DC 20001
Phone: 202/638-5200   Fax: 202/638-6740

A handsome Tudor-style building constructed in 1918, the Henley Park Hotel is distinctive with battlements, plaques, and 119 gargoyles on its exterior. Originally known as Tudor Hall, an upscale apartment complex that was home to many senators and representatives, the building was renovated in 1982, reopening as a small European-style luxury hotel. Meeting space is available in the Eton Room, designed primarily for business, and is equipped with built-in screens. To accommodate small to mid-size executive meetings or gatherings, the hotel offers elegantly appointed hospitality suites of various sizes and arrangements. All furnishings are of the Queen Anne or Chippendale styles. Formal private or corporate functions may be held in the Coeur de Lion, the hotel's restaurant, where an opulent bilevel room with mirrored pillars, stained glass windows, and exquisite detailing makes for an elegant setting. The restaurant's name is derived from the crest of Richard the Lion Heart located above the lobby archway. The Henley Park Hotel's downtown Washington, D.C., location puts it within easy walking distance of numerous attractions, including the Smithsonian's National Museum of American Art and the National Portrait Gallery, the J. Edgar Hoover F.B.I. Building, and the District of Columbia convention center.

Member of Historic Hotels of America

Location: The Henley Park Hotel is one block west of Mt. Vernon Square, four blocks from Metro Center metrorail station, and 5 miles from National Airport. The hotel is accessible via I-395.

Function Space: 668 square feet; 1 room; restaurant also available (2,600 square feet)

Capacity—Conference: 24; Reception: 175; Banquet: 55

Equipment On-site: Audiovisual equipment available; secretarial services, fax, photocopier available

Food Service: Catering/food service available; restaurant and lounge

Overnight Accommodations: 96 rooms

Access: On-site parking; open year-round

Payment: Check, credit card

HOTEL SOFITEL
1914 Connecticut Avenue NW
Washington, DC 20009
Phone: 202/797-2000 Fax: 202/328-1984

THE graceful 1906 Beaux Arts building that rises above clusters of embassies along fashionable Connecticut Avenue was first known as the Highlands. Built on one of the city's highest elevations, the Highlands opened as a luxury apartment hotel that was soon at the center of Washington's diplomatic and social circles, home to legislators and diplomats alike. Today the Hotel Sofitel offers French elegance, old-fashioned charm, and modern conveniences for visitors to the nation's capital and boasts oversized suites and the largest guest rooms in Washington. Each comfortably furnished room features its own work and study areas, computer and fax lines, armoires with safes, and other amenities; guests also have complimentary use of a nearby fitness center. The hotel's restaurant, the Trocadero Cafe, is known for its fine French cuisine, and the adjoining Pullman Bar is an intimate setting for drinks. Conference facilities are available for business meetings, din-

ners, and receptions, and a valet parking service allows conference attendees easy hotel access. Nearby attractions include the lively Adams Morgan and Dupont Circle neighborhoods, with their clubs, art galleries, and ethnic restaurants, and Georgetown and the National Mall are just minutes away by cab.

Location: The Hotel Sofitel is located five blocks north of Dupont Circle in northwest Washington, D.C., 15 to 20 minutes from National Airport.

Function Space: 2,000 square feet; 3 rooms

Capacity—Conference: 35; Reception: 100; Banquet: 80; Theater: 40

Equipment On-site: Audiovisual equipment available

Food Service: Catering/food service available; restaurant, bar, 24-hour room service

Overnight Accommodations: 145 rooms

Access: On-site (valet) parking; open year-round

Payment: Credit card (AmEx, Diners, MC, Visa)

THE KALORAMA GUEST HOUSE
1854 Mintwood Place NW, Washington, DC 20009
Phone: 202/667-6369 Fax: 202/319-1262

THE Kalorama Guest House, built in about 1900, enjoys a splendid location in the city's historic Adams Morgan district, known for its charming turn-of-the-century Victorian townhouses, ethnic dining, antique shops, and art galleries. Also nearby are the National Zoo, Rock Creek Park, and numerous embassies. Downtown Washington is just minutes away by cab or subway. The Kalorama Guest House happily borrows its traditions from English bed and breakfasts, French hostelleries, and Italian pensiones while maintaining its American identity. Overnight guests are treated to a continental breakfast, and sherry is served in the parlor in the afternoon. Rooms are individually furnished with both antiques and reproductions, and framed historic sheet music and magazine covers on the walls add an early twentieth-century touch. Comfortable parlor rooms furnished with late Victorian and Edwardian antiques and period prints are available for informal business meetings and other gatherings.

Location: Kalorama Guest House is located in northwest Washington's Adams Morgan district at Kalorama Park, between Columbia Road and Connecticut Avenue. The Woodley Park-Zoo metrorail station is just a half-mile away.
Function Space: 900 square feet; 3 rooms
Capacity—Conference: 20; Reception: 30; Banquet: 20; Theater: 25
Equipment On-site: Fax, copier, 24-hour answering service available; renter must supply own audiovisual equipment
Food Service: Breakfast with room
Overnight Accommodations: 31 rooms
Limitations/Restrictions: Restrictions on smoking; must supply own food/beverages; no pets
Access: Limited on-site parking; open year-round
Payment: Major credit card or company check in advance

MERIDIAN INTERNATIONAL CENTER
Meridian House
1630 Crescent Place NW, Washington, DC 20009
Phone: 202/667-6800   Fax: 202/939-5506

CALLED by some the finest example of French eighteenth-century urban architecture in the United States, the Meridian House was designed by John Russell Pope, who was also the architect of the Jefferson Memorial. Pope built the elegant house, named for its proximity to the meridian line that bisected the District of Columbia, as a retirement home for American Ambassador Irwin Laughlin in 1920. With its limestone facade and classical Louis XVI style, the house is reminiscent of the eighteenth-century estates of the Île-de-France. Guests passing through the famous solid oak doors are greeted in a two-story foyer, its curving double stairway ascending to the Reception Gallery, which displays many original furnishings, such as wrought-iron and marble-top tables and Waterford crystal torchiers. Other decorative flourishes in the principal rooms include eighteenth-century over-door paintings, French brass hardware, and ornate lighting fixtures. Traveling art exhibitions also are on display at both the Meridian House and its counterpart next door, the White-Meyer House (see the following entry). Outdoors, visitors can enjoy the pebbled courtyard and formal garden, shaded by 41 linden trees imported from Europe.

Listed in the National Register of Historic Places

Location: Meridian House is located a block from Meridian Hill Park in northwest Washington, D.C., and 1.5 miles north of the White House off Sixteenth Street.

Function Space: 2,500 square feet; 4 rooms
Capacity—Conference: 50; Reception: 500;
Banquet: 150; Theater: 150; capacities may vary
according to room configuration
Equipment On-site: Sound system, including
cassette and CD players, and pull-down screens;
additional audiovisual equipment must be
rented from outside source
Food Service: Renter may select outside
 caterer with demonstrated experience
Limitations/Restrictions: No smoking; no
red-staining foods or beverages (red wine,
Bloody Mary mix, cranberries, etc.);
dancing limited to certain areas
Access: Handicapped accessible; on-site
parking; open year-round
Payment: Check

MERIDIAN INTERNATIONAL CENTER

White-Meyer House
(Mailing address)
1630 Crescent Place NW
(Street address)
1624 Crescent Place NW, Washington, DC 20009
Phone: 202/667-6670   Fax: 202/939-5506

THE White-Meyer House, a red brick Georgian
mansion shaped by two prominent architects,
each a designer of Smithsonian buildings on the
National Mall, has been beautifully renovated
and restored. John Russell Pope, who designed
the National Gallery of Art, built the grand
house in 1912 for diplomat Henry White, former
U.S. ambassador to France. During World War I
the house was briefly used as the French mission
and was the scene of many high-level strategic
meetings. Eugene Meyer purchased the home in
1929 and commissioned Charles A. Platt, who
designed the Freer Gallery of Art, to remodel the
interior in a simpler, more elegant style. Meyer,
later publisher of the *Washington Post*, entertained
frequently and his guests included Eleanor
Roosevelt, Adlai Stevenson, and John and Robert
Kennedy. Discussions around Meyer's dining
room table eventually led to the creation of the
U.S. Department of Health, Education, and
Welfare. The White-Meyer House is connected
to the Meridian House (see the preceding entry)
through the gardens, and much of the original
landscaping and gardens has been preserved.

Listed in the National Register of Historic Places

Location: The White-Meyer House is located
a block from Meridian Hill Park in northwest
Washington, D.C., and 1.5 miles north of the
White House off Sixteenth Street.
Function Space: 2,500 square feet; 5 rooms
Capacity—Conference: 50; Reception: 500;
Banquet: 150; Theater: 150; capacities may
vary according to room configuration
Equipment On-site: Sound system, including
cassette and CD players, and pull-down screens;
additional audiovisual equipment must be rented from outside source; state-of-the-art translation equipment makes the site especially useful
for international meetings.
Food Service: Renter may select outside caterer
with demonstrated experience
Limitations/Restrictions: No smoking; no red-
staining foods or beverages (red wine, Bloody
Mary mix, cranberries, etc.); dancing limited
to certain areas
Access: Handicapped accessible; on-site
parking; open year-round
Payment: Check

THE MORRISON-CLARK INN

(Mailing address)
1015 L Street NW
(Street address)
Massachusets Avenue and Eleventh Street NW
Washington, DC 20001
Phone: 202/898-1200 or 800-332-7898
Fax: 202/289-8576

IN 1864 businessmen David Morrison and Reuben Clark each owned a new elegant townhouse in a posh Massachusetts Avenue neighborhood. A later owner of Clark's townhouse added a Chinese Chippendale porch and a Shanghai mansard roof, following a trip to the Orient, and the houses eventually merged to form a mansion. In 1923 it became the Soldiers, Sailors, Marines and Airmen's Club, an inexpensive hotel for servicemen staying in the capital. First Ladies traditionally served as the club's honorary chairwomen, and both Mamie Eisenhower and Jacqueline Kennedy devoted a good deal of time as volunteers. Following a 1987 restoration and renovation, the Morrison-Clark opened as an inn, and since then its award-winning restaurant serving Southern-influenced cuisine has been a local favorite. Guest rooms are individually furnished with period antiques, and room rates include a continental breakfast, a shoe shine, and a morning paper. Meeting facilities include a conference room and smaller breakout rooms, and the courtyard is also used for special events. The inn is within walking distance of the convention center, Chinatown, and metrorail stations, and the city's numerous cultural attractions are close by as well.

Listed in the National Register of Historic Places; member of Historic Hotels of America

Location: The Morrison-Clark Inn is on the corner of Eleventh and L Streets NW and is 45 minutes from Dulles International Airport and 20 minutes from National Airport.
Function Space: 1,000 square feet; 4 rooms
Capacity—Conference: 35; Reception: 150
Equipment On-site: Audiovisual equipment and business services available
Food Service: Breakfast with room; restaurant; room service
Overnight Accommodations: 54 rooms
Limitations/Restrictions: Restrictions on smoking (permitted in some guest rooms); food and beverages must be provided by hotel; no pets
Access: On-site parking; open year-round
Payment: Cash, check, credit card, direct billing

NATIONAL TRUST FOR HISTORIC PRESERVATION

1785 Massachusetts Avenue NW
Washington, DC 20036
Phone: 800-944-6847 or 202/588-6018
Fax: 202/558-6038

BUILT in 1916 in the Beaux Arts style as one of Washington's first luxury apartment buildings, 1785 Massachusetts Avenue was once home to some of the city's most distinguished citizens, including industrialist Andrew Mellon, diplomat Robert Woods Bliss, and hostess Perle Mesta. Originally the building housed six apartments, which were converted into British government offices in 1940. A variety of professional businesses and associations later occupied the building until 1977, when it was purchased and renovated by the National Trust for Historic Preservation for use as its headquarters. Many of the original features remain, including decorative herringbone parquet wood flooring, carved mar-

National Trust for Historic Preservation

ble fireplace mantels, and solid mahogany doors with brass hardware. An oval-shaped reception area welcomes visitors into the executive board-room and conference room, where crystal chandeliers hang from 14½-foot-high ceilings and antique mirrors in classic-design ornamental moldings decorate the walls. The National Trust is located in a colorful urban setting, just east of Dupont Circle and within walking distance of embassies, chanceries, and the historic Adams Morgan neighborhood.

National Historic Landmark; listed in the National Register of Historic Places

Location: The National Trust headquarters building is at the intersection of Eighteenth and Massachusetts Avenue at Dupont Circle, 5 minutes from downtown/national monuments in Washington, D.C. Union Station is 15 minutes away; National and Dulles Airports are within 20 and 45 minutes, respectively. The Trust is a block and a half from the Dupont Circle metro-rail station.

Function Space: 1,581 square feet; 2 rooms; an additional 392-square-foot foyer is available

Capacity—Conference: 15; Reception: 35–150; Banquet: 15–40; Theater: 90

Equipment On-site: Speaker's podium, tables, and chairs included in rental; audiovisual equipment may be rented from an outside source
Food Service: Kitchenette available; list of preferred caterers provided
Limitations/Restrictions: The National Trust meeting space is for nonprofit use, although exceptions are sometimes made; insurance, provided by the renter, is required; on-site parking is unavailable; smoking and propane tanks are prohibited; hours of availability: 8:00 A.M. to 8:00 P.M. Monday through Friday.
Access: Handicapped accessible; parking nearby
Payment: Check

THE OLD POST OFFICE

1100 Pennsylvania Avenue NW
Washington, DC 20004
Phone: 202/289-4224   Fax: 202/898-0653

BOUNDED by historic Pennsylvania Avenue, the National Mall, and the Ellipse, the Federal Triangle is a remarkable complex of monumental architecture. Rising above it all and America's Main Street is the grand 12-story Old Post Office, Washington's first modern "skyscraper." Built in 1899 in the Richardsonian Romanesque Revival style, the Old Post Office's trademark 315-foot clock tower boasts an impressive panoramic view of the capital. The building's steel frame is covered by a thick layer of granite, and it was the first government building designed with its own electrical power plant. During the 1960s and 1970s preservationists fought to save the building from demolition, and today the Old Post Office is home to the National Endowment for the Arts, the National Endowment for the Humanities and other federal agencies. The building's massive 10-story glass-enclosed atrium, whose ground floor and stage are

available for receptions, banquets, meetings and other large gatherings, is adjacent to specialty shops and an international food court. The National Park Service provides free tours of the clock tower, where visitors may see on display the Congressional Bells, a Bicentennial gift from Great Britain, which are rung on special occasions.

Listed in the National Register of Historic Places

Location: The Old Post Office is located in Washington's historic Federal Triangle district at Twelfth Street NW and Pennsylvania Avenue, one block from the National Mall and across the street from the Federal Triangle metrorail stop. Washington National Airport is 15 minutes away; Dulles and Baltimore/Washington International Airports are 25 and 30 minutes away, respectively.
Function Space: 1 room
Capacity—Reception: 2,000; Banquet: 350–400; Theater: 550
Equipment On-site: Public address system and stage
Food Service: Renter selects caterer
Limitations/Restrictions: No smoking
Access: Handicapped accessible
Payment: Check

RENAISSANCE MAYFLOWER HOTEL

1127 Connecticut Avenue NW
Washington, DC 20036
Phone: 202/347-3000   Fax: 202/466-9082

THE Mayflower Hotel's career as a local landmark began with Calvin Coolidge's 1925 inaugural ball, held just two weeks after the hotel opened. Since then, the Mayflower has welcomed international political figures, royalty, and numerous celebrities. It was here that FDR worked on his 1933 inaugrual address ("the only thing we have to fear is fear itself"), and for years FBI Director J. Edgar Hoover lunched at the hotel nearly every day that he was in town. Glittering with more gold leaf than any building in the country except the Library of Congress when it opened, the Mayflower underwent extensive renovation work during the early 1990s, which led to the discovery of a 25-foot skylight that had been blacked out in World War II. Conference and banquet facilities feature fine decor, including marble, crystal, and rich wood amenities, and the Mayflower hosts groups of as few as 10 for a breakfast meeting or as many as 1,000 for a formal state dinner. Guest room rates include a number of complimentary services, including coffee and morning newspaper, a wake-up call, a downtown limousine service, a shoe shine, and a fitness center. The Mayflower, located in the heart of Washington's business district, is just a short walk from fashionable shops, metrorail stops, and the White House.

Listed in the National Register of Historic Places; member of Historic Hotels of America

Location: The Renaissance Mayflower Hotel is easily accessible from all directions via major interstate highways. The hotel is only four blocks from the White House, 15 minutes from Washington National Airport, 10 minutes from Union Station, and is located next to Farragut North metrorail station.

Function Space: 35,000 square feet; 23 rooms
Capacity—Conference: 14–140; Reception: 25–1,000; Banquet: 10–900; Theater: 50–1,150
Equipment On-site: Complete audiovisual equipment including projection gear, sound systems, video playback, technical personnel; business services available
Food Service: Catering/food service available; a master chef works exclusively with meeting planners; three restaurants, 24-hour room service
Overnight Accommodations: 659 rooms
Access: Handicapped accessible
Payment: Cash, check, credit card

THE SWANN HOUSE

1808 New Hampshire Avenue NW
Washington, DC 20009
Phone: 202/265-7677   Fax: 202/265-6755
E-mail: SwannHouse@aol.com

LOCATED in Washington's colorful Dupont Circle Historic District, the Swann House is a handsome brick Victorian mansion, built in the Richardsonian Romanesque style in 1883. Architect Walter Paris, a famous local watercolorist, designed the house, which is characterized by its distinctive arched front porch, multicolored roof shingles, and lush landscaping. The Swann House is an elegant setting for business meetings, corporate retreats, receptions, luncheons, and other gatherings. Its lovely, bright interiors feature elaborate mantels, fluted woodwork, 12-foot-high ceilings, crystal chandeliers, French doors, and a sunroom with wet bar that overlooks a private garden and pool. Overnight guests stay in beautifully appointed rooms and enjoy an abundant continental breakfast in the sun room. The Swann House is conveniently located near the heart of downtown Washington, and nearby Adams Morgan and Georgetown are known for their excellent restaurants and dynamic neighborhoods.

Location: The Swann House is located at the corner of New Hampshire Avenue and Swann Street, four blocks blocks from the Dupont Circle metrorail stop in Northwest Washington, D.C. National Airport and Dulles International Airport are within 20 and 45 minutes, respectively.
Function Space: 1,500 square feet; 4 rooms
Capacity—Conference: 50–70; Reception: 150; Banquet: 50–70; Theater: 50
Equipment On-site: Audiovisual equipment can be rented from outside source; fax and photocopier available
Food Service: Breakfast with room; catering/food service available
Overnight Accommodations: 4 rooms
Limitations/Restrictions: No smoking; no red wine
Access: On-site parking (limited); open year-round
Payment: Check, credit card (MC, Visa)

TABARD INN

1739 N Street NW, Washington, DC 20036
Phone: 202/785-1277   Fax: 202/785-6173

THE oldest continuously operated hotel in Washington, D.C., the Tabard Inn opened for business in 1914 and comprises three Victorian townhouses built in the 1890s. The inn is named for the hostelry in Chaucer's *Canterbury Tales*, and its bar has long been a favorite with local jour-

nalists and publishers. Edward Everett Hale is said to have penned his classic short story *The Man Without a Country* in the inn's attic, and the hotel has appeared in numerous novels, including John Grisham's *The Pelican Brief*. During World War II the inn housed female naval officers. In the 1970s it was threatened with demolition, but the inn's neighbors put up a spirited fight and today the Tabard remains a fixture in the Dupont Circle Historic District. The inn provides a variety of room setups for gatherings, including business meetings, formal dinners, cocktail parties, and afternoon tea. The Tabard Inn Restaurant cuisine has a country flair, derived in part from the inn's Tabard Farm in the Shenandoah, which supplies fine seasonal produce. Guest room rates include a complimentary breakfast.

Listed in the National Register of Historic Places

Location: The Tabard Inn is at 1739 N Street, two blocks from Dupont Circle metrorail station and 5 minutes from downtown/national monuments in Washington, D.C. Union Station is 15 minutes away; National and Dulles Airports are within 20 and 45 minutes, respectively.
Function Space: 4,000 square feet; 4 rooms
Capacity—Conference: 60; Reception: 150; Banquet: 120
Equipment On-site: Audiovisual equipment and business services available
Food Service: Breakfast with room; catering and food service available; restaurant and bar
Overnight Accommodations: 40 rooms
Access: Open year-round
Payment: Check, credit card (MC, Visa)

THE WASHINGTON CLUB

15 Dupont Circle, Washington, DC 20036
Phone: 202/483-9200   Fax: 202/483-1195

AN ornate four-story Italianate house in the center of Washington's fashionable Dupont Circle district, the Patterson House was completed in 1902 for Robert Patterson, editor-in-chief of *The Chicago Tribune*, and his wife. The house, with its grand white marble facade and glazed terracotta ornamentation, is architect Stanford White's only intact building in the nation's capital, but the building holds other important distinctions as well. Patterson House served as a temporary White House in 1927 when the Executive Mansion was being repaired, and it was here that President Calvin Coolidge received Charles Lindbergh following his historic transatlantic flight. The house was used as a civil defense shelter during World War II, and in 1951 the building was purchased by the Washington Club, a women's literary and cultural organization founded shortly after the Civil War. The club's interior, which features design work by Tiffany and Sons, showcases a formal marble staircase leading to the second-floor drawing room, ballroom, and dining room. Meeting space is available on the first and second floors, which have remained relatively unchanged over the years.

National Historic Landmark; listed in the National Register of Historic Places

Location: The Washington Club is located at Dupont Circle, one block from the Dupont Circle metrorail station (Red Line) and 5 minutes from downtown/national monuments in Washington, D.C. Union Station is 15 minutes away; National and Dulles Airports are within 20 and 45 minutes, respectively.

Function Space: 6,168 square feet; 3 rooms

Capacity—Conference: 150; Reception: 325; Banquet: 200; Theater: 200

Equipment On-site: Lectern, wireless and wired microphones, slide projector and screen available; all other audiovisual equipment must be rented from an outside source; all tables and chairs are included in rental price, not including linens; pay telephone available

Food Service: Renter may choose in-house food service or caterer

Limitations/Restrictions: The Washington Club meeting space is for nonprofit use, although exceptions are sometimes made; insurance, provided by the renter, is required; on-site parking is unavailable; smoking and propane tanks are prohibited; hours of availability: 9:00 A.M. to 9:00 P.M. daily

Access: Partially handicapped accessible; open September through July

Payment: Cash or check (no credit cards)

WOODROW WILSON HOUSE

2340 S Street NW, Washington, DC 20008
Phone: 202/387-4062   Fax: 202/483-1466

AFTER Woodrow Wilson left the presidency in 1921, he and his wife, Edith, began a quiet life in Washington's Kalorama neighborhood, in the heart of Embassy Row. In their elegant 1915 townhouse the Wilsons hosted occasional dinner parties, and their distinguished guest lists included British Prime Minister David Lloyd George and French Premier Georges Clemenceau. Wilson was the only president to live in Washington when not in office, and his home today, furnished just as it was when he lived here, is the only presidential museum in the capital. Items in the library illustrate Wilson's life as an educator, president, and world statesman; on display are the books he authored on political theory and government, his inaugural medal, and a gold presentation chest presented by a grateful City of London in 1918 for his peace efforts. Groups may meet at the house for receptions, luncheons, dinners, meetings, and weddings, and space is available in the dining room, library, drawing room, and solarium. Outdoor events are held on the garden terraces and on the porch.

National Historic Landmark; listed in the National Register of Historic Places; National Trust for Historic Preservation Historic Site

Location: The Wilson House is in Washington, D.C.'s Embassy Row neighborhood; from Dupont Circle, travel north on Massachusetts Avenue for five blocks, turn right onto 24th Street, then right onto S Street.
Function Space: 4 rooms
Capacity—200 standing indoors, 40 seated; 200 standing outdoors, 125 seated
Equipment On-site: Podium
Food Service: Approved caterers list provided
Limitations/Restrictions: No smoking
Access: Handicapped accessibility to house but not to garden; open year-round
Payment: Check

Woodrow Wilson House
(Victor Boswell. Courtesy of the National Trust for Historic Preservation)

FLORIDA

BOCA RATON

BOCA RATON HISTORICAL SOCIETY— TOWN HALL

71 N. Federal Highway, Boca Raton, FL 33432
Phone: 407/395-6766 Fax: 407/395-4049

ARCHITECT Addison Mizner had ambitious plans for the Mediterranean-style community and resort he envisioned during the heady days of Florida's real estate boom in the 1920s. Although the boom went bust, Mizner's plan for a town hall, modified by William E. Alsmeyer, did come to fruition in 1927. A local landmark with its signature gold dome, the Town Hall housed city offices until 1983, when it was turned over to the Boca Raton Historical Society, which restored the building and maintains it as a historic site. With its characteristic Mediterranean flourishes—its white exterior, arched entrances, fanlit windows, and tile and pine floors—the Town Hall preserves other elements of historic Boca Raton, as seen in its archives and permanent displays of maps, photographs, and documents. Graceful meeting facilities are available for both business and social events, including the Council Chambers, the Library, and the Mayor's Office, which accommodate corporate meetings, cocktail receptions, luncheons and dinners, and small private gatherings. Special rental rates are available to society members and nonprofit organizations, and the society can arrange for special group tours of local historic sites.

Listed in the National Register of Historic Places

Location: The Town Hall is located in downtown Boca Raton, between West Palm Beach and Fort Lauderdale, and is accessible via I-95.
Function Space: 2,100 square feet; 3 rooms
Capacity—Conference: 50; Reception: 130; Banquet: 80; Theater: 100
Equipment On-site: Slide projector, large TV with VCR, photocopier, fax available
Food Service: Full-service kitchen available; list of recommended caterers provided
Overnight Accommodations: Can arrange for special discount at historic Boca Raton Resort and Club
Limitations/Restrictions: No smoking; no candles; no nails in walls; tablecloths must be used on antique tables
Access: Handicapped accessible; on-site parking; open year-round
Payment: Cash, check

DELRAY BEACH

THE COLONY HOTEL AND CABAÑA CLUB

(Mailing address)
P.O. Box 970
Delray Beach, FL 33447
(Street address)
525 E. Atlantic Avenue, Delray Beach, FL 33483
Phone: 561/276-4123 or 800-552-2363 (reservations)
Fax: 561/276-0123
E-mail: info-fla@thecolonyhotel.com

THE Mediterranean Revival-style Colony Hotel and Cabaña Club, with its red-tiled roof, sparkling white facade, and twin domed towers, is a designated Delray Beach historic landmark and has been an elegant fixture on Florida's "Gold Coast" since its construction in 1926. Martin Luther Hampton designed the hotel, along with a number of other Addison Mizner buildings, to cater to Florida's growing winter flock of snow-birds. The Colony has been owned and operated by the same family since 1935 and is one of the few remaining "hospitality nomad" resorts, with a sister hotel in Maine serviced by the same staff during the Florida hotel's off-season. The Music Room and the dining room are available for meetings, receptions, dances, and other func-tions, and groups may gather in the skylit lobby as well, which is filled with the original Fixx Reed white wicker furniture. The comfortable guest rooms, named for state birds and fish, are accessible by the only still-functioning hand-operated Otis elevator in South Florida. At the hotel's Cabaña Club guests can enjoy lunch and take a dip in the heated saltwater pool. Art gal-leries, fine dining, polo, golf, tennis, and night-clubs are all available in Delray Beach as well.

Delray Beach Historic Landmark

Location: The Colony Hotel is located at the intersection of East Atlantic Avenue and North Federal Highway in downtown Delray Beach. Palm Beach and Fort Lauderdale International Airports are 20 and 45 minutes away, respectively; Miami International Airport is 1.25 hours away. The hotel is accessible via I-95 and the Florida Turnpike. Bus service connects to the Tri-Rail train system.
Function Space: 4,600 square feet; 2 rooms
Capacity—Conference: 90; Reception: 200; Banquet: 200
Equipment On-site: Audiovisual equipment and fax available
Food Service: Full food service and high tea available
Overnight Accommodations: 64 rooms
Limitations/Restrictions: No smoking indoors

Access: Handicapped accessible; on-site parking; open November–April
Payment: Cash, check, credit card

GAINESVILLE

HISTORIC THOMAS CENTER
(Mailing address)
P.O. Box 490, Station 30, Gainesville, FL 32602
(Street address)
302 NE 6th Avenue, Gainesville, FL 32601
Phone: 352/334-2197   Fax: 352/334-2314

BUILT in the Mediterranean Revival style in 1910, the Historic Thomas Center has served a variety of uses since businessman William Rueben Thomas built it for his family's home. The 1920s Florida land boom drew thousands to the state, and Thomas responded by converting his 21-room home into a resort hotel and adding a wing. Numerous distinguished visitors to the University of Florida stayed at the hotel, including Helen Keller and Robert Frost. The hotel operated for 40 years, closing in 1968, and then functioned as Santa Fe Community College until 1975. After four years of rehabilitation, the building reopened as the Thomas Center and was recognized as an excellent example of historic preservation and adaptive use. As Gainesville's cultural center, this historic struc-ture, located in the Northeast Historic Gainesville District and surrounded by gardens, maintains art galleries, 1920s period rooms, local history exhibits, and performance space in the Spanish Court. Meeting rooms for business and social events include the Thomas family's parlor, library, kitchen and breakfast room.

Listed in the National Register of Historic Places

Location: The Historic Thomas Center is located in downtown Gainesville and is accessible via I-75 and Highway 441. The Gainesville Regional Airport is 10 minutes away.
Function Space: 3,076 square feet; 5 rooms
Capacity—Conference: 80; Reception:150; Banquet: 80; Theater: 100
Equipment On-site: Overhead and slide projectors
Food Service: Renter selects caterer; kitchen available
Limitations/Restrictions: No smoking; no lit candles; alcohol permitted—kegs outside, only on porch
Access: Handicapped accessible; on-site parking; open year-round
Payment: Cash, check

LAKE WALES

CHALET SUZANNE COUNTRY INN AND RESTAURANT

3800 Chalet Suzanne Drive, Lake Wales, FL 33853
Phone: 941/676-6011   Fax: 941/676-1814

A cheerful mix of pastel-hued structures, fairy-tale architecture, and colorful gardens, the Chalet Suzanne is an award-winning country inn filled with the delightfully unexpected. The chalet was built in 1924, and the Hinshaw family has operated the inn and restaurant since 1931, when the widowed Bertha Hinshaw opened the place for business, continually adding to it the remarkable and sometimes unusual treasures she acquired in her world travels. Renowned for its gourmet cuisine and world-famous homemade soup (which even went to the moon with the Apollo astronauts), the chalet serves meals in a multilevel setting overlooking its private lake. An on-site ceramist turns out replicas of Norwegian ashtrays, in which the inn's soups are served and which customers often buy as souvenirs; visitors are also welcome to tour the on-site soup cannery. The comfortable country guest rooms are brightly decorated and vary in size, and room rates include a full breakfast. Guests can enjoy the lake and relaxing patio settings or take a dip in the pool. From its central Florida location, Chalet Suzanne is convenient to numerous attractions, including Disney World, Cypress Gardens, and Bok Tower Gardens.

Listed in the National Register of Historic Places

Location: Chalet Suzanne is 4 miles north of Lake Wales, between US 27 and 17, one-half hour from Disney World. Private airstrip available.
Function Space: 500 square feet; 5 rooms
Capacity—Conference: 20; Banquet: 150
Equipment On-site: Slide projector, fax
Food Service: Breakfast with room; full-service restaurant, lounge
Overnight Accommodations: 30 rooms
Access: Handicapped accessible; on-site parking; open year-round
Payment: Major credit card

MIAMI

MIAMI RIVER INN

118 SW South River Drive, Miami, FL 33130
Phone: 305/325-0045 or 800-HOTEL-89
Fax: 305/325-9227
E-mail: miami100@ix.netcom.com

FROM its riverfront location, the Miami River Inn comprises a group of historic early twentieth-century buildings graced with a tropical architecture and ambiance. Located in the oldest part of the city, where travelers on Henry Flagler's Florida East Coast Railroad disembarked, the inn enjoys a view of downtown Miami from its extensive and flower-filled grounds. Each guest room is individually decorated and furnished with antiques, while offering all the modern conveniences. Beautiful, lush tropical gardens surround the pool area, where guests can relax over a complimentary breakfast and afternoon tea. The lobby library maintains historical publications on Miami, and visitors will find museums, galleries, restaurants, and shopping just a short walk away. The nearby metrorail makes the Bayside Festival Marketplace, Coconut Grove, and other interesting stops easily accessible.

Listed in the National Register of Historic Places

Location: The Miami River Inn is located across from the Miami River and the downtown area and is accessible via I-95.
Function Space: 800 square feet; 2 rooms
Capacity—Conference: 60; Reception: 50 (inside), 100+ (outside); Banquet: 50 (inside), 100+ (outside)
Equipment On-site: TV/VCR, overhead and slide projectors, chalkboard, fax and photocopy machines, message center, computer use/hookup
Food Service: Catering and full kitchen available
Overnight Accommodations: 40 rooms
Limitations/Restrictions: No smoking; no pets
Access: Handicapped accessible, off-street parking; open year-round
Payment: Credit cards and business checks

MIAMI BEACH

INDIAN CREEK HOTEL
2727 Indian Creek Drive, Miami Beach, FL 33140
Phone: 305/531-2727 Fax: 305/531-5651

SET in the midst of Miami Beach's historic Art Deco District, the Indian Creek Hotel enjoys both a beautiful and a convenient location, as it faces the creek and is just a block from the ocean. The fully restored hotel, built in 1936, was honored by the Miami Design Preservation League for outstanding restoration. A multilingual staff is on hand to assist guests and groups meeting for conferences, retreats, business meetings, or other events. In addition to two conference rooms, office suites and a business center are also available, and the hotel is just eight blocks from the convention center. Each guest room boasts modern amenities as well as authentic Art Deco furniture. Dining options include a cafe restaurant and bar, room service, and poolside service. The landscaped grounds and tropical gardens give the hotel a secluded atmosphere, even though Miami Beach's fine restaurants, shops, and lively nightspots are just minutes away.

Location: The Indian Creek Hotel is one block from the beach, 15 minutes from Miami International Airport, and 10 minutes from downtown Miami.
Function Space: 760 square feet; 2 rooms
Capacity—Conference: 30; Reception: 200 (lobby and garden also available); Banquet: 20; Theater: 50
Equipment On-site: Audiovisual equipment available; business center on-site
Food Service: Catering/food service available; restaurant, bar, room and poolside service
Overnight Accommodations: 61 rooms

Lafayette Hotel *(Courtesy of the Lafayette Hotel)*

Access: Handicapped accessible; open year-round
Payment: Cash, check, credit card

LAFAYETTE HOTEL

944 Collins Avenue, Miami Beach, FL 33139
Phone: 305/673-2262   Fax: 305/534-5399

THE Lafayette Hotel, Henry Malone's 1934 eclectic Mediterranean Revival creation, enjoys a beachside location in the center of Miami's famed Art Deco Historic District. The 10-block district is recognized for its Art Deco, Streamline Revival, and Mediterranean Revival architectural treasures. A fashionable "on the beach" hotel during the 1930s, the Lafayette was used to house military personnel during World War II. In 1991 the hotel's owners, the Cattarossi family, began an award-winning restoration and renovation of both the exterior and the interior. Pseudo-Art Deco ornamentation from the 1970s was removed, and the original tile, wooden floors, wrought-iron railings, and vintage elevator have been preserved. The relaxed Mediterranean atmosphere is enhanced by tropical plants, fresh flowers, tiled patios, garden, fountains, and Gino Cattarossi's original stained glass work. Conferences and receptions are held in the Mediterranean-style meeting room, which is equipped with fax and modem lines and portable phones. Groups may also use the garden area for indoor and outdoor gatherings.

Listed in the National Register of Historic Places

Location: The Lafayette Hotel is 10 minutes from downtown Miami and 20 minutes from Miami International Airport. From the airport, take 836 east to 395 (MacArthur Causeway) to Miami Beach, left on Collins Avenue. From the north or south, take I-95, then Exit 5 to 395.

Function Space: 2,000 square feet; 1 room
Capacity—Conference: 40; Reception: 120
Equipment On-site: Audiovisual and business services available
Food Service: In-house or outside catering available
Overnight Accommodations: 55 rooms
Limitations/Restrictions: No smoking
Access: Handicapped accessible; on-site parking; open year-round
Payment: Cash, business check

THE PARK CENTRAL HOTEL

640 Ocean Drive, Miami Beach, FL 33139
Phone: 305/538-1611   Fax: 305/534-7520
E-mail: parkcent@sobe.com

ONCE the playground of celebrities in the 1930s, Miami's Ocean Drive and historic Art Deco District continue to draw enchanted visitors. The 1937 Park Central Hotel, with its trademark portals above the entrance and its lavender, blue, and mint exterior, was beautifully restored in 1986. The interior features a Nautical Moderne decor, and each guest room and suite is furnished with a mahogany ceiling fan, palm-printed carpet, original period furniture, and authentic black-and-white photography from the 1930s. Meeting space for business and corporate gatherings is available in Mezzaine South, an oceanfront boardroom, and in the Florida Room, which juts out over the sculpture garden and pool area. The room features two walls of floor-to-ceiling glass (blackout curtains can be used for more privacy), a hardwood floor, and a 10-foot ceiling. On-site dining includes the Casablanca, a full-service restaurant offering new world cuisine, and the pool area Park Central Bar. Both the beach and the sea of bright Art Deco architecture in South Beach make for pleasant strolls and sightseeing, and the variety of restaurants, cafes, nightclubs, art galleries, and shops provide something for everyone.

Listed in the National Register of Historic Places; member of Historic Hotels of America

Location: The Park Central Hotel is 10 miles from downtown Miami on 836 W, and 12 miles from Miami International Airport. The hotel is accessible via 836 W, 826 N, I-95, and the Florida Turnpike.
Function Space: 2,000 square feet; 2 rooms
Capacity—Conference: 35; Reception: 50; Banquet: 35; Theater: 50
Equipment On-site: VCR and monitor, overhead projector and screen; limited photocopying and typing service available
Food Service: Catering/food service available; two restaurants
Overnight Accommodations: 120 rooms
Limitations/Restrictions: In-house catering only; no pets
Access: Public areas handicapped accessible; on-site parking; open year-round
Payment: Cash, check, credit card

RICHMOND HOTEL

1757 Collins Avenue, Miami Beach, FL 33139
Phone: 305/538-2331   Fax: 305/531-9021

MIAMI Beach's most famous Art Deco architect, L. Murray Dixon, designed the Richmond Hotel, one of the first oceanfront hotels on the city's famed Collins Avenue. The Richmond opened just prior to the outbreak of World War II in 1941, and today the small luxury hotel is a restored landmark in Miami's historic Art Deco District. The Verandah Cafe serves American Southern cuisine, and guests may dine indoors or out, enjoying the verandah dining terrace; the coconut palm-studded patio is also a good place to enjoy cool ocean breezes. Meeting space is available in the cafe, and torchlit receptions and buffets are held on the lawn, which can be canopied. A number of amenities and recreational facilities are available at the Richmond, including a spa, a rooftop solarium, and a fitness center. The pool area, with its distinctive Art Deco fountain, is adjacent to the hotel's private white sand beach. Comfortable guest rooms offer garden, city, ocean, and oceanfront views, and overnight guests enjoy a complimentary breakfast.

Listed in the National Register of Historic Places; cited by Miami Beach Development Corporation for excellence in restoration

Location: The Richmond Hotel is on the oceanfront on Collins Avenue, 4 miles from downtown Miami via 836 and 17 blocks from A1A north; Miami International Airport is 7 miles west; bus service a half-block away.
Function Space: 750 square feet; 1 room
Capacity—Conference: 20; Reception: 30; Theater: 50; 200 can be accommodated outdoors
Equipment On-site: Hotel will arrange for required audiovisual equipment
Food Service: Breakfast with room; catering/food service available; restaurant, limited room service available
Overnight Accommodations: 99 rooms
Limitations/Restrictions: No pets
Access: Handicapped accessible; open year-round
Payment: Cash, traveler's check, credit card

THE RITZ PLAZA

1701 Collins Avenue, Miami Beach, FL 33139
Phone: 305/534-3500   Fax: 305/531-0900

A landmark in Miami's internationally known Art Deco District, the Ritz Plaza was built in 1940 in the Deco style known as Art Moderne. The 12-story structure is a striking blend of smooth-faced stone, metal, and concrete with crisp, clean lines, making the Ritz Plaza another distinctive success for architect L. Murray Dixon. In 1990 the hotel reopened following a multimillion dollar restoration that earned it several awards for excellence in historic preservation. Early photographs of the hotel guided the accurate restoration of the lobby and public spaces, and all of the comfortable guest rooms, with city and ocean views, were refurbished. Although the bathrooms were modernized, the original cast-iron bathtubs and ceramic tile remain. Business and social events are accommodated in five function rooms, and visitors will enjoy one of the Ritz Plaza's most interesting features—the circular poolside restaurant with its 18-foot-high ceiling and garden and ocean views. From its oceanfront location, the hotel is just a short walk from the Theater of the Performing Arts, the convention center, and the New World Symphony.

Listed in the National Register of Historic Places; member of Historic Hotels of America

Location: The Ritz Plaza is 4 miles from downtown Miami and 7 miles from Miami International Airport.
Function Space: 6,600 square feet; 5 rooms
Capacity—Conference: 25; Reception: 500; Banquet: 180; Theater: 250

Equipment On-site: Audiovisual equipment available through outside source
Food Service: Catering/food service available; two restaurants, bar
Overnight Accommodations: 132 rooms
Access: Open year-round
Payment: Credit card (AmEx, Discover, MC, Visa)

MOUNT DORA

LAKESIDE INN

100 N. Alexander Street, Mount Dora, FL 32757
Phone: 800-972-7175   Fax: 352/735-2642

THE Lakeside Inn has been a favorite winter destination since it opened as the Alexander House, a 10-room hotel, in 1883. Later named for its waterfront location on Lake Dora, the inn developed into its characteristic style during the 1920s and 1930s, and it is to that appearance that it has been restored. The Lakeside comprises the 1908 Colonial Manor, the Beauclaire Restaurant, the Gate House, the Sunset Cottage, and the English Tudor-style Gables and Terrace buildings that former President Calvin Coolidge dedicated during his stay in 1931. A variety of events, ranging from corporate meetings and retreats to receptions and formal dinners, are accommodated in the banquet and conference rooms. American regional cuisine is served in the inn's acclaimed Beauclaire Dining Room, and Tremain's Lounge offers cocktails and vintage music. The inn's classic architecture, sweeping verandahs, and landscaped grounds evoke the feeling of Old Florida, and the nearby village of Mount Dora with its antique shops and galleries adds to the quaint atmosphere. Swimming, tennis, volleyball, and canoeing are among the available activities, and guest room rates include a continental breakfast.

Listed in the National Register of Historic Places; member of Historic Hotels of America

Location: The Lakeside Inn is located 25 miles northwest of Orlando and is within an hour of both the Atlantic and Gulf beaches. It is accessible via US 441, I-4 (15 miles away) and I-75 (15 miles away), and I-95 (40 miles away). Airport service is available at Orlando, Daytona, and Sanford, 1 hour, 45 minutes, and 45 minutes away, respectively.
Function Space: 5,396 square feet; 5 rooms
Capacity—Conference: 170; Reception: 250; Banquet: 170; Theater: 170
Equipment On-site: Overhead and slide projectors, VCR and monitor, microphone, flip charts; fax, photocopier, e-mail service available
Food Service: Breakfast with room; food service available; restaurant, lounge, room service
Overnight Accommodations: 88 rooms
Limitations/Restrictions: Restrictions on smoking
Access: Handicapped accessible; on-site parking; open year-round
Payment: Check or credit card

PALM BEACH

THE CHESTERFIELD HOTEL

363 Cocoanut Row, Palm Beach, FL 33480
Phone: 407/659-5800   Fax: 407/659-6707

SINCE 1926 this Mediterranean Revival-style hotel has been a Palm Beach landmark. Known for a half century as the Vienta, the hotel came under new ownership in 1989 and was renamed the Chesterfield, after the English author and statesman Lord Chesterfield (1694–1773). The interior decor is in the style of an English country manor, and a traditional English tea is served each afternoon. In the beautifully furnished rooms and suites, guests will find potpourri sachets and a variety of deluxe English toiletries. Small groups may meet in the charming wood-paneled Fireside Library, one of Oscar de la Renta's favorite rooms, and larger groups are accommodated in the elegant poolside Pavilion Room. The on-site Leopard Room Restaurant and Lounge is a favorite Palm Beach night spot, offering gourmet dining and live entertainment. Located just two blocks from world-famous Worth Avenue, the Chesterfield is just minutes from Lake Worth, several ocean beaches, and the Henry Morrison Flagler Museum.

Location: The Chesterfield Hotel is on Cocoanut Row (363), 15 minutes from the Palm Beach International Airport, and accessible via US Highway 1, I-95, and the Florida Turnpike. Fort Lauderdale is 45 minutes away and Miami is 1.5 hours away.
Function Space: 900 square feet; 2 rooms.
Capacity—Conference: 60; Reception: 54; Banquet: 54; Theater: 60
Food Service: Catering/food service available; restaurant, lounge, room service
Overnight Accommodations: 53 rooms

Access: Handicapped accessible; complimentary valet parking; open year-round
Payment: Cash, check, credit card

ST. PETE BEACH

THE DON CESAR BEACH RESORT AND SPA

3400 Gulf Boulevard, St. Pete Beach, FL 33706
Phone: 813/360-1881   Fax: 813/367-3609

A 1928 landmark on Florida's Gulf Coast, the Don CeSar Beach Resort and Spa is a spectacular hotel whose monumental grandeur can be envisioned just by hearing its nicknames—the "Pink Palace" and the "Legendary Castle on the Beach." Also affectionately called "the Don," the hotel boasts luxurious interiors with its lofty ceilings, rich furnishings, marble fountains, and European art. As a full-service convention hotel, the award-winning Don CeSar offers numerous meeting and banqueting facilities in a variety of styles, ranging from ballrooms and a beach pavilion to conference rooms and a boardwalk for outdoor catered events. Each guest room features a water view and a marble bath, and 37 suites and 2 penthouses are also available; a morning paper is delivered to each. The resort offers a variety of dining options, including casual fine dining and the easygoing atmosphere of a bar and grill. Retail shops, children's and spouses' programs, and a health spa are available; swimming, deep sea and drift fishing, tennis, and golf are among the many activities guests can enjoy. Guests can also observe the Don's magnificent beachfront location while riding catamarans, waverunners, and aquabikes.

Listed in the National Register of Historic Places; member of Historic Hotels of America

The Don CeSar Beach Resort and Spa

Location: The Don Cesar Beach Resort and Spa is located on the island of St. Pete Beach, off the coast of St. Petersburg, 35 minutes from Tampa International Airport and 30 minutes from the St. Petersburg/Clearwater Airport. The resort is accessible via I-275.

Function Space: 39,900 square feet; 14 rooms

Capacity—Conference: 50; Reception: 650; Banquet: 420

Equipment On-site: Audiovisual equipment and business services available

Food Service: Catering/food service available; four restaurants, four lounges, 24-hour room service

Overnight Accommodations: 275 rooms

Limitations/Restrictions: No pets

Access: Handicapped accessible; on-site parking; open year-round

Payment: Credit card

St. Petersburg

RENAISSANCE VINOY RESORT
501 Fifth Avenue, North, St. Petersburg, FL 33701
Phone: 813/894-1000   Fax: 813/894-1970 (sales)

THE salmon-colored Vinoy Park Hotel began its history as the center of St. Petersburg's social scene in 1925. Among the hotel's noted guests were Presidents Calvin Coolidge and Herbert Hoover, Babe Ruth, F. Scott Fitzgerald, and Ernest Hemingway. The luxurious Mediterranean-style resort also did duty as a training facility for the Army Air Corps during World War II, and military cooks and bakers learned their trade here as well. The grand hotel closed in 1974, reopening as the Renaissance Vinoy Resort in 1992 following a painstaking renovation and restoration. Overlooking Tampa Bay and the marina (where the hotel's boat slips are available to guests), the

Vinoy offers complete resort facilities on St. Petersburg's scenic waterfront. Conference and banquet facilities include elegant ballrooms, a formal boardroom and breakout rooms, and a tea garden adjacent to the croquet lawn. Guest rooms are richly appointed, and 20 handsome suites offer the finest in executive amenities. Five restaurants, a lounge, and a comprehensive fitness center and spa are on-site, as are a championship golf course and a tennis complex offering four different court surfaces.

Listed in the National Register of Historic Places; member of Historic Hotels of America

Location: The Renaissance Vinoy Resort is at the intersection of Fifth Avenue NE and Beach Drive NE in the city of St. Petersburg. St. Petersburg/Clearwater International and Tampa International Airports are within 15 and 25 minutes, respectively; airport shuttle service is available. The resort is also easily accessible via Interstates 4, 75, 275, and 375.

Function Space: 23,000 square feet; 18 rooms

Capacity—Conference: 350; Reception: 500; Banquet: 450; Theater: 500

Equipment On-site: Audiovisual equipment and business services available

Food Service: Catering/food service available; five restaurants, lounge, 24-hour room service

Overnight Accommodations: 360 rooms

Access: Handicapped accessible; on-site parking; open year-round

Payment: Cash, credit card

Renaissance Vinoy Resort

GEORGIA

ATHENS

TAYLOR-GRADY HOUSE

634 Prince Avenue, Athens, GA 30601
Phone: 706/549-8688   Fax: 706/613-0860

IN 1844 planter and cotton merchant General Robert Taylor built his majestic Greek Revival antebellum mansion, whose 13 Doric columns are said to represent the original colonies. Like many others, Taylor moved to Athens so that his sons could attend the University of Georgia. In 1863, Major William S. Grady, while home on furlough from the Confederate army, purchased the house from the Taylors. His son, Henry W. Grady, who lived here from 1865 until 1868 when he graduated from the university, became managing editor of the *Atlanta Constitution.* An impressive orator, the young Grady was a spokesman for the New South, calling for reconciliation between the North and the South after the Civil War. Today the Taylor-Grady House is a public museum, beautifully restored and decorated with elegant period furnishings. The ballroom and grounds are available for both public and private functions. The house is located just outside historic downtown Athens and the picturesque Georgia campus, the oldest state-chartered university in the United States.

National Historic Landmark; listed in the National Register of Historic Places

Location: The Taylor-Grady House is 1 mile from downtown Athens; the Athens Ben-Epps Airport is 15 minutes away, and Atlanta's Hartsfield Airport is 65 miles southwest.
Function Space: 800 square feet; 1 room
Capacity—Conference: 75; Banquet: 65
Equipment On-site: Must be obtained from outside source
Food Service: Renter selects caterer; kitchen available
Limitations/Restrictions: No smoking, dancing, amplifiers or electric music inside house
Access: Handicapped accessible; on-site parking; open year-round
Payment: Check or money order

ATLANTA

THE ABBEY RESTAURANT

163 Ponce de Leon Avenue, Atlanta, GA 30308
Phone: 404/876-8532

AN acclaimed restaurant and local landmark, the Abbey is a remarkable Gothic Revival structure built in 1915 as a Methodist-Episcopal church. The building's 50-foot arched and vaulted ceiling rises above huge stained glass windows that recall the medieval cathedrals of Europe. Decorated with tapestries, statuary, monks' chairs, and copperware, the Abbey became a estaurant in 1968 and is a unique setting for business luncheons and dinners, weddings, receptions, cocktail parties and other gatherings. Meeting space includes banquet facilities and private dining rooms, and catering for outdoor events is also available. The extensive menu is continental, the wine list is renowned, the service is French, and the staff is appropriately clad in Old World attire. Special menus and arrangements may be worked out in advance by contacting the abbess.

Location: The Abbey Restaurant is 3 minutes from downtown Atlanta, two blocks from MARTA service, and 15 minutes from Hartsfield International Airport.
Function Space: 5,000 square feet; 4 rooms
Capacity—Conference: 500; Reception: 500; Banquet: 400; Theater: 500
Equipment On-site: Audiovisual equipment and business services available
Food Service: Lunch, dinner, banquets
Access: On-site parking; open year-round
Payment: Cash, check, credit card

ACADEMY OF MEDICINE

Atlanta Medical Heritage
875 W. Peachtree Street, Atlanta, GA 30309
Phone: 404/874-3219 Fax: 404/872-0601
E-mail: maa@atlanta.com

CONVENIENTLY located in midtown Atlanta, the Academy of Medicine is a beautifully restored meeting facility available for business, civic, cultural, and social events. The Academy, built in 1941 for the Medical Association of Atlanta, was designed by Philip Shutze and is an outstanding example of elegant neoclassical architecture. During the 1940s and 1950s the facility was a training center and library for local doctors. Use of the building declined with the onset of medical specialization and as hospitals were required to maintain their own libraries. Atlanta Medical Heritage, Inc., was established to own and operate the building, and under its auspices this architectural treasure has been restored. Recessed windows, rounded archways, marble floors, and classical detailing are found throughout the building, and the authentic period furnishings and fabrics add to the formal atmosphere. Small conferences are easily accommodated in the Gold Room or the library, and the dining room and auditorium are ideal for large groups. The handsome rotunda, with its Czechoslovakian crystal chandelier from the *Gone with the Wind* movie set, is also available for use.

Listed in the National Register of Historic Places

Location: The Academy of Medicine is in midtown Atlanta, three blocks from MARTA subway service and 15 minutes from Hartsfield International Airport.
Function Space: 4,000 square feet; 5 rooms
Capacity—Conference: 250; Reception: 300; Banquet: 100; Theater: 254
Equipment On-site: Podium, tables, chairs, and piano included in rental; video conferencing equipment and screen available
Food Service: Renter provides licensed and insured caterer
Limitations/Restrictions: No smoking (permitted outside only); renter provides own beverages; no food or beverages in auditorium

Academy of Medicine

Access: Handicapped accessible; on-site parking; open year-round
Payment: Cash, personal check

ANTHONYS
3109 Piedmont Road, Atlanta, GA 30305
Phone: 404/262-7379   Fax: 404/261-6009

THE Pope-Walton House, a dazzling historic plantation house, is home to Anthonys, which offers fine dining and a glimpse of the antebellum past. In 1797, Wiley Woods Pope began building the house, which would take years to complete. During Sherman's March to the Sea, Union troops stormed through the house, occupied only by Mary Elizabeth Pope Walton, her infant daughter, and a young slave girl, Sarah, who helped to hide the family silver. The home escaped destruction because of the presence of the newborn, Lulu Belle. In 1963 the house was moved, piece by piece, from its original site near Washington, Georgia, to a wooded three-acre site in Buckhead 117 miles away. The house was meticulously restored, and even the attic retains its original lumber. A restaurant since 1967, Anthonys offers private dining rooms of varied design, including a rustic brick kitchen with open hearth fireplace, elegant and chandeliered parlors, an enclosed front porch with a view of the grounds, and two working wine cellars. Consistently rated one of the finest restaurants in the country, Anthonys specializes in contemporary and Southern cuisine.

Listed in the National Register of Historic Places

Location: Anthonys is located north of downtown Atlanta and is accessible via I-85 and I-75.
Function Space: 7,500 square feet; 10 rooms

(groups from 10 to 200 individually or 600 as total capacity)
Capacity—Conference: 220; Reception: 600; Banquet: 220; Theater: 250
Equipment On-site: Sound system, business services can be prearranged
Food Service: Dinner; breakfast and lunch for 20 or more; catering
Access: Handicapped accessible; on-site parking; open year-round
Payment: Company check, direct billing, credit card

THE MANSION RESTAURANT
179 Ponce de Leon Avenue, Atlanta, GA 30308
Phone: 404/876-0727

LOCATED close to downtown Atlanta, the Mansion is an excellent example of late nineteenth-century Shingle Style architecture. The Peters family, hailing from Philadelphia, owned hundreds of acres surrounding what is now called the Mansion, the home they built in 1885. It was a private residence until 1970, when it was established as a restaurant. Eleven dining rooms, each unique, are available for business lunches and dinners, weddings, receptions, cocktail parties—even fashion shows. The opulent mansion is richly furnished and offers a variety of settings for business and private events, ranging from the grand Magnolia Room to the elegant library and the large cupola-topped gazebo. Three rooms tie into the courtyard, with its fountain and pool, to form a quadrangle that accommodates as many as 400. The menu highlights Southern specialties and features American cuisine, including seafood from the Gulf, prime Western beef, pheasant in peach sauce, and veal. The staff can also assist with special menus, party coordination, and entertainment.

Listed in the National Register of Historic Places;
Atlanta Landmark Building

Location: The Mansion is 3 minutes from down-town Atlanta, 15 minutes from Hartsfield International Airport, and is accessible via I-75/85.
Function Space: 4,500 square feet; 11 rooms
Capacity—Conference: 500; Reception: 500; Banquet: 400; Theater: 200
Equipment On-site: Audiovisual equipment available
Food Service: Lunch, dinner, banquets
Access: Handicapped accessible; on-site parking; open year-round
Payment: Cash, check, credit card

AUGUSTA

THE OLD GOVERNMENT HOUSE
432 Telfair Street, Augusta, GA 30901
Phone: 706/821-1812

AS one of Augusta's oldest public buildings, the Old Government House is a pivotal link to the city's early history. Built in 1801, it was first used as the Richmond County government headquarters, then later as the seat of city government before passing into private hands. Among its many owners was Samuel Hale, later mayor of Augusta, who in 1821 bought the house and converted it from a government building into a magnificent residence, adding the Regency porch and wrought-iron fence. The mansion was restored during the late 1980s to its nineteenth-century appearance, and today the grounds are reminiscent of the famous antebellum gardens that once surrounded the house. The elegant interiors boast Greek Revival fireplaces and a Victorian staircase,

and the central hall, dining room, and parlor are beautiful settings for intimate gatherings. A new two-story addition behind the house forms a reception area—including a balcony for orchestras—for groups numbering up to 300. The Old Government House is available for meetings, weddings, receptions, dinner parties, banquets, and other events and is also open for tours by appointment.

Listed in the National Register of Historic Places;
Georgia Trust Best Adaptation for Renovation award, 1989

Location: The Old Government House is located in downtown Augusta and is accessible via I-20 and Highway 25.
Function Space: 5,000 square feet; 10 rooms
Capacity—Conference: 200; Reception: 300; Banquet: 300
Equipment On-site: Audiovisual equipment and business services available
Food Service: Catering/food service available; full catering kitchen available, list of preferred caterers provided
Limitations/Restrictions: No smoking
Access: Handicapped accessible; on-site parking; open year-round
Payment: Cashier's check

THE PARTRIDGE INN
2110 Walton Way, Augusta, GA 30904
Phone: 706/737-8888 Fax: 706/731-0826

LIKE many other Northerners, Morris Partridge spent his winters in Augusta. But unlike Northern snowbirds on holiday, Partridge pursued a career as a hotelier with grand plans. He opened a small inn in the 1890s and continued to expand over the years; by 1929 the Partridge Inn was outfitted with a quarter-mile of galleried porches and balconies. In 1923, in a crowning moment, the inn hosted a brilliant banquet honoring President Warren G. Harding. Threatened with demolition during the 1980s, the renovated and refurbished inn opened again in 1988. A variety of meeting facilities are available for business conferences, retreats, receptions, and special events; these include the ballroom and dining room, which can accommodate groups of more than 100, the Board Room, the Club Room, and the penthouse. Guests stay in beautiful traditionally furnished rooms and enjoy a complimentary full Southern breakfast buffet. The inn's dining room and Veranda Bar & Grill are local favorites and are acclaimed for their Sunday brunch and outdoor dining, respectively. Other guest services include the inn's own Historic Gallery Tour, use of the pool and nearby health club, and use of the park and tennis courts next door.

Listed in the National Register of Historic Places; member of Historic Hotels of America

Location: The Partridge Inn is in Augusta's historic Summerville residential area, about 5 miles from I-20 (Washington Road, Exit 65) and just minutes from Bush Field Airport. Atlanta is 2.5 hours away, and Columbia, South Carolina, is just an hour away.
Function Space: 6,510 square feet; 6 rooms
Capacity—Conference: 80; Reception: 225; Banquet: 120; Theater: 120
Equipment On-site: Inn can arrange for all needed audiovisual equipment; light typing, photocopying, fax service available
Food Service: Breakfast with room; catering/food service available; two restaurants
Overnight Accommodations: 155 rooms

Limitations/Restrictions: No pets
Access: Handicapped accessible; on-site parking; open year-round
Payment: Cash, credit card

CLARKESVILLE

GLEN-ELLA SPRINGS COUNTRY INN

(Mailing address)
Route 3, Box 3304, Clarkesville, GA 30523
(Street address)
1789 Bear Gap Road, Turnerville, GA 30523
Phone: 706/754-7295   Fax: 706/754-1560

EVER since it was built in the late nineteenth century, Glen-Ella Springs has welcomed visitors seeking the cool mountain breezes of northeastern Georgia. The inn is situated on 17 acres along Panther Creek at the edge of the Chattahoochee National Forest, amid meadows, herb and perennial gardens, and a restored mineral spring. The cozy and elegant inn, whose long covered porches provide a peaceful view of mountains and forest, underwent an award-winning restoration in 1986. The inn offers a range of accommodations, and each guest room is individually furnished with antiques and locally handcrafted pieces. Room rates include a complimentary full breakfast; Sunday brunch and dinner (most evenings) are served, and the varied and changing menu is classic American and New Southern cuisine. A full-service conference center is available for meetings, retreats, seminars, and other activities. A spacious sun deck surrounds the pool, and there are numerous walking and hiking trails in the area. Other nearby recreational activities include golf, white-water rafting, and boating, and the area is also known for its folk art, pottery, and antique shops.

Listed in the National Register of Historic Places

Location: Glen-Ella Springs is located 4 miles off US 441, 15 miles north of Clarkesville and approximately 90 miles north of Atlanta via I-85 to I-985, Exit 45. From US 441, turn left onto Historic Old 441 at Turnerville and follow signs; last 2 miles on gravel road. Two hours to airport service in Atlanta and Greeneville-Spartanburg, South Carolina.

Function Space: 900 square feet; 1 room

Capacity—Conference: 30; Reception: 75; Banquet: 60; Theater: 60

Equipment On-site: VCR, overhead projector, screen; fax and photocopier available; guest rooms have voice mail

Food Service: Breakfast with room; catering/food service available; dining room

Overnight Accommodations: 16 rooms

Limitations/Restrictions: No smoking indoors; customer supplies own alcohol, not sold on-site

Access: Handicapped accessible; on-site parking; open year-round

Payment: Check or credit card

COLQUITT

TARRER INN

155 S. Cuthbert Street, Colquitt, GA 31737

Phone: 912/758-2888   Fax: 912/758-2825

NESTLED in the plantation region between Albany, (Georgia), Tallahassee, (Florida), and Dothan, (Alabama), the Tarrer Inn is an excellent example of Southern hospitality and service—even the coins are washed. Originally built in 1861 as a boarding house, the inn became Hunter House in 1905, offering the town's many visitors lodging and dining. Now known as the Tarrer Inn and owned by the citizens of Miller County, it was renovated in 1994 to recapture the elegant spaciousness of its public rooms and Victorian treasures. A grand staircase ushers guests up to their rooms, each of which is embellished with a distinctive motif and furnished with Victorian antiques. The Inn's banquet halls, dining room, and parlor are dramatically designed and can accommodate a variety of events, ranging from business seminars to afternoon teas. In the Garden Room, the chef accents the rich heritage of Southern cooking with a gourmet touch, using the local abundance of fresh ingredients and game. Rates include a generous continental breakfast, and guests enjoy hunting, horseback riding, and health club privileges. Bicycles are provided, and tennis and golf can be arranged.

Listed in the National Register of Historic Places

Location: Tarrer Inn, located on Colquitt's town square, is just off US 27 and GA 91, in Georgia's Plantation Trace travel region.

Function Space: 950 square feet; 3 rooms

Capacity—Conference: 140; Reception: 500; Banquet: 120

Equipment On-site: TV, VCR, overhead projector; computer, fax, photocopier available

Food Service: Breakfast with room; catering/food service available; restaurant

Overnight Accommodations: 12 rooms

Limitations/Restrictions: No smoking in rooms; alcoholic beverages limited to beer and wine

Access: Handicapped accessible; on-site parking; open year-round

Payment: Credit card (AmEx, MC, Visa)

COLUMBUS

SPRINGER OPERA HOUSE

(Mailing address)
P.O. Box 1626
(Street address)
103 Tenth Street, Columbus, GA 31902
Phone: 706/324-5714   Fax: 706/324-4681

DESIGNATED the official state theater of Georgia in 1971 by then-governor Jimmy Carter, the Springer Opera House has been a Southern cultural institution for more than a century. Francis Joseph Springer, a native of France, arrived in Columbus prior to the Civil War and built the theater in 1871. A host of famous figures appeared here, including Ethel Barrymore, Oscar Wilde, John Philip Sousa, Lillie Langtry, William Jennings Bryan, Will Rogers, and Franklin D. Roosevelt. During the 1930s the theater became a movie house, since touring companies no longer crisscrossed the nation as they once had. In 1965 an effort to save and restore the theater began, and today the Springer Opera House presents entertainment year-round. A Victorian lobby leads to the red-plush-and-gilt theater with its curving double balconies, tulip lights, high proscenium arch, and huge brass chandelier. The theater also houses a museum that highlights the work of the Springer's most celebrated personalities, as well as a library and archives. A variety of meeting facilities, including the main stage area, are available for performances, meetings, receptions, parties, and lectures. Guided tours by appointment provide a behind-the-scenes look at an active, working theater.

National Historic Landmark; listed in the National Register of Historic Places

Location: The Springer Opera House is accessible via I-185 and Highways 27 and 80 and is located 4 miles from Columbus Municipal Airport and 120 miles southwest of Atlanta.
Function Space: 2,500 square feet; 5 rooms
Capacity—Conference: 784; Reception: 175; Banquet: 150; Theater: 784
Equipment On-site: Sound and lighting system available
Food Service: Full kitchen and half-kitchen available
Limitations/Restrictions: No smoking; no food or drink in theater
Access: Handicapped accessible; on-site parking; open year-round
Payment: Cashier's check

JEKYLL ISLAND

JEKYLL ISLAND CLUB HOTEL

371 Riverview Drive, Jekyll Island, GA 31527
Phone: 912/635-2600   Fax: 912/635-2818

NAMES from America's Gilded Age—including Rockefeller, Morgan, and Pulitzer—are representative of those who gathered together to purchase Jekyll Island from a private owner in 1886. Two years later, the elite group opened the first season of their barrier island winter hunting retreat, returning to their clubhouse and cottages year after year until World War II. In 1947 the state of Georgia purchased the island, which is open to the public, and the turreted clubhouse is now the Jekyll Island Club Hotel, the centerpiece of the island's historic district. A full-service resort, the restored hotel offers complete conference, meeting, and banqueting facilities, fine dining, and nightly entertainment. The club's exquisite decor is what one would expect in a millionaires' haven, as seen in the columned archways, leaded art glass, original heart pine floors, and Rumford fireplaces. Guest rooms feature mahogany beds, amoires, and modern amenities, and many come with fireplaces and/or jacuzzi tubs. Tours of the historic district offer a look at the many gorgeous "cottages" and the art of historic preservation. There is no shortage of recreation available at the island, which offers 63 holes of golf, as well as tennis, biking, fishing, and numerous water sports.

National Historic Landmark; listed in the National Register of Historic Places; member of Historic Hotels of America

Location: Jekyll Island is 6 miles off the coast of Georgia, between Savannah, Georgia, and Jacksonville, Florida. The Jekyll Island Club Hotel is on the island's western (intercoastal) edge. Automobile access is via I-95 to US 17 to the Jekyll Island Causeway. Small private aircraft may use the island runway; Brunswick Airport, 18 miles away, and Savannah and Jacksonville Airports serve commercial carriers.
Function Space: 6,200 square feet; 9 rooms
Capacity—Conference: 42; Reception: 350; Banquet: 160; Theater: 240

Jekyll Island Club Hotel *(Courtesy of Jekyll Island Museum)*

Equipment On-site: Overhead and slide projectors, VCR/monitors, screens, flip charts; photocopy, fax, typing, and computer services available
Food Service: Catering/food service available; dining room, pub, deli-bakery, and room service
Overnight Accommodations: 134 rooms
Limitations/Restrictions: Restrictions on smoking
Access: Handicapped accessible; on-site parking; open year-round
Payment: Cash, check, credit card

NEWNAN

THE OLD GARDEN INN

51 Temple Avenue, Newnan, GA 30263
Phone: 770/304-0594   Fax: 770/304-9003

LOCATED in the College-Temple Historic District, the Old Garden Inn offers a charming, quiet respite just 45 minutes from downtown Atlanta. Built in 1904, the classic Greek Revival inn, with its wraparound Ionic portico, opens onto a beautifully kept lawn amid lush, green foliage. The interiors feature an English cottage-style decor, and the Grand Hall, with its 132 beveled window panes, is both casual and elegant. Meeting space at the inn is available with the rental of all five guest rooms (which includes a private cottage). Each guest room has its own private, modern bath and comes with English toiletries, robes, and wall-mounted hair dryers. Rates include a full breakfast, coffee, and other beverages. A refrigerator stocked with wines and soft drinks is available throughout the day, as is a cappuccino machine. Visitors will also find historic home tours, art and design studios, and antique shops among the nearby attractions.

Location: The Old Garden Inn is 35 minutes southwest of Hartsfield International Airport in Atlanta, and is accessible via I-85 (Exit 9) and Highway 34.
Function Space: 800 square feet; 1 room
Equipment On-site: Computer, fax service
Food Service: Breakfast with room
Overnight Accommodations: 4 guestrooms, 1 cottage; meeting space available with rental of all 5 rooms
Limitations/Restrictions: Restrictions on smoking—permitted on porches
Access: On-site parking; open year-round
Payment: Credit cards (AmEX, MC, Visa), cash, check

NORCROSS

FLINT HILL PLANTATION

539 South Peachtree Street, Norcross, GA 30071
Phone: 770/263-7669   Fax: 770/246-0764

AN authentic antebellum home built in 1835, this two-story columned house was once the center of a 500-acre working plantation, and its traditional plantation architecture is the very picture of the storied Old South. Civil War veteran Steven McElroy, who served as mayor of Norcross several times, purchased the house in 1870 and promptly renovated it in the High Victorian style. Flint Hill was renovated again in 1905 in the Simple Victorian style and, finally, in 1935, converted to the Colonial style. The McElroys sold the home in 1979, and in 1986, after 18 months of restoration and preservation work, Flint Hill opened as a special events facility. Authentic period lighting, wall

The Old Garden Inn

coverings, antiques, and period furnishings recall much of the interior's original appearance. Other features of particular note include original paneling and plasterwork visible throughout the house, the fireplace and antique mantel found in each of the eight rooms, and in one room the rare original buttermilk and blueberry paint. Located in the Norcross Historic District, the plantation hosts weddings, reunions, garden parties, and private gatherings and is also well suited for business meetings and conferences.

Listed in the National Register of Historic Places

Location: Flint Hill Plantation is 20 to 25 minutes from downtown Atlanta and is accessible via I-85.
Function Space: 3,000 square feet; 1 room
Capacity—Conference: 150; Reception: 300; Banquet: 150; Theater: 150
Equipment On-site: Audiovisual equipment, business services available
Food Service: In-house catering
Limitations/Restrictions: Smoking outside only; client provides alcohol

Access: Handicapped accessible; on-site parking; open year-round
Payment: Check or credit card (AmEx, MC, Visa)

ROSWELL

PRIMROSE COTTAGE

674 Mimosa Boulevard, Roswell, GA 30075
Phone: 770/594-2299   Fax: 770/594-8121

MORE mansion than cottage, this historic ante-bellum two-story home was built in 1839 for the widowed Eliza King Hand, daughter of Roswell King. Soon after Mrs. Hand, her father, and her three children moved in, early town settlers established the Roswell Presbyterian Church in the parlor of Primrose Cottage. Mrs. Hand and her second husband, Nicholas J. Bayard of Savannah, lived at the cottage until the Civil War. The first permanent home in Roswell, the cottage was constructed in a mere seven months. It was built in the simple but pleasing New England style, reminiscent of the homes King knew during his early years in Connecticut. Four large, square rooms on each floor open to wide central halls, and extending across the back of the house is a beautiful verandah. A glass-walled garden ballroom, designed to reflect the home's history and architectural integrity, is the most recent addition to the tree-shaded site. Primrose Cottage is available for corporate meetings, receptions, theme parties, and other catered events.

Listed in the National Register of Historic Places

Location: Primrose Cottage is located 20 to 25 minutes north of downtown Atlanta.
Function Space: 2,600 square feet; 4 rooms

Capacity—Conference: 150; Reception: 200; Banquet: 150; Theater: 150
Equipment On-site: Audiovisual equipment, business services available
Food Service: In-house catering
Limitations/Restrictions: Smoking outside only; client provides alcohol; corkage fee
Access: Handicapped accessible; on-site parking; open year-round
Payment: Check or credit card (AmEx, MC, Visa)

SAVANNAH

THE KEHOE HOUSE

123 Habersham Street, Savannah, GA 31401
Phone: 912/232-1020   Fax: 912/231-1587

BUILT in 1892, the Kehoe House is an impressive red brick Victorian mansion with Renaissance Revival features, originally home to William Kehoe, an Irish immigrant. He arrived in Savannah as a child, was apprenticed as an iron molder, and in 1874 founded Kehoe Iron Works under the name of Wm Kehoe Company. His house, now a luxury European-style inn, sits right on Columbia Square and is part of the renowned Savannah Historic District. The mansion, beautifully restored in 1990, boasts a number of fine features, including hand-woven carpets, pine, oak, and maple floors, and in the Double Parlor are the original chandeliers, noted for their marble centers. All of the guest rooms and suites have been individually designed and decorated with period furnishings. A gourmet breakfast is served each morning, and complimentary hors d'oeuvres are served daily during the cocktail hour. An English afternoon tea is available by reservation. The handsome conference room, with its comfortable leather chairs and fireplace, is well suited for business meetings and seminars, and an experienced concierge is on hand to assist in selecting among the many fine restaurants and entertainment venues in the area.

Located in a National Historic Landmark district; listed in the National Register of Historic Places

Location: Savannah is four hours from Atlanta and two hours from Charleston, South Carolina. Savannah International Airport is 20 minutes away via I-16.

Function Space: 2,376 square feet; 2 rooms
Capacity—Conference: 10; Reception: 45
Equipment On-site: Will arrange audiovisual equipment rental; computer and fax
Food Service: Breakfast with room; in-house food service and outside caterer available
Overnight Accommodations: 15 rooms
Limitations/Restrictions: No smoking; no pets
Access: Handicapped accessible; on-site parking; open year-round
Payment: Credit card

The Kehoe House *(Olivia Jane Williams)*

HAWAII

HILO

SHIPMAN HOUSE BED AND BREAKFAST

131 Ka'iulani Street, Hilo, HI 96720

Phone: 808/934-8002 or 800-MAP-THIS

E-mail: bighouse@ilhawaii.net

BUILT in 1900, the Shipman House is just four blocks from historic Hilo town, on the lush green side of Hawaii Island. Local children refer to the house as "the castle"; located in the Reed's Island neighborhood, it is one of the few remaining Victorian mansions in the state. A striking exterior feature is the three-story rounded tower with a conical roof, further accented by the circular verandah and the curved bay windows (with handmade glass) on both the first and second floors. Also of note is the porte cochere, whose high step accommodated turn-of-the-century horse and buggy passengers. The house overlooks the fern-lined gorge of Waikapu Stream, which offers a contrast to the extensive lawns, gardens, and swaying palm trees surrounding the house. The inn was renovated by the Shipmans' great-granddaughter's family, and the house has many of its original features and furnishings. Space is available for business meetings, receptions, and other gatherings. A short walk away is Hilo's historic downtown, which in the nineteenth century drew whaling ships, traders, and volcano explorers. Swimming, golf, tennis, and other activities are available nearby, and spectacular natural scenery abounds nearly everywhere.

Shipman House *(Barbara Andersen)*

Listed in the National Register of Historic Places

Location: The Shipman House is approximately a half-mile off Highway 19 in the city of Hilo on the Island of Hawaii (Big Island). Hilo International Airport is 10 minutes away. Taxi service is available.
Function Space: 791 square feet; 2 rooms
Capacity—Conference: 12; Reception: 150; Banquet: 12
Equipment On-site: Audiovisual equipment available from outside source; other business services can be arranged
Food Service: Breakfast with room; catering/food service available, renter may select caterer
Overnight Accommodations: 5 rooms
Limitations/Restrictions: Not wheelchair accessible; restrictions on smoking (in designated outdoor areas only); inn does not sell alcohol, may be purchased from caterer; renter provides insurance; for large groups, special transportation arrangements are required until wooden bridge is replaced in 1997
Access: On-site parking; open year-round
Payment: Credit card

HONOLULU

THE ROYAL HAWAIIAN

2259 Kalakaua Avenue, Honolulu, HI 96815
Phone: 808/923-7311 or 800-325-3535 (reservations)
Fax: 808/924-7098

THE Royal Hawaiian, or "Pink Palace" as it is also known, occupies a site on Waikiki Beach that at various times was the playground of King Kamehameha I, the summer home of Queen Kaahumanu, and a royal coconut grove. Royal con-

nections were further established here when the hotel opened in 1927 and Princess Kawananakoa signed in as the first registered guest. Built in a Spanish-Moorish style with Mission overtones, the hotel was a rest and recreation center for military personnel serving in the Pacific Fleet during World War II, reopening to the public in 1947. The Royal Hawaiian welcomes guests with a flower lei greeting and fresh banana bread on arrival; other guest amenities include multilingual concierge services, specialty shops, and even instruction in Hawaiian music and making flower leis. Meeting and banqueting facilities range from the Lurline Room, with its private ocean terrace, to the regally decorated Regency Room and the Monarch Room, where dinner shows are held. The Ocean Lawn and Coconut Grove offer beautiful outdoor settings for large events as well. Dining options include the Royal Luau, held every Monday on the Ocean Lawn, and the Surf Room, overlooking Waikiki's sandy white beach.

Location: The Royal Hawaiian is on Waikiki Beach, 4 miles from downtown Honolulu.
Function Space: 22,242 square feet; 4 rooms
Capacity—Reception: 2,000; Banquet: 1,200; Theater: 400; 66,000 square feet of outdoor meeting space available for up to 2,000
Equipment On-site: Audiovisual equipment and business services available
Food Service: Two restaurants, bar, 24-hour room service
Overnight Accommodations: 527 rooms
Access: Handicapped accessible; valet parking; open year-round
Payment: Cash, check, credit card

SHERATON MOANA SURFRIDER

2365 Kalakaua Avenue, Honolulu, HI 96815

Phone: 808/922-3111 or 800-782-9488

Fax: 808/923-0308

SMALL hostelries on Waikiki's gorgeous beach-front had been in business since the 1880s, but at the turn of the century this famous stretch of coastline was changed forever with the completion of its first hotel—the four-story, 75-room Moana. Oliver Traphagen's gracious 1901 design, distinguished by its elegant porte cochere, incorporates Colonial, Beaux Arts, Queen Anne, and neoclassical styles, and the hotel's open lobby, verandahs, and courtyards were built to take full advantage of the refreshing trade winds. Over the years the Moana has grown to three beachfront wings connected by a luxury shopping arcade. The center-piece, however, is the 75-foot-tall historic banyan tree in the courtyard, where the popular radio program *Hawaii Calls* was broadcast between 1935 and 1975. During the 1980s the hotel underwent a monumental $50 million restoration that also led to the creation of its Historical Room, which features a variety of hotel memorabilia, including 1930s woolen swimsuits. Indoor and outdoor banqueting and meeting facilities include ballrooms, a boardroom, and rooftop terraces, and the Moana Surfrider's private beach is available for receptions as well. Guest services include full concierge service, a fresh flower lei greeting, a children's program, and walking tours of Old Waikiki with costumed guides.

Listed in the National Register of Historic Places

Location: The Sheraton Moana Surfrider is located on Waikiki Beach, just minutes from downtown Honolulu.

Function Space: 15,300 square feet; 9 rooms (including outdoor terraces and courtyard)

Capacity—Conference: 120; Reception: 300; Banquet: 220; Theater: 275; private beach accommodates up to 300 for receptions

Equipment On-site: Audiovisual equipment available

Food Service: Four restaurants, snack bar, 24-hour room service

Overnight Accommodations: 791 rooms

Access: Handicapped accessible; valet parking; open year-round

Payment: Cash, check, credit card

IDAHO

BLACKFOOT

SHILLING HOUSE

81 N. Shilling Avenue, Blackfoot, ID 83221
Phone: 208/785-3606 or 800-785-3606
Fax: 208/785-6534

IN 1890, William Behle, a local physician and surgeon, built this two-story Italianate home that is now part of the North Shilling Historic District. A prominent local citizen, Behle also served as county coroner and built a drugstore on Main Street, while his daughter Mattie became Idaho's first woman pharmacist. His home, now the Shilling House Reception Center, was built of locally kilned red brick and features Queen Anne detailing, large box bay windows, and stained glass windowpanes. One hundred years after its construction, the house was beautifully restored to its original Victorian appearance by Angelen and Eugene Parrish. The original brass chandeliers still accentuate the elegantly appointed living room, but modern conveniences, including a new full kitchen, are found here as well. The house and its landscaped grounds easily accommodate a variety of functions, including private parties, weddings, receptions, and business meetings. The Shilling House and the historic district are named for Watson N. Shilling, an early Blackfoot settler and trader whose wire to Salt Lake City announced the death of General George A. Custer at the Battle of Little Bighorn in 1876.

Listed in the National Register of Historic Places

Location: The Shilling House is centrally located in Blackfoot on I-15, 25 miles from airports in both Idaho Falls and Pocatello. Salt Lake City, Utah, and Boise, Idaho, are 200 and 250 miles away, respectively.
Function Space: 1,500 square feet; 3 rooms
Capacity—Conference: 60; Reception: 200+; Banquet: 65; Theater: 80; landscaped patio area available for large groups May–October
Equipment On-site: TV/VCR, overhead projector, screen
Food Service: Full food service and refreshments available
Limitations/Restrictions: No smoking (permitted outside only)
Access: Handicapped accessible; on-site parking; open year-round
Payment: Cash, check, bank card (MC, Visa)

The Shilling House

ILLINOIS

CHICAGO

BISMARCK HOTEL

171 W. Randolph, Chicago, IL 60611
Phone: 312/236-0123   Fax: 312/236-3440

LOCATED in the heart of Chicago's Loop, the Bismarck Hotel has been a meeting place for business and political leaders since it was built in 1927. A luxury hotel designed to service business, the Bismarck enjoys proximity to the Board of Trade and City Hall and is within walking distance of the financial district, theaters, and Magnificent Mile shopping. It is also just a short courtesy van ride away from the Art Institute, State Street Mall, Water Tower Place, and the Tribune, Wrigley, and Hancock buildings. A variety of meeting rooms are available for large conferences, receptions, and parties, as well as smaller meetings and gatherings. The Bismarck's stunning Palace Lobby, with its rich ornamentation, imported stained glass, and marble staircases, accommodates 400, while parlor and conference rooms seat 20 to 50 conference style. Hotel guests have access to fine specialty shops and other services on site, and a private health and fitness club across the street is also available. Daily meals are served in the Crown Room, which features fine gourmet dining, and Gate 3½, the Loop's exclusive sports bar.

Location: The Bismarck Hotel is in downtown Chicago, 35 minutes from O'Hare International Airport.
Function Space: 15,000 square feet; 12 rooms
Capacity—Reception: 400; Banquet: 450; Theater: 400
Equipment On-site: Audiovisual equipment and business services available
Food Service: Catering/food service available; two restaurants, piano bar
Overnight Accommodations: 500 rooms
Limitations/Restrictions: Smoking and non-smoking areas; no outside food or beverage service
Access: Handicapped accessible; open year-round
Payment: Cash, check, credit card (AmEx, Diners Club, Visa)

OMNI AMBASSADOR EAST

1301 North State Parkway, Chicago, IL 60610
Phone: 312/787-7200   Fax: 312/787-4760

IT came as no surprise to the friends of engineering student Ernest Byfield that he should go into the hotel business. Coming from a long line of hoteliers, Byfield was a natural and his 17-story Ambassador East quickly became a popular address when it opened in 1926. Its splendidly restored interior highlights many of its original features—from the Italian marbled lobby to the crystal chandeliers. In 1938 Byfield opened his renowned restaurant named for the Pump Room in Bath, England, where fashionable Londoners gathered in the eighteenth century. Byfield's Pump Room has also been a popular meeting place for well-known figures, including numerous Hollywood celebrities eager to dine at the famed Booth One, favored by John Barrymore, Elizabeth Taylor, and Liza Minnelli. Meeting space is available in a classically furnished boardroom, private dining rooms, and conference rooms; facilities can also accommodate large cocktail parties or receptions. Located in Chicago's Gold Coast, the Omni Ambassador East is just minutes from the Loop and within walking distance of Michigan Avenue's business and fine shopping areas.

Member of Historic Hotels of America

Location: The Omni Ambassador East is located two blocks north of Division; Union Station is 12 minutes away, and Midway and O'Hare International Airports are within 35 and 55 minutes, respectively. The hotel is three blocks from CTA Subway.
Function Space: 6,500 square feet; 8 rooms
Capacity—Conference: 42 Reception: 225; Banquet: 120; Theater: 133
Equipment On-site: Audiovisual equipment and business services available
Food Service: Catering/food service available; restaurant; 24-hour room service
Overnight Accommodations: 275 rooms
Limitations/Restrictions: Nonsmoking floors available
Access: Open year-round
Payment: Cash, check, credit card

PALMER HOUSE HILTON
17 E. Monroe Street, Chicago, IL 60603
Phone: 312/726-7500   Fax: 312/917-1735

JUST 13 days after Potter Palmer opened his first Palmer House, the Great Chicago Fire of 1871 reduced his impressive hotel to smoldering ruins. But with crews working around the clock, Palmer opened his second—and more lavish—hotel just across the street in 1873. This magnificent hotel was replaced in 1925 but never closed

during construction, as guests lodged in the newly built sections while crews tore down the remaining half. During the 1980s the hotel underwent a multimillion-dollar renovation that preserved its historical ambiance and charm, and Florentine artisan Lido Lippi, known for his work on the Sistine Chapel, restored Louis Pierre Rigal's turn-of-the-century Greek mythology ceiling paintings. The Palmer House Hilton's extensive meeting facilities include three major ballrooms; the Empire Room, renowned for its High French Empire design; and Conference Center 7, a 40,000-square-foot complex on the seventh floor with 37 custom meeting rooms. The center's lounge areas, concierge services, separate food service, and access to a special block of guest rooms allow corporate and industry meetings to function during major conventions at the hotel. Located in the Loop, the city's business and financial district, the hotel is within walking distance of many of Chicago's cultural attractions.

Location: The Palmer House Hilton is located within Chicago's Loop and is 35 minutes from O'Hare International Airport and 30 minutes from Midway Airport. "El" train and bus service is available within one block of the hotel, and Chicago's major expressways (90, 94, 80, and 55) are just minutes away.
Function Space: 113,000 square feet; 78 rooms
Capacity—Reception: 2,000; Banquet: 1,600; Theater: 1,800
Equipment On-site: Audiovisual equipment available and comprehensive business center on-site
Food Service: Catering/food service available; 5 restaurants, room service
Overnight Accommodations: 1,639 rooms
Access: Handicapped accessible; open year-round
Payment: Cash, check, credit card

REGAL KNICKERBOCKER HOTEL

163 E. Walton Place, Chicago, IL 60611
Phone: 312/751-8100   Fax: 312/751-0370

BUILT in 1927, the year so many of America's grand old luxury hotels opened for business, the Regal Knickerbocker was originally known as the Davis. In 1996 the hotel completed a $15 million renovation, and the handsome decor is accented with a European flair. Over the years the Regal Knickerborcker has been the setting for numerous prominent gatherings, ranging from conventions and business meetings to dinner dances and notable weddings. The baroque-style Crystal Ballroom features a 28-foot gilded ceiling and a large illuminated Plexiglas dance floor, and smaller banquet rooms in the former tower casinos (said to be speakeasys during Prohibition) are available as well. The gracious guest rooms are larger than average, and rates include morning coffee, a newspaper, and a shoeshine. Situated atop the Magnificent Mile of Chicago's Gold Coast, the hotel is convenient to numerous Chicago attractions and landmarks, as well as the city's finest dining, shopping, and entertainment.

Member of Historic Hotels of America

Location: The Regal Knickerbocker Hotel is located at Walton Place and Michigan Avenue, 1 mile from Union Station, and 9 and 14 miles from Midway and O'Hare International Airports, respectively.
Function Space: 18,000 square feet; 12 rooms
Capacity—Reception: 750; Banquet: 400; Theater: 600
Equipment On-site: Audiovisual equipment, fax, photocopier available
Food Service: Catering/food service available; restaurant and bar; 24-hour room service
Overnight Accommodations: 305 rooms
Access: Open year-round
Payment: Major credit card

The Whitehall Hotel

THE WHITEHALL HOTEL

105 E. Delaware Place, Chicago, IL 60611
Phone: 312/944-6300   Fax: 312/573-6250

THE Whitehall Hotel opened in 1928 as one of Chicago's prestigious apartment buildings and was converted into a hotel in 1972. Following a 1994 restoration, this local landmark once again boasts an elegant, old-fashioned atmosphere. The renovation preserved the hotel's traditional, stylish decor while incorporating the latest modern conveniences. Meetings, weddings, and other events are accommodated in the hotel's conference and banquet facilities. The richly decorated guest rooms include a wide array of amenities, including multiline telephones with voice mail, computer capabilities, and (in some rooms) a fax machine. Dining options include Whitehall Place, once known as the Whitehall Club, which serves modern continental cuisine in an elegant setting. A sidewalk cafe offers alfresco dining during warmer months. From its location in the heart of the Gold Coast, the Whitehall Hotel offers complimentary downtown transportation and is just steps away from the Magnificent Mile, the John Hancock Center, and Chicago's lakefront. It is also easily accessible to the Loop, the city's central business district.

Location: The Whitehall Hotel is located in downtown Chicago, 20 miles from O'Hare International Airport, 3 miles from Amtrak service, and 1 mile from I-90/94 and I-55 expressways.
Function Space: 2,500 square feet; 6 rooms
Capacity—Conference: 60; Reception: 150; Banquet: 80; Theater: 100
Equipment On-site: Audiovisual equipment available
Food Service: Catering/food service available; restaurant, lounge; 24-hour room service
Overnight Accommodations: 221 rooms
Access: Handicapped accessible; open-year round
Payment: Major credit card

EVANSTON

THE HOMESTEAD
1625 Hinman Avenue, Evanston, IL 60201
Phone: 847/475-3300   Fax: 847/570-8100

EVANSTON architect Philip Danielson designed and built the Colonial-style Homestead in 1927 as a residence and hotel. With the onset of the Depression and World War II, Danielson and his wife, Ruby, an interior decorator, ran the hotel themselves, overseeing the Homestead for 30 years. The Homestead sits on a charming residential street adjacent to downtown Evanston and is just two blocks from Lake Michigan and Northwestern University. It borders Evanston's Lakeshore National Historic District and offers beautiful, well-appointed guest rooms. Trio, one of the top-rated restaurants in metropolitan Chicago, is located on the first floor and serves "American fusion" cuisine, a lively mix of French and Italian ingredients with Asian overtones. Meeting space is available in the library, its shelves lined with American fiction. Evanston is both a pleasant suburb and a cosmopolitan city, boasting six museums, a renowned dance company, fine specialty shopping,

The Homestead

art galleries, and sophisticated and varied dining. Several miles of walking and cycling paths run through lakefront parks, and a nearby health club offers special rates to the Homestead's guests.

Location: Evanston is 30 minutes from downtown Chicago and 35 minutes from O'Hare International Airport and Midway Airport. The Homestead is three blocks from the Chicago and Northwestern Railway and the CTA, which both provide regular commuter service to Chicago.
Function Space: 400 square feet; 1 room
Capacity—Conference: 18; Reception: 30; Banquet: 18
Food Service: Restaurant on-site, or renter may choose caterer
Overnight Accommodations: 35 hotel rooms, 55 apartments (apartments are usually not available for overnight stays)
Limitations/Restrictions: Restrictions on smoking
Access: Open year-round
Payment: Cash, check, credit card (AmEx, MC, Visa)

GALENA

DESOTO HOUSE HOTEL

230 S. Main Street, Galena, IL 61036
Phone: 815/777-0090   Fax: 815/777-9529

THE Galena Historic District offers a visitors a charming mid-nineteenth century atmosphere amid picturesque surroundings and rolling countryside, and much of Galena's mining and riverboat past remain. Most of the town's structures are listed in the National Register of Historic Places, including the three-story brick Desoto House, built in 1855 and handsomely restored in the late 1980s. The hotel has welcomed such noted guests as Abraham Lincoln, Ralph Waldo Emerson, Mark Twain, Susan B. Anthony, and Theodore Roosevelt, and it also served as Ulysses S. Grant's presidential campaign headquarters. Guest rooms are attractively decorated with period furnishings, and meeting facilities include small, intimate rooms as well as the spacious Victorian Ballroom. On-site food service is provided by the Courtyard Restaurant, the Green Street Tavern (a casual corner pub), and the Generals' Restaurant, named for Galena's nine Civil War generals. Nearby attractions include steamboat excursions on the Mississippi and Galena Rivers, Galena's historic lead mine and museum, Grant's home, and a variety of architecturally important sites that are open for tours.

Listed in the National Register of Historic Places

The DeSoto House Hotel

Location: Galena is in the northwest corner of Illinois and is accessible via Highway 20.
Function Space: 2,500 square feet; 5 rooms
Capacity—Conference: 20–40; Reception: 40–100; Banquet: 20–48; Theater: 40–90
Equipment On-site: Overhead and slide projectors, screen, TV/VCR, podium
Food Service: Full-service banquet facilities; two restaurants, tavern
Overnight Accommodations: 55 rooms
Limitations/Restrictions: Outside catering of food and beverage is not permitted
Access: Handicapped accessible; on-site parking; open year-round
Payment: Cash, check, credit card

JOLIET

JOLIET UNION STATION

(Mailing address)
81 N. Chicago Street
(Street address)
50 E. Jefferson Street, Joliet, IL 60432
Phone: 815/727-9753   Fax: 815/727-2324

IN the early days of the railroads, before there was a Union Station depot in Joliet, seven railroads at ground level crisscrossed the city's commercial center. Particularly bothersome were the tracks that ran directly between the county courthouse and City Hall, so Joliet filed suit against the Rock Island Railroad to have the tracks removed. In 1912 the stately French Renaissance-style Union Station designed by Jarvis Hunt was built a block from where the disputed trackage once passed. Still active today, Joliet Union Station offers an elegant setting for meetings, weddings, receptions, and trade shows. Rooms that at one time were designated as a smoking room, a retiring room, and a waiting room for travelers are now used for corporate meetings and social gatherings. The refurbished interior is especially impressive on the second floor, with its marble floors, two-story arched windows, 45-foot-high ceiling, and a graceful stone balcony that sweeps across the entire face of the building. The station is within walking distance of other historic sites, such as the Rialto Square Theater and the Joliet Public Library.

Listed in the National Register of Historic Places

Location: Joliet Union Station is approximately 45 minutes southwest of Chicago on I-55; 60 minutes to O'Hare International Airport, 45 minutes to Midway Airport. Metra and Amtrak train service available at Union Station.
Function Space: 6,570 square feet; 3 rooms
Capacity—Conference: 100; Reception: 250–500; Banquet: 250–300; Theater: 100
Equipment On-site: Podium, tables, chairs, included in rental; audiovisual equipment may be rented from an outside source
Food Service: Catering available
Limitations/Restrictions: Restrictions on smoking; insurance must be provided by renter
Access: Handicapped accessible; on-site parking; open year-round
Payment: Cash, check, credit card (MC, Visa)

LAKE FOREST

GORTON COMMUNITY CENTER

400 E. Illinois Road, Lake Forest, IL 60045
Phone: 847/234-6060   Fax: 847/234-4715

A contributing structure to historic Lake Forest, the Gorton Community Center has been a local landmark since its construction in 1900. First known as the Central School and renamed the Gorton School in 1912 after long-time Lake Forest mayor Edward F. Gorton, the school finally closed in 1971, reopening the next year as a privately funded community center. Since then, additions and renovations have made the facility a popular gathering place for both social and business functions. A variety of meeting rooms accommodate business and club meetings, reunions, receptions, performances, luncheons and dinners, and other gatherings. The traditional Community Room, which seats up to 170 for a sit-down dinner, features a fireplace, 14-foot-high ceilings, and a retractable screen, while the auditorium seats 343 and has professional lighting and sound systems. There are also smaller conference and meeting rooms, and two fully equipped, commercial-sized kitchens are available for professional catering. Groups are welcome to decorate to personalize their events, and the center offers special rates to residents and nonprofit organizations.

Location: Lake Forest is 45 minutes north of downtown Chicago and approximately 30 minutes from O'Hare International Airport.
Function Space: 9,932 square feet; 8 rooms
Capacity—Conference: 150; Reception: 200; Banquet: 150; Theater: 343
Equipment On-site: Slide and overhead projectors, screens, fax machine

Food Service: Client may choose caterer; two kitchens available
Limitations/Restrictions: No smoking; alcohol requires a special license
Access: Handicapped accessible (first floor only); on-site parking; open year-round
Payment: Check

MOLINE

WILLIAM BUTTERWORTH MEMORIAL TRUST

The Deere-Wiman House
817 Eleventh Avenue, Moline, IL 61265
Butterworth Center (Hillcrest)
1105 Eighth Street, Moline, IL 61265
Phone: 309/765-7970   Fax: 309/765-9656

THE William Butterworth Memorial Trust operates two historic homes within a half-block of each other as meeting facilities for nonprofit organizations. Overlooking the Mississippi River, downtown Moline, and the John Deere Plow Works, "Overlook," now called the Deere-Wiman House, was built for Charles and Mary Deere in 1872. Charles was the son of John Deere, whose successful manufacture of the steel plow was critical to Midwestern agricultural development. Charles and Mary gave Hillcrest, built in 1892, to their daughter, Katherine, and her husband, William Butterworth, as a wedding present. The house has a particularly noteworthy library, constructed in 1917, that was designed in the Italian Renaissance style and showcases an eighteenth-century ceiling painting done on canvas for the Dandolo family of Venice. In the music room is a grand piano and the Butterworth organ, whose main section consists of 26 ranks of pipes. Installed in 1909, the organ is considered one of the finest in the Midwest and is still in use today.

Location: Moline is two hours west of Chicago and two hours east of Des Moines, Iowa, off I-80, and is served by the Quad City Airport, less than 5 miles from the Deere-Wiman House and the Butterworth Center. The houses are at the intersection of Eleventh Avenue and Eighth Street, with easy access to I-80 via I-74. Metrolink service stops right in front of the Deere-Wiman House.

Function Space: 5,000 square feet; 10 rooms

Capacity—Conference: 150; Reception: 200; Banquet: 50

Equipment On-site: TV/VCR, overhead projector, screen; fax available

Food Service: Caterers list provided

Limitations/Restrictions: No smoking; no alcohol allowed; use of facilities restricted to nonprofit organizations

Access: Handicapped accessible at Deere-Wiman, accessible with assistance at Butterworth; on-site parking; open September through June 30

Payment: Donation to the William Butterworth Memorial Trust

OAK PARK

FRANK LLOYD WRIGHT HOME AND STUDIO

951 Chicago Avenue, Oak Park, IL 60302

Phone: 708/848-1976   Fax: 708/848-1248

MANY of the signature characteristics of Frank Lloyd Wright's Prairie Style of architecture— horizontally, strong geometric forms, and environmental harmony—found their earliest expression in the architect's own home. Built in 1889, the house was subject to Wright's ongoing experimentation, and his six children became accustomed to returning home from school to find that their father was changing the house yet again. In

Studio facade, Frank Lloyd Wright Home and Studio *(Jon Miller, Hedrich-Blessing)*

1898, Wright added a handsome studio, and today the drafting room is available for dinners and receptions. It was here that Wright designed more than 150 structures, later presenting his plans to clients in the studio's octogonal library. Wright left Oak Park in 1909 and the house was eventually subdivided into apartments, but beginning in 1974 a 13-year effort restored the house to its 1909 appearance. Groups holding an event here must be members of the Inglenook Society of the Frank Lloyd Wright Home and Studio Foundation, and site tours are provided during group events. The house is located in the Frank Lloyd Wright Prairie School Historical District, and Oak Park boasts 25 of the architect's buildings, the largest concentration of Wright structures in the world.

National Historic Landmark; listed in the National Register of Historic Places; National Trust for Historic Preservation Historic Site

Location: The house and studio are located 10 miles west of downtown Chicago and are accessible via I-290; at Harlem Avenue, exit north. Continue to Chicago Avenue, turn right, and proceed three blocks.
Function Space: 1 room
Capacity—Reception: 60; Banquet: 24
Food Service: Approved caterers list provided
Limitations/Restrictions: No smoking, dancing, or amplified music; no political or religious functions; fundraisers limited to those that benefit the Foundation; function space is available only to Inglenook Society members
Access: Open year-round
Payment: Check

PAXTON

REMEMBRANCE HALL

(Mailing address)
c/o Royce Baier
440 E. Pells Street
(Street address)
103 N. Market Street, Paxton, IL 60957
Phone: 217/379-2811   Fax: 217/379-4452

AT one time the tallest brick building on the Illinois Central Railroad between Chicago and Cairo, Illinois, this three-story structure has been the scene of community gatherings for well over a century. Remembrance Clark, who arrived in Paxton from Bangor, Maine, in 1860, built what was then known as Clark's Hall in 1867. Retail stores occupied the first floor, the second floor housed business offices, and for years the third floor hosted a variety of meetings, lectures, and traveling shows. In the early 1990s the Paxton Foundation, Inc., led by President Royce Baier, began restoring and renovating the building, now

called Remembrance Hall. The exterior, with its original windows and awnings, has been restored, and the hall has been given a new roof, floors, and ceilings as well. The elegant first floor, available for receptions, conferences, and seminars, is decorated in a grand Victorian style and features solid hardwood wainscoting, brass chandeliers, print wallpaper, and period floor covering.

Location: Paxton is 30 miles north of Champaign-Urbana via I-57 and is at the crossroads of Routes 9 and 45. Train, bus, and taxi service is available 10 miles south in Rantoul. Remembrance Hall is just a mile from Paxton Municipal Airport, and Willard Airport at the University of Illinois is 40 miles away.
Function Space: 3,500 square feet; 1 room
Capacity—Conference: 500; Reception: 450; Banquet: 500
Equipment On-site: Sound system
Food Service: Catering/food service available
Limitations/Restrictions: No smoking
Access: Handicapped accessible; on-site parking; open year-round
Payment: Cash, check

INDIANA

INDIANAPOLIS

MORRIS-BUTLER HOUSE

1204 N. Park Avenue, Indianapolis, IN 46202
Phone: 317/636-5409   Fax: 317/636-2630

LOCATED in the Old Northside Historic District of Indianapolis, the restored Morris-Butler house has been called the city's best-kept secret. Architect Dietrich Bohlen built the house, one of the few remaining examples of Second Empire architecture in Indianapolis, in 1865 for businessman John Morris and his family. Morris lost the house through bankruptcy in 1878, and the Butler family later moved in, occupying the Victorian mansion until 1958. Alarmed that so many of the city's beautiful old homes were being torn down, Eli Lilly of Lilly Pharmaceuticals restored the mansion, which is now a house museum. The house today is filled with antiques and an excellent collection of Victorian decorative arts and furnishings that capture the flavor of upper-middle-class family life in the mid- to late nineteenth century. All three floors are open for tours, including the richly ornate formal parlor and the family's private living quarters, and groups renting facilities may arrange in advance for house tours at a discounted rate. The conference/banquet room is located in the house, but away from museum areas to ensure privacy, and the courtyard area can also be rented.

Listed in the National Register of Historic Places

Location: The Morris-Butler House is accessible via I-65, I-70, I-74, I-69, US 31, and US 40; a bus stop is a half-block away; 15 minutes from Indianapolis International Airport. The house is five blocks east of Meridian (US 31) and is within 10 minutes of downtown hotels, restaurants, and shopping.
Function Space: 700 square feet; 1 room
Capacity—Conference: 30; Reception: 50; Banquet: 30; Theater: 30
Equipment On-site: Slide projector, cart, screen
Food Service: Caterer's kitchen available
Limitations/Restrictions: No smoking; alcohol may be served but not sold on-site
Access: On-site parking; open year-round except December 24 through mid-January
Payment: Check, credit card (MC, Visa)

THE VICTORIAN MANOR

3050 N. Meridian, Indianapolis, IN 46208
Phone: 317/925-4800   Fax: 317/926-7658

BUILT in 1904, the Victorian Manor (formerly known as the Schnull-Rauch House) is one of the few existing French Romanesque houses in the city. The house was home to Gustav and Tillie Schnull and, later, their daughter, Gertrude, and her husband, John G. Rauch. Today the three-story mansion is an elegant setting for business meetings, weddings and receptions, dinners, and dances. The rich interiors, enhanced with oriental carpets, museum-quality paintings, crystal chandeliers, and hand-carved oak trim, generate a warm and luxurious ambiance. Business meetings are held in the boardroom, complete with a small stage, while the ballroom and reception area accommodate both conferences and parties. The formal North Parlor features a Steinway grand piano, and sliding parlor doors can expand areas as needed. Individual rooms or the entire house can be rented, and groups may also use the beautiful curving verandah and outside grounds for larger warm-weather events.

Listed in the National Register of Historic Places

Location: The Victorian Manor is next to the Children's Museum at 30th and N. Meridian, 5 minutes from downtown Indianapolis. The house is accessible via I-74, I-69, I-70 and I-65 and is 20 minutes from Indianapolis International Airport.
Function Space: 2,500 square feet; 5 rooms
Capacity—Conference: 100; Reception: 150; Banquet: 125; Theater: 150
Equipment On-site: TV, VCR and other equipment available for rent
Food Service: Exclusive caterer available
Limitations/Restrictions: No smoking indoors

Access: Handicapped accessible; on-site parking; open year-round
Payment: Check

SOUTH BEND

NORTHERN INDIANA CENTER FOR HISTORY
(includes Copshaholm, Carriage House, and Oliver Gardens)
808 W. Washington, South Bend, IN 46601
Phone: 219/235-9664   Fax: 219/235-9059

OPERATED by the Northern Indiana Historical Society, Inc., the Center for History is a fascinating complex that includes galleries, museums, a library, and an impressive Romanesque Queen Anne-style 38-room mansion. The house was built for Joseph Doty Oliver, president of the Oliver Chilled Plow Works. Copshaholm, the three-story house, was completed in 1896 and maintains its original furnishings, such as furniture dating from the late eighteenth century, porcelains, glass, and silver. Each room on the ground floor has its own distinct parquetry, and there are leaded glass windows throughout the house. The two-story granite Carriage House, built about the same time as Copshaholm and also in the Romanesque Queen Anne style, is available for meetings. It retains its late-nineteenth-century atmosphere, and its sliding front doors are original as well. The historic Oliver Gardens may also be rented for receptions and gatherings. Created in 1907, the gardens include the only Italianate garden in South Bend. Although Copshaholm is not used for meetings, house tours

Copshaholm, Northern Indiana History Center

can be arranged for groups renting the Carriage House and/or gardens.

Location: The Northern Indiana Center for History is located eight blocks west of downtown South Bend. The Michiana Regional Airport is five minutes away, and Amtrak and South Shore rail service is available. South Bend is 2 hours from downtown Chicago and 2.5 hours from Indianapolis.
Function Space: 2,000 square feet; 1 room
Capacity—Conference: 50; Reception: 200; Banquet: 100
Food Service: Renter arranges catering
Limitations/Restrictions: No smoking
Access: Handicapped accessible; on-site parking; open year-round
Payment: 20 percent deposit, full payment 7 days prior to event

WABASH

HONEYWELL CENTER
275 W. Market Street, Wabash, IN 46992
Phone: 219/563-1102 or 800-626-6345
Fax: 219/563-0873

MARK C. Honeywell, a Wabash native and cofounder of what is today Honeywell, Inc., began building his original 45,000-square-foot multipurpose center in the early 1940s. The Art Deco-style center was intended as a cultural, conference, and recreation facility, and Honeywell established the Honeywell Foundation, Inc., as an endowed charitable corporation to own, maintain, and operate the center. Most of its original features, including light fixtures designed by Honeywell, a marble staircase, rift-cut oak paneling, and the original gymnasium and roller skating rink, remain today. In 1994 the foundation opened a $14 million, 75,000-square-foot addition that includes a 1,500-seat theater, a large lobby-gallery-reception area, and a restaurant. The addition also includes bronze sculptures, a large activity plaza, an outdoor dining terrace, and a 33-foot life-size replica of the deck of Honeywell's yacht, a piece he originally made for one of his homes. The block-long center is adjacent to the 90-building downtown district that is listed in the National Register of Historic Places. Today the center hosts more than 3,200 events and 220,000 visitors annually.

Location: The center is located on State Road 15 in downtown Wabash and is accessible via Highway 24.
Function Space: 15,000 square feet; 8 rooms
Capacity—Meeting rooms: few as 10; Ford Theater: 1,500
Equipment On-site: Tables, chairs, TV/VCRs, slide and overhead projectors
Food Service: Complete food and beverage service for banquets, receptions, and meeting breaks; three-way liquor license
Limitations/Restrictions: All room reservations subject to approval by the Board of Directors of the Honeywell Foundation, Inc.; smoking prohibited in the center
Access: Handicapped accessible; on-site parking; open year-round except on major holidays
Payment: Cash, check, credit card

IOWA

AMANA

AMANA COLONIES CONVENTION AND VISITORS BUREAU

39 - 38th Avenue, Suite 100, Amana, IA 52203
Phone: 800-245-5465   Fax: 319/622-6395

ESTABLISHED in 1855, the Amana Colonies have long been one of Iowa's leading tourist destinations. The roots of the colony stretch back to the early eighteenth-century German state of Hessen, where the Community of True Inspiration, or the Amana Church, was founded. Persecuted church members arrived in America, settling first in Buffalo, New York, then later purchasing 26,000 acres of land south of Cedar Rapids. The colony operated in a communal way of life until members voted to end the communal system in 1932. Today the entire settlement comprises seven villages and more than 400 historic sites and buildings. Crafts people still produce furniture, woolens, baskets, and other crafts in traditional ways, and museums and other village structures further document the history and customs of the colonies. Hearty German meals, many from recipes originating in the days of the communal kitchens, are still served family-style and continue to be a hallmark of Amana's hospitality. Facilities for meetings, receptions, and other gatherings are available at the Ox Yoke Inn (1865), the Colony Inn (1860), the Museum of Amana History (1870), and the Amana Community Church in the Village of Homestead (1865).

Listed in the National Register of Historic Places

Location: The Amana Colonies are located north, off I-80 (Exit 225), on US Route 151; 17 miles south of Cedar Rapids on US Route 151; 18 miles west of Iowa City on US Route 6. The Cedar Rapids Municipal Airport is 15 minutes away.

Museum of Amana History, Amana Colonies
(Courtesy of Amana Heritage Society)

Ox Yoke Inn

Function Space: 1,622 square feet; 2 rooms
Capacity—Conference: 30; Reception: 100;
Banquet: 130; Theater: 120
Equipment On-site: Slide and overhead
projectors, TV, fax and photocopy service

Colony Inn

Function Space: 1,000 square feet; 2 rooms
Capacity—Conference: 25; Reception: 50;
Banquet: 50; Theater: 50
Equipment On-site: TV, VCR, overhead
projector, flip chart

Museum of Amana History

Function Space: 1,200 square feet; 2 rooms
Capacity—Reception: 50; Theater: 80
Equipment On-site: Slide projector and screen

Amana Community Church

Function Space: 2,500 square feet; 2 rooms
Capacity—Conference: 50; Reception: 75;
Theater: 180

Food Service: Catering/food service available at
the **Ox Yoke Inn** and the **Colony Inn**
Overnight Accommodations: Hotels, bed and
breakfasts nearby
Limitations/Restrictions: Restrictions on
smoking
Access: All facilities handicapped accessible,
except the **Amana Community Church**; on-
site parking; open year-round
Payment: Cash, check, credit card

CEDAR RAPIDS

BRUCEMORE

2160 Linden Drive, SE, Cedar Rapids, IA 52403
Phone: 319/362-7375   Fax: 319/362-9481

SET in a 26-acre estate of formal gardens and rolling lawns, this Queen Anne-style home to three notable Iowa families offers a look at stylish upper-class Midwestern living. Caroline Sinclair, widow of industrialist T. M. Sinclair, built the house in 1886, but 20 years later she traded homes with the George Bruce Douglas family. Inherited by Margaret Douglas Hall in 1937, Brucemore was donated by Mrs. Hall to the National Trust for Historic Preservation in 1981. The three-story house built of darkened red brick with limestone trim features 14 fireplaces and an array of chimneys, gables, and turrets. In the Great Hall is the Wagnerian *Ring Cycle* mural painted on-site in the 1910s. The estate remains a center for cultural, philanthropic, and educational activities and is available to nonprofit organizations; for-profit organizations that wish to meet here must be corporate members of Brucemore. Space is available for meetings in the Hall-Perrine Conference Room, formerly the master bedroom, and receptions can be held in the mansion or on the grounds, which may be tented. House tours are included in the rental fee.

Listed in the National Register of Historic Places;
National Trust for Historic Preservation Historic Site

Location: Brucemore is located in the center of
Cedar Rapids; from I-380 take Exit 22 at
29th Street and follow signs.
Function Space: 300 square feet; 1 room
Capacity—Conference: 10; Reception: 125;
Banquet: 40

Brucemore *(Ron Blunt. Courtesy of the National Trust for Historic Preservation)*

Food Service: Approved caterers list provided
Limitations/Restrictions: Restrictions on smoking; alcohol service must comply with state law; for-profit organizations must be corporate members of Brucemore
Access: Handicapped accessible; on-site parking; open February through December
Payment: Check following invoice

DES MOINES

HOTEL FORT DES MOINES

Tenth and Walnut, Des Moines, IA 50309
Phone: 515/243-1161 or 800-532-1466 (reservations)
Fax: 515/243-4317

WHEN the Hotel Fort Des Moines opened with great fanfare in 1919, the ultramodern facility was well on its way to becoming the grande dame of Iowa hostelries. The H-shaped, 11-story structure exhibits classical detailing in its limestone and granite base and in the decorative ornamentation on the top floor. One of its featured amenities was ice water circulated to guest rooms and sterilized with ultraviolet light. Hotel Fort Des Moines continues to offer state-of-the-art amenities in an elegant, old-fashioned atmosphere. Over the years the hotel has welcomed numerous prominent figures, among whom were presidents and premiers (including 11 U.S. presidents and Soviet leader Nikita Khrushchev) and a king (Elvis Presley). Extensive convention and meeting room facilities are available, including ballrooms and conference rooms to accommodate large or small gatherings. Hotel dining options include the Gotham Club, featuring fine steaks, seafood, and pasta; Chequers Lounge, an English-style pub; and a traditional coffee shop. Guests can also take advantage of the health club, with its colorful lap pool. The hotel's downtown location makes it convenient to a number of attractions, such as the state capitol, Drake University, and house and history museums.

Listed in the National Register of Historic Places

Location: Des Moines is at the intersection of I-80 and I-35, and the Hotel Fort Des Moines is located off of I-235, the main interstate through town. The hotel is just 4.5 miles from Des Moines International Airport.
Function Space: 32,000 square feet; 21 rooms
Capacity—Conference: 100; Reception: 2,000; Banquet: 550; Theater: 1,000
Equipment On-site: Audiovisual equipment available; dataport hookups in all rooms; satellite teleconferencing available; fax and copier service available

Food Service: Catering/food service available; two restaurants, lounge
Overnight Accommodations: 242 rooms
Access: Handicapped accessible; on-site parking; open year-round
Payment: Cash, check, major credit cards

DUBUQUE

RYAN HOUSE

(Mailing address)
P.O. Box 266
Dubuque, IA 52004-0266
(Street address)
1375 Locust, Dubuque, IA 52001
Phone: 319/557-9545   Fax: 319/583-1241

THE irrepressible William "Hog" Ryan, whose fortune was mainly derived from the meat packing business, owned this impressive High Italianate villa built in 1873. In the style of the Gilded Age, the Ryan House was lavishly decorated with fine imported fixtures and furnishings and boasted a solid walnut staircase, marble fireplaces, embossed wallpaper, and crystal chandeliers. This home in downtown Dubuque was the scene of numerous meetings of notable figures, including General Ulysses S. Grant, whose likeness is found on the front gateposts. Today, Ryan House continues to host meetings, receptions, and parties in a setting that has beautifully retained its Victorian charm and opulence. Full food service is available, including customized Victorian meals featuring a historical presentation. A house museum of the Dubuque County Historical Society, the mansion is also a stop on the Society's Victorian House Tour and Progressive Dinner circuit.

Listed in the National Register of Historic Places

Location: Dubuque is located in eastern Iowa on the Mississippi River, 3.5 hours from Des Moines and Chicago and within 90 minutes of Cedar Rapids. The Ryan House is accessible via US Highways 20, 52, 61, 151. Airport service is nearby at Dubuque Regional Airport.
Function Space: 991 square feet; 3 rooms
Capacity—Conference: 45; Reception: 175; Banquet: 45
Equipment On-site: Audiovisual equipment available
Food Service: Catering/food service available
Limitations/Restrictions: No smoking
Access: On-site parking; open year-round
Payment: Check, credit card; payment due day of event less a $100 deposit

PELLA

THE PELLA OPERA HOUSE

(Mailing address)
P.O. Box 326
(Street address)
611 Franklin Street, Pella, IA 50219
Phone: 515/628-8628   Fax: (call first) 515/628-8628

THIS handsomely restored three-story brick opera house in downtown Pella has been at the center of community life in one fashion or another since it was built in 1900. The opera house flourished in the early twentieth century until movies upstaged live productions in small theaters such as this one. Over the years it was used for a variety of purposes until, in 1986, concerned citizens launched a $2 million effort to renovate the historic building. In 1990 the rejuvenated Pella Opera House, with its colorful stained glass windows and turn-of-the-century detailing, again opened for business. In addition to theatrical and musical events, receptions, meetings, and other business and social events are held here. The theater seats 324 under an authentic and ornate "tin ceiling" and offers both a state-of-the-art media booth and a beautifully restored 1920s theater organ. Private foyers and the Great Hall, which can be partitioned into smaller meeting rooms, are also available for rent.

Listed in the National Register of Historic Places

Location: Pella is 40 miles east of Des Moines on Highway 163.
Function Space: 5,000 square feet; 4 rooms (including 324-seat theater)

Capacity—Conference: 100; Reception: 350–500; Banquet: 210; Theater: 250–324
Equipment On-site: Public address system, overhead and slide projectors, VCR, piano; fax, clerical, and photocopy service available
Food Service: Caterers available
Limitations/Restrictions: No smoking; food and beverages must be provided by approved caterers
Access: Handicapped accessible; on-site parking; open year-round including holidays
Payment: Check

The Pella Opera House

KANSAS

COTTONWOOD FALLS

THE GRAND CENTRAL HOTEL

(Mailing address)
P.O. Box 506
(Street address)
215 Broadway, Cottonwood Falls, KS 66845
Phone: 316/273-6763 Fax: 316/273-8381

THE Grand Central Hotel is built on land grant-ed to Martin V. B. Merrick by President Abraham Lincoln in 1862 under the Military Bounty Land Act. Merrick had served as a private in Captain Henry's company, Grays Indian Disturbances, and had sent Isaac Alexander out to locate the land three years earlier. The land changed hands a number of times as Americans poured into Kansas during the years of westward expansion, but in 1881 M. M. Young purchased the proper-ty, opening the Grand Central Hotel in 1884. Filled with an old-fashioned Western flair and the charm of a country inn, the Grand Central Hotel and Grill reopened in 1995 following a beauti-ful restoration. The 10 unique and oversized guest rooms are individual-ly "branded" with the carefully select-ed historic brands of Chase County ranches. Room rates include a conti-nental breakfast, and the popular grill room serves an excellent menu featur-ing the finest of steaks. Meeting rooms are available for weddings, receptions, board meetings, small corporate retreats, and other functions. Located in the Flint Hills Historic District, the Grand Central Hotel is just one block west of Scenic Byway 177.

Location: The Grand Central Hotel, located 18 miles west of Emporia, is accessible via Highway 50 and I-35 and is 150 miles from Kansas City (both Kansas and Missouri) and 180 miles from Kansas City International Airport. The Wichita Mid-Continent Airport is 80 miles southwest, and a grass landing strip for small air-craft is 1 mile from Cottonwood Falls. Car rental is available in Emporia.
Function Space: 550 square feet; 2 rooms
Capacity—Conference: 40; Reception: 50; Banquet: 35; Theater: 75
Equipment On-site: TV, VCR, overhead projector, podium; fax, copying, secretarial services available
Food Service: Breakfast with room; catering/food service available; restaurant
Overnight Accommodations: 10 rooms
Access: Handicapped accessible; on-site parking; open year-round
Payment: Cash, traveler's checks, credit card

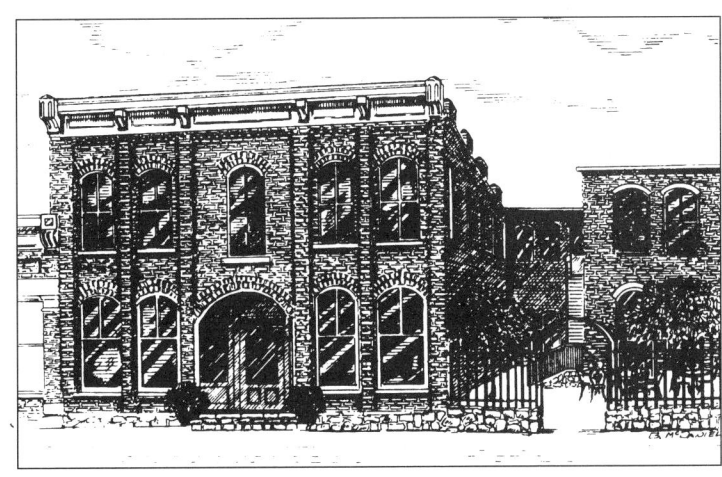

The Grand Central Hotel

STRONG CITY

TALLGRASS PRAIRIE NATIONAL PRESERVE

Route 1, Box 14, Strong City, KS 66869
Phone: 316/273-8494 Fax: 316/273-8247

CATTLE baron Stephen F. Jones's magnificent nineteenth-century mansion and cattle barn occupy a splendid setting in the Flint Hills, surrounded by a rich, though now rare, tallgrass prairie landscape. Constructed in 1881, the three-story house rises majestically above the vast reaches of its Great Plains estate and boasts a handsome Second Empire-style mansard roof. The house, the huge three-story barn overlooking Fox Creek, and the nearby hilltop one-room schoolhouse were all built of hand cut and dressed native white limestone. Formerly known as the Z Bar/Spring Hill Ranch, the preserve offers a unique atmosphere for meetings and gatherings, with a parlor in the house available for small groups (15 to 20), and a barn that comfortably accommodates up to 100. Part of the barn has been set aside as a theater, complete with hay-bale seating. Tours of the house, outbuildings, and schoolhouse can be arranged, and the Southwind Nature Trail, a 1 3/4 mile walk, offers wonderful views of the native grasses and wild-flowers that grace the countryside. A movement is under way to bring the preserve into the fold of the National Park system, but until that is accomplished, public access is limited.

National Historic Landmark; listed in the National Register of Historic Places

Location: The Tallgrass Prairie National Preserve is located 2 miles north of Strong City on Highway 177, 16 miles south of Council Grove and 20 miles west of Emporia. Nearest major airports are Wichita (90 miles) and Kansas City, Missouri (157 miles). Airport service is also available in Emporia and Manhattan, 20 and 60 miles away, respectively.

Function Space: 2,434 square feet; 3 rooms

Capacity—Conference: 100 (barn); Reception: 20 (house); Banquet: 80 (barn); Theater: 80 (barn)

Equipment On-site: Slide projector and screen; fax machine; tables and chairs included in rental

Food Service: Catering through local restaurant

Limitations/Restrictions: No smoking

Access: Limited handicapped accessibility (assistance is available); on-site parking; open spring and fall

Payment: Check

Tallgrass Prairie National Preserve *(Roger Weaver)*

KENTUCKY

HARRODSBURG

SHAKER VILLAGE OF PLEASANT HILL
3501 Lexington Road, Harrodsburg, KY 40330
Phone: 800-734-5611   Fax: 606/734-5411

THE largest restored community of its kind in the United States, the Shaker Village of Pleasant Hill comprises 33 historic nineteenth-century buildings on 2,700 acres of bluegrass farmland. The Shakers were a religious sect that arrived in America from England in 1774, and their communities flourished until the mid-nineteenth century. Costumed interpreters on-site offer insight into the village's history and the daily life of its residents, and visitors may take a self-guided walking tour that includes stops at 15 restored buildings. Skilled artisans continue to ply nineteenth-century trades, and the storied Shaker music is performed daily in the 1820 Meeting House, April through October. Horse-drawn wagon rides and riverboat trips aboard the *Dixie Belle* on the scenic Kentucky River combine to transport visitors back to another era. Meetings may be held in newly restored buildings designed to accommodate receptions, business meetings and breakout sessions, and other gatherings. The restored buildings comfortably house overnight guests, whose rooms are furnished with authentic Shaker reproductions and handwoven bedspreads and rugs. At the Trustees'

Office Inn, guests and meeting participants will find a menu featuring delicious Kentucky fare.

National Historic Landmark; listed in the National Register of Historic Places

Location: Shaker Village is 30 minutes from Lexington and 90 minutes from Louisville, and is accessible via US 68.
Function Space: 3,000+ square feet; 4 rooms
Capacity—Conference: 85; Reception: 85; Banquet: 50; Theater: 50
Equipment On-site: Overhead and 35mm slide projectors, screens, fax machine
Food Service: Dining room; menus and mealtimes arranged for group dining
Overnight Accommodations: 81 rooms
Limitations/Restrictions: All food must be provided by Shaker Village; local law prohibits sale of alcoholic beverages (Shaker Village will arrange setups for groups that wish to host receptions)
Access: Handicapped accessible to meeting rooms A and B, dining room; on-site parking; open year-round
Payment: Check, credit card (MC or Visa)

Shaker Village of Pleasant Hill

LOUISVILLE

THE CAMBERLEY BROWN HOTEL

335 W. Broadway, Louisville, KY 40202
Phone: 502/583-1234   Fax: 502/561-8443

EVER since J. Graham Brown, a millionaire lumberman, opened his hotel in 1923, the Brown Hotel has been a Louisville landmark. The first person to sign the guest register was David Lloyd George, former prime minister of Great Britain, and a parade of other dignitaries and celebrities soon followed. A major renovation during the 1980s reconfigured the hotel's original 600 guest rooms into 292 spacious, beautifully appointed accommodations. At the same time, a meticulous restoration of the Brown's detailed plaster molding, woodworking, stained glass, crystal chandeliers, and gilt-embellished medallion ceiling returned the interior to its original grand appearance. Function and conference rooms, including the Crystal Ballroom, which hosts the city's most opulent events, are available for a full range of business meetings and social gatherings. The acclaimed English Grill offers fine dining and a seasonal menu, and J. Graham's Bar and Grill is known as the birthplace of the famous "Hot Brown" sandwich. Shops, a 24-hour fitness center, concierge services, and many other conveniences are available on-site. Complimentary van shuttle service is available to and from the airport, and nearby attractions include Theater Square and Churchill Downs, home of the Kentucky Derby.

Listed in the National Register of Historic Places;
member of Historic Hotels of America

Location: The Camberley Brown Hotel is located in the heart of downtown Louisville and is accessible via I-65, I-64, and I-71. Complimentary trolley service available to downtown locations and complimentary airport transportation to Louisville International Airport.
Function Space: 17,309 square feet; 13 rooms
Capacity—Conference: 50; Reception: 700; Banquet: 400; Theater: 500
Equipment On-site: Audiovisual equipment available; in-room faxes
Food Service: Full-service catering, three restaurants, lounge, 24-hour room service
Overnight Accommodations: 292 rooms
Limitations/Restrictions: Restrictions on smoking; smoking and nonsmoking rooms available
Access: Handicapped accessibility; on-site parking; open year-round
Payment: Cash, credit card

SPRINGFIELD

MAPLE HILL MANOR BED AND BREAKFAST

2941 Perryville Road, Springfield, KY 40069
Phone: 606/336-3075 or 800-886-7546

SET on a peaceful rural hilltop under ancient maple trees, Maple Hill Manor was built in 1851 for Thomas McElroy as a wedding present to his wife, Sarah Maxwell. The 13-room mansion, which once overlooked a huge tobacco plantation, sits on 14 scenic acres. The house was built in the Federal style with Italianate detailing and is considered one of the best-preserved historic homes in the Bluegrass Region. The manor boasts $13^1/2$-foot ceilings, 9-foot windows, and nine fireplaces and is decorated with period furnishings. In the foyer, with its decorative stenciling, is an impressive freestanding cherry spiral staircase. The beautifully furnished guest rooms are spacious, and rates include a full breakfast served on fine china. Guests also enjoy a complimentary homemade dessert and beverage in the evening. Meeting space is available in the parlor and the dining room, which are connected by a pocket sliding door, for small groups, and the manor can cater lunch and dinner as well. Outdoors is large patio area, and a picnic table and grills are available for guests' use. Lincoln Homestead Park, Perryville Battlefield, and Shaker Village are just a short drive away.

Listed in the National Register of Historic Places; a designated Kentucky Landmark Home

Location: Springfield is on US 150, 45 minutes from Louisville International and Lexington Airports.

Function Space: 800 square feet; 2 rooms

Capacity—Conference: 30; Reception: 30; Banquet: 30

Equipment On-site: B & B can arrange for audiovisual equipment with prior notice

Food Service: Breakfast with room; food service available

Overnight Accommodations: 7 rooms

Limitations/Restrictions: No smoking in building

Access: On-site parking; open year-round

Payment: Cash, check, credit card (MC, Visa)

LOUISIANA

BATON ROUGE

OLD STATE CAPITOL

(Mailing address)
P.O. Box 94125, Baton Rouge, LA 70804
(Street address)
100 North Boulevard at River Road
Baton Rouge, LA 70801
Phone: 504/342-0500   Fax: 504/342-0316

A Gothic masterpiece overlooking the Mississippi River, the Old State Capitol is a sparkling white castle on a bluff and is as magnificent as it is historic. Architect James Harrison Dakin's original capitol was completed in 1849, and it was here that the state legislature voted to secede from the Union in 1861. The capitol was burned by Union soldiers in 1862, but the state government returned to the restored building in 1882 and continued to meet there for the next 50 years. Today the Old State Capitol houses the Center for Political and Governmental History, the state's official repository of film and video archives. The center also maintains a museum that includes interactive displays on Louisiana's lively political past, and there are exhibits on the Louisiana Purchase and the Huey Long assassination. The building itself is a monument to Gothic architecture, and the rich interior evokes medieval splendor with its amber glow, marble floors, spiral staircase, stained glass windows, and pointed archways. The Rotunda and the Senate Chamber are available for receptions and special events after-hours, and the elegant conference and public meeting rooms

may be used for meetings, conferences, lectures, and other gatherings during the day.

National Historic Landmark; listed in the National Register of Historic Places

Location: The Old State Capitol is accessible via I-10, I-110, and Highway 61.
Function Space: 7,280 square feet; 4 rooms
Capacity—Conference: 200; Reception: 500; Banquet: 200; Theater: 200
Food Service: Catering available
Limitations/Restrictions: No smoking; licensed caterers only; no red wine
Access: Handicapped accessible; open year-round
Payment: Check

DARROW

TEZCUCO PLANTATION

3138 Highway 44, Darrow, LA 70725
Phone: 504/562-3929   Fax: 504/562-3923

TEZCUCO, whose name is of Atztec origin meaning "resting place," was built by Benjamin Tureaud in 1855, and it was one of the last of the antebellum plantation homes completed before the Civil War. The main house is a Greek Revival raised cottage that contains a fine collection of nineteenth-century antique furnishings and showcases the expert craftsmanship of the home's interiors, including detailed plasterwork and the original hand-painted false graining on the doors and window sashes. Beyond the main house surrounded by glorious live oaks, visitors will find along the paths formal gardens and a number of historic plantation structures, including a chapel, a blacksmith shop, a carriage house, museums, and 10 guest cottages. Overnight guests are treated to a full creole breakfast served in their cottages and are welcome to take a complimentary tour of the main house. The country-style cottages are furnished with antiques, artifacts, and private libraries. Meeting rooms are located in the Tezcuco Plantation Restaurant, which has been elegantly refurbished in the Victorian style.

Listed in the National Register of Historic Places

Location: Located in the historic River Road district, Tezcuco Plantation is 45 miles from New Orleans International Airport and 30 miles from Baton Rouge Airport; 5.5 miles from I-10.
Function Space: 1,410 square feet; 3 rooms
Capacity—Conference: 25; Banquet: 25; Theater: 50
Equipment On-site: TV/VCR, overhead and slide projectors, flip charts, microphone available (for rent)
Food Service: Breakfast with guest room (meeting room rental discounted with lunch or buffet

served; continental breakfast, mid-morning and afternoon breaks available); meeting room rental includes water and coffee throughout the day
Overnight Accommodations: 17 rooms
Limitations/Restrictions: No outside catering
Access: On-site parking; open year-round
Payment: Cash, approved company check, credit card

NEW IBERIA

SHADOWS-ON-THE-TECHE
317 East Main Street, New Iberia, LA 70560
Phone: 318/369-6446   Fax: 318/365-5213

IN 1831 wealthy planter David Weeks built one of the most famous antebellum houses in the South, known today as Shadows-on-the-Teche. Located in New Iberia's historic district and overlooking Bayou Teche, the mansion combines neoclassical design elements, including a bold facade

Tezcuco Plantation

Shadows-on-the-Teche *(Ron Blunt. Courtesy of the National Trust for Historic Preservation)*

National Historic Landmark; listed in the National Register of Historic Places; National Trust for Historic Preservation Historic Site

Location: Shadows-on-the-Teche is at the intersection of Highways 182 and 14, 30 minutes southeast of Lafayette, and is accessible via I-10 and Highway 90.
Function Space: 600 square feet; 1 room
Capacity—Conference: 35; Reception: 200
Equipment On-site: Slide projector and screen, TV, VCR, tables and chairs
Food Service: Exclusive caterer
Overnight Accommodations: Available nearby
Limitations/Restrictions: No smoking; site prefers use of approved caterer
Access: Handicapped accessible; free street parking; open year-round
Payment: Check

with eight Doric columns, with a French Colonial floorplan. The elegantly restored sugar plantation house was home to four generations of the Weeks family and is filled with original furnishings. In 1922 the builder's great-grandson William Weeks Hall returned to Shadows and discovered an incredible collection of 17,000 family letters, photographs, and receipts in 40 trunks in the attic, providing visitors with one of the best-documented house tours in the country. During the 1920s he restored the house and its renowned gardens, featuring the live oaks and camellias planted by his great-grandmother in the 1830s. Hall also entertained celebrities such as Henry Miller, Anais Nin, Walt Disney, Cecil B. DeMille, and Elia Kazan, who left their autographs on an interior door, and D. W. Griffith filmed his silent movie *The White Rose* at Shadows in 1923. A meeting room is provided for group programs and presentations, and the gardens and porches are available for receptions and cocktail parties.

NEW ORLEANS

THE COLUMNS HOTEL

3811 St. Charles Avenue, New Orleans, LA 70115
Phone: 504/899-9308 or 800-445-9308
Fax: 504/899-8170

THIS stately and elegant hotel, with its prominent columns, is the last remaining example of renowned architect Thomas Sully's grand Italianate homes built between 1883 and 1885. Originally a private residence, the Columns was also a boarding house, and as a small hotel it has long been a favorite gathering spot for locals. Gilded bronze chandeliers, dark mahogany walls, and a beautiful coffered ceiling give the Victorian Lounge, one of the city's hottest nightspots, its charming, European pub atmosphere. Guest rooms vary from the simple to the grand, and overnight guests enjoy a complimentary continental breakfast. Sunday jazz brunches are served in the Albertine Tea Room, which is available for private parties. Conferences, receptions, and other functions may also be held in the Columns' restored period rooms. Streetcars pass right by the hotel's front door, ready to take visitors to the city's innumerable nearby attractions, including the Central Business District, Riverwalk, the Superdome, Convention Center, and the French Quarter.

Listed in the National Register of Historic Places

Location: The Columns is located on "the Avenue," as New Orleanians call fashionable St. Charles Avenue, on the the city's famed streetcar line and just blocks from the historic garden district.
Function Space: 2,500 square feet; 4 rooms
Capacity—Conference: 30; Reception: 300; Banquet: 60 (one room), 150 (four rooms); Theater: 60
Equipment On-site: Audiovisual equipment and business services available
Food Service: Breakfast with room; catering available; lounge
Overnight Accommodations: 19 rooms
Limitations/Restrictions: No smoking
Access: Handicapped accessible; open year-round
Payment: Cash, traveler's checks, credit card (AmEx, MC, Visa); personal checks in advance

LE PAVILLON HOTEL
833 Poydras Street, New Orleans, LA 70140
Phone: 504/581-3111   Fax: 504/522-5543
E-mail: Lepavsales@aol.com

LE Pavillon, one of New Orleans' most historic and beautifully preserved turn-of-the-century buildings, is situated on what was once the site of one of Louisiana's great plantation homes. The 10-story hotel incorporates Greek Revival design elements and is an architectural classic amid the city's modern high rises. Built in 1907 as the New Hotel Denechaud, the renovated Le Pavillon Hotel is also known as "the belle of New Orleans" and is an achievement in historic preservation. The exquisite interiors feature ornate woodwork, marbles, original art, antique furnishings, and crystal chandeliers. Among its luxurious suites, of note is the Antique Plantation Suite, that is true to the character of New Orleans, with its authentic Louisiana antiques and plantation-style mosquito-netted beds. Versatile conference and meeting facilities accommodate a variety of business and social functions, and the hotel's downtown location is just steps away from the city's business district and civic buildings. Other amenities include the opulent Crystal Room, which serves regional cuisine, the Gallery Lounge, a heated rooftop pool, and a fitness center. Le Pavillon also continues its long tradition of serving complimentary peanut butter and jelly sandwiches nightly in the elegant lobby.

Listed in the National Register of Historic Places; member of Historic Hotels of America

Location: Le Pavillon Hotel is 13 miles from New Orleans International Airport and is accessible via I-10. The hotel is six blocks from the Greyhound Bus terminal and the Amtrak station.
Function Space: 9,063 square feet; 7 rooms
Capacity—Conference: 50; Reception: 350; Banquet: 150; Theater: 225
Equipment On-site: Audiovisual equipment available through outside source; business services arranged through concierge
Food Service: Catering/food service; restaurant and lounge, 24-hour room service
Overnight Accommodations: 219 rooms
Access: Handicapped accessible; valet parking; open year-round
Payment: Cash, check, all major credit cards

PORT ALLEN

POPLAR GROVE PLANTATION

3142 N. River Road, Port Allen, LA 70767-3530
Phone: 504/344-3913   Fax: 504/343-8701

SURROUNDED by beautiful gardens in a serene rural setting, Poplar Grove Plantation sits on the bank of the Mississippi River, offering visitors a pleasing river overlook from its lovely wraparound verandah. Originally, Poplar Grove was the Bankers' Pavilion at the 1884 World's Industrial and Cotton Exposition held in New Orleans. Thomas Sully, one of Louisiana's leading architects, designed the intriguing structure, incorporating elements of Chinese, Italianate, Eastlake, and Queen Anne styles into a "galleried pavilion." In 1886 the pavilion was transported by barge up the Mississippi River to Port Allen, where it became the home of sugar planter Horace Wilkinson. Five generations of the Wilkinson

family have lived at Poplar Grove, and family members continue to welcome visitors to this private residence. Several rooms are available for parties and special functions, and group tours of the home may be made with advance reservation.

Listed in the National Register of Historic Places; subject of Historic American Buildings Survey

Location: Poplar Grove Plantation is 10 minutes west of Baton Rouge, 1.5 hours from New Orleans, and 5 minutes from I-10. Airport service is available at Baton Rouge Metro and New Orleans International.
Function Space: 1,500 square feet; 3 rooms
Capacity—Conference: 40; Reception: 150; Banquet: 45
Food Service: Renter selects caterer
Limitations/Restrictions: No smoking
Access: On-site parking; open year-round, except major holidays
Payment: Check

ST. FRANCISVILLE

ROSEDOWN PLANTATION AND HISTORIC GARDENS

12501 Highway 10, St. Francisville, LA 70775
Phone: 504/635-3332

AN arching colonade of majestic oaks lines Oak Avenue, the stunning approach to Rosedown Plantation. Set in the heart of Plantation Country, Rosedown occupies 1,000 acres and boasts 14 historic structures. The Greek Revival main house anchors a plantation brimming with history and aesthetic delights. Built in 1835 by David and Martha Turnbull, the mansion is filled with the works of America's finest cabinetmakers, as well as wall coverings, chandeliers, silver, and marble statuary from Europe. The 28-acre Rosedown garden, among the nineteenth century's most famous horticultural collections, is now considered one of the nation's five most important gardens. Inspired by the post-Renaissance gardens they visited during their grand tour of Europe in 1828, the Turnbulls developed formal gardens with classical landscaping and experimented with exotic imported flora. In 1956, Catherine Fondren Underwood purchased the plantation, which had been occupied by the Turnbull family for more than a century, and launched an extensive and costly private restoration. The house, with its well-documented rare collection of original furnishings, is maintained as a house museum, while the guest house offers overnight accommodations, a continental breakfast, a mansion tour, and access to the grounds.

Listed in the National Register of Historic Places

Location: Rosedown is 25 miles north of Baton Rouge and is accessible via Highway 61.
Function Space: 800 square feet; 1 room
Capacity—Conference: 12–40; Reception: 20–200; Banquet: 20–30; Theater: 85
Equipment On-site: Projector screen for both laser disc and VHS cassettes
Food Service: Breakfast with room; catering/food service available for dinners and receptions
Overnight Accommodations: 12 rooms
Limitations/Restrictions: Restrictions on smoking; bar setups provided, client provides alcohol
Access: Handicapped accessible (limited); on-site parking; open year-round
Payment: Cash, check, credit card

Rosedown Plantation

MAINE

FALMOUTH

QUAKER TAVERN BED & BREAKFAST

377 Gray Road (Route 26/100)
Falmouth, ME 04105-2520
Phone: 207/797-5540   Fax: 207/797-7599
E-mail: aol.com.quaker.bb

ORIGINALLY known as Hall's Tavern, the Quaker Tavern was built by Quakers Nicholas and Experience Hall in about 1800. A lovely Federal-style clapboard country tavern, it is the center-piece of a 13-acre farm surrounded by forests near the coast of southern Maine. Each guest room has a fireplace and an antique bed, and a candlelight full breakfast is served in the dining room or the wicket room. Small meetings, workshops, and other gatherings are accommodated in the inn's two parlors. Over the centuries Falmouth's traditional industries have been farming and fishing, thus much of area's rural character remains. Downtown Portland is just minutes away, with its many restored nineteenth-century buildings, museums, waterfront, and the childhood home of Henry Wadsworth Longfellow.

Listed in the National Register of Historic Places

Location: The Quaker Tavern is accessible via the Maine Turnpike at Routes 26 and 100. Falmouth is located just outside Portland in southern Maine.
Function Space: 250 square feet; 2 rooms

Capacity—Conference: 8-10; Reception: 15–20; Banquet: 8–10
Equipment On-site: Cable, VTR, VCR, phone
Food Service: Breakfast with room
Overnight Accommodations: 3 rooms
Limitations/Restrictions: Restrictions on smoking; two cats on premises
Access: On-site parking; open year-round
Payment: Cash, credit cards (MC, Visa)

KENNEBUNKPORT

CAPTAIN LORD MANSION

(Mailing address)
P.O. Box 800
(Street address)
Corner of Pleasant and Green Streets
Kennebunkport, ME 04046-0800
Phone: 207/967-3141   Fax: 207/967-3172
E-mail: captain@biddeford.com

DURING the War of 1812, the British blockade of the New England coast halted local commerce and threw those in the shipping industry out of work. Nathaniel Lord, a wealthy merchant and shipbuilder, hired unemployed shipwrights to build his three-story mansion overlooking the Kennebunkport River. The mansion was occupied by Lord's descendants until the early 1970s, when it became a bed and breakfast inn. Repainted its traditional "colonial yellow," the mansion is topped by an octagonal cupola reached by a four-story spiral staircase. Interior features include trompe l'oeil hand painted doors, original "pumpkin pine" wide floor boards, and 14 working fireplaces. Large, luxurious guest rooms, furnished with rich fabrics, European paintings, and fine period antiques, come with modern comforts as well. Overnight guests will also enjoy a full three-course breakfast served family-style in the country kitchen. Consistently rated one of the finest B&Bs in the country, the mansion is especially suitable for hosting small meetings and retreats. The charming seaside village of Kennebunkport offers a variety of recreational activities, shops, and dining options.

Listed in the National Register of Historic Places

Location: Kennebunkport is on the coast in southern Maine, and the Captain Lord Mansion is 6 miles from the Maine Turnpike (I-95). The Portland Jetport is 30 miles north, and Boston is 90 miles away. Taxi and limousine service available.
Function Space: 900 square feet; 2 rooms
Capacity—Conference: 14; Reception: 25; Theater: 14
Equipment On-site: Slide and overhead projectors, screen; photocopying, fax, and typing service available
Food Service: Breakfast with room; catered lunch available

Overnight Accommodations: 20 rooms
Limitations/Restrictions: No smoking; client supplies alcohol (inn can supply setups)
Access: On-site parking; open year-round
Payment: Company check or credit card (MC, Visa)

PORTLAND

PORTLAND REGENCY HOTEL
20 Milk Street, Portland, ME 04101
Phone: 207/774-4200 or 800-727-3436
Fax: 207/775-2150

A centerpiece of the Old Port's Waterfront District, the Portland Regency Hotel occupies what was once an armory for Maine's National Guard. The neo-Gothic Romanesque armory, built in 1895, also saw civilian service, as the building's large drill hall was often used as a civic auditorium. During World War II the navy used the facility as a recreation center, and later it

Portland Regency Hotel

functioned as a warehouse. In 1984 the armory was purchased for conversion to a hotel, and three years later the Portland Regency opened for business. With the exception of added skylight windows, the exterior of the building was preserved intact; the interiors feature spacious, traditionally furnished guest rooms, detailed brick fireplaces, and turreted corners. A variety of meeting spaces, including a ballroom and an executive boardroom, are available for business and social functions, and the hotel offers full-service catering and menu customization. The Market Street Grille serves breakfast and dinner daily, lunch weekdays, and Sunday brunch, and the Armory is a comfortable setting for drinks and light fare. Shopping, dining, and cultural venues are all nearby, and just two blocks away is the city's working waterfront.

Member of Historic Hotels of America

Location: The Portland Regency Hotel is located downtown, 10 miles north of Portland International Jetport, and is accessible via I-95.
Function Space: 5,200 square feet; 7 rooms
Capacity—Conference: 50; Reception: 350; Banquet: 150; Theater: 250
Equipment On-site: Audiovisual equipment and business services available
Food Service: Catering/food service available; restaurant and bar, room service
Overnight Accommodations: 95 rooms
Access: Handicapped accessible; on-site parking; open year-round
Payment: Cash, check, credit card

ROCKLAND

CAPTAIN LINDSEY HOUSE INN
5 Lindsey Street, Rockland, ME 04841
Phone: 207/596-7950   Fax: 207/596-2758
E-mail: Kebarnes@midcoast.com

LOCATED in downtown Rockland among a number of historic seaport buildings is the Captain Lindsey House, which has its own enchanting nineteenth-century maritime flavor. George Lindsey, son of one of the area's early settlers, built his brick home in 1835. It became one of Rockland's first hotels when it opened as an inn and tavern in 1859. After serving as the Camden-Rockland Water Company headquarters from 1922 to 1994, the Captain Lindsey Inn was restored and returned to its former occupation as a full-service inn by the Barnes family. Typical of a sea captain's home, the inn is filled with artifacts and furnishings collected from around the world. On-site is the Waterworks Pub and Restaurant, which offers favorite New England dishes and creative surprises. Overnight guests are served complimentary continental breakfasts and afternoon tea. The inn is available for small conferences, retreats, and other gatherings. The Farnsworth Museum, home of the Wyeth family's Maine collection, and windjammer sailing vessels are among the nearby attractions.

Location: The Captain Lindsey House Inn is approximately 50 minutes from Augusta and 1.5 hours from Bangor and Portland; accessible via I-95, which is 45 minutes away. Nearest airport service is in Portland and at Knox County Airport.
Function Space: 600 square feet; 3 rooms
Capacity—Reception: 15; Banquet: 18
Equipment On-site: Fax and modem

Food Service: Breakfast with room; restaurant
Overnight Accommodations: 9 rooms
Limitations/Restrictions: No smoking; no children under 10 years of age
Access: Handicapped accessible; on-site parking; open year-round
Payment: Credit card (MC, Visa)

SOUTHWEST HARBOR

THE CLAREMONT HOTEL
P.O. Box 137, Southwest Harbor, ME 04679
Phone: 207/244-5036   Fax: 207/244-3512

BEAUTIFULLY situated at the mouth of Somes Sound on Mt. Desert Island, the Claremont opened for its first summer season in 1884. Retired sea captain Jesse Pease built the hotel to attract the growing number of tourists in Maine, and after his death in 1900 his wife, Grace, continued as manager for the next 17 years. The tradition of family ownership continued with the Phillips family, who ran the Claremont until 1968, and since then the McCues have owned the hotel, overseeing a 1994 renovation and the addition of new cottages. The hotel's Victorian-style main building boasts splendid mountain and ocean views, and accommodations are also available in two large guest houses and 12 traditional log cottages set in woods of spruce and pine. The handsome Clark Point Room, with its fireplace and cathedral ceilings, is available for business and social gatherings, including small conferences, seminars, lectures, receptions, cocktail parties, and private dinners. Recreational facilities include a clay tennis court, badminton, bicycles, rowboats, and a groomed croquet court, scene of the Claremont's annual week-long single-elimination croquet tournament. Golf, freshwater

swimming, and Acadia National Park are nearby as well.

Listed in the National Register of Historic Places

Location: Southwest Harbor is located just south of Bar Harbor, and the Claremont Hotel is accessible via the Maine Turnpike, Route 3, and Route 102.
Function Space: 900 square feet; 1 room
Capacity—Conference: 75; Reception: 90; Banquet: 75; Theater: 90
Equipment On-site: Audiovisual equipment available
Food Service: Bed-and-breakfast or modified American plan rates; catering/food service available; dining room
Overnight Accommodations: 45 rooms
Limitations/Restrictions: No smoking; food and beverages provided by hotel only
Access: Handicapped accessible; on-site parking; hotel open mid-June to mid-October; cottages open late May to late October
Payment: Cash, check

YORK

BRECKINRIDGE PUBLIC AFFAIRS CENTER OF BOWDOIN COLLEGE
201 US Route 1, York, ME 03909-1635
Phone: 207/363-3620

SET on a 23-acre estate bordering the York River, the Breckinridge Public Affairs Center offers complete conference and meeting facilities for groups of 10 to 28. Organizations meeting at the center have sole occupancy of the handsome main building, River House, and the grounds, which were constructed in 1905 as a summer retreat.

Nineteen guests can be accommodated overnight on-site; for larger groups a nearby hotel is available. River House's third-floor conference room seats 28 meeting participants around tables, and three smaller rooms on the first floor are useful for smaller group sessions. Meals are planned and served with attention to each group's health requirements and work schedule. For relaxing, guests have use of a clay tennis court, a 110-foot circular saltwater swimming pool, and croquet and volleyball courts. The attractive grounds also feature formal gardens, wildflower fields, and walking paths. Extra services, such as poolside lobster bakes and cocktail parties, may be scheduled as well, and the center is also available for day meetings on a limited basis. The client's exclusive use of the center makes it especially suitable for board meetings, academic symposia, staff retreats, and training programs.

Listed in the National Register of Historic Places

Location: The Center is located just off I-95 in York and is 15 minutes from Pease Airport in Portsmouth, New Hampshire, 70 minutes north of Logan International Airport in Boston, and 45 minutes south of the Portland International Jetport in Portland.

Function Space: 840 square feet; 1 room (3 additional sitting rooms available for informal sessions)

Capacity—Conference: 28; Theater: 45

Equipment On-site: VCR, fax service available; other equipment may be rented from outside source

Food Service: All meals included in conference package

Overnight Accommodations: 16 rooms (other accommodations nearby)

Limitations/Restrictions: No smoking; groups may provide their own alcoholic beverages, served by staff; Center is for nonprofit, academic, and public affairs-oriented groups—exceptions may be made

Access: Handicapped accessible; on-site parking; open April to July and mid-September to Thanksgiving

Payment: Deposit in advance, payment within 30 days of event

Breckinridge Public Affairs Center *(Bruce McMillan)*

MARYLAND

ANNAPOLIS

CHARLES CARROLL HOUSE OF ANNAPOLIS, INC.

107 Duke of Gloucester Street
Annapolis, MD 21401
Phone: 410/269-1737   Fax: 410/269-1746

CHARLES Carroll, the only Roman Catholic to sign the Declaration of Independence, was born in this house in 1737, and it remained his principal urban residence until 1821. In the early 1770s he enlarged the brick house, which had been built by his father about 50 years earlier, and improved the landscaping and gardens. Despite the restrictions he faced in voting and practicing law because of his religion, Carroll carved out a successful political career for himself, and he was considered the wealthiest man in the country at the time of his death in 1832. While living here he composed his "First Citizen" letters, which encouraged the rights of local citizens against Lord Baltimore's authority, and he served in the Maryland Senate and, later, in the U.S. Senate. Among the guests the Carrolls entertained were George Washington and the Marquis de Lafayette, and in April 1783 outdoor celebrations were held here to mark the end of the War for Independence. The home's historic rooms and terraced boxwood gardens overlooking Spa Creek are available for wedding receptions, seminars, conferences, and private events. House tours by appointment are also available. Located in the Annapolis Historic District, the Carroll House is just a short walk from the city's waterfront shops and restaurants.

Located in a National Historic Landmark district; listed in the National Register of Historic Places

Location: Charles Carroll House is 30 minutes from Baltimore and 50 minutes from Washington, D.C., and is accessible via Route 50.
Function Space: 1,859 square feet; 5 rooms
Capacity—Conference: 75; Reception: 150; Banquet: 75; Theater: 125; outside terrace (may be tented): 200
Equipment On-site: Audiovisual equipment available
Food Service: Preferred caterers list provided
Limitations/Restrictions: No smoking; wine/beer permitted, no hard liquor
Access: Handicapped accessible; on-site parking; open year-round
Payment: Cash or check

GIBSON'S LODGINGS OF ANNAPOLIS

110 Prince George Street, Annapolis, MD 21401
Phone: 410/268-5555

A complex of historic and modern guest houses, Gibson's Lodgings boasts an attractive location in Maryland's capital city, and visitors will find many of Annapolis's colonial and maritime charms within easy walking distance. The restored Patterson House, a Georgian townhouse completed in 1786 by local businessman Richard MacCubbin, occupies a site where the late-seventeenth-century "Old Courthouse" once stood. The Berman House, renovated in 1985 and described as being a tri-gable variation of the Homestead style, was built in 1888 for a prominent merchant family. A century later, the Lauer House was built, combining modern architecture with nineteenth-century furnishings. A large conference room, featuring Victorian decor, is available in the Lauer

House, and both the Patterson and Berman Houses offer comfortable parlors for meetings and gatherings. Guest rooms are furnished with antiques, and overnight guests enjoy a full continental breakfast. Located near the U.S. Naval Academy, Gibson's Lodgings are convenient to a number of other attractions, including the harbor, with its restaurants and shops, the State House, and numerous restored historic houses and buildings dating back to the eighteenth century.

Located in a National Historic Landmark district; listed in the National Register of Historic Places

Location: Gibson's Lodgings is 30 minutes from Baltimore and 50 minutes from Washington, D.C., and is accessible via Route 50. The inn is located a half-block from the City Dock.
Function Space: 1,100 square feet; 3 rooms
Capacity—Conference: 30; Reception: 30; Banquet: 30; Theater: 30
Equipment On-site: VCR, overhead projector, flip charts

Food Service: Breakfast with room; catered lunch, all-day coffee/soda service, cookie break
Overnight Accommodations: 21 rooms
Limitations/Restrictions: No smoking
Access: Handicapped accessible, on-site parking; open year-round
Payment: Credit card (MC, Visa)

HISTORIC INNS OF ANNAPOLIS
58 State Circle, Annapolis, MD 21401
Phone: 410/263-2641   Fax: 410/268-3813

NESTLED in the heart of this colonial city, three of the four restored buildings that compose the Historic Inns of Annapolis are directly across the street from the State House, where General George Washington resigned his commission as commander of American forces in 1783 and the Treaty of Paris was ratified in 1784, officially ending the War for Independence. The buildings date from 1727 to 1820, the oldest being the Governor Calvert House, a two-story brick building that was

Gibson's Lodgings of Annapolis

once home to two Maryland governors named Calvert. A short walk away is the Maryland Inn, on Church Circle, an elegant brick house built in 1776 where 11 delegates of the 1786 U.S. Congress stayed. The restored guest rooms feature original and reproduction antiques as well modern conveniences. The Governor Calvert Conference Center offers state-of-the-art audiovisual equipment and meeting space in 10 rooms, and other types of business meetings, parties, and social events may be held in private function rooms at the Maryland Inn. Eighteenth-century dining is available at the Treaty of Paris Restaurant at the Maryland Inn; also on-site are the Drummer's Lot Pub and the King of France Tavern.

Located in a National Historic Landmark district; listed in the National Register of Historic Places; member of Historic Hotels of America

Location: The Historic Inns of Annapolis are 40 minutes from Baltimore and 45 minutes from Washington, D.C.
Function Space: 8,000 square feet; 12 rooms
Capacity—Conference: 100; Reception: 300; Banquet: 250; Theater: 300
Equipment On-site: Audiovisual equipment available
Food Service: Catering/food service available; restaurant, tavern, pub
Overnight Accommodations: 137 rooms
Limitations/Restrictions: No outside food and beverage service in function rooms
Access: Handicapped accessible; on-site parking; open year-round
Payment: Cash, major credit card

BALTIMORE

ADMIRAL FELL INN
888 S. Broadway, Baltimore, MD 21231
Phone: 410/522-7377   Fax: 410/522-0707

THE Admiral Fell in is a luxury urban inn and business conference center located at the water's edge in Historic Fell's Point, Baltimore's original seaport. This vibrant community is known for its charming Belgian block streets, antique shops, art galleries, pubs, and waterfront docking. The inn comprises eight connected buildings dating from 1790 to 1910, and over the years it has been a ship chandlery, a theater, a boarding house for sailors, and a seamen's YMCA. Guest rooms feature Federal-style furnishings, and the hotel's elegant decor with nautical accents reflects the area's maritime legacy. Several on-site dining options are available, including the inn's main restaurant, Savannah, which serves Southern cuisine, the casual Point Restaurant, and the Sea Witch Restaurant and Raw Bar. The inn's rooftop conference and banquet facilities offer a striking 360-degree view of the downtown skyline, the Inner Harbor, and the working waterfront community. Just a short water taxi ride away is Baltimore's famed Inner Harbor, whose attractions include Little Italy, Oriole Park at Camden Yards, the National Aquarium, and a number of museums and theaters.

Member of Historic Hotels of America

Location: The Admiral Fell Inn is located at Market Square at Thames Street, Fell's Point, a half-mile from Baltimore's Inner Harbor. The inn is accessible via I-95 and I-83 and is 12 miles from Baltimore/Washington International Airport and 3 miles from Penn Station.
Function Space: 4,920 square feet; 7 rooms

Capacity—Conference: 30; Reception: 150; Banquet: 120; Theater: 130; Classroom: 60
Equipment On-site: Overhead and slide projectors, screens, flip charts, podium; fax and photocopying available
Food Service: Catering/food service available; three restaurants
Overnight Accommodations: 80 rooms
Limitations/Restrictions: No smoking; inn provides all food and beverage service
Access: Handicapped accessible; valet parking available, parking nearby; open year-round
Payment: Major credit card or billing with credit approval

BROOKLANDVILLE

MARYVALE CASTLE
11300 Falls Road, Brooklandville, MD 21022
Phone: 410/252-3528
Fax: 410/252-3528 (same as phone)

A bit of Camelot and merry olde England is to be found in the Greenspring Valley, where Maryvale Castle stands. Built by the Wickes family in 1917, the gray stone castle was modeled after England's famous Warwick Castle and features English Gothic arched windows, diamond-paned leaded glass windows and doors, iron-studded doors, and a porte cochere. In 1945 the Sisters of Notre Dame de Namur purchased the castle and surrounding 183 acres, and the castle now houses the Maryvale Preparatory School. The Great Hall, library, chapel, and solarium, all on the first floor, are available for public use. Maryvale's magnificent Great Hall showcases a molded plaster ceiling, European oak-paneled walls with Tudor-style carvings, and baroque chairs, while monks' stalls line the outside corridor. The Great Hall

opens onto a flagstone terrace overlooking the gorgeous lawn, where events may also be held. The paneled chapel, the library with its Tudor-style ceiling, and the stone-walled solarium with a brick-tile floor and a huge fireplace also evoke the feel of an old English manor house. In addition to the striking gardens, a large variety of wildflowers are found at Maryvale, which has been designated as a Chesapeake Audubon Society wildlife sanctuary.

Location: Maryvale is 2 miles north of 695 Baltimore Beltway from Falls Road Exit 23, and 30 minutes from Baltimore/Washington International Airport.
Function Space: 4 rooms
Capacity—Conference: 60; Reception: 80–150; Banquet: 60
Equipment On-site: Audiovisual equipment available to rent
Food Service: In-house catering
Limitations/Restrictions: No smoking
Access: Limited handicapped accessibility; on-site parking; open year-round
Payment: Cash, check

CHESTERTOWN

GREAT OAK MANOR BED & BREAKFAST
10568 Cliff Road, Chestertown, MD 21620
Phone: 410/778-5943
Fax: 410/778-5943 (same as phone)

BEAUTIFULLY situated on the banks of the Chesapeake, Great Oak Manor occupies 12 quiet acres of Maryland's Eastern Shore. Built of bricks from the ballast of W. R. Grace sailing ships, the 25-room mansion was constructed in 1938 and has been designated as a Maryland Historic Home.

The inn's stately decor adds to its regal atmosphere, extending from the handsome library to the individually appointed guest rooms. Room rates include a deluxe continental breakfast and late afternoon refreshments. In addition to hosting small meetings, receptions, reunions, and other functions, Great Oak Manor offers full small-conference-center services, including meals tailored to individual requirements, privacy guaranteed with no other guests at the inn, and a 15-passenger van for use to and from area restaurants. Next door to the inn is the Landing, which offers Great Oak Manor guests swimming, tennis, golf, yacht charters, and complete restaurant and bar facilities. Guests also have access to a private beach, and just eight miles away is a treasure of the Eastern Shore, the historic colonial village of Chestertown, founded in 1706 and brimming with quaint shops and restaurants.

Location: The Great Oak Manor is about 1.5 hours from Washington, D.C., Philadelphia, and Baltimore.
Function Space: 900 square feet; 2 rooms
Capacity—Conference: 26; Reception: 75; Banquet: 25; Theater: 28
Equipment On-site: Overhead projector, screen, flip chart stands, VCRs, fax, computer/telephone hookup
Food Service: Breakfast with room; food service for all meals and breaks available
Overnight Accommodations: 10 rooms, accommodates 20
Limitations/Restrictions: Smoking permitted in designated areas only
Access: Handicapped accessibility limited; on-site parking; open March 15 to February 15
Payment: Check, credit card (MC, Visa)

THE WHITE SWAN TAVERN
231 High Street, Chestertown, MD 21620
Phone: 410/778-2300   Fax: 410/778-4543

LOCATED in the Chestertown Historic District, this two-story brick structure now known as the White Swan Tavern offers both hospitality and a remarkable look back at the eighteenth century. John Lovegrove operated a tannery on the site, then sold the property to Joseph Nicholson in 1733. Nicholson, a member of the Committee of Correspondence and actively involved in the American Revolution, built what is now the front portion of the present structure. John Bordley bought the house in 1793 and enlarged the residence, and throughout the first half of the nineteenth century various innkeepers ran a tavern here. From 1854 until 1977 the building housed a variety of businesses. A three-year restoration of the site began in 1978 with an archeological dig, which turned up a number of interesting finds, including brick and flagstone paving in the tavern yard, glassware, coins, and polished black marble that was used in the original fireplace surround. Many of the artifacts found at the site are on display at the house, which has been restored to its appearance in Bordley's time. Overnight guests stay in restored period rooms and receive a full continental breakfast. The tavern is also available for weddings, receptions, and small conferences.

Located in a National Historic Landmark district; listed in the National Register of Historic Places; recognized by the Society for the Preservation of Maryland Antiquities, 1982

Location: The White Swan Tavern is accessible via MD Route 213; local taxi and water taxi service available. Baltimore-Washington International Airport and Philadelphia International Airport are approximately 1.5 hours away; Easton Airport is 40 miles away.
Function Space: 620 square feet; 2 rooms
Capacity—Conference: 20–30 (per room); Reception: 75 (total); Banquet: 75 (total)
Food Service: Breakfast with room; catering/food service can be arranged
Overnight Accommodations: 6 rooms
Limitations/Restrictions: No smoking
Access: Handicapped accessible; on-site parking; open year-round
Payment: Check

London Town House & Gardens *(Courtesy of London Town Foundation, Inc.)*

EDGEWATER

LONDON TOWN HOUSE & GARDENS
839 Londontown Road, Edgewater, MD 21037
Phone: 410/222-1919   Fax: 410/222-1918

BUILT at about 1760, this striking red brick London townhouse on the South River waterfront near Annapolis was home to cabinetmaker William Brown. Brown was licensed to operate the ferry from Annapolis to London Town, which was once a busy port. By the mid-eighteenth century, however, the town was in decline and the enterprising Brown was never as successful as one would expect of the mansion's owner. London Town was virtually abandoned by 1800, and in the 1820s the house became the Anne Arundel County Almshouse; some of the county's poorest residents lived here in the course of the next 140 years. During the 1970s the mansion was restored and opened as a museum. Adjacent to the house are eight acres of modern woodland gardens filled with native and exotic species, and garden paths lead through wooded and water vistas and the Azalea Glade. Beneath the lawns archeologists continue to find evidence of buildings from London Town's early past. Available meeting space includes an enclosed pavillion overlooking the South River, an adjoining conference room, and an outdoor area that can be tented.

National Historic Landmark; listed in the National Register of Historic Places

Location: London Town House & Gardens is located 5 miles south of Annapolis off Route 2 South, and is 35 minutes south of Baltimore and 45 minutes east of Washington, D.C. Baltimore/Washington

International Airport is approximately 30 minutes away.

Function Space: 1,173 square feet; 2 rooms, plus 800-square-foot tent.

Capacity—Conference: 100; Reception: 175; Banquet: 100; Theater: 125

Equipment On-site: Podium, projector, screen TV/VCR

Food Service: Preferred caterers list provided

Overnight Accommodations: Available nearby

Limitations/Restrictions: No smoking; alcoholic beverages require liquor license

Access: Handicapped accessibility to Visitor Center, access to house and gardens difficult; on-site parking; open year-round

Payment: Check

ELKRIDGE

BELMONT MANOR HOUSE AND MEETING FACILITY

6555 Belmont Woods Road, Elkridge, MD 21227

Phone: 410/796-4300   Fax: 410/796-4565

SINCE 1738 visitors have been coming to Belmont Manor, Caleb Dorsey's secluded Georgian mansion set on 80 acres of peaceful fields and woodlands. The estate is now used as a conference center, but today's guests still enjoy the elegance of the main house, its formal gardens, and the tree-lined country lanes. Ten to 45 guests can be accommodated in one of three meeting facilities, and up to 200 guests for a garden reception. Meeting areas are in the manor itself, graced with period furnishings, the smaller Dobbin House, and the stable, once the home of the international race horse Billy Barton. The stable is a modern conference site with a rustic exterior, and its French doors open to a view of the woods. Belmont Manor offers exclusive use of its facilities to visiting organizations to ensure a private working environment, and conference center services include customized meal plans, overnight accommodations, and a variety of recreational opportunities, such as swimming, tennis, volleyball, and walking and fitness trails.

Location: Belmont Manor is located 8 miles from Baltimore/Washington International Airport; 20 minutes to downtown Baltimore, 45 minutes to downtown Washington, D.C., and National Airport. Amtrak and MARC service less than 15 minutes away.

Function Space: 2,514 square feet; 4 rooms

Capacity—Conference: 45; Reception: 75 (inside), 200 (outside); Banquet: 45; Theater: 50

Equipment On-site: Audiovisual equipment and business services available

Food Service: Three daily meals included in conference package

Overnight Accommodations: 21 rooms

Access: On-site parking; open year-round

Payment: Deposit and direct billing

FREDERICK

TYLER SPITE HOUSE

(Mailing address)

P.O. Box 3669

(Street address)

112 W. Church Street, Frederick, MD 21701

Phone: 301/831-4455

Fax: 301/831-4455 (same as phone)

DR. John Tyler, known as the first to perform cataract surgery in the United States, built his three-story Federal-style mansion in 1814 to prevent the city of Frederick from extending a road across his property. Under cover of darkness, Tyler had the foundation of his house built to block the planned route of the road, and he was seen the next morning in his rocking chair on the the site of his new home. Not surprisingly, the structure became known as Spite House. Today the house is a lovely bed-and-breakfast inn boasting 13-foot ceilings, eight fireplaces, cherry and mahogany antiques, and oriental rugs in each room. Small business meetings, training sessions, receptions, and other gatherings are held in the dining room and the spacious library. Overnight guests are treated to a full breakfast in the formal dining room or on the formal patio garden, where there is a pool for guests' use. Right outside the inn's front door guests can board horse-drawn carriages and tour historic Frederick's numerous sites, including the law office of Francis Scott Key, author of "The Star Spangled Banner."

Listed in the National Register of Historic Places

Location: The Tyler Spite House is halfway between Washington, D.C., and Baltimore (45 miles each way) and is accessible via I-70,

I-270, US 15, and US 40. Washington National, Dulles, and Baltimore/Washington International Airports are less than an hour from Frederick.
Function Space: 413 square feet; 2 rooms
Capacity—Conference: 30; Reception: 30; Banquet: 30; Theater: 10
Equipment On-site: Audiovisual equipment and business services available
Food Service: Breakfast with room; catering/food service available
Overnight Accommodations: 15 rooms
Limitations/Restrictions: No smoking
Access: On-site parking; open year-round
Payment: Credit card

GAITHERSBURG

KENTLANDS MANSION
320 Kent Square Road, Gaithersburg, MD 20878
Phone: 301/258-6425   Fax: 301/258-6428

SOON after Frederick A. Tschiffely built his large brick country estate in 1900, it became known to locals as "The Bricks." The name was changed to Kentlands following Otis Beall Kent's purchase of the house in 1942. He set about dramatically remodeling and enlarging the mansion to make way for his impressive collection of oriental rugs, books, artwork, and jewels. Kent also added modern greenhouses, ponds, and lakes. Now owned by the city of Gaithersburg for public use, the elegant house features 22-foot ceilings with denture molding, dark wood paneling, and crystal chandeliers. Kentlands welcomes groups for a wide variety of social and business functions, ranging from weddings and receptions to teas and business meetings. The first-floor meeting rooms, which accommodate up to 130 guests, include the dining room, a

Kentlands Mansion

formally furnished parlor, a banquet room, and a music room with a hand-painted ceiling. Small business meetings are easily accommodated in the executive conference room and classroom on the second floor. Also available for outdoor events is the Kentlands Green.

Location: Kentlands is accessible from I-270 north, Routes 124 and 28; Washington National Airport is 40 minutes away; metrorail station 10 minutes away.
Function Space: 2,500 square feet; 6 rooms
Capacity—Conference: 10–115; Reception: 130; Banquet: 110; Theater: 115 (adjoining rooms)
Equipment On-site: TV/VCR, overhead projector, podium, easels
Food Service: Renter arranges catering/food service
Limitations/Restrictions: No smoking; no red wine; no large amplifiers
Access: Handicapped accessible; on-site parking; open year-round
Payment: Cash, check, credit card (MC, Visa)

LAUREL

MONTPELIER MANSION

(Mailing address)
9401 Montpelier Drive
(Street address)
Route 197 and Muirkirk Road, Laurel, MD 20708
Phone: 301/953-1376   Fax: 301/953-7572

AT the turn of the century, Abigail Adams, traveling to Washington to join her husband, President John Adams, stayed at Montpelier Mansion, which she described as a "large, handsome, elegant

Montpelier Mansion *(Mary Jurkiewicz. Courtesy of the Maryland-National Capital Park and Planning Commission)*

house, where I was received with my family, and with what we might term true English Hospitality." Her hosts were Major Thomas and Ann Snowden, who welcomed the Washingtons and other prominent visitors to their impressive 9,000-acre estate. The Snowden family first purchased property here in 1669, and as their income from agriculture and an ironworks grew, so did their substantial landholdings. The Montpelier Mansion was built in 1783, a five-part red brick Georgian structure consisting of a main block, two hyphens, and two wings. Thomas and Ann Snowden's son Nicholas, who established a successful cotton mill known as the Laurel Factory, inherited the estate in 1803. A room-by-room inventory of his possessions following his death in 1831 has guided the furnishing of select rooms to their early nineteenth-century appearance. A private residence until 1961, the mansion today is available for meetings, receptions, luncheons, and dinners, and a number of cultural events are held here as well.

National Historic Landmark; listed in the National Register of Historic Places

Location: Montpelier Mansion is at Route 197 and Muirkirk Road in Laurel, a quarter-mile west of the Baltimore/Washington Parkway (Route 295). The mansion is 25 minutes from Washington, D.C., and Baltimore.
Function Space: 515 square feet; 2 rooms
Capacity—Conference: 70; Reception: 100; Banquet: 45; Theater: 70
Equipment On-site: Slide projector, movie screen, TV/VCR
Food Service: Caterers list available
Limitations/Restrictions: No smoking; food permitted only in specified areas; list of regulations is provided to renter
Access: Partial handicapped accessibility; on-site parking; open March through November
Payment: Cash, check, money order, credit card

RIVERDALE

RIVERSDALE
4811 Riverdale Road, Riverdale, MD 20737
Phone: 301/864-0420   Fax: 301/927-3498

AFTER fleeing political turmoil at home and the approach of France's Revolutionary army, Flemish aristocrat Henri Stier arrived in what is now Riverdale, just outside the young nation's capital. In 1801 he began building his plantation home, a five-part stucco-covered brick mansion featuring both Flemish and American design elements. Steir went back to Europe in 1803, never to return to the United States, but through a lively correspondence with his daughter, Rosalie, she and her husband George Calvert completed the house as he had intended. Plans to restore the Victorianized mansion to its antebellum appearance were dramatically halted with the discovery of the family letters, whose discussions on the home's construc-

tion and decoration allowed Riversdale to be accurately returned to its early nineteenth-century appearance instead. Among the other noteworthy figures who later lived at Riversdale was Senator Hattie Caraway, the first woman elected to the Senate, who was in residence from 1929 to 1933. Today Riversdale, recognized as an excellent example of historic preservation, provides visitors with a look at early-nineteenth-century plantation life of owners, servants, and slaves. A meeting room and a gallery are available for social and business events, and groups meeting here can arrange for guided tours of the house.

Listed in the National Register of Historic Places

Location: Riversdale is 15 minutes from downtown Washington, D.C., and 30 minutes from Baltimore and is accessible via US Route 1, I-95, MD 410, and MD 201. Metrobus service is available.
Function Space: 1,430 square feet; 2 rooms
Capacity—100 persons maximum
Equipment On-site: Slide projector and screen
Food Service: Preferred caterers list provided
Limitations/Restrictions: No smoking
Access: Handicapped accessible; on-site parking; open year-round
Payment: Check

STEVENSVILLE

KENT MANOR INN
500 Kent Manor Drive, Stevensville, MD 21666
Phone: 410/643-7716   Fax: 410/643-8315

SITUATED on a 226-acre plantation with a mile and a half of waterfront on the Chesapeake Bay, the Kent Manor Inn is an excellent example of

Riversdale *(Steven Abramowitz. Courtesy of the Maryland-National Capital Park and Planning Commission)*

Italianate architecture. The three-story, cupola-topped house boasts expansive walk-out porches and exquisite craftsmanship. In 1651, Thomas Wetherall was granted land that would later become the site of Kent Manor, and from the turn of the century until 1898 the Smyth family and their heirs owned the estate. The original portion of the house was built in about 1820, and the center section was added just prior to the Civil War, with marble fireplaces in each room on the first and second floors. Known variously as Brightsworth Inn and Kent Hall in the early twentieth century, the inn was completely restored in 1987. The lovely guest rooms are furnished in the Victorian style, as is the inn's renowned restaurant, whose cuisine reflects an Eastern Shore influence. Three meeting rooms are available in the main house, and the Guest House Gazebo accommodates larger groups.

Maryland Historic Site; member of Historic Hotels of America

Location: The Kent Manor Inn is located just off Route 50 on Maryland's Eastern Shore, 20 minutes from Annapolis and 50 minutes from Washington, D.C., and Baltimore. Baltimore/Washington International Airport is 35 minutes away, and the Bay Bridge Airport, a private facility, is adjacent to the inn.

Function Space: 3,140 square feet; 4 rooms
Capacity—Conference: 50; Reception: 150; Banquet: 150; Theater: 175
Equipment On-site: TV/VCR, overhead projector and screen, flip charts; other audiovisual equipment readily available; fax, photocopier available
Food Service: Catering/food service available, restaurant
Overnight Accommodations: 24 rooms
Limitations/Restrictions: No smoking
Access: On-site parking; open year-round
Payment: Cash, check, credit card (MC, Visa)

MASSACHUSETTS

BOSTON

BOSTON CENTER FOR THE ARTS
539 Tremont Street, Boston, MA 02116
Phone: 617/426-5000   Fax: 617/426-5336

LOCATED in Boston's South End—one of the largest historic districts in the country, covering more than 500 acres—the Boston Center for the Arts (BCA) comprises a four-acre complex. BCA's centerpiece is the 23,000-square-foot Cyclorama, built in 1884, that sits beneath a 125-foot glass dome. Cycloramas made for popular entertainment during the late nineteenth century, as visitors came to view the large, encircling paintings that often depicted historic events and created a "you-are-there" sensation. The original painting in Boston's Cyclorama was Paul Dominique Philippoteaux's *The Battle of Gettysburg* (now seen in Gettysburg), which measured 50 by 400 feet and weighed 2.9 tons. By the 1890s interest in cycloramas declined and the Boston Cyclorama was used to host other events, including roller polo championships and boxing matches. The Tremont Garage occupied the building in the early twentieth century, and it was here that Albert Champion invented the AC spark plug in 1907. In 1923 the Cyclorama became home to the Boston Flower Exchange, but since 1970 the handsome, battlemented building has been part of the BCA. Each year the center coproduces programs in the Cyclorama, whose dramatic interiors are available for large meetings, receptions, exhibitions, and other gatherings.

Listed in the National Register of Historic Places

Location: The Boston Center for the Arts is located between Berkeley and Clarendon Streets in Boston's South End. The BCA is just 3 miles from Logan International Airport and is accessible via local transit.
Function Space: 23,000 square feet; 1 room
Capacity—Conference: 876; Reception: 1,200–1,850; Banquet: 876; Theater: 876
Food Service: Preferred caterers list provided
Limitations/Restrictions: No open bar; live and high-volume music hours limited to 10:30 P.M.–1:00 A.M., Wednesday through Saturday
Access: Handicapped accessible; on-site parking; open year-round
Payment: Business check, cashier's check, money order

BOSTON PARK PLAZA HOTEL
64 Arlington Street, Boston, MA 02116
Phone: 617/426-2000 or 800-225-2008
Fax: 617/423-1708
E-mail: info@bostonparkplaza.com

SITUATED in the heart of the Back Bay, the Boston Park Plaza Hotel has been a landmark since 1927 in a city renowned for its historic sites. Pioneering hotelier E. M. Statler, who was the first to provide radios, stationery, and closets in guest rooms, built the Boston Park Plaza, his last hotel, as the flagship of his grand hotel empire. A recipient of the President's Gold Medal for Environmental Achievement, the hotel has maintained its reputation for innovation through its environmental action program, which has become a model for the hospitality industry. With some of the largest meeting space available anywhere, the Boston Park Plaza can accommodate everything from small business meetings and parties to huge, lavish weddings and conventions for 1,700. Space includes the old-world Imperial Ballroom, with its six opera-style boxes, the Plaza Castle Exhibit Hall, and a complete conference center. A wide variety of graciously appointed guest rooms and suites are available, with rooms designed for families and VIPs. Services and amenities include a fitness club, shops, a pharmacy, a travel agency, concierge service, five restaurants, and live entertainment. The Boston Park Plaza is within walking distance of business and government centers and many of the city's historic sites.

Member of Historic Hotels of America

Location: The Boston Park Plaza is just steps away from the Boston Public Garden and the Boston Common, and is a block from the Massachusetts Turnpike (I-90 West); the hotel is also easily accessible via I-93. Logan International Airport is 3 miles away.
Function Space: 40,000 square feet; 35 rooms
Capacity—Conference: 1,000; Reception: 1,700; Banquet: 1,200; Theater: 1,800
Equipment On-site: Audiovisual equipment and business services available
Food Service: five restaurants, lounge, bar, 24-hour room service
Overnight Accommodations: 960 rooms
Limitations/Restrictions: Designated smoking rooms available
Access: Handicapped accessible; on-site parking; open year-round
Payment: Credit card (AmEx, DC, Discover, En Route, MC, Visa)

THE COLLEGE CLUB

44 Commonwealth Avenue, Boston, MA 02116
Phone: 617/536-9510   Fax: 617/247-8537

THE College Club is housed in an 1865 classic Victorian brownstone located in Boston's Back Bay Historic District. In 1890 local college-educated women formed the club to promote higher education for women, and in the 1920s the group purchased the single-family townhouse for their own use. Today the club, open to both women and men, continues to meet here and makes its elegant facilities available for dinner parties, luncheons, weddings, receptions, and business gatherings. Meetings and afternoon teas are held in the Members Room, overlooking Commonwealth Avenue, and the richly decorated room may also be used en suite with the stately Drawing Room, which features 18-foot-high ceilings and classic decor. The dark and intimate dining room is available for dinner parties, and special menus can be arranged. Exquisite guest rooms are furnished with period antiques and reproductions. The club is within walking distance of the Theater District, Beacon Hill, and the Public Garden.

Location: The College Club is accessible via the Massachusetts Turnpike, the Southeast Expressway (Route 3), and Route 93, and is 5 minutes from the Back Bay train station, 15 minutes from Logan International Airport, and 1½ blocks from the Arlington MBTA station.
Function Space: 2,500 square feet; 2 rooms
Capacity—Conference: 18; Reception: 100; Banquet: 60; Theater: 75
Food Service: In-house catering/food service available
Overnight Accommodations: 9 rooms
Limitations/Restrictions: No smoking

Access: Parking available at the nearby 500 Boylston Street Garage; guest rooms available year-round, functions may be held mid-September to mid-June
Payment: Cash, check, credit card (MC, Visa)

THE LENOX HOTEL

710 Boylston Street, Boston, MA 02116
Phone: 617/536-5300 Fax: 617/267-1237

KNOWN to many as "that charming little hotel in Boston," the Lenox Hotel in Boston's Back Bay Historic District is adjacent to some of the city's modern landmarks, including the Hynes Convention Center, the Prudential Center Mall, and Copley Place. But the Lenox is also just a short walk away from many of Boston's historic landmarks as well, such as fashionable Newbury Street, Copley Square, the Boston Public Library, the Theater District, and the famous public gardens, and the financial district is just five minutes away by car. Built in 1900, the hotel offers spacious rooms in Colonial and French Provincial decor, and all guest rooms come with voice mail and modem ports. Some guest rooms are even equipped with in-room fax machines and cellular phones, and seven meeting rooms are available for both business meetings and social events. Complete food service is available, highlighting New England fare from the area's farms and waters. On-site is the Upstairs Grille, with its country inn atmosphere, and the hotel's pub offers a selection of beers and ales from around the world.

Location: The Lenox Hotel, in the heart of the Back Bay, is one block from Route 90, four blocks from Storrow Drive, and one block from Copley subway station. Logan International Airport is 3.5 miles away.

Function Space: 4,500 square feet; 7 rooms
Capacity—Conference: 35; Reception: 200; Banquet: 130; Theater: 200
Equipment On-site: Audiovisual equipment and business services available
Food Service: Catering/food service available; restaurant, bar
Overnight Accommodations: 214 rooms
Limitations/Restrictions: Smoking and nonsmoking rooms available
Access: Handicapped accessible, on-site parking; open year-round
Payment: Major credit card

MUSEUM OF FINE ARTS

465 Huntington Avenue, Boston, MA 02115
Phone: 617/369-3205 Fax: 617/536-1319

ESTABLISHED in 1870, the Museum of Fine Arts (MFA) is housed in a stately neoclassical building constructed in 1908. One of the five largest museums in the country, the MFA is renowned for its outstanding collections of Asiatic art and also maintains excellent collections of paintings, sculpture, decorative arts, textiles, prints, drawings, and photographs. The museum offers an elegant venue for meetings, dinner parties, reunions, receptions, and luncheons. An especially striking setting is the Koch Gallery, with its classical features and European master paintings adorning the walls. The Remis Auditorium seats 380, utilizes state-of-the-art presentation technology, and accommodates concerts, lectures, performances, and films, while the Mabel Louise Riley Seminar Room, overlooking the Garden Court, welcomes smaller gatherings. Outdoor events are held in the Galleria in the West Wing, the museum's spacious contemporary addition. Groups meeting at the museum can arrange for private tours of the collections or special shows.

Location: The MFA is located in Boston's Back Bay and is accessible via Route 95, Route 93, and the Massachusetts Turnpike.
Function Space: 10,000 square feet; 4 rooms
Capacity—Reception: 1,000; Banquet: 200–400; Theater: 380
Equipment On-site: Slide, film, and overhead projectors, VCR
Food Service: Catering available
Limitations/Restrictions: No smoking; food and drink not permitted in galleries; no fundraisers permitted
Access: Handicapped accessible; on-site parking; open year-round
Payment: Initial rental deposit plus final billing

Shirley-Eustis House
(Courtesy of Shirley-Eustis House Association)

SHIRLEY-EUSTIS HOUSE

33 Shirley Street, Boston, MA 02119
Phone: 617/442-2275   Fax: 617/442-2270

SHIRLEY Place, the only remaining country house in America built by a British royal colonial governor, was constructed in 1747 for Royal Governor William Shirley. The magnificent Georgian mansion was also the home of Jean-Baptiste du Buc, councilor to Louis XVI of France, who lived here in exile during the French Revolution from 1791 to 1793. William Eustis, governor of the Commonwealth of Massachusetts, purchased the house in 1819, and it was here that the Marquis de Lafayette was fêted in 1824. By the turn of the century, the mansion had become a tenement house and was later abandoned. Although neglect had left the building in a state of decline,

no substantial renovations had been made to the house, and the restoration of the 1980s has returned it to its splendid early nineteenth-century Federal period appearance. Today the Shirley-Eustis mansion is a house museum, filled with early nineteenth-century French furnishings and some eighteenth-century American antiques. Receptions, parties, lectures, meetings, and other gatherings are held in the Great Hall, a double-cubed room with 25-foot-high ceilings and an exquisite staircase, and additional meeting rooms are available as well.

National Historic Landmark; listed in the National Register of Historic Places; named best restored historic house in Boston by the Boston Preservation Alliance, 1991

Location: The Shirley-Eustis House is located in Roxbury, 10 minutes from the Boston Common,

and 5 minutes from I-93 (Exit 18)—left on Massachusetts Avenue, right on Shirley Street. The house is also accessible via the MBTA Orange Line to "Ruggles," then bus #15 to Shirley Street.
Function Space: 2,500 square feet; 3 rooms
Capacity—Conference: 65; Reception: 150; Banquet: 60
Food Service: Catering/food service can be arranged
Limitations/Restrictions: No smoking; no food or beverages in two historically furnished rooms
Access: On-site parking; open June to September
Payment: Check

BREWSTER

OLD SEA PINES INN
2553 Main Street, Box 1026, Brewster, MA 02631
Phone: 508/896-6114   Fax: 508/896-8322

THE Old Sea Pines Inn, built in 1900 at the center of the vast Brewster estate on Cape Cod, was in the early part of the century an exclusive boarding school for young women. The inn has maintained its turn-of-the-century charm and decor, contributing to a community of classic, old Yankee homes on the New England seacoast. Meeting space is available in the restored large formal dining room that opens to a spacious outdoor dining deck. From here guests enjoy a view of the gardens and grounds surrounded by trees. Overnight guests are treated to a full breakfast and stay in rooms with early twentieth-century period furnishings and names like Petticoat Tree and Headmaster. Located in Old King's Highway Historic District, the inn is close to wonderful, unpopulated beaches, golf courses, bike trails, and fine restaurants, and excellent

shopping abounds as well. Also nearby is the Cape Cod Museum of Natural History and the Cape Cod National Seashore.

Location: Brewster is on the bay side of Cape Cod, 90 miles from Boston via Route 3. Hyannis Airport is 25 minutes west on Route 6.
Function Space: 1,656 square feet; 2 rooms
Capacity—Conference: 72; Reception: 80; Banquet: 84; Theater: 90; the two rooms open into one large room, accommodating up to 130
Equipment On-site: Audiovisual equipment, secretarial/computer services available
Food Service: Breakfast with room; catering/food service available
Overnight Accommodations: 21 rooms
Limitations/Restrictions: No smoking
Access: Handicapped accessible; on-site parking; open March to December
Payment: Cash, check, credit card

CAMBRIDGE

HOOPER-LEE-NICHOLS HOUSE
159 Brattle Street, Cambridge, MA 02138-3300
Phone: 617/547-4252   Fax: 617/661-1623

THE Hooper-Lee-Nichols House evolved as a succession of prominent families—not all of them included in the extended house name—contributed to the mansion's compelling 300-year history. Physician Richard Hooper built his small, medieval two-story house in about 1685. During the 1730s, Cornelius Waldo, a Boston merchant, did some dramatic remodeling, adding a third story and giving the home its elegant Georgian appearance. In 1758, Joseph Lee purchased the house on Brattle Street, which became known as Tory Row because of the neighborhood's political sympathies. Lee fled his mansion with the coming of the war and was the only Tory owner permitted to return after the Revolution. George Nichols acquired the house in 1850 and installed scenic—and rare—wallpaper by Dufours of Paris, issued in the early nineteenth century. The rare seventeenth-centry Delft tiles surrounding two of the fireplaces were added by Nichols' grandson, Austin T. White, during a Colonial Revival remodeling phase. The Cambridge Historical Society, which owns the house today, performed a substantial exterior restoration during the 1980s. In addition to hosting dinners, meetings, and small receptions, the house is open for public tours.

Listed in the National Register of Historic Places; garden honored by Massachusetts Horticulture Society

Location: The Hooper-Lee-Nichols House is located in the Old Cambridge Historic District, less than a mile from Harvard Square, and is accessible via I-93.
Function Space: 847 square feet; 2 rooms
Capacity—Conference: 50; Reception: 75; Banquet: 40; an outdoor area that may be tented is also available
Equipment On-site: Slide and overhead projectors, screen; folding chairs and buffet tables available for outdoor use
Food Service: Preferred caterers list provided
Limitations/Restrictions: No smoking; no liquor sold on premises; no amplified or loud music; 12:00 P.M. curfew
Access: Partial handicapped accessibility (excluding bathrooms); on-site parking; open year-round
Payment: Cash or check; no credit cards

CENTERVILLE

THE INN AT FERNBROOK

481 Main Street, Centerville, MA 02632
Phone: 508/775-4334 Fax: 508/778-4455
E-mail: sal@capecod.net

RENOWNED landscape architect Frederick Law Olmsted designed the grounds surrounding Fernbrook, an exquisite Victorian mansion built in 1881. Located in Centerville's historic district on Cape Cod, the inn was designed to ensure privacy, as no two rooms share the same wall. Rooms have a light, airy ambiance, and the antique furnishings, oriental carpets, and hardwood floors of cherry, maple, and oak add to the turn-of-the-century atmosphere. A meeting room is available for business meetings, receptions, small banquets, and other events. Three of the individually furnished guest rooms are named for Fernbrook's prior owners: Howard Marstons, founder of Fernbrook; Cardinal Francis Spellman, archbishop of New York, whose guests here included John F. Kennedy and Richard Nixon; and Dr. Herbert Kalmus, inventor of Technicolor, who hosted Cecile B. DeMille, Gloria Swanson, and Walt Disney. Room rates include a full gourmet breakfast (a continental breakfast is available as well), and guests will also enjoy relaxing in the Sweetheart Rose Garden or inspecting the grounds adorned with flower beds, arbors, ponds, and exotic trees. The inn is just minutes from Hyannis and a short drive from the Old King's Highway, with its many art galleries, pottery and antique shops, and restaurants.

Listed in the National Register of Historic Places

Location: The Inn at Fernbrook is just off Route 28 in Centerville, a half-mile from Craigville Beach.

Function Space: 795 square feet; 1 room
Capacity—Conference: 35; Reception: 55; Banquet: 32; Theater: 40
Equipment On-site: Audiovisual equipment and business services available through local outside source
Food Service: Breakfast with room; catering service available
Overnight Accommodations: 7 rooms
Limitations/Restrictions: Restrictions on smoking; no beverages sold on-site, guests supply their own; no children or pets
Access: On-site parking; open year-round
Payment: Check, all major credit cards

CHATHAM

CHATHAM BARS INN

(Mailing address)
P.O. Box 666
(Street address)
297 Shore Road, Chatham, MA 02633
Phone: 508/945-0096   Fax: 508/945-4978
E-mail: salescbi@chathambarsinn.com

CHATHAM Bars Inn is a beautifully restored landmark situated on 22 acres of pristine Cape Cod seashore overlooking Pleasant Bay and the Atlantic Ocean. Built in 1914 as a hunting lodge, this grand oceanfront resort once charmed clientele such as Henry Ford, William Rockefeller, and Holland's royal family. Many of the guest rooms feature balconies and spectacular views, while the seaside cottages provide spacious living rooms and homey amenities. A variety of meal options are available, ranging from the candlelit Main Dining Room, which serves classic New England cuisine, to the Beach House Grill and the North Beach Tavern. Beautiful terraces and magnificent themed gardens surround the inn, adding splashes of color to the coastal landscape and providing tranquil settings for relaxation. With over a quarter-mile of private beach, the inn also offers an outdoor pool, a fitness room, tennis, and golf. Deep sea fishing, picnics via launch to the Outer Bar, beachside lobster and clam bakes, and a complimentary children's program are available as well. The fully equipped meeting and conference facilities also come with ocean views.

Member of Historic Hotels of America

Location: Chatham is located at the elbow of Cape Cod, two hours from Boston and five hours from New York City. Barnstable Municipal Airport in Hyannis is 25 miles away.
Function Space: 10,412 square feet; 6+ rooms
Capacity—Conference: 100; Reception: 350; Banquet: 350; Theater: 350
Equipment On-site: Audiovisual equipment and business services available
Food Service: Catering/food service available; three restaurants
Overnight Accommodations: 155 rooms
Limitations/Restrictions: Restrictions on smoking
Access: Handicapped accessible; on-site parking; open year-round
Payment: Cash, check, credit card

DANVERS

GLEN MAGNA FARMS

(Mailing address)
Danvers Historical Society
P.O. Box 381
(Street address)
Ingersoll Street, Danvers, MA 01923
Phone: 508/777-1666   Fax: 508/777-5028

THE original foundation of this beautiful country estate dates back to the 1690s, and during the War of 1812 a simple farmhouse was built on the site. For 144 years "The Farm" was home to the Peabody and Endicott families, whose members enlarged and improved the house until it became an elegant summer residence. The house as it now stands was built in 1893, a delightful three-story, white clapboard Colonial Revival set on 11 acres in the Salem Village Historic District. The Farm was renamed "Glen Magna" sometime in the nineteenth century, after a family estate in England. The home's wraparound porch overlooks the beautiful lawn and grounds, and the bright, airy interiors reflect a cheerful and relaxed summer atmosphere. Groups may meet in the parlor, drawing room, library, and dining room. Outdoors, a wisteria-laden pergola anchors Glen Magna's award-winning English perennial gardens, embellished with fountains and statuary. Also on the grounds are the Derby Summer House, which Samuel McIntyre built in 1793, and the reproduction of Francis Peabody's original 1840 gazebo. Glen Magna welcomes visitors for weddings and receptions, private parties, corporate meetings, and other functions.

Listed in the National Register of Historic Places

Location: Danvers is located in northeastern Massachusetts, and Glen Magna Farms is accessible via Routes 89, 93, and 95 to 128 North.
Function Space: 1,864 square feet; 4 rooms
Capacity—Conference: 70; Reception: 125; Banquet: 130; Theater: 70; outdoor tenting available for additional space
Equipment On-site: Slide projector and screen, podium and amplifier
Food Service: Approved caterers list available
Limitations/Restrictions: No smoking; approved caterers only; no cash bars; some space may be off limits during event, contract will specify conditions
Access: On-site parking; open year-round
Payment: Check

DEDHAM

ENDICOTT ESTATE

656 East Street, Dedham, MA 02026
Phone: 617/326-0012

IN 1904, Henry Endicott, a founder of the Endicott-Johnson Shoe Corporation, lost his Dedham homestead to fire. Said to have interpreted the event as a divine order to rebuild, Endicott obeyed, and the result was a long, graceful three-story Colonial Revival mansion with Georgian overtones. Endicott's widow, Katherine, willed the house and property to Dedham in 1967 for educational, civic, social, and recreational purposes. Today the mansion occupies 15 acres of lush grounds; it accommodates a wide variety of social and business functions, including meetings, seminars, conventions, conferences, receptions, banquets, and reunions and is also used for commercial photography and filming. Events can be held indoors or out in a relaxed but elegant atmosphere.

The Grand Ballroom accommodates banquets and dancing, as well as lectures and meetings. The adjoining rooms feature period furnishings, mahogany paneling, oriental carpets, and marble fireplaces; upper-level special-function rooms are suited for smaller gatherings such as workshops and group meetings.

Location: The Endicott Estate is located south of Boston in Dedham, 1½ miles from Route 128, 4 miles from I-95, and 12 miles from the Massachusetts Turnpike. Commuter rail service is within walking distance of the estate.
Function Space: 2,384 square feet; 10 rooms
Capacity—Conference: 100; Reception: 200; Banquet: 150; Theater: 100
Food Service: Endicott Estate can arrange catering, or client can make own arrangements; kitchen available
Limitations/Restrictions: No smoking; open bar only, preapproved servers only
Access: Handicapped accessible; on-site parking; open year-round
Payment: Cash, check

DEERFIELD

DEERFIELD INN

81 Old Main Street, Deerfield, MA 01342
Phone: 800-926-3865   Fax: 413/773-8712
E-mail: Drfldinn@shaysnet.com

SINCE 1884 travelers have happily stopped by this authentic New England country inn for food and lodging. The inn is in the heart of historic Old Deerfield, a 300-year-old village that was once an outpost of Colonial America and in many ways is still an early New England frontier community. On the nearby working farms, bones and axeheads remaining from a 1704 Indian massacre are still found. Built at the corner of "The Street" is the graceful Deerfield Inn, a white clapboard two-story mansion. Each of the guest rooms, furnished with antiques and period reproductions, is named after a person connected with village history. The inn's renowned full-service restaurant specializes in New American cuisine with an international touch, and some of the regional dishes have come straight out of the village library's old recipe books. Banquets, weddings, and other social events are hosted here, and the inn also provides full meeting services for conferences, business meetings, and retreats. Numerous outdoor activities, including boating, fishing, skiing, and golf are available nearby, and 13 house museums are open for tours as well.

Located in a National Historic Landmark district; listed in the National Register of Historic Places

Deerfield Inn

Winsor House Inn

Location: The Deerfield Inn is located 5 miles south of Greenfield on Routes 5 and 10 North, Exit 24, off I-91 North, or Exit 25 off I-91 South, and is 55 minutes from Bradley International Airport, 2 hours from Boston/Logan International Airport, and 3.5 hours from New York City.
Function Space: 2,250 square feet; 3 rooms
Capacity—Conference: 20; Reception: 130; Banquet: 50; Theater: 50
Equipment On-site: Overhead and slide projectors, screen, public address system, flip charts, in-room modem hookup, photocopier, fax
Food Service: Full-service restaurant and bar
Overnight Accommodations: 23 rooms
Limitations/Restrictions: No smoking in inn; off-premise alcohol to be consumed in room only; no pets, seeing/hearing dogs only
Access: Handicapped accessible; on-site parking; open year-round except December 24–26
Payment: Corporate check

DUXBURY

WINSOR HOUSE INN
390 Washington Street, Duxbury, MA 02332
Phone: 617/934-0991   Fax: 617/934-5955

IN 1803 merchant and sea captain Nathaniel Winsor built this handsome two-story clapboard Georgian mansion for his daughter, Nancy, and her husband, John Howland. A prominent family, the Winsors enjoyed Duxbury's prosperity, derived from the shipbuilding industry and merchant sea trade. In 1915, Daniel Winsor, a 19-year-old British naval intelligence officer who had left Duxbury with his parents as an infant, inherited the family homestead. He returned in 1932 with his wife, Marie, and opened the house as an inn. The Winsor House has been restored and once again welcomes visitors with its colonial atmosphere and decor. The inn can accommodate a variety of meetings and gatherings, ranging from a small, intimate party of 10 to a reception for 110. Overnight guests enjoy a full innkeeper's breakfast, and the inn's restaurant is open daily for lunch and dinner; also on-site is an old English-style pub. The beach, tennis, and golf are all nearby, and the inn offers a 36-foot cutter-rigged Cape Dory sailboat for charter.

Location: Duxbury/Winsor House is located 35 miles south of Boston's Logan International Airport and is accessible via Route 3.
Function Space: 1,625 square feet; 3 rooms
Capacity—Conference: 65; Reception: 110; Banquet: 80; Theater: 65
Food Service: Breakfast with room; catering/food service available; restaurant and pub
Overnight Accommodations: 3 rooms
Limitations/Restrictions: Restrictions on smoking
Access: On-site parking; open year-round
Payment: Cash, check, credit card (AmEx, Discover, MC, Visa)

EDGARTOWN

THE HARBOR VIEW RESORT

(Mailing address, Sales Department)
One International Place, Twelfth Floor
Boston, MA 02110
(Street address)
131 N. Water Street, P.O. Box 7
Edgartown, MA 02539
Phone: 617/261-7300 (sales), 508/627-7000 (hotel), or 800-ISLANDS   Fax: 617/330-8870

SINCE 1891 the Harbor View Hotel has graced the shore at Edgartown on Martha's Vineyard, its 300-foot verandah looking out to sea. The restored hotel has retained its Victorian charm, and the refurbished guest rooms, many with harbor views, all come with modern amenities. Accommodations are also available in two townhouses, and seven boat slips are on hand for guests arriving by sea. Extensive conference facilities are available year-round, and the full-service resort's beachside location and distance from the mainland make it ideal for retreats. In addition to state-of-the-art conference and banquet rooms, the Harbor View offers outdoor dining and meeting space, lighthouse receptions, and clambakes on the beach. Recreational activities include swimming, tennis, and golf, and downtown Edgartown, with its brick sidewalks and charming gardens, boutiques and art galleries, is within walking distance of the resort. Among the Harbor View's neighbors are nineteenth-century whaling captains' homes and plenty of elm trees, and the numerous island attractions are just minutes away, including deep-sea fishing, biking, fishing, and wildlife tours.

Listed in the National Register of Historic Places; member of Historic Hotels of America

Location: Edgartown is on the eastern end of Martha's Vineyard. The Harbor View Hotel is 10 minutes from Martha's Vineyard Airport, and there is regular 45-minute ferry service to New Bedford, Hyannis, and Woods Hole.
Function Space: 27,792 square feet; 15 rooms
Capacity—Conference: 55; Reception: 200; Banquet: 140; Theater: 175
Equipment On-site: Audiovisual equipment, business and concierge services available
Food Service: Catering/food service available; three restaurants, room service
Overnight Accommodations: 113 rooms
Access: Handicapped accessible; on-site parking; open year-round

Payment: Cash, check, credit card (AmEx, Carte Blanche, DC, MC, Visa)

FALMOUTH

GRAFTON INN

261 Grand Avenue, South
Falmouth Heights, MA 02540
Phone: 508/540-8688   Fax: 508/540-1861

Grafton Inn

IN about 1850, what is now the Grafton Inn began to take shape on Cape Cod's Falmouth Heights. The area had been an encampment for Queen Awashonks of the Narragansett Indians in the seventeenth century, and by 1686 settlers incorporated Falmouth as a town. In the late nineteenth century Falmouth became a popular resort, attracting visitors from around the world. So the locale already had quite an established history when Leslie Dodge, from Grafton, Massachusetts, set about enlarging the existing structure in 1905. A stylish three-story Queen Anne building on the beachfront Grand Avenue in the Falmouth Heights Historic District, the Grafton Inn was constructed of tongue-and-groove white pine, which allows for the wood's expansion and contraction caused by storms and ocean moisture. The completely renovated inn is decorated in soft colors and accented with fresh flowers from the English garden. Guest rooms are decorated with period furnishings, antiques and original artwork, and overnight guests can enjoy a full breakfast taken on the porch. Many of Cape Cod's most popular activities, including swimming, bike riding, deep-sea fishing, and island cruises are just a short walk away.

Location: The Grafton Inn is located on the south side of Cape Cod, 70 miles from both Boston and Providence; from I-95 to I-195 to Route 28 South.
Function Space: 800 square feet; 1 room
Capacity—Conference: 15–20
Equipment On-site: TV/VCR, tables, chairs, speaker's podium, fax
Food Service: Breakfast with room; breakfast and lunch served on-site
Overnight Accommodations: 11 rooms
Limitations/Restrictions: No smoking
Access: On-site parking; open February to December
Payment: Cash, bank and traveler's checks, credit card

GLOUCESTER

GRAND BANKS FISHING SCHOONER
ADVENTURE

Gloucester Adventure, Inc.
(Mailing address)
P.O. Box 1306
(Street address)
4 Harbor Loop, Gloucester, MA 01930
Phone: 508/281-8079 Fax: 508/281-2393

THE last American dory trawler still in service by 1953, the *Adventure* retired after 27 years of fishing the North Atlantic's outer banks. Built in 1926 with a deck measuring 121 feet, 6 inches, the trawler operated with a full sailing rig, diesel engine, and 14 dories. During the course of its career, the schooner brought in a record $4 million worth of cod and other ground fish. From 1954 to 1988, it was known as "The Queen of the Windjammers" and served as a pleasure cruise ship sailing along the Maine coast. Donated in 1988 to the city of Gloucester, the *Adventure's* home port and a community rich in seafaring heritage, the knockabout schooner is now open for tours and hosts a variety of educational programs. It offers a unique setting for business and committee meetings and other gatherings in the galley and the captain's cabin, which are furnished with tables, benches, and chairs. The deck is ideal for receptions, cocktail parties, and other events. Groups meeting on board receive a tour of the historic schooner.

National Historic Landmark; listed in the National Register of Historic Places

Adventure *(Hazel Andrea-Stuart ©1994)*

Location: The *Adventure* can be found at Harbor Loop, downtown Gloucester, a half-mile from the northern end of Route 128. Boston's Logan International Airport is one hour by car, and its commuter rail line is a half-mile away.
Function Space: 500 square feet; 2 rooms
Capacity—Conference: 74; Reception: 74; Banquet: 30
Equipment On-site: VCR
Food Service: Catering and food service can be arranged, or renter may select caterer
Limitations/Restrictions: No smoking except in designated areas
Access: On-site (mostly metered) parking available; open April to November
Payment: Check, credit card

HINGHAM

THE OLD SHIP MEETINGHOUSE

(Mailing address)
107 Main Street
(Street address)
90 Main Street, Hingham, MA 02043
Phone: 617/749-1679

AS the oldest meeting house in continuous ecclesiastical use in the United States, the Old Ship Meeting House in historic Hingham has been a gathering place since it was built 1681. Townspeople raised the frame of the building in three days, and each parish member was assessed a share of the total cost of 430 pounds. Known as the "Old Ship," the building was constructed of oak, its roof resembling an inverted ship's hull. The frame and walls of the Old Ship are original, but the side galleries were added in 1730 and 1755. The original seats were backless benches, replaced with box pews in 1755. Although the interior fea-

tured various styles over the years, including Victorian decor during the latter half of the nineteenth century, it was returned to its seventeenth- to eighteenth-century appearance during a 1930 restoration. Today groups may use the Old Ship for lectures and concerts, and facilities are also available for meetings and receptions in Fellowship Hall in the Parish House, a three-story Victorian built in 1865. Guided group tours of the Old Ship can be arranged when booking an event.

National Historic Landmark; listed in the National Register of Historic Places

Location: Hingham is 20 miles southeast of Boston and is accessible via Route 3A.
Function Space: 5,000 square feet; 1 room
Capacity—Conference: 200
Equipment On-site: TV, VCR
Food Service: Renter selects caterer; kitchen available
Limitations/Restrictions: No smoking; no food or beverages in Old Ship Meeting House
Access: Handicapped accessible; open year-round
Payment: Check

IPSWICH

CASTLE HILL

The Trustees of Reservations
(Mailing address)
P.O. Box 563
(Street address)
290 Argilla Road, Ipswich, MA 01938
Phone: 508/356-4351   Fax: 508/356-2143

THE area that is now Castle Hill was once inhabited by the Agawam Indians, but by 1634 it was planned as the site of a fort to protect English settlement. In 1910, farmer John Brown sold the land to industrialist Richard Teller Crane Jr. He hired David Adler to design his Great House, a three-story, 59-room Stuart mansion completed in 1928. Ten paneled rooms were acquired from eighteenth-century London townhouses, but perhaps the most remarkable room is the paneled library, noted for its seventeenth-century lime-wood carvings, from the manor of the Earl of Essex at Cassiobury Park. Today the library contains books from Ireland's Castle Killeen, including the only Parliamentary Register in North America. The Crane family lived at Castle Hill until 1949, when they bequeathed the house and 1,400 acres to the Trustees of Reservations for the preservation of the landscaped grounds and surrounding natural areas. The magnificent estate, which overlooks expansive lawns, formal gardens, and Ipswich Bay's white sandy beach, offers comprehensive services for corporate gatherings ranging from business meetings to cocktail parties. Rentals include exclusive use of the Great House and grounds, and arrangements can be made for gourmet meals, hot air balloons, and even fireworks.

Location: Ipswich is in northeastern Massachusetts, and Castle Hill is accessible via Route I-95/Route 128 north to Route 1A to Route 133 east. Castle Hill is 50 miles north of Boston.
Function Space: 3,141 square feet; 3 rooms
Capacity—Conference: 200+; Reception: 300+; Banquet: 200; Theater: 150
Equipment On-site: Equipment available for rent from outside source
Food Service: Full-service kitchen available for outside caterer
Access: On-site parking; open year-round
Payment: Check

LENOX

BLANTYRE

(Mailing address)
P.O. Box 995
(Street address)
16 Blantyre Road, Lenox, MA 01240
Phone: 413/637-3556 (season); 413/298-1661 (winter)
Fax: 413/637-4282

A stunning Tudor-style mansion set in the foothills of the Berkshires, Blantyre welcomes visitors with much the same generous hospitality as the aristocratic castle and grand Scottish manors it is modeled after. The turreted mansion, with its porte cochere, stone gargoyles, and carved friezes, sits perched above 85 acres of an immaculate greensward, flower beds, and towering trees. Built in 1902, Blantyre is a luxurious and relaxing setting for group functions ranging from wedding parties to executive retreats. Meetings are held in the elegant Music Room, which is furnished with antiques dating from 1760. French doors open onto a covered terrace that is available for breakout sessions. Eight suites and rooms accommodate overnight guests in the main house; additional accommodations are available in the Carriage House and cottages. Blantyre's country house cuisine, accented with French culinary techniques, is served in the mahogany-paneled main dining room; meals may also be served in the Conservatory or on the terrace in summer. On-site recreational facilities include a pool, tennis courts, and croquet lawns.

Location: Blantyre is in the Berkshire Hills, 130 miles from Boston/Logan International Airport and 1.75 hours from Hartford's Bradley International. The estate is accessible via I-90, Exit 2 (Lee), and Route 7.

Function Space: 1,080 square feet; 1 room
Capacity—Conference: 35; Reception: 150;
Banquet: 135; Theater: 45
Equipment On-site: Slide and overhead projec-
tors, screen, VCR and monitor, flip chart, black-
board; newspapers; fax, typing service available
Food Service: Full food service; dining room
Overnight Accommodations: 23 rooms
Limitations/Restrictions: No children under
the age of 13
Access: Handicapped accessible; on-site parking;
open early May to early November
Payment: Cash, check, credit card (AmEx, MC,
Visa)

SEVEN HILLS COUNTRY INN

40 Plunkett Street, Lenox, MA 01240
Phone: 413/637-0060   Fax: 413/637-3651

THE Seven Hills Country Inn, located in the heart
of the Berkshires, was originally a farmhouse built
in the 1750s, and over the centuries the house has
changed dramatically. In 1885 the refurbished
house was dubbed "Norwood," one of the first of
the large estates built in Lenox. Norwood became
"Shipton Court" in 1911 under its new owner,
Mrs. Emily Meredith Read Spencer, whose additions to the structure doubled its size. Finally, in
1951, Leonard Bernstein christened the house
"Seven Hills," and its new owners, Larry and
Sophie Hewitt, converted the building into an inn.
More than a summer resort, the inn also hosts conferences, business retreats, banquets, weddings,
and other functions. Guest rooms are located in
both the manor house and the terrace house, and
the inn's interiors showcase antiques, hand-carved
fireplaces, and leaded glass windows dating back
to the Shipton Court era. The inn is situated on 27
acres of gardens and countryside, and an outdoor
pool and tennis courts are on the grounds. The
Berkshires region offers dozens of lakes and rivers
for boating, fishing, and swimming, and plenty of
country lanes for biking and walking. Downhill
and cross-country skiing are available throughout
the area.

Location: The Seven Hills Country Inn is
located in western Massachusetts, one hour
from airport service in Albany, New York,
80 minutes from Hartford, Connecticut, and
two hours from Boston; accessible via the
Massachusetts Turnpike.
Function Space: 2,400 square feet; 5 rooms
Capacity—Conference: 150; Reception: 300;
Banquet: 200; Theater: 250
Equipment On-site: Overhead and slide
projectors, public address system; computer,
fax, steno available
Food Service: Catering/food service available;
restaurant
Overnight Accommodations: 52 rooms
Limitations/Restrictions: No smoking
Access: Handicapped accessible; on-site parking;
open year-round
Payment: Cash, check, credit card

LYNN

DIAMOND DISTRICT BREAKFAST INN

142 Ocean Street, Lynn, MA 01902
Phone: 617/599-4470   Fax: 617/595-2200

JUST a short walk from the ocean in the fashionable historic Diamond District, this 17-room
Georgian clapboard mansion recalls the locale's
glittering past. At the turn of the century, wealthy
businessmen and factory owners, many from
Boston, built luxurious mansions in the area,

which became known as the Diamond District. Architect Thomas M. James, who also designed the Schubert Theater in Boston, built the mansion in 1911 for P. J. Harney, a Lynn shoe manufacturer. A grand staircase winds three floors above a gracious foyer, and the home is decorated with antiques and oriental rugs. The large living room, finished in Mexican mahogany, offers an ocean view, and French doors lead to a verandah that overlooks the gardens and the sea. Guest rooms are named for types of shoes or shoe parts, such as Slipper, Oxford, Pump, High Top, and Button Boot. A full breakfast is served in the formal dining room each morning. In addition to the beach, local attractions include the Mary Baker Eddy Home, Lynn Woods, and the historic sights of Salem, Marblehead, and Boston are nearby.

Listed in the National Register of Historic Places

Location: Diamond District Breakfast Inn is located 8 miles northeast of Boston's Logan International Airport, near Route 1A North and 129 East; one block from bus service.

Diamond District Breakfast Inn

Function Space: 825 square feet; 2 rooms
Capacity—Conference: 20
Equipment On-site: Fax
Food Service: Breakfast with room; in-house or outside catering can be arranged
Overnight Accommodations: 8 rooms
Limitations/Restrictions: No smoking; no alcohol
Access: On-site parking; open year-round
Payment: Cash, check, traveler's checks, credit cards (AmEx, MC, DC, Discover, Visa)

MARBLEHEAD

KING HOOPER MANSION
8 Hooper Street, Marblehead, MA 01945
Phone: 617/631-2608

A grand sight on the Salem Maritime Trail, the King Hooper Mansion is a stately Georgian house in the Marblehead Historic District. Greenleaf Hooper, a candlemaker, built the house in 1728, and his son Robert, a wealthy shipping merchant, added the front section in 1745. Local seamen called the younger Hooper "King" because of his genial demeanor and reputation for fairness. Now home of the Marblehead Arts Association, the mansion's public rooms are available for hosting a variety of corporate functions and social events. Renters may use the wine cellar, the dining room, a small gallery, and a charming front parlor on the first floor, as well as the third-floor ballroom, furnished with a Steinway grand piano. The home features traditional Colonial decor, and in addition to the interior rental space, the pleasing garden may also be used. Nearby attractions include many historic buildings, shops, and restaurants in this "sailing capital" seaside town, and Salem and Boston are close by.

Listed in the National Register of Historic Places

Location: Marblehead is 15 miles northeast of Boston and is accessible via I-95.
Function Space: 7,000 square feet; 6 rooms
Capacity—Conference: 50; Reception: 50; Banquet: 50 (total capacity: 100 persons maximum)
Equipment On-site: May be rented from outside source
Food Service: Renter selects caterer, two kitchens available
Limitations/Restrictions: No smoking; alcoholic beverages limited to wine and ale; no amplifiers
Access: Handicapped accessibility ground floor only; street parking available; open year-round
Payment: Check or credit card (MC, Visa)

MARSHFIELD

ISAAC WINSLOW HOUSE
(Mailing address)
P.O. Box 531
(Street address)
Webster and Careswell Streets (Route 139)
Marshfield, MA 02050
Phone: 617/837-5753

JUDGE Isaac Winslow, grandson of *Mayflower* passenger and Pilgrim Governor Edward Winslow, built this clapboard Colonial mansion in 1699, and the house remained in the Winslow family until 1822. Of note are the exceptionally fine Jacobean staircase, the unusually high ceilings, and a "secret room," possibly used for Tory gatherings in the Revolutionary era. Owner Dr. Isaac

Winslow, who remained loyal to England, saved the lives of many townspeople during a 1778 smallpox epidemic, and apparently those efforts allowed him to retain his property after the war. In 1844 statesman Daniel Webster bought the house, and although he never lived in it, some of his letters and possessions remain here. In 1920, on the occasion of the 300th anniversary of the Pilgrim landing, the Winslow House Association was formed to purchase and restore the house. A high-ceilinged tea room was added to connect the house harmoniously with a refurbished 1880s barn. Also on the grounds are an herb garden, a blacksmith shop, and a carriage house containing a Concord stagecoach, a brougham, and Webster's phaeton. Tours of the house are available at an additional per-person charge.

National Historic Landmark; listed in the National Register of Historic Places (Daniel Webster law office)

Location: The Isaac Winslow House is 34 miles south of Boston's Logan International Airport and 14 miles north of Plymouth; the house is accessible via Route 3 to Route 139.
Function Space: 1,000 square feet; 2 rooms
Capacity—Conference: 25–50; Reception: 30–75 (indoors), 200 (yard and patio); Banquet: 25–50; Theater: 75; renters have use of the tea room, barn room, yard, patio, and kitchen
Equipment On-site: Screen, telephone; tables and chairs for 75 included in rent
Food Service: Preferred caterers list provided
Limitations/Restrictions: No smoking indoors; licensed caterer required for food service; cash bar requires town liquor license; facilities available from 9:00 A.M. to 9:00 P.M., Monday through Saturday

Access: Handicapped accessibility limited, bathrooms are *not* wheelchair accessible; on-site parking; open mid-May through mid-October
Payment: Cash, check

NANTUCKET

THE ALBERT G. BROCK CONFERENCE CENTER

(Mailing address)
P.O. Box 1500
(Street address)
53 Main Street, Nantucket, MA 02554
Phone: 508/228-0104 or 800-344-4044
Fax: 508/228-5166
E-mail: agbrock@nantucket.net

LOCATED in Nantucket's Old Historic District, the Union Building that houses the Albert G. Brock Conference Center was built after the Great Fire of 1846. Marsha Fader and John D. Brock's restoration and renovation of the property gave special attention to the conference center located on the second floor. The building is filled with Greek Revival trim, plaster cornices, and medallions, and the conference room has been beautifully returned to its original use as a meeting place. The room, with its warm Victorian tones, evokes the true spirit of Nantucket in its reflection of the locale's history and seclusion. Columns and exquisite scrollwork were added in the late nineteenth century. Guests can easily move from the lecture and presentation area to a more formal conference table or to the adjoining kitchen and library workspace. Surrounded by historic structures, the center and the nearby inns and hotels offer a good point of departure for exploring the area's many charms along its cobbled streets and scenic waterfront.

Location: The Albert G. Brock Conference Center is located in the center of town in the Old Historic District; trip by ferry to Nantucket from Hyannis is 2 hours, 15 minutes; 20 minutes by plane. Hyannis is 1.5 hours from Boston and Providence; 5 hours from New York City.
Seasonal shuttle service, taxis, car and bike rentals available on island; cars may be brought over on the ferry by advance reservation only.
Function Space: 788 square feet; 1 room
Capacity—Reception: 50–70; Theater: 40; additional kitchen and library space (450 square feet)
Equipment On-site: Audiovisual equipment, speaker's podium, tables and chairs
Food Service: Kitchen facility available; renter selects caterer; center staff available for assisting in coffee breaks
Limitations/Restrictions: No smoking; food permitted in kitchen and library only; no handicapped accessibility; no on-site parking
Access: Open year-round
Payment: Check

Albert G. Brock Conference Center

JARED COFFIN HOUSE

(Mailing address)
P.O. Box 1580
(Street address)
29 Broad Street, Nantucket, MA 02554
Phone: 508/228-2400   Fax: 508/228-8549
E-mail: jchouse@nantucket.net
http://www.nantucket.net/lodging/jchouse

NANTUCKET, famous for its nineteenth-century whaling industry, maintains numerous historic and preserved buildings from the island's colorful past. A landmark site in the heart of Nantucket's Old Historic District is the Jared Coffin House, comprising six buildings, the centerpiece of which is Jared Coffin's brick mansion. Coffin, a prosperous ship owner, built the graceful three-story mansion in 1845. The 60 guest rooms are decorated with antiques or period reproductions, and many rooms are furnished with canopied beds. Jared's, the inn's renowned restaurant, serves local cuisine (including Nantucket Bay scallops in season) and traditional New England fare in an elegant atmosphere amid fine whaling ship paintings. The dark-paneled Tap Room, a local favorite, offers lunch and dinner and, during the summer season, dining on the patio, surrounded by flower boxes and gardens. Restored and preserved, the mansion offers a pleasant island gathering place and holds a place of honor among the mansions and shingle cottages that line Nantucket's cobblestone streets.

Located in a National Historic Landmark district; listed in the National register of Historic Places

Location: The Jared Coffin House is located in Nantucket's Old Historic District and is accessible by ferry and plane from Hyannis.
Function Space: 869 square feet; 3 rooms

Capacity—Conference: 20; Reception: 150; Banquet: 70; Theater: 30
Equipment On-site: Overhead and slide projectors, flip charts; fax and printer available
Food Service: Full food service available; two restaurants
Overnight Accommodations: 60 rooms
Limitations/Restrictions: Restrictions on smoking
Access: On-site parking; open year-round
Payment: Cash, check, credit card

NEW MARLBOROUGH

GEDNEY FARM INN

(Mailing address)
Star Route 70
(Street address)
Route 57, New Marlborough, MA 01230
Phone: 413/229-3131
Fax: 413/229-3131 (same as phone)

LOCATED in the old Berkshire village of New Marlborough, the Old Inn on the Green and Gedney Farm are surrounded by 200 acres of country fields and pastures. The restored inn, circa 1760, served as a relay stop on the post road from Westfield to Albany. The farm's barns are designed after the great Normandy barns of nineteenth-century France and were built at the turn of the twentieth century as a breeding farm. Now an old Berkshire high country lodge, Gedney Farm offers a rural setting for exclusive executive retreats and business meetings for small groups. A variety of meeting and work spaces, including an auditorium, a conference room, and a reception area, are available in the former horse barn, whose original architectural features have been preserved. All meals can be catered to suit each group's needs.

Across from the horse barn the former cattle barn now houses elegant guest rooms and suites, many with granite fireplaces. The farm is also available for other special events, including weddings, receptions, and banquets. Biking, hiking, cross country and downhill skiing, golf, swimming, and other activities are all available nearby.

Listed in the National Register of Historic Places; named 1992 "Outstanding Conference Facility" by New Jersey Meeting Planners Association

Location: New Marlborough is located in south-western Massachusetts in the Berkshires, approxi-mately 2.5 hours from New York City and Boston. It is accessible via I-90 and Route 57.
Function Space: 2,500 square feet; 4 rooms
Capacity—Conference: 12–200; Reception: 200; Banquet: 200; Theater: 200
Equipment On-site: Audiovisual equipment, fax, phone conferencing, photocopier available
Food Service: Catering/food service available; full banquet kitchen on premises; dining rooms, cafe
Overnight Accommodations: 21 rooms
Limitations/Restrictions: Restrictions on smoking
Access: Handicapped accessible; on-site parking; open year-round
Payment: Cash, check, major credit card

NEWBURYPORT

THE PHOENIX ROOM OF NEWBURYPORT

19 Inn Street, Newburyport, MA 01950
Phone: 508/463-3301   Fax: 508/465-6653

THE Phoenix Building was first built in 1809 to house the Phoenix Marine & Fire Insurance Company in downtown Newburyport. Just two years later, a devastating fire swept through the city's center, destroying 250 buildings, including the Phoenix Building. As its name may suggest, the building did rise from the ashes and six months later it was rededicated, one of the first structures to be rebuilt. Located in the Newburyport Historic District, the elegant Phoenix Building remains a source of architectural and historical significance and flourishes as a center hosting business and social events. Occupying the entire third floor of the building, the Phoenix Room has been fully restored, and the ballroom is again seen in its grand, original Federal-style appearance. Period decor, a brass chandelier, a high-arched ceiling, and six-foot-high multipaned windows overlooking the city add to the room's bright and engaging atmos-phere. A variety of social events, such as weddings, luncheons, fundraisers, and corporate meetings, including dinners, seminars, and promotional events, are easily accommodated. Smaller rooms for breakout sessions are also available.

Listed in the National Register of Historic Places

Location: Newburyport is located in the north-eastern corner of Massachusetts and is accessible via I-95 (exit 57) to Route 113.
Function Space: 2,100 square feet; 3 rooms
Capacity—Conference: 150; Reception: 100–150; Banquet: 100–120; Theater: 150
Equipment On-site: Cordless microphone and podium; VCR, slide projector and screen avail-able for rental
Food Service: Catering/food service available
Overnight Accommodations: Available nearby
Limitations/Restrictions: No smoking; open bar only; exclusive caterer
Access: Parking in municipal lots; open year-round
Payment: Cash or check

NORTHAMPTON

THE HOTEL NORTHAMPTON

36 King Street, Northampton, MA 01060
Phone: 413/584-3100   Fax: 413/584-9455
E-mail: info@hotelnorthampton.com

BUILT in 1927, the five-story brick Colonial Revival Hotel Northampton rises above its glass-enclosed conservatory, whose hanging plants, wicker chairs, and palm-leaved chandeliers create a relaxing atmosphere. Lewis Wiggins filled his hotel with museum-quality antiques, adding to his collection on a daily basis and bringing on a full-time antiquarian curator with a staff of 15. Adjacent to the hotel is Wiggins Tavern, which Benjamin Wiggins established in 1786. It was originally located in Hopkinton, New Hampshire, but Lewis, a descendant of Benjamin, had the tavern dismantled and brought to the hotel, where its hand-hewn beams, stone and brick hearths, and carved paneling were carefully reassembled. The Northampton's function rooms, of varying size and style, range from the Grand Ballroom, with its high ceilings and arched windows, to smaller meeting space for business meetings, seminars, and other gatherings. Rates include a complimentary breakfast, and many of the hotel's comfortable guest rooms afford balcony views of downtown; some of the luxurious suites also feature jacuzzis and fireplaces. The surrounding area offers a variety of cultural and recreational activities, including museums, theaters, boating, and hiking.

Listed in the National Register of Historic Places; member of Historic Hotels of America

The Hotel Northampton

Location: Hotel Northampton is 2.5 hours from Boston and 35 miles north of Hartford Airport via I-91.
Function Space: 5,600 square feet; 5 rooms
Capacity—Conference: 150; Reception: 300; Banquet: 180; Theater: 250
Equipment On-site: Complete audiovisual equipment available; fax, photocopier, typing available
Food Service: Breakfast with room; catering/food service available; two restaurants
Overnight Accommodations: 77 rooms
Access: Handicapped accessible; on-site parking; open year-round
Payment: Cash, check, credit card

SALEM

HAWTHORNE HOTEL

On the Common, Salem, MA 01970
Phone: 508/744-4080   Fax: 508/745-9842
E-mail: Info@Hawthornehotel.com

IN the 1920s the citizens of Salem launched a public subscription drive to build the Hawthorne Hotel, named for renowned author Nathaniel Hawthorne, who spent the first 10 years of his life in Salem and was later a frequent visitor. Completed in 1925, the Federal-style hotel has a refined and elegant New England atmosphere and is furnished with handsome eighteenth-century reproductions. Conference facilities accommodate board meetings and larger business gatherings, and the ballroom, with its view of Salem Common seen through large Palladian windows, has long been the setting of magnificent receptions. Dining options at the hotel include Nathaniel's Restaurant, known for its seasonal American cuisine, and the Tavern on the Green, which offers light fare and live entertainment. A twentieth-century landmark in the Salem Common Historic District, the hotel is within walking distance of numerous historic sites and attractions, including the House of the Seven Gables, the Peabody Essex Museum, the Salem Witch Museum, Salem 1630 Pioneer Village, and Pickering Wharf.

Listed in the National Register of Historic Places; member of Historic Hotels of America

Location: The Hawthorne Hotel is accessible via I-95 or US 1 to Route 128 North, and from Boston's Logan Airport by following Route 1A north 15 miles.
Function Space: 6,070 square feet; 6 rooms

Capacity—Conference: 150; Reception: 350; Banquet: 200; Theater: 350
Equipment On-site: Audiovisual equipment, photocopier, fax available
Food Service: Catering/food service available; two restaurants, bar, room service
Overnight Accommodations: 89 rooms
Access: Handicapped accessible; on-site parking; open year-round
Payment: Credit card

STOCKBRIDGE

CHESTERWOOD

(Mailing address)
P.O. Box 827
(Street address)
4 Williamsville Road, Stockbridge, MA 01262
Phone: 413/298-3579 ext. 19   Fax: 413/298-3973
TTY: 413/298-3579

DANIEL Chester French, creator of two of America's greatest public monuments (*The Minute Man*, 1875, and *Abraham Lincoln*, 1922, for the Lincoln Memorial) spent 35 summers here at his home and studio in the Berkshires. Henry Bacon, the architect of the Lincoln Memorial in Washington, D.C., also designed the Colonial Revival home (1901) and studio (1898) for French, who laid out the estate's gardens and idyllic woodland walks. On display in French's studio are some of the nearly 500 pieces of sculpture, molds, and life casts that document his singular creativity and prolific output. During a career that spanned a half century, French created more than 100 works of public sculpture that embellish major buildings and landscape designs throughout the country. Chesterwood is open for public tours, and meeting space is available in the 1919 Woodshed meeting room. The Studio Piazza offers a charming setting for open-air dining, and outdoor areas, including the Studio Garden Fountain Court, Residence Terrace, Formal Garden, Upper Garden, and lawn, also are available. Meeting facilities and grounds may be rented for weddings, receptions, corporate functions, parties, and as backdrops for advertising photography.

National Historic Landmark; listed in the National Register of Historic Places; Massachusetts Historic Landmark; National Trust for Historic Preservation Historic Site

Chesterwood *(Ron Blunt. Courtesy of the National Trust for Historic Preservation)*

Location: Stockbridge is just south of I-90, off Route 183 in western Massachusetts.
Function Space: 1,200 square feet; 1 room
Capacity—Conference: 40; Reception: 70; Banquet: 30; Theater: 50; manicured grounds also available; client must rent tents for grounds rentals
Equipment On-site: Slide projector and screen, public address system, VCR with large monitor; podium, tables, chairs; phone, fax, and photocopier available
Food Service: Renter selects caterer; small galley in woodshed; planning guide provided for all renters; brochures available on request
Limitations/Restrictions: No smoking indoors; insurance certificate required; insurance must have liquor liability clause if alcoholic beverages are served
Access: Limited handicapped access to buildings and grounds; rest rooms and museum shop are handicapped accessible; on-site parking; open May 1 to October 31
Payment: Payment in advance

THE RED LION INN

Main Street, Stockbridge, MA 01262
Phone: 413/298-5545   Fax: 413/298-5130

IN 1773, Silas Pepoon established a tavern on Main Street under the sign of the Red Lion, and his business became a popular stop for coaches traveling between Albany and Boston. Mr. and Mrs. Charles Plumb purchased the building in 1862, and Mrs. Plumb acquired much of the fine antique furniture and china found at the inn today. More than a century later, the small tavern had grown to accommodate 100 guests and was known as the Stockbridge House. Fire destroyed the entire building in 1896, but less than a year later the rebuilt hotel was open for business. The last of the nineteenth-century hotels still operating in the Berkshires, the Red Lion is pictured in Norman

Rockwell's painting *Main Street, Stockbridge*. Refurbished meeting rooms are available for conferences, business meetings, receptions, and social gatherings. Bed-and-breakfast guest rooms are available, and New England cuisine is served in the elegant dining room, the Widow Bingham Tavern, and the Lion's Den, a pub featuring live nightly entertainment. A pool and exercise room are available on-site, and golf, tennis and skiing are nearby. The inn is also convenient to the Norman Rockwell Museum, Chesterwood, the Mission House, and other historic sites.

Member of Historic Hotels of America

Location: The Red Lion Inn is located off Exit 2 on the Massachusetts Turnpike (I-90). From Exit 2, take Route 102 west to Stockbridge; the inn is on Main Street on the corner at the intersection of Routes 102 and 7. Nearest airports are Albany Airport, New York (1 hour), and Bradley Airport, Hartford, Connecticut (1.5 hours); Boston and New York City are 2 and 3 hours away, respectively.

The Red Lion Inn

Function Space: 2,700 square feet; 4 rooms
Capacity—Conference: 20; Reception: 100; Banquet: 75; Theater: 60
Equipment On-site: Audiovisual equipment and business services available
Food Service: Catering/food service available; two restaurants and pub
Overnight Accommodations: 108 rooms
Limitations/Restrictions: Restrictions on smoking
Access: Handicapped accessible; on-site parking; open year-round
Payment: Cash, check, credit card

WENHAM

WENHAM MUSEUM—BURNHAM HALL
132 Main Street, Wenham, MA 01984
Phone: 508/468-2377   Fax: 508/468-5535

AS part of the Wenham Museum complex, the recently renovated but still rustic "old barn" known as Burnham Hall offers a charming meeting place amid several historic structures. Built in 1934, the hall is adjacent to the museum, which is also flanked by the seventeenth-century Claflin-Richards house. The house was originally a two-room saltbox built in about 1660 for Robert McClaflin, whose family name was later shortened. In the late seventeenth century the clapboard house was enlarged to three stories and four rooms. Today the period-furnished rooms reflect the different eras of its occupants, from the Colonial decor of McClaflin's time to the early Victorian style of the Richards family, who owned the house from the mid-nineteenth century until 1921. Also on-site is a Wenham ice industry exhibit chronicling the town's famous export, the authentic nine-teenth-century Merrill Shoe Shop, and a genealogical library. The museum features changing exhibits from its stellar collection of costumes, antique toys, and textiles and features a permanent display of more than one thousand dolls from philanthropist Mary Richards Horton's collection. Groups renting Burnham Hall may arrange for house tours.

Listed in the National Register of Historic Places

Location: Wenham is located in northeastern Massachusetts; from Route 128 north, Exit 20A and follow Route 1A north 2.3 miles; museum is on the right before Wenham Town Hall. Boston's Logan International Airport is 30 minutes away. The museum is a 10-minute walk from the South Hamilton train depot.
Function Space: 1,092 square feet; 1 room
Capacity—Conference: 100; Reception: 100; Banquet: 100; Theater: 100
Equipment On-site: Microphone, podium, screen
Food Service: Renter selects caterer; kitchen available
Limitations/Restrictions: No smoking; may serve but not sell alcoholic beverages
Access: Handicapped accessible; on-site parking; open year-round
Payment: Cash, check

WEST BROOKFIELD

SALEM CROSS INN
(Mailing address)
P.O. Box 553
(Street address)
260 W. Main Street, West Brookfield, MA 01585
Phone: 508/867-8337   Fax: 508/867-0351

THE Salem Cross Inn, so named for the Salem Cross mark on its front door meant to deter witch-craft and deviltry, was built in 1705 by the grand-son of Peregrine White, who was born on the *Mayflower* in Plymouth Harbor. Wood fences and fieldstone now enclose the inn's 600-acre farm, once the campground of the Wampanoags. The site endured the strain of eighteenth-century Indian raids, the French and Indian wars, and the American Revolution, and relics from the area's historic past are still found in the planting field. The richly paneled inn is furnished with American antiques, and visitors will find numerous treasures of the past here, such as the Chestnut Room's enormous fieldstone fireplace and the 42-foot-long chestnut ceiling beams made by colonial artisans. Other rooms showcase chandeliers, redware jugs, pierced tin lanterns, and old prints, as well as anti-quarian books, maps, and documents. The inn serves traditional New England fare, featuring squash muffins, seafood, beef, chowders, and Indian pudding, and guests can further enhance their dining experience with a meal cooked using the country's only known operating Clock Jack, circa 1700, a device that ensures large pieces of meat are evenly cooked.

Listed in the National Register of Historic Places

Location: West Brookfield is located in central Massachusetts, approximately 35 minutes west of Worcester on Route 9. The inn is approximately one hour from Boston's Logan International Airport and Hartford's Bradley International Airport.
Function Space: 900 square feet; 4 rooms; for meetings, meal service for up to 50 participants; up to 200 may be accommodated for receptions, and even larger groups may be accommodated outdoors with tent rentals
Food Service: Restaurant
Limitations/Restrictions: No smoking; outside liquor not permitted
Access: Handicapped accessible; on-site parking; open year-round
Payment: Cash

WOBURN

BALDWIN'S RESTAURANT
2 Alfred Street, Woburn, MA 01801
Phone: 617/932-9812

IN 1643, Deacon Henry Baldwin built a small one-room dwelling in North Woburn, the first of six phases in its evolution as Woburn's oldest building. The deacon's great-grandson, the dashing Colonel Loammi Baldwin, was a noted regional figure during the Revolution and served as superintendent of construction of the Middlesex Canal. From his orchards the colonel brought into prominence the popular Baldwin Apple, and in 1803 he enlarged his home and converted it into a Federal-style mansion. The family library, eventually numbering 4,000 volumes, was considered the finest collection of engineering books in the country. The colonel's sons, Loammi and George, also engineers, constructed the Boston and Lowell

Railroad between 1831 and 1836. In 1971 the historic mansion was moved to its present site, and in 1983 it was beautifully renovated for use as a restaurant. Baldwin's ballroom and private meeting rooms are available for business meetings, receptions, banquets, and other special occasions. Open for lunch and dinner, Baldwin's offers a menu featuring a fine selection of veal, fish, steak, and pasta dishes.

Listed in the National Register of Historic Places

Location: Woburn is 8 miles north of Boston and is accessible via I-95 and Route 38.
Function Space: 3,000 square feet; 9 rooms
Capacity—Private rooms accommodate 5 to 60 guests
Food Service: Restaurant
Access: Handicapped accessible; on-site parking; open year-round
Payment: Credit card

WORCESTER

MECHANICS HALL
321 Main Street, Worcester, MA 01608
Phone: 508/752-5608   Fax: 508/754-8442

ARTISANS and tradesmen built the stunning Mechanics Hall for the Worcester County Mechanics Association in 1857, and today many architectural historians consider it the country's finest pre-Civil War concert hall. Henry David Thoreau, Charles Dickens, John Philip Sousa, Teddy Roosevelt, Elizabeth Cady Stanton, Mel Torme, and Ella Fitzgerald are just some of the legendary figures who have been applauded here. Sweeping grand staircases ascend to the Great Hall, recognized for its outstanding acoustics and admired for its richly decorated coffered ceiling, original fresco paintings, and rows of decorative Corinthian pilasters. The hall's original muted paint scheme has been returned, following its discovery under a century's worth of accumulated coatings. The crowning showpiece of the Great Hall is the 1864 Worcester Organ, with its bold baroque facade; the 52-stop instrument is the oldest unaltered four-keyboard organ in the Western hemisphere. The Great Hall seats 1,600, but considerably smaller groups may meet in the other available rooms, including the Dickens Room, formerly a parlor; the stylish Boydon Salon, a contemporary reception area enclosed by a two-story glass facade; the refined Washburn Hall; and the Board Room.

Listed in the National Register of Historic Places

Location: Mechanics Hall is located in downtown Worcester, 39 miles west of Boston, and is accessible via the Massachusetts Turnpike (I-90) and Route 290. Amtrak and local bus service is available.

Function Space: 14,945 square feet; 5 rooms

Capacity—Conference: 450; Reception: 1,500; Banquet: 700; Theater: 1,600

Equipment On-site: Complete audiovisual equipment, digital recording studio, and professional light and sound technician services available; hall also has an assistive loop hearing system

Food Service: Recommended caterers list provided; full liquor service and professional bar staff available

Overnight Accommodations: 250 rooms available within walking distance

Limitations/Restrictions: No smoking

Access: Handicapped accessible; three parking areas near rear entrance; open year-round

Payment: Check or money order

MICHIGAN

GROSSE POINTE SHORES

EDSEL AND ELEANOR FORD HOUSE
1100 Lake Shore Road
Grosse Pointe Shores, MI 48236
Phone: 313/884-4222   Fax: 313/884-5977

THE only child of automobile magnate Henry Ford, Edsel Ford, and his wife, Eleanor, spent three years building their English Cotswold-style home. The pair traveled with architect Albert Kahn to England, researching architectural styles and structural detailing that were then incorporated into their 60-room mansion overlooking Lake St. Clair. The Fords moved into the house in 1929 during Edsel's 22-year service as president of the Ford Motor Company. Intended to house the family's stunning art collection, the mansion was designed at a high level of craftsmanship, with English artisans brought in to construct an authentic Cotswold-style stone shingle roof. Stained glass medallions accentuate the leaded glass windows, and the ceilings are hand plastered with decorative motifs. Original artwork by Cezanne and Matisse are on view, and much of the house and its contents—including oriental rugs and antique English and French furnishings—appear as they did when the Fords lived here. The grounds showcase the work of Jens Jensen, one of the country's leading landscape architects, who used only plants and trees indigenous to the Midwest. At her death in 1976, Eleanor Ford left the house and grounds for public use.

Listed in the National Register of Historic Places

Location: The Edsel and Eleanor Ford House is approximately 15 minutes from downtown Detroit, 1 hour north of Toledo, Ohio, and 4.5 hours from Chicago. Detroit City Airport and Detroit Metro Airport are 20 and 35 minutes away, respectively, and the house is accessible via I-94, I-696, and I-75.
Function Space: 17,000 square feet; 4 rooms (winter) or 5 rooms (summer)
Capacity—Banquet: 220/280; Theater: 300/350
Equipment On-site: Audiovisual equipment available
Food Service: Catering/food service available
Limitations/Restrictions: No smoking
Access: Handicapped accessibility; on-site parking; open year-round
Payment: Check, due day of event

MACKINAC ISLAND

LAKE VIEW HOTEL
1 Huron Street, Mackinac Island, MI 49757
Phone: 906/847-3384 (winter number: 906/643-6202)
Fax: 906/847-6283 (winter fax: 906/643-6441)

LAKE View Hotel, in the heart of the historic village, is one of the oldest continuously operated hotels on Mackinac Island. Built by Reuben Chapman in 1858, the hotel was originally known as Lake View House and for more than a century was operated by Chapman family members. In 1964, Harry Ryba, who made the island famous for its fabulous fudge, purchased the hotel from Chapman's grandson. Ryba's renovation and expansion of the building resulted in new guest rooms, banquet and conference facilities, two restaurants, and an impressive four-story atrium featuring the island's only indoor heated swimming pool. From banquets to business meetings, the Lake View accommodates a variety of social and corporate events, and several grades of guest rooms in both modified American and European plans are available. Since cars are not permitted on the island, visitors here enjoy a peaceful, relaxing step back in time. The Lake View Hotel captures much of the past with its Victorian-style atmosphere and nineteenth-century vernacular resort architecture. Three specialty shops are located on site, and the island also offers tennis, golf, sunset cruises, and historic sites, including Old Fort Mackinac, built in 1780.

State of Michigan Registered Historic Site

Location: Mackinac Island is accessible by an 18-minute passenger ferry boat ride from either St. Ignace or Mackinac City, on either end of Mackinac Bridge, which links Michigan's Upper and Lower Peninsulas. The island also has a paved runway for both private and charter planes. Commercial air service is available from Detroit Metro and Chicago O'Hare to Pellston Regional Airport, 16 miles south of the Mackinac Bridge. The island is accessible via I-75; exit 337 to boat lines.

Function Space: 3,000 square feet; 2 rooms
Capacity—Conference: 200; Reception: 250; Banquet: 165; Theater: 200
Equipment On-site: Projectors, microphone, podium; faxing and copying available
Food Service: Banqueting services, two restaurants
Overnight Accommodations: 85 rooms
Limitations/Restrictions: Restrictions on smoking; no pets; no cars are allowed on island—travel by foot, bicycle, or horse and carriage only
Access: Handicapped accessible; open mid-May through mid-October
Payment: Credit card (Discover, MC, Visa)

Lake View Hotel

MONROE

SAWYER HOMESTEAD

320 E. Front Street, Monroe, MI 48161
Phone: 313/242-0168

THE first white settler in Monroe, Francois Navarre, built himself a cabin on land acquired from the Potawatomi Indians in 1785. Nearly a century later the cabin, which had served as headquarters for General Winchester prior to the Battle of River Raisin in 1813, was demolished and Sawyer Homestead was constructed on the site. Dr. Alfred I. Sawyer, a leader in the field of homeopathy and twice the mayor of Monroe, had lived in the cabin with his family from 1859 to 1870, but in 1873 they moved into the new 15-room, cupola-topped Italianate mansion. The staircase was built with logs from the Navarre cabin, and the back wing of the house is a replica of that cabin. The house is now headquarters for the Monroe Women's Center, which restored the building during the 1980s. The house and grounds retain their Victorian charm, and the mansion is available for receptions, showers, dinners, and other special events. Other historic attractions in Monroe, which was renamed for the fifth U.S. president and was home to General George Custer, are the River Raisin Battlefield and the Navarre Anderson Trading Complex, portions of which date back to the late eighteenth century.

Listed in the National Register of Historic Places; state of Michigan historic site; City of Monroe historic place

Location: Monroe is less than 10 minutes from I-75 and within an hour of I-94, I-275, and US 23, and is 30 miles south of Detroit and Ann Arbor, 15 miles north of Toledo, Ohio, and 35 miles south of Windsor, Ontario, Canada.

Local airport (small aircraft), Amtrak, and bus service available.
Function Space: 3,000+ square feet; 6 rooms
Capacity—Conference: 100; Reception: 150; Banquet: 100
Equipment On-site: Slide projector and screens; other rentals available through local library
Food Service: Rental includes kitchen facilities, coffee pots, punch bowls, snack trays, cups, tables and chairs; wineglasses and silverware also available. Caterers list available
Limitations/Restrictions: No smoking
Access: Handicapped accessibility (first floor); on-site parking; open year-round
Payment: Check

PETOSKEY

STAFFORD'S PERRY HOTEL

Bay and Lewis Streets, Petoskey, MI 49770
Phone: 616/347-4000   Fax: 616/347-0636

BUILT in 1899 when Petoskey already boasted 11 resort hotels, the Perry was the town's first brick hotel, and it has remained a landmark in the historic Gaslight District ever since. For a century, Petoskey has been a popular Midwestern summer retreat, characterized by Victorian homes and "gingerbread" cottages set on rolling hills overlooking Little Traverse Bay. Today, Stafford's Perry is the only original downtown hotel still in existence, and its restoration has enhanced the yellow and white building's old-fashioned charm. Meeting space is available for conferences and business gatherings, and social events such as weddings, reunions, and other private parties are also welcome. The bright guest rooms, individually appointed, feature colorful turn-of-the-century wallpaper patterns, and some rooms offer balconies and views of the bay.

Dining options include the H. O. Rose Room, which serves international and American fare, and the Noggin Room Pub. Numerous recreational activities are available nearby, including skiing, golf, and boating, and Traverse City, Mackinac Island, and Tahquamenon Falls make for easy day trips. In town, art studios, antique galleries, parks, and the picturesque Penn Plaza railroad depot offer pleasant diversions as well.

Listed in the National Register of Historic Places

Location: Petoskey is located at the foot of Lake Michigan's Little Traverse Bay, 17 miles from airport service in Pellston, 70 miles from Traverse City, 3.5 hours from Grand Rapids, and 5 hours from Detroit. Petoskey is accessible via Highways 31 and 131.
Function Space: 2,000 square feet; 3 rooms
Capacity—Conference: 75; Reception: 35–150; Banquet: 35–150; Theater: 75
Equipment On-site: TV/VCR, overhead projector, screen, fax
Food Service: Catering/food service available; restaurant, pub, lounge
Overnight Accommodations: 80 rooms
Limitations/Restrictions: No pets
Access: Handicapped accessibility; on-site parking; open year-round
Payment: Credit card or direct bill

ROCHESTER

MEADOW BROOK HALL
Oakland University, Rochester, MI 48309-4401
Phone: 810/370-3140   Fax: 810/370-4260

INSPIRED by the English country houses of the sixteenth century, the 100-room Meadow Brook Hall is a magnificent architectural landmark, possessing a quality of craftsmanship that would perhaps be irreplaceable today. In 1929, Alfred G. and Matilda Dodge Wilson, widow of the late auto pioneer John Dodge, completed their $4 million mansion that boasts Tudor and Elizabethan-era design elements and occupies a manorial, parklike setting. In 1957 the Wilsons gave the 1,400-acre estate, as well as a $2 million cash donation, to found Oakland University. Following Matilda's death 10 years later, ownership of their residence transferred to the university, whose is commitment to the preservation and interpretation of the architecture, grounds, and original art and furnishings includes sharing the mansion and its history with the community. Meadow Brook Hall, which opened to the public in 1971, can accommodate large receptions and conferences, and the spacious grounds can be tented to increase capacity. The hall is also open for daily public tours.

Listed in the National Register of Historic Places and the Michigan Register of Historic Sites

Location: Meadow Brook Hall is approximately 25 miles north of Detroit on the east campus of Oakland University and 5 minutes from I–75. Bishop International/Flint and Detroit Metropolitan Airports are approximately 45 and 75 minutes away, respectively.

Meadow Brook Hall

Function Space: 5,557 square feet; 10 rooms
Capacity—Conference: 18 (56 total); Reception: 200 (620 total, additional 800 with tent); Banquet: 120 (296 total, plus additional 400 in tent); Theater: 150 (200 total, additional 600 in tent); Classroom: 50 (80 total); summer tent overlooks gardens and grounds adjacent to house
Equipment On-site: Lectern with microphone included at no charge, additional audiovisual equipment available for rental; fax and photocopying also available
Food Service: On-site caterer provides full food and beverage service; Meadow Brook Hall is licensed for alcoholic beverages

Limitations/Restrictions: Meadow Brook Hall is a cultural program of Oakland University; original furnishings and art objects remain in place to enhance the Meadow Brook experience, and guests using the house must respect guidelines for use of the facility; no smoking inside the house; guests may not bring food or beverages into the house; residential guests are required to sign in on arrival and sign out on departure
Access: Handicapped accessible; on-site parking; open year-round
Payment: Cash, check, credit card (MC, Visa)

MINNESOTA

LUTSEN

CASCADE LODGE

HC3 Box 445, Lutsen, MN 55612
Phone: 218/387-1112 or 800-322-9543
Fax: 218/387-1113

SERENELY overlooking Lake Superior, the Cascade Lodge enjoys a picturesque setting in the midst of Cascade State Park. The main lodge dates back to 1939, although some of the surrounding cabins were built in the 1920s. Guests may stay in the main lodge, motel units, cabins, (some of which come with fireplaces and kitchenettes), or the Cascade House, which accommodates 12 people. Open year-round, the lodge offers a full range of recreational activities, and excellent hiking and cross-country ski trails through a forest of birch, pine, and maple start at the lodge; the area also offers fishing, biking, canoeing, tennis, and golf. At nearby Lutsen Mountain skiers will find the longest runs and steepest drops in the upper Midwest. The rustic on-site North Shore Restaurant, with its north woods decor and lake view, offers breakfast, lunch, and dinner, and features local seafood and home-baked desserts. The living room of the main lodge, with its relaxing lakeside view, is available for meetings and social events.

Location: Cascade Lodge is 100 miles north of Duluth and about five hours from Minneapolis/St. Paul, midway between Lusten and Grand Marais, in the Cascade State Park on Highway 61. Air service is available in Duluth.
Function Space: 580 square feet; 1 room
Capacity—Conference: 40; Reception: 60; Theater: 50
Equipment On-site: VCR, overhead projector, fax
Food Service: Restaurant
Overnight Accommodations: 30 rooms
Limitations/Restrictions: Nonsmoking in Main Lodge; alcoholic beverages are not served
Access: On-site parking; open year-round
Payment: Cash, check, credit card

PIPESTONE

HISTORIC CALUMET INN

104 W. Main Street, Pipestone, MN 56164
Phone: 507/825-5871 Fax: 507/825-4578

LOCATED in the Pipestone Commercial Historic District, the Historic Calumet Inn is continuing its tradition as a grand hotel. Built jointly with a bank at the corner of Hiawatha Avenue and Main Street in 1888, the hotel opened on Thanksgiving Day and replaced Pipestone's first grand hotel, which had been destroyed by fire the year before. The Calumet's name comes from the word French fur traders used to refer to Indian ceremonial pipes. Sioux quartzite, the primary building stone, was quarried from nearby Jasper, and quarries surrounding Pipestone provided darker stone for the hotel's trim. In 1900 and again in 1913 the hotel was enlarged, and an extensive renovation and restoration of the building was completed in 1981. Visitors may dine in the dining room and relax in Eddie's Pub; meetings and social events are held in the Pocahontas Room. What was once the bank is now the lounge, and today the old vault functions as a wine cellar. Nearby attractions include Pipestone National Monument and Fort Pipestone, and numerous historic buildings can be seen or visited on downtown walking tours.

Listed in the National Register of Historic Places

Location: The Calumet Inn is located six blocks east of Highways 75 and 23 on Main Street, or four blocks north of Highway 30. Pipestone is 50 miles from airport service in Sioux Falls, South Dakota. Daytime taxi service is available.
Function Space: 1,000 square feet; 1 room
Capacity—Conference: 30; Reception: 75; Banquet: 60; Theater: 75
Equipment On-site: TV/VCR, chalkboard, fax, photocopy machine
Food Service: Breakfast with room; dining room, lounge, pub
Overnight Accommodations: 38 rooms
Limitations/Restrictions: No pets
Access: Handicapped accessible; on-site parking; open year-round
Payment: Cash, check, credit card (AmEx, DC, Discover, MC, Visa)

RED WING

ST. JAMES HOTEL
406 Main Street, Red Wing, MN 55066
Phone: 612/388-2846 or 800-252-1875
Fax: 612/388-5226

THE city of Red Wing, situated between picturesque limestone bluffs on the Mississippi River, enjoyed great prosperity in the 1870s as the world's primary wheat market, and as testament to

their success local businessmen built the St. James Hotel in 1875. The Lillyblad family ran the hotel for 72 years, and proprietress Clara Lillyblad's reputation for excellent dining was such that trains would regularly stop so that passengers could come in for a meal. Reflecting Clara's legendary repasts, the Hotel St. James offers several dining options in its two restaurants and "very British" pub. The Italianate hotel was restored to its 1870s appearance shortly after its centennial anniversary and is graciously furnished with Victorian antiques and reproductions. The individually appointed guest rooms are named for nineteenth-century riverboats, and many rooms enjoy river views. A wide range of function rooms with period settings are available for corporate meetings, educational programs, receptions, and other events. Located in the downtown historic district, the St. James Hotel is convenient to shopping and the historic pottery area, and Levee Park is right outside the hotel's back door.

Listed in the National Register of Historic Places; member of Historic Hotels of America

Location: Red Wing is located 60 miles south of the Twin Cities and the Minneapolis/St. Paul International Airport. The St. James Hotel is located on Highway 61 and is accessible via I-94 and Highways 63 and 58. Cab and bus service available.
Function Space: 14,385 square feet; 12 rooms
Capacity—Conference: 40; Reception: 350; Banquet: 300; Theater: 300
Equipment On-site: Audiovisual equipment, fax, photocopier available
Food Service: Catering/food service available; two restaurants, pub
Overnight Accommodations: 60 rooms
Limitations/Restrictions: Restrictions on smoking; no pets

Access: Handicapped accessible; on-site parking; open year-round
Payment: Check or credit card

St. Paul

The Saint Paul Hotel
350 Market Street, St. Paul, MN 55102
Phone: 612/292-9292   Fax: 612/228-9506

HANDSOME Italian Renaissance Revival architecture distinguishes the Saint Paul Hotel, a luxury European-style hotel built in 1910. Comfortable guest rooms are equipped with PC adapters, voice mail, and well-lit workspace, and a complimentary morning newspaper is delivered daily. A variety of meeting spaces are available for business and social functions, including an executive boardroom, ballrooms, and meeting rooms for breakout sessions or other small gatherings. Seven suites are also available for meetings of 10 or fewer. Writing tablets, candy, ice water, and telephones are all standard in hotel meeting rooms. The Saint Paul boasts two award-winning restaurants—the St. Paul Grill, an East Coast-style bar and grill, and the Cafe, which serves American regional cuisine. Located in the center of Minnesota's capital city, the hotel is within walking distance of the St. Paul Convention Center, the Landmark Center, and the renowned Ordway Music Center, and the city's indoor skyway system connects the hotel to business, retail, and entertainment venues. Complimentary transportation to business and entertainment centers is also available.

Member of Historic Hotels of America

Location: The Saint Paul Hotel is in downtown St. Paul, accessible from I–35E and I–94.
Function Space: 11,000 square feet; 9 rooms
Capacity—Conference: 450; Reception: 500; Banquet: 350; Theater: 260
Equipment On-site: Audiovisual equipment and business services available, including fax, telex, administrative support, shipping and receiving
Food Service: Catering/food service available; two restaurants on-site; room service
Overnight Accomodations: 254 rooms
Limitations/Restrictions: Restrictions on smoking; no outside catering or food permitted
Access: Handicapped accessible; on-site parking; open year-round
Payment: Direct bill

Stillwater

Washington County Historic Courthouse
101 W. Pine Street, Stillwater, MN 55082
Phone: 612/430-6233   Fax: 612/430-6245

PERCHED on "Zion's Hill," overlooking the Mississippi River, Washington County's magnificent courthouse is the oldest standing courthouse in Minnesota. Following the Civil War, plans for westward expansion and a successful economy resulted in both a thriving community and the need for a new, grand courthouse. The 1870 landmark structure above Stillwater boasts 11 chimneys and features a double portico of stacked arches and a graceful dome capped by a small cupola. Architect Augustus F. Knight gave the brick courthouse an Italianate touch, and the handsome building is surrounded by gently sloping lawns. For more than a century the courthouse operated as the county's administrative and judicial center; in

Washington County Historic Courthouse
(Gudrun Nordby)

1975 the last of the county offices moved out. Today the historic courthouse is an excellent example of adaptive use and hosts a variety of social and business gatherings, including meetings, seminars, lectures, weddings, reunions, and concerts. Group tours by appointment are available, and history-related exhibits and historical reenactments are just some of the activities to be found at the courthouse.

Listed in the National Register of Historic Places

Location: Stillwater is 25 miles from St. Paul on the Mississippi River and 40 miles from Minneapolis/St. Paul Interntional Airport; accessible via I–94.

Function Space: 2,200 square feet; 1 room
Capacity—Conference: 50–100; Reception: 200; Banquet: 200; Theater: 125
Equipment On-site: Equipment available for rent (TV/VCR, public address system, overhead projector, tables); chairs provided
Food Service: Client selects caterer
Limitations/Restrictions: No smoking; alcohol limited to beer, wine, champagne
Access: Handicapped accessible; on-site parking; open year-round
Payment: Check, in advance

MISSISSIPPI

JACKSON

FAIRVIEW INN

734 Fairview Street, Jackson, MS 39202
Phone: 601/948-3429   Fax: 601/948-1203

RECALLING the South's antebellum era with its classical facade, the Fairview Inn was actually built in 1908. Robert Closson Spencer, a close associate of Frank Lloyd Wright, built the three-story Colonial Revival mansion for lumber tycoon Cyrus G. Warren. The house is one of the few architec-turally designed homes remaining in Jackson, and since 1930 it has been in the Simmons family. Set on two lush acres with formal gardens and beautiful lawns, the house is flanked by flowering magnolia and crepe myrtle trees. The richly decorated foyer, from its Venetian marble floor to its transept ceiling, offers an elegant setting for the large crystal chandelier that once hung in the Byrne Plantation home in Natchez. Overnight guests stay in charmingly decorated rooms filled with antiques and in the morning are treated to a full breakfast. Since opening in 1993, the Fairview Inn has become a popular site for weddings, although its lovely garden room may be used for a variety of other functions as well. Small meetings and conferences may be held in the carriage house or in the library, amid Civil War books and a collection of miniature pewter soldiers.

Fairview Inn

Listed in the National Register of Historic Places

Location: The Fairview Inn is in the residential Belhaven neighborhood of Jackson, the state capital, and is accessible via I–55, Exit 98A. Taxi service is available from Jackson International Airport, 10 miles from the inn.
Function Space: 3,200 square feet; 3 rooms
Capacity—Conference: 50; Reception: 500; Banquet: 150; Theater: 200
Equipment On-site: Phone, fax, photocopying, dataport, typewriter; other equipment may be rented from outside source
Food Service: Breakfast with room, catering/food service provided on-site
Overnight Accommodations: 8 rooms
Limitations/Restrictions: No smoking; no outside food brought in; alcoholic beverages may be provided by host
Access: Handicapped accessible; on-site parking; open year-round
Payment: Check or credit card

LONG BEACH

RED CREEK INN, VINEYARD & RACING STABLE

7416 Red Creek Road, Long Beach, MS 39560
Phone: 601/452-3080   Fax: 601/452-4450

THIS circa-1899 raised French cottage is situated on 11.5 acres of fragrant magnolias and ancient live oaks, two of which are registered with the Live Oak Society. The three-story brick and cypress inn is furnished with antiques, and rooms have distinctive Victorian, French, and English decor. Red Creek's gracious atmosphere is enhanced by a 64-foot front porch with swings, as well as the inn's six fireplaces, wooden radios, and a working Victrola and pump organ. The newest additions to the inn

are the vineyard and the stables, which are still under development. The Red Creek Inn hosts a variety of functions in the dining room and living room, ranging from business meetings to receptions, and the grounds may be tented to accommodate larger groups; guest room rates include a continental-plus breakfast. Located near the beach yet out in the country, the Red Creek Inn is a convenient base from which to explore miles of beach along the Mississippi coast. Numerous golf courses, casinos, and other attractions are nearby, including several historic sites, such as "Beauvoir," Jefferson Davis's last home.

Location: The Red Creek Inn is 7 miles from Gulfport-Biloxi Regional Airport and 20 minutes west of Biloxi via I–10 or Highway 90.
Function Space: 675 square feet; 2 rooms
Capacity—Reception: 50; Banquet: 10; use of grounds can accommodate up to 200
Equipment On-site: VCR, fax, typewriter
Food Service: Breakfast with room; inn will assist in arranging catering
Overnight Accommodations: 7 rooms (the inn can place additional guests at other nearby accommodations)
Limitations/Restrictions: No smoking; no pets indoors
Access: On-site parking; open year-round
Payment: Cash, check

NATCHEZ

MONMOUTH PLANTATION

36 Melrose Avenue, Natchez, MS 39120

Phone: 601/442-5852 or 800-828-4531

Fax: 601/446-7762

MEXICAN war hero General John Anthony Quitman purchased Monmouth Plantation in 1826 as a gift for his new wife, Eliza Turner. Built in 1818, Monmouth was originally a two-story Federal-style brick mansion, but in 1854 the general transformed the house into an imposing Greek Revival structure. Visitors included Jefferson Davis and Henry Clay. Several of the Quitman daughters lived here during the Civil War, but Union damage to the house began a period of deterioration. Today the restored mansion, considered one of the most romantic inns in America, boasts an antebellum splendor on 26 acres of beautifully landscaped grounds and gardens. Nestled in the woods are the original plantation stables that now serve as a meeting facility for group retreats and corporate gatherings. The inn itself features elegant period art and furnishings, and guest room rates include a full Southern breakfast. Located in historic Natchez, Monmouth offers a tantalizing look at the Old South, and nearby attractions include more than 500 antebellum structures and the Natchez Trace Parkway, originally an Indian trail and later a pioneer route, which stretches to Nashville, Tennessee.

National Historic Landmark; listed in the National Register of Historic Places; member of Historic Hotels of America

Location: Natchez is located on the Mississippi River in southwestern Mississippi at the intersection of Highways 61 and 84 and is 3 hours from New Orleans, 1.5 hours from Baton Rouge,

Louisiana; 2 hours from Jackson.

Function Space: 1,680 square feet; 1 room

Capacity—Conference: 35; Reception: 115; Banquet: 80; Theater: 125

Equipment On-site: Slide and overhead projectors, screen, VCR and monitor, flip charts, fax

Food Service: Breakfast with room; catering/food service available; restaurant and full-service bar

Overnight Accommodations: 27 rooms and suites

Limitations/Restrictions: No smoking

Access: Handicapped accessible; on-site parking; open year-round

Payment: Check, credit card

VICKSBURG

SOUTHERN CULTURAL HERITAGE COMPLEX

(Mailing address)

P.O. Box 150, Vicksburg, MS 39181-0150

(Street addresss)

1021 Crawford Street, Vicksburg, MS 39180

Phone: 601/631-2997   Fax: 601/634-4519

RECOGNIZED as an important Mississippi landmark, the Southern Cultural Heritage Complex comprises the buildings and grounds once belonging to the historic St. Francis Xavier Convent and Academy. The city block of buildings date from 1830 to 1953 and trace American architectural history from the original Greek Revival convent to a mid-twentieth-century gymnasium. The Sisters of Mercy purchased the older facilities in 1860, but by 1862 closed the school to assist wounded Union and Confederate soldiers throughout Mississippi. At different times armies from both the North and the South used Cobb House as a barracks, and it was here´that Jefferson Davis addressed the citizens of Vicksburg in 1869 following his release from prison. In 1868 the Sisters built a new, four-story convent building, now regarded as one of the best preserved examples of nineteenth-century Gothic Revival architecture in the state. After relocating to modern facilities, the Sisters sold their school to the city of Vicksburg in 1994 for use as an artistic, cultural, and educational center. Small corporate board meetings and large receptions are easily accommodated, and the center will provide guests with a slide presentation and tour of the complex upon request.

Listed in the National Register of Historic Places; designated Mississippi Landmark

Location: The Southern Cultural Heritage Complex is located in the heart of Vicksburg's downtown historic district and is accessible via I–20.

Function Space: 7,000 square feet; 3 rooms
Capacity—Conference: 250; Reception: 500; Banquet: 300; Theater: 300
Equipment On-site: Slide projector, screen, public address system
Food Service: In-house or outside catering; coffee and snacks available; several restaurants are located within easy walking distance
Overnight Accommodations: Available nearby
Limitations/Restrictions: No smoking; alcohol may be consumed but not sold on-site
Access: Auditorium handicapped accessible; on-site parking, open year-round
Payment: check, credit card (MC, Visa)

MISSOURI

KANSAS CITY

SOUTHMORELAND ON THE PLAZA— AN URBAN INN

116 E. 46th Street, Kansas City, MO 64112
Phone: 816/531-7979   Fax: 816/531-2407

SOUTHMORELAND on the Plaza has earned awards both for its service as an inn and as an excellent example of historic preservation. The three-story Colonial Revival mansion, built in 1913, was completely renovated and opened for business in 1990. As an urban inn, Southmoreland on the Plaza offers amenities especially attractive to business travelers, including variable breakfast menus and times, airport shuttle availability, and workspace, as well as the comforts of home. The guest rooms are named and decorated for prominent Kansas City figures, such as Thomas Hart Benton, Satchel Paige, and Clara and Russell Stover. Groups of 14 or fewer may use the entire first floor, which includes the New England-style dining room, solarium, living room, and covered verandah. Groups also can arrange for a picnic on the verandah or order gourmet sack lunches to take along on afternoon outings. Guest rates include breakfast, afternoon wine and hors d'oeuvres, and sports and dining privileges at a nearby historic private club. The inn is located in the Southmoreland Historic District and is within walking distance of the Crown Center and the Nelson-Atkins Art Gallery and Museum.

Location: Southmoreland is a block and a half off the Country Club Plaza, 20 minutes south of downtown Kansas City and 20 minutes from I–70. Kansas City International Airport is 15 miles northwest via I–29.
Function Space: 950 square feet; 4 rooms
Capacity—Conference: 18
Equipment On-site: VCR, overhead projector and screen, dry-erase easels; fax and photocopier available
Food Service: Breakfast with room, catering/food service available
Overnight Accommodations: 12 rooms
Limitations/Restrictions: No smoking
Access: Handicapped accessible; on-site parking; open year-round
Payment: Check or credit card (AmEx, MC, Visa)

ST. LOUIS

CROWNE PLAZA MAJESTIC

1019 Pine Street, St. Louis, MO 63101
Phone: 314/436-2355 or 800-451-2355
Fax: 314/436-0223

A remarkable renovation and restoration during the 1980s returned the Crowne Plaza Majestic to its original 1913 grandeur, when it was designed as an elegant European-style hotel. The nine-story Italian Renaissance Revival hotel is furnished in comfortable, neutral tones with coffered ceilings, antiques, and fine reproduction furniture. The spacious, larger-than-average guest rooms and suites are individually furnished with poster beds and chintz fabrics, and guests receive complimentary in-room coffee service and a continental breakfast. Smaller get-togethers can be held in Just Jazz, the hotel's lively restaurant and nightspot, while larger groups gathering for business meetings or parties can meet in the private salons. Just Jazz, which features contemporary American cuisine and some of the finest live jazz in the Midwest, offers an intimate atmosphere amid red oak, marble, and brass decor. From its downtown location, the Crowne Plaza Majestic is convenient to a number of fine restaurants and shops, as well as other attractions, including Busch Stadium and the spectacular Gateway Arch.

Listed in the National Register of Historic Places; member of Historic Hotels of America

Location: The Crowne Plaza Majestic is located in downtown St. Louis, between 10th and 11th Streets on Pine Street, and is four blocks from I–40/64. The hotel is 20 minutes from St. Louis Lambert International Airport and just two blocks from a Metrolink stop.
Function Space: 1,800 square feet; 2 rooms
Capacity—Conference: 45; Reception: 120; Banquet: 90; Theater: 50
Equipment On-site: Audiovisual equipment and business services available
Food Service: Breakfast with room; restaurant, room service
Overnight Accommodations: 91 rooms

Grandel Theatre *(Alise O'Brien)*

Access: Handicapped accessible; on-site parking; open year-round
Payment: Cash, check, credit card

GRANDEL THEATRE

(Mailing address)
Grand Center, Inc.
634 N. Grand Boulevard #10A
St. Louis, MO 63103
(Street address)
3610 Grandel Square, St. Louis, MO 63108
Phone: 314/533-1884   Fax: 314/533-3345

THE distinctive Grandel Theatre, which opened in 1992, was St. Louis's first new theater in a quarter century, but it is housed in a beautiful Romanesque Revival church built back in 1884. Constructed from a design by Lewis Frederick Rice, the theater maintains the Greek cross design in its original woodwork and its 50-foot buttressed ceilings. The Grand Hall, with its striking 26-foot-high vaulted ceiling and 12-foot arched leaded glass windows, enhances the Old World atmosphere. The lobby will hold up to 120 people for a reception, and the theater seats 470 (320 on the orchestra level, 150 in the balcony). The renovated building features modern amenities, including catering facilities and an elevator, but noteworthy architectural features have been preserved as well, such as the carved newel posts on the staircase. The Grandel Theatre is part of the historic Grand Center Arts and Entertainment District, which comprises a number of cultural and educational facilities.

Location: The Grandel Theatre is 10 minutes from downtown, a half-mile

from Grand Metrolink Station, and is easily
accessible to I–70, I–64/40, and I–44.
Function Space: 9,800 square feet; 3 rooms
Capacity—Conference: 225; Reception: 225;
Banquet: 150; Theater: 470
Equipment On-site: Basic sound system and
podium; other audiovisual equipment available
through outside source
Food Service: Catering available
Limitations/Restrictions: No smoking
Access: Handicapped accessible; on-site parking;
open year-round
Payment: Cashier's check

HYATT REGENCY ST. LOUIS AT UNION STATION

(Mailing address)
One Union Station
(Street address)
1820 Market, St. Louis, MO 63103
Phone: 314/231-1234   Fax: 314/923-3970

Hyatt Regency St. Louis at Union Station

THE Hyatt Regency St. Louis captures the
grandeur of America's railroading past in its
remarkable setting—the restored St. Louis Union
Station, which at its peak was the country's largest
and busiest railroad terminal. Built in 1894, the
restored Romanesque structure is the centerpiece of
a revitalized 100-acre area comprising specialty
shops, restaurants, entertainment venues, a bier-
garten, and even an 11-acre glass-enclosed train
shed with an indoor lake, in addition to four active
train tracks. The Hyatt's main lobby, formerly the
station's Grand Hall, boasts a spectacular six-story
barrel-vaulted ceiling, magnificent stained glass
windows, and the famous "Whispering Arch," and
the guest rooms also reflect the station's turn-of-
the-century elegance. The flexible meeting and
banqueting facilities can accommodate functions
ranging from small meetings to conferences and
large receptions. American cuisine is featured at the
hotel's renowned Station Grille, and the exclusive
private dining room of station architect Theodore
Carl Link, with its "railroad baron" atmosphere,
is available for functions. Located downtown, the
Hyatt is convenient to the city's business and
financial centers, as well as Busch Stadium and
the Gateway Arch.

National Historic Landmark; listed in the National
Register of Historic Places; member of Historic Hotels
of America

Location: The Hyatt Regency St. Louis at Union Station is 20 minutes from Lambert Field International Airport and is on the Gateway Arch/Airport MetroLink Lightrail System.
Function Space: 35,000 square feet; 22 rooms
Capacity—Conference: 72; Reception: 1,800; Banquet: 1,500; Theater: 1,600

Equipment On-site: Complete audiovisual equipment and business services available
Food Service: Catering/food service available; two restaurants, room service
Overnight Accommodations: 538 rooms
Access: Handicapped accessible; on-site parking; open year-round
Payment: Major credit card

MONTANA

LEWISTOWN

THE SKY BALLROOM, MEGAHERTZ BUILDING

223 W. Main, Lewistown, MT 59457

Phone: 406/538-8531

Fax: 406/538-8531 (Same as phone)

KENT and Bell, designers of Montana's state capitol building, are also credited with Lewistown's first bank, the Bank of Fergus County. This handsome Renaissance Revival/Beaux Arts structure of sandstone and brick was built in 1904, but in 1930 the bank building became home to the Elks, which operated here for the next 30 years. In 1992, Megahertz Fabrics bought the historic building and began a complete rehabilitation. The main floor retains its original hardwood, beamed, paneled 14-foot ceilings and beveled glass doors. Created by the Elks, the Sky Ballroom features a ceiling of painted clouds and a 2,000-square-foot maple dance floor. The Sky Ballroom hosts weddings, parties, reunions, meetings, and conferences, and restaurants and overnight accommodations are nearby. Lewistown is a particularly good base from which to explore central Montana, and numerous cross-country ski runs, some on old mining and logging trails, are less than an hour away. There are also plenty of opportunities for hunting and fishing in the area, and during the summer the CR Kendall Gold Mine offers free tours.

Location: Lewistown is located in central Montana, 100 miles southeast of Great Falls and 130 miles north of Billings on Highway 87; Lewistown Airport, 1.5 miles away, serves small commuter planes from Great Falls and Billings only.

Function Space: 2,500 square feet; 1 room

Capacity—Conference: 150; Reception: 150; Banquet: 100

Equipment On-site: Microphone not needed; CD/cassette player and speakers available; piano; tables and chairs included in rental

Food Service: Outside catering and kitchen preparation area available

Limitations/Restrictions: No smoking; facility not handicapped accessible

Access: Parking nearby; open year-round

Payment: Check, credit card (Discover, MC, Visa)

Megahurtz Building
(Jane Raven OKeefe)

RED LODGE

THE POLLARD

(Mailing address)
P.O. Box 650
(Street address)
2 North Broadway, Red Lodge, MT 59068
Phone: 406/446-0001   Fax: 406/446-0002

BORN on the Fourth of July in 1893, the Pollard was the first brick building in the historic mining town of Red Lodge, and over the years the hotel acquired a number of other historic associations. Guests included William Jennings Bryan, Frederic Remington, Buffalo Bill Cody, Calamity Jane, and the noted Indian scout Jeremiah "Liver Eatin' " Johnson. The Pollard changed hands in 1991 with the flip of a coin, and the restored hotel's rich pine furnishings and oak paneling once again impart a Western turn-of-the-century atmosphere. Conference facilities accommodate business meetings, retreats, and social gatherings, and guest rooms are available with mountain views, hot tubs, and steam baths. Room rates include breakfast, and the hotel's restaurant, Greenlee's at the Pollard, offers traditional and contemporary fare that changes seasonally, as well as an award-winning wine list. A health club, racquetball courts, and sauna are available, while numerous outdoor recreational opportunities abound in the surrounding Big Sky country. Located in the Red Lodge Historic District, the Pollard is situated at the end of the Beartooth Highway, within reach of the scenic wonders of Yellowstone and the Grand Tetons.

Listed in the National Register of Historic Places; member of Historic Hotels of America

Location: Red Lodge is just north of the Wyoming border, 60 miles from the airport at either Billings, Montana, or Cody, Wyoming.
Function Space: 2,000 square feet; 3 rooms
Capacity—Conference: 50; Reception: 75; Banquet: 30; Theater: 60
Equipment On-site: TV, VCR, overhead and slide projectors; photocopying and faxing available

The Pollard

Food Service: Breakfast with room; banquet service available; restaurant
Overnight Accommodations: 36 rooms
Limitations/Restrictions: No smoking
Access: Handicapped accessible; on-site parking; open year-round
Payment: Cash, check, credit card (AmEx, Discover, MC, Visa)

THREE FORKS

SACAJAWEA INN

(Mailing address)
P.O. Box 648
(Street address)
5 Main Street, Three Forks, MT 59752
Phone: 406/285-6575   Fax: 406/285-4210
E-mail: sacinn@aol.com

WITH its long, welcoming front porch that runs the length of the building, the Sacajawea Inn has been a pleasing stop for travelers since the early 1900s. Portions of the inn built in 1882 were rolled on logs from their original location near the confluence of the Jefferson, Madison, and Gallatin Rivers to the inn's present site on higher ground. The main building was completed in 1910 as a stop for passengers traveling to Yellowstone National Park on the Milwaukee Railroad. Today the renovated three-story Sacajawea Inn combines modern amenities with its turn-of-the-century atmosphere and antique-inspired furnishings. Modern conference facilities, as well as indoor and outdoor dining options, are available for business and social events, and guests stay in comfortable rooms decorated with an old-fashioned touch. The Sacajawea Inn is a good base for retracing Lewis and Clark's footsteps in southwestern Montana and exploring the Gallatin Valley and nearby Yellowstone National Park. There are also excellent opportunities in the area to fish, ski, golf, hike, bike, and canoe.

Listed in the National Register of Historic Places

Location: Three Forks is 28 miles west of Bozeman and 50 miles east of Butte. Airport service is available in town and in Bozeman. The Sacajawea Inn is 2 miles from I–90 (Exit 278).
Function Space: 1,000 square feet; 1 room
Capacity—Conference: 60; Reception: 80; Banquet: 90; Theater: 90
Equipment On-site: Public address system, overhead and slide projectors
Food Service: Restaurant
Overnight Accommodations: 33 rooms
Limitations/Restrictions: No smoking; beer and wine license
Access: Handicapped accessible; on-site parking; open year-round
Payment: Check, credit card (AmEx, MC, Visa)

Sacajawea Inn

NEBRASKA

CRAWFORD

FORT ROBINSON STATE PARK

(Mailing address)
P.O. Box 392
(Street address)
3200 W. Highway 20, Crawford, NE 69339
Phone: 308/665-2900 Fax: 308/665-2906

THE Sioux Expedition established Camp Robinson in 1874 to protect the Red Cloud Indian Agency, which was responsible for distributing goods to area tribes. In September 1877 the Sioux warrior Crazy Horse, who had surrendered 889 members of his tribe at the camp just four months earlier, was killed while trying to escape. The camp was renamed a fort in 1878, and it later became a regimental headquarters calvary post. During the late 1930s the U.S. Olympic equestrian team trained at the fort, and German POWs were held here during World War II, after which the area was turned over to the Department of Agriculture as a research station. Today the fort encompasses 22,000 acres and a number of restored historic buildings, including late-nineteenth- and early-twentieth century officers' quarters, that provide guest lodging. Howard Dodd Hall, located in the lodge, is available for business and social events. Also on-site is the Fort Robinson Museum and the Trailside Museum, and recreational activities include stagecoach, trail, and hayrack rides, swimming, golf, biking, rodeo events, and chuck wagon cookouts.

Location: Fort Robinson State Park is located in northwestern Nebraska on Highway 20.
Function Space: 1 room
Capacity—150 seated
Equipment On-site: TV/VCR
Food Service: Catering/food service available; restaurant
Overnight Accommodations: 22 rooms in lodge; 24 cabins, 7 brick units, ranch house, former officers' quarters also available
Limitations/Restrictions: Alcohol not allowed in park without permit (2-hour maximum); permit available at Park Office
Access: Limited handicapped accessibility; on-site parking; open April to mid-November
Payment: Cash, check, credit card (MC, Visa)

OMAHA

THE WESTIN AQUILA HOTEL

1615 Howard Street, Omaha, NE 68102
Phone: 402/342-2222 Fax: 402/342-2569

AS a prototype for the modern urban building, the four-story, U-shaped Aquila Court building comprised offices, shops, an art institute, and apartments when it opened in 1924. The Cook family of Chicago built the Aquila Court in downtown Omaha, naming it for family patriarch Aquila Cook. Filling half a city block, the neoclassical building features Italian design elements, having drawn much of its inspiration from the Bargello Palace in Florence, Italy. After serving as Omaha's premier office building for nearly seven decades, it reopened in 1995 as the city's only luxury hotel, and even with its conversion from offices much of the Aquila's architectural and historical integrity remains intact. Built of buff Indiana limestone, the hotel's elegant interiors include Brazilian cherry wood floors, travertine stone walls, mahogany woodwork, oriental rugs, tapestries, and crystal chandeliers. Twenty luxury suites overlook the courtyard and reflecting pool, and meeting space is available for a variety of social and business gatherings. The full-service, upscale Amadeus Room serves continental cuisine, and cocktails are available at Dr. Eugene's Pub, named for a dentist whose office was in the Aquila Court for many years. The hotel is within walking distance of theaters and the historic Old Market district.

Listed in the National Register of Historic Places; member of Historic Hotels of America

Location: The Westin Aquila is just off I-80 in downtown Omaha and is 3 miles from Eppley Airfield; the hotel offers complimentary airport shuttle service on the half-hour.
Function Space: 6,500 square feet; 9 rooms
Capacity—Conference: 40; Reception: 200; Banquet: 140; Theater: 200
Equipment On-site: Audiovisual equipment and business services available
Food Service: Catering/food service available; restaurant, pub, 24-hour room service
Overnight Accommodations: 146 rooms
Access: Handicapped accessible; on-site parking; open year-round
Payment: Credit card

NEVADA

LAS VEGAS

HUNTRIDGE THEATRE

1208 E. Charleston Boulevard
Las Vegas, NV 89104
Phone: 702/477-7069   Fax: 702/477-0887

HI, Neighbor and *Hellzapoppin'* were on the bill when the Huntridge Theatre opened in 1944. The theater is one of the few remaining examples of postmodern theater architecture left in the United States, and in a city known for its spectacular newer buildings, the Huntridge is an important link to another era. Distinguished by its 75-foot sign overhead, the theater was restored and renovated in 1992, and many of its original decorative features remain. Today the theater is an active venue for concerts, plays, and musicals and is also available for rehearsal space, video production, lectures, large business meetings and conventions, and other presentations. The stage measures 59 feet wide by 24 feet deep with a 40-foot proscenium. Other features include a 50-foot movie screen, production and dressing rooms, complete sound and lighting systems, and a 700-square-foot loading dock and roll-up door to center stage. Las Vegas's world-famous hotels on the Strip are just minutes away, and nearby Hoover Dam makes for both a fascinating and easy day trip.

Listed in the National Register of Historic Places

Location: The Huntridge Theatre is 4 minutes from downtown Las Vegas and 15 minutes from McCarran International Airport. The theater is accessible via I-15 and Highway 95; Los Angeles is 4.5 hours away and Phoenix is 6 hours away.
Function Space: 12,000 square feet; 1 room
Capacity—Theater: 600 seated, 800 concert-style
Equipment On-site: Extensive sound, light, and other audiovisual equipment, including a 50-foot movie screen
Food Service: Catering/food service available
Limitations/Restrictions: No smoking
Access: Handicapped accessible; on-site parking; open year-round
Payment: Cash, check

VIRGINIA CITY

GOLD HILL HOTEL

(Mailing address)
P.O. Box 710
(Street address)
1540 S. Main Street, Gold Hill
Virginia City, NV 89440
Phone: 702/847-0111

WITH the discovery of the Comstock Lode on January 8, 1859, the face of the West was forever changed as miners, businessmen, adventurers, and thousands of others poured into the area. Virginia City and her sister city, Gold Hill, sprang up and quickly became a bustling industrial center of the Far West. Wealth from the mines helped build San Francisco and Reno, encouraged Nevada's statehood, and supported Union efforts during the Civil War. In the early days of the Comstock Lode rush, the Gold Hill Hotel (originally known as the Vesey Hotel) opened for business, and is the oldest hotel in the state. Located in the Comstock Historic District, the hotel comprises the original rubble stone structure, with its covered boardwalk, and a newer building with additional guest rooms and period furnishings. The area's remarkable past is kept alive at the hotel in a number of ways, including its Old West atmosphere and decor, its weekly dinner and lecture series on Comstock and Western history, and its organized walking tours of local historic sights. Meetings, private parties, and other gatherings are accommodated in the old hotel's Great Room or in the Bullion Room.

Located in a National Historic Landmark district; listed in the National Register of Historic Places

Location: Virginia City is 35 minutes southeast of Reno and 20 minutes north of Carson City, the state capital. The Gold Hill Hotel is located one mile south of Virginia City on Highway 342 and is accessible via Highways 395 and 341. Airport service is available in Reno.

Function Space: 1,800 square feet; 2 rooms

Capacity—Conference: 100; Reception: 80; Banquet: 80; Theater: 100

Equipment On-site: TV, projector and screen, loudspeakers

Food Service: Catering/food service available, restaurant, lounge, and saloon

Overnight Accommodations: 13 rooms

Access: Handicapped accessible (limited); on-site parking; open year-round except three weeks in January

Payment: Deposit and advance payment

NEW HAMPSHIRE

ASHLAND

GLYNN HOUSE VICTORIAN INN

(Mailing address)
P.O. Box 719
(Street address)
43 Highland Street, Ashland, NH 03217
Phone: 603/968-3775   Fax: 603/968-3129

SITUATED in the midst of the White Mountains in the picturesque village of Ashland is the Glynn House Victorian Inn. The beautiful surrounding scenery is especially breathtaking during the fall, and Squam Lake, made famous in the film *On Golden Pond*, is just minutes away. The inn itself is a lovely Queen Anne-style house built in 1896, featuring a gingerbread wraparound porch. Inside, Queen Anne furniture, ornate oriental wallpaper, and carved oak woodwork combine to create an elegant atmosphere. Meeting space is available in the parlor and adjacent dining room for both business and social occasions. Guest rooms are individually appointed with period furnishings, and some rooms come with fireplaces and jacuzzis. A full gourmet breakfast is included in the guest room rates, and groups meeting at the inn can arrange for a special lunch or dinner; the innkeeper is a retired executive chef whose specialty is continental cuisine with an American flair. From its location on a quiet, tree-lined street, the inn is a good base from which to explore the Lakes and White Mountains regions, with its covered bridges, antique shops, and fine dining. Skiing, fishing, biking, nature trails, and other recreational activities are all nearby as well.

Listed in the National Register of Historic Places

Location: The Glynn House is just off I-93 (Exit 24) in the central Lakes and White Mountains regions, and is two hours from Boston. Nearest airports are in Manchester, 45 minutes away, and Boston and Portland, Maine, two hours away. Bus service is available.
Function Space: 600 square feet; 2 rooms
Capacity—Conference: 30; Reception: 35; Banquet: 35; Theater: 50
Equipment On-site: Overhead projector, TV monitors; fax and computer service available
Food Service: Breakfast with room; food service available; dining room
Overnight Accommodations: 9 rooms
Limitations/Restrictions: No smoking; no pets; groups provide own alcohol
Access: On-site parking; open year-round
Payment: Cash, check, credit card (AmEx, MC, Visa)

BRETTON WOODS

THE MOUNT WASHINGTON HOTEL AND RESORT

Route 302, Bretton Woods, NH 03575
Phone: 603/278-1000   Fax: 603/278-3457

NESTLED in the heart of New Hampshire's majestic White Mountains and 18,000 acres of national forest, the Mount Washington Hotel and Resort has been welcoming guests since industrialist Joseph Stickney built his magnificent Italianate hotel in 1902. The sparkling white and red-roofed hotel has hosted a cavalcade of who's who in American history, including presidents, performers, tycoons, and other prominent figures such as Thomas Edison, Babe Ruth, and Alfred Hitchcock. Closed in 1943 because of the war, the hotel was the scene of the historic Bretton Woods Monetary Conference held the following year, thus becoming the birthplace of the International Monetary Fund and the World Bank. Renovation and restoration efforts during the 1990s were extensive, right down to reglazing the antique clawfoot bathtubs, and have given Stickney's Victorian "grande dame" a new luster. The elegant octagonal dining room offers a dinner menu that changes daily, and guest dine to the strains of the hotel's own orchestra. The resort offers an extensive, full-service meetings package and an endless list of recreational activities, including golf, tennis, horseback riding, mountain biking, skating, hayrides, and carriage and sleigh rides, as well as live entertainment and diverse dining options.

National Historic Landmark; listed in the National Register of Historic Places

The Mount Washington Hotel and Resort

Location: The resort is located on Route 302 at the base of the Presidential Mountain Range, approximately 20 miles off I-93 and 165 miles north of Boston; Twin Mountain Airport and Mount Washington Regional Airport are just 8 and 15 miles away, respectively; airport service is also available at Manchester Municipal Airport, 105 miles away.

Function Space: 19,000 square feet in 19 rooms; 8,100 square feet of exhibition space, and 18,000 square feet in separate dining rooms

Capacity—Conference: 350; Reception: 1,000; Banquet: 750; Theater: 700; Classroom: 350

Equipment On-site: Audiovisual equipment, podiums, tables, chairs; copier, fax, limited secretarial services available

Food Service: Complete in-house catering service; three restaurants, two dining rooms, lounges

Overnight Accommodations: 195 rooms; additional 135 rooms at the resort are in the Bretton Arms Country Inn (1896, National Historic Landmark), the Bretton Woods Motor Inn, and the Townhomes at Bretton Woods; all properties located within a half-mile radius and accessible by complimentary resort shuttle

Limitations/Restrictions: No pets

Access: Handicapped accessible; on-site parking; Grand Hotel open mid-May to mid-October; Country Inn, Motor Inn, and Townhomes open year-round

Payment: Cash, check, credit card, direct billing

CLAREMONT

GODDARD MANSION BED AND BREAKFAST

25 Hillstead Road, Claremont, NH 03743

Phone: 603/543-0603 Fax: 603/543-0001

BUILT in 1905 as a summer home for Claremont industrialist Frank Maynard, this gabled 18-room mansion enjoys gorgeous mountain views in pleasant surroundings. The elegant mansion was named for a later owner, who also owned the Goddard Bakery, but today as a bed and breakfast it offers a relaxing setting for lodging and meetings. Guest rooms are individually decorated in the style indicated by their names, such as the French Country Room, the Cloud Room, and the Victorian Room. A baby grand piano in the living room and a restored 1939 Wurlitzer jukebox with 78s add to the mansion's cheerful atmosphere. In the morning, a natural breakfast, including homemade muffins served with preserves made from homegrown fruit, is provided and served family-style. Both summer and winter recreational activities abound in the area, and golf, swimming, biking, and tennis are all nearby. Cross-country and alpine skiing are just a short drive away, and quiet country roads lead to great hiking trails and scenic views of spectacular foliage in the fall.

Location: Claremont is accessible via I-91, I-93, I-89, and Route 103; airport service for private planes is available in Claremont; Lebanon Airport is a half-hour away, Manchester Airport, 1.5 hours away, and Logan International Airport and Bradley International Airport (Connecticut) are 2 hours away. Local taxi service is available.
Function Space: 985 square feet; 3 rooms
Capacity—Conference: 15; Reception: 60; Banquet: 20
Equipment On-site: TV/VCR, stereo system, fax

Food Service: Breakfast with room; on-site catering available; outside caterer may also be chosen
Overnight Accommodations: 10 rooms
Limitations/Restrictions: No smoking indoors, permitted on porches, tea house; no pets
Access: Handicapped accessible; on-site parking; open year-round
Payment: Cash, check, credit card

DIXVILLE NOTCH

THE BALSAMS GRAND RESORT HOTEL

Lake Gloriette on Route 26

Dixville Notch, NH 03576

Phone: 603/255-3400 or 800-255-0600

Fax: 603/255-4221

E-mail: The Balsams@aol.com

PRESIDENTIAL candidates win their first votes in the primaries and general elections from the citizens of Dixville Notch, who gather in the Ballot Room of the Balsams Grand Resort Hotel just after midnight on Election Day to cast their ballots. Originally a rustic 25-room hunting lodge when it was built in 1866, the Balsams expanded in the 1890s and again in 1918, adding facilities in New England countryside and Alpine architecture. The resort occupies some 15,000 acres in New Hampshire's White Mountains region, which offers spectacular surroundings for a variety of winter and summer recreation. A wide range of function rooms accommodate groups of 10 to more than 400. Guest rates include all meals, nightly entertainment, and children's programs. The main dining room serves American and continental cuisine, while seasonal lunches are available at the Cafe, the Golf Club House, and the Ski Base Lodge. Also on-site are a lake and boathouse; 27 holes of golf, and both clay and hard tennis courts.

Member of Historic Hotels of America

Location: Dixville Notch is located in northern New Hampshire on Route 26.
Function Space: 40,000+ square feet; 19 rooms
Capacity—Conference: 250; Reception: 425; Banquet: 600; Theater: 600
Equipment On-site: 16mm, 35mm, overhead, slide, and video projectors, TVs and VCRs; photocopying, faxing, steno, and paging available
Food Service: Full American plan; full-service catering; dining room, three restaurants
Overnight Accommodations: 212 rooms
Limitations/Restrictions: Restrictions on smoking; beverages for public consumption must be purchased from the hotel; drinking age 21; no pets; jackets for gentlemen after 6:00 P.M.; no business meetings July, August, and winter holiday season
Access: Handicapped accessible; on-site parking; open late May to mid-October and mid-December to early April
Payment: Cash, check, credit card (AmEx, Discover, MC, Visa)

EXETER

THE INN OF EXETER
90 Front Street, Exeter, NH 03833
Phone: 603/772-5901   Fax: 603/778-8757

THIS handsome brick Georgian inn on the campus of Phillips Exeter Academy was built in 1932 as a guest house for visiting dignitaries and the families of students. While it still serves that original purpose, the inn has expanded its clientele and offers a charming setting for conferences, business functions, and social occasions. Guest rooms feature modern amenities and are furnished with period

antiques. The inn has maintained a tradition of casual yet elegant award-winning dining, and its rich decor and ambiance make it a comfortable meeting place for lunch or dinner. Wedding ceremonies, reunions, and other social gatherings are held in the inn's lovely courtyard and old-fashioned gazebo. Within walking distance of the inn are a number of historic sites and downtown shopping, as well as the Phillips Exeter Academy, established in 1781.

Location: The Inn of Exeter is 20 minutes from Portsmouth and one hour from Boston's Logan International Airport; Manchester Airport is 40 minutes away. The inn is accessible via I-95 and Route 108.
Function Space: 3,308 square feet; 7 rooms
Capacity—Conference: 60; Reception: 175; Banquet: 100; Theater: 150
Equipment On-site: Projectors, TV, VCR, screens, flip charts; fax, computer, photocopying, and conference calls available
Food Service: Catering/food service available
Overnight Accommodations: 47 rooms
Access: Handicapped accessible; on-site parking; open year-round
Payment: Major credit card guarantee

KINGSTON

KINGSTON 1686 HOUSE

(Mailing address)
P.O. Box 248
(Street address)
127 Main Street (on the common)
Kingston, NH 03848
Phone: 603/642-3637

NOT surprisingly, the Kingston 1686 House is the oldest house in this historic town; perhaps more unexpectedly, the main house has remained intact after more than three centuries. One of the few existing examples in the United States of a full, two-story house with an arch-supported central chimney and a superimposed hipped roof, the Kingston House maintains a number of other interesting features. The original wide pine floorboards, the beehive bake oven, hand-cut beams, and the pulpit staircase all contribute to the colonial atmosphere. Built in 1686, the house was acquired by the Reverend Benjamin Choat, Kingston's first minister, for use as a parsonage and family home. After signing the Declaration of Independence in Philadelphia, Kingston resident Dr. Josiah Bartlett returned to town with seedling trees, and in memory of Mrs. Choat he planted a European linden tree, which still stands just outside the house. From 1836 until the early 1950s the prominent Clark family owned the house; in 1972 the complex, which includes the house, barn, and other facilities, was converted into a restaurant and lounge. The restaurant offers hearty meals and fine spirits; large banqueting groups can be accommodated, and smaller business dinner rooms seat 10 to 30.

Location: Kingston is a half-hour from Manchester and Portsmouth, New Hampshire, and one hour north of Boston. It is both 15 minutes west of I-95 and north of I-495, and a quarter-mile west of Route 125. Nearest airports are in Manchester and Boston.
Function Space: 2,400 square feet; 4 rooms
Capacity—Banquet: 130; smaller business dinner rooms for 10 to 30 also available
Food Service: Restaurant
Access: Handicapped accessible; on-site parking; open year-round
Payment: Cash, check, credit card

Kingston 1686 House

New Jersey

Cape May

Carroll Villa Bed and Breakfast at the Mad Batter Restaurant

19 Jackson Street, Cape May, NJ 08204
Phone: 609/884-9619   Fax: 609/884-0264

ONE of the oldest seaside resorts in the country, Cape May is chock-full of splendid Victorian structures and nineteenth-century architecture, yet only a handful of Victorian hotels remain. One of them is the Carroll Villa, located in the Cape May Historic District, just a half-block from the ocean, beaches, and promenade. Built in 1882 in the style of an Italian villa, the reno- vated and restored hotel is known for its fun and lively atmosphere. The Victorian guest rooms are furnished with period antiques and modern amenities, and in the morning guests enjoy a Mad Batter's breakfast. A fine gourmet restau- rant, the Mad Batter offers a creative menu fea- turing international cuisine and serves breakfast, lunch, and dinner; dining alfresco on the front verandah comes with an ocean view. The spa- cious and unique meeting areas—a skylit Victorian dining room and a glass enclosed (or open) secluded garden terrace—accommodate corporate meetings, workshops, reunions, wed- dings, and rehearsal dinners. Available breakout facilities include an antique-wicker-filled living room and sculpture garden terrace. The Carroll Villa is within walking distance of historic house tours, horse and buggy tours, swimming, fish- ing, and boating.

Located in a National Historic Landmark district; listed in the National Register of Historic Places

Location: Cape May is on the southernmost tip of New Jersey, 45 minutes from Atlantic City Airport, two hours from Philadelphia and three hours from New York City; to Carroll Villa, take the Garden State Parkway south to Cape May, turn left on Jackson Street. Cape May is also accessible via New Jersey Transit bus service.
Function Space: 2,400 square feet; 2 rooms
Capacity—Conference: 60; Reception: 75; Banquet: 70; Theater: 70
Equipment On-site: TV, VCR, projector screen, blackboards
Food Service: Breakfast with room; full-service restaurant
Overnight Accommodations: 22 rooms
Limitations/Restrictions: No smoking; no on-site parking
Access: Open year-round
Payment: Check

Chalfonte Hotel

(Mailing address)
P.O. Box 475
(Street address)
301 Howard Street, Cape May, NJ 08204
Phone: 609/884-8409   Fax: 609/884-4588

AN impressive landmark building in the heart of the Cape May Historic District, the Chalfonte Hotel was built in 1876 and is the oldest building in this seaside Victorian town. Local Civil War hero Colonel Henry Sawyer, who was captured by the South and exchanged for General Robert E. Lee's son, built the Chalfonte as a boarding house. From the Satterfields of Virginia, who owned the hotel from 1910 to 1973, came the hotel's renowned tra-

Chalfonte Hotel

dition of Southern hospitality and Southern cooking. Overnight guests stay in simply appointed rooms with marble-topped dressers, ceiling fans, and original furnishings, and both a full breakfast and dinner are included in the room rate. The shotgun-shaped Magnolia Room, formerly the ballroom, is now the dining room, but guests may also take their meals on the newly restored side porch. The King Edward Bar offers a secluded and old-fashioned setting for drinks. A traditional summer hotel (with no heating), the Chalfonte entertains generations of families year after year, sponsors a wide array of cultural and artistic activities, and offers a relaxing, gracious setting for weddings, reunions, private parties, and workshops.

Located in a National Historic Landmark district; listed in the National Register of Historic Places

Location: Cape May, on the southernmost tip of the New Jersey shore, is 2 hours from Philadelphia and 3.5 hours from New York City or Washington, D.C. The Chalfonte Hotel is just two blocks from the beach.

Function Space: 800 square feet; 1 room (additional meeting space in hotel lobby, bar, and on the porches)

Capacity—Conference: 50; Banquet: 200; Theater: 70

Equipment On-site: Slide projector and screen; fax and photocopying available

Food Service: Breakfast and dinner with room; restaurant

Overnight Accommodations: 62 rooms

Limitations/Restrictions: Restrictions on smoking (public areas only); no elevator available; outside food and beverages not permitted in public meeting areas

Access: Street parking; open Memorial Day to Columbus Day

Payment: Personal check, credit card (MC, Visa)

EASTAMPTON

SMITHVILLE MANSION

Burlington County Cultural and Heritage
Department
Smithville Road, P.O. Box 6000
Eastampton, NJ 08060
Phone: 609/265-5068   Fax: 609/265-5022

ONCE the center of a unique and thriving workers'
community, Smithville Mansion remains a testament to the American entrepreneurial spirit. The
Greek Revival mansion, now the centerpiece of
Burlington County Park, was built in about 1840
in what was then the village of Shreveville. In
1865, Hezekiah Bradley Smith bought the nearly
deserted town, renamed it Smithville, and set about
converting the local factories from cotton manufacture to production of one-quarter of the nation's
woodworking machinery. During the 1880s, Smith
had great success in producing the "Star," a high-
wheel bicycle, whose novel design featured a large
back wheel and a small front wheel. After Smith's
death in 1887 his descendants owned the house
until 1962, and in 1975 the county came into pos-
session of the mansion, its annex (which included
Smith's billiard room and bowling alley), and the
village for use as a cultural and heritage center. The
mansion is being restored to Smith's era
(1865–1887), and several meeting areas are available for receptions, meetings, and other gatherings.
Tours of the mansion are given Wednesdays and
Sundays, May through October.

Location: The Smithville Mansion is 2 miles east
of Mt. Holly, 22 miles from downtown
Philadelphia, and is accessible via Route 38 and
Route 206.
Function Space: 3, 271 square feet; 3 rooms

Capacity—Conference: 75; Reception: 125
(two rooms + hallway); Banquet: 125 (two
rooms + hallway)
Food Service: No food or catering services
provided, no on-site food preparation or
storage; department will recommend caterers
experienced with the site
Limitations/Restrictions: Restrictions on
smoking; insurance and fees required
Access: Partially handicapped accessible;
on-site parking; open April to November
Payment: Cash, check

NEWARK

THE NEWARK MUSEUM

(Mailing address)
P.O. Box 540
(Street address)
49 Washington Street, Newark, NJ 07101-0540
Phone: 201/596-6639   Fax: 201/596-6353

JOHN Cotton Dana, a city librarian, founded the
Newark Museum in 1909, and his vision for an
institution that excels both in collecting and teach-
ing continues to this day. Renowned for its pioneering collection of African art as well as its
American, Asian, and Tibetan collections, the
museum showcases its treasures in a splendid complex, the result of a 1989 renovation that nearly
doubled its gallery space. The museum has space
available for business meetings, receptions, luncheons, banquets, and other business or celebratory
gatherings both during the day and in the evening.
Meeting space includes Engelhard Court, the
museum's original skylight court that opens to
three surrounding galleries; the Alice Ransom
Dreyfuss Memorial Garden, an isolated area known

for its unique lawn art; and the Billy Johnson Auditorium. Special themed events may also be held in the appropriate galleries. Members of the Newark Museum Business Partners Program are entitled to exclusive use of additional meeting and conference facilities, which include space in Ballantine House, a restored classic Victorian house next door to the museum. Groups may also arrange for special guided tours of the museum and its exhibitions when booking their events.

National Historic Landmark and listed in the National Register of Historic Places (Ballantine House); recipient of the American Institute of Architects 1992 Honor Award (Newark Museum)

Location: The Newark Museum is located in downtown Newark at Washington Park and is accessible via the New Jersey Turnpike, Garden State Parkway, and Route 78. New York City is 30 minutes away, and airport service is available at Newark International.
Function Space: Approximately 1,000 square feet; 3 rooms
Capacity—Conference: 100; Reception: 400; Banquet: 220; Theater: 275 + 20 handicapped
Equipment On-site: Slide projector, VCR; auditorium control booth; fax and photocopying available
Food Service: On-site cafe and two catering kitchens
Limitations/Restrictions: No smoking; no propane ovens at facility; no food or beverages allowed in galleries; decorations limited because of exhibitions, only votive/hurricane candles allowed
Access: Handicapped accessible; on-site parking; open year-round
Payment: 50 percent deposit, balance due date of event; extra services/equipment billed two weeks after event

PRINCETON

MORVEN
55 Stockton Street, Princeton, NJ 08540
Phone: 609/683-4495   Fax: 609/497-6390

A handsome Georgian-turned-Federal-style mansion, Morven was built in 1758 and was the home of Richard Stockton, a signer of the Declaration of Independence, and his wife, Annis Boudinot Stockton, a poet. The mansion was later enlarged by their son, Richard, a U.S. senator, and grandson, Robert, a commodore in the navy. Robert, a naval hero who banned flogging in the navy and claimed California from the Spanish, also added the columned front porch, which features a colorful century-old wisteria vine. Morven remained in the Stockton family for 150 years, and from 1950 until 1980 it served as the official residence of New Jersey's governors. Today the restored rooms reflect the different eras in the mansion's history, and the renowned gardens once more blossom as they did in the eighteenth and nineteenth centuries. A new theme garden based on Mrs. Stockton's poetry has been created as well. Morven is available for conferences, business meetings, receptions, and other gatherings, and groups may use the ground-floor rooms of the house or the 1930s Art Deco pool house and terrace. Morven is within walking distance of Princeton University and the homes of Albert Einstein, Woodrow Wilson, and T. S. Eliot.

National Historic Landmark; listed in the National Register of Historic Places

Location: Princeton is five miles northeast of Trenton, 45 minutes from Philadelphia and 1 hour 15 minutes from New York City. Morven is within walking distance of the train station.

Function Space: 2,400 square feet; 4 rooms
Capacity—Conference: 40; Reception: 100;
Banquet: 90
Equipment On-site: TV, VCR, slide projector,
screen, microphone, podium
Food Service: List of approved caterers and
catering kitchen available
Limitations/Restrictions: No smoking
Access: On-site parking
Payment: Check

SPRING LAKE

NORMANDY INN

21 Tuttle Avenue, Spring Lake, NJ 07762
Phone: 908/449-7172   Fax: 908/449-1070

LOCATED just a half-block from the beach on the
New Jersey shore, the Normandy Inn treats its visitors to gentle ocean breezes on its porch and hearty
breakfasts in its dining room. The inn was built as
a private residence in 1888 as an Italianate villa
with Queen Anne flourishes. It was once known as
the Audenried House and was moved to its present
location in the early 1900s. The elegant interiors
feature striking Colonial Revival and neoclassic
touches—such as an antique English tall-case clock
and marble sculptures—and each guest room is
uniquely decorated with antique Victorian furnishings. The scenic oceanfront village of Spring Lake
includes small shops and boutiques, tree-lined
streets, splendid turn-of-the-century estates, and a
wide range of restaurant options. Guests at the
Normandy Inn are provided with complimentary
bicycles, great for exploring the tranquil town.
Golf, tennis, and horseback riding are available
nearby, not to mention deep-sea fishing and thoroughbred racing. Corporate retreats, business meetings, and social gatherings are all welcomed here.

Listed in the National Register of Historic Places

Location: Spring Lake is located on the central
New Jersey shore and is accessible via the
Garden State Parkway and I-195.
Function Space: 800 square feet; 2 rooms
Capacity—Conference: 20; Reception: 50;
Banquet: 30
Equipment On-site: VCR, overhead projector,
slide projector, screen, copier, fax; PC available
Food Service: Breakfast included with room;
lunch and dinner available
Overnight Accommodations: 19 rooms
Limitations/Restrictions: No smoking
(outdoors only)
Access: On-site parking; open for business
meetings September to May
Payment: Check

SUMMIT

REEVES-REED ARBORETUM

165 Hobart Avenue, Summit, NJ 07901-2908
Phone: 908/273-8787   Fax: 908/273-6869

THE Reeves-Reed Arboretum is an educational
conservancy that promotes protection of the natural environment. The area was part of a farm during
the Revolutionary era, and in 1889 John Hornor
Wisner established his country estate here, con-
structing a Colonial Revival mansion that is now
the arboretum's administrative center. Calvert
Vaux, a partner of Frederick Law Olmsted,
designed the spectacular landscape. In 1916 the
Reeves family bought the estate, adding to the gardens and daffodil collections, and in 1968 the
Reeds became the last private owners. They created
the patterned herb garden and opened woodland
trails as well. In 1974, through the efforts of the

Reeds and local citizens, the property was preserved as an arboretum. The beautiful, peaceful landscape comprises 12.5 acres of woodlands, formal gardens, fields, and lawns, and allows plant and wildlife to be studied and enjoyed in a natural setting. The grounds are open daily, year-round, free of charge. The grounds and the Wisner House are available for meetings, weddings, and special events.

Listed in the National Register of Historic Places and the New Jersey Register of Historic Places

Location: The Reeves-Reed Arboretum is 35 minutes from New York City (non-rush hour) and 20 minutes from Morristown, New Jersey. The arboretum is accessible via Route 78, the Garden State Parkway, and the New Jersey Turnpike. Route 24, off Route 78, leads to Hobart Avenue exit; turn left over highway. Newark and Morristown airports are 20 minutes away; train, bus, and taxi service available.
Function Space: 2,500 square feet; 4 contiguous rooms
Capacity—Overall capacity: 200 standing, 73 seated; if rooms used singly, conference: 35, reception 35
Equipment On-site: Slide and overhead projectors, lectern with microphone
Food Service: Client selects caterer; kitchen available, renter/caterer responsible for setup and cleanup
Limitations/Restrictions: Restrictions on smoking; no alcoholic beverages
Access: Handicapped accessible; on-site parking limited, street parking available; open year-round
Payment: Check

NEW MEXICO

ALBUQUERQUE

LA POSADA DE ALBUQUERQUE

125 Second Street, NW, Albuquerque, NM 87102
Phone: 505/242-9090 or 800-777-5732 (reservations)
Fax: 505/242-8664

ORIGINALLY known as the Hilton of Albuquerque, La Posada de Albuquerque was the setting for the announcement of owner Conrad Hilton and Zsa Zsa Gabor's 1942 wedding engagement. The hotel lobby was also the scene of "Mayor" Claude Tingley's lively political gatherings in the 1940s and 1950s. When the hotel opened in 1939, it was claimed to be the tallest building in the state by virtue of its 16-foot rooftop Hilton sign, and it remains an important downtown landmark. La Posada was completely restored in 1984 and renovated in 1996, given all the modern conveniences while preserving its historical character, and all of the guest rooms feature hand-crafted furniture and Spanish tiles. Conrad's Downtown serves cuisine from Spain and the Yucatan in a casual, Art Deco atmosphere, and the Lobby Bar offers live weekend entertainment. A variety of function rooms are available for business and social events, including a ballroom, a boardroom, and a gallery. Located in downtown Albuquerque, the hotel is just one block from the convention center and minutes from historic Old Town Plaza and some of the many golf courses in the area.

Listed in the National Register of Historic Places; member of Historic Hotels of America

Location: La Posada is 7 miles from Albuquerque International Airport and is accessible via I-25 and I-40.
Function Space: 8,076 square feet; 6 rooms
Capacity—Conference: 160; Reception: 300; Banquet: 200; Theater: 200
Equipment On-site: Audiovisual equipment available; full business services available within walking distance of the hotel
Food Service: Catering/food service available; restaurant, bar, room service
Overnight Accommodations: 114 rooms
Access: Handicapped accessible; on-site parking; open year-round
Payment: Credit card

AZTEC

AZTEC MUSEUM AND PIONEER VILLAGE

125 N. Main Avenue, Aztec, NM 87410
Phone: 505/334-9829   Fax: 505/334-2344

LOCATED in the Four-Corners region in northwestern New Mexico, the city of Aztec has retained its strong associations to the past through the Aztec Museum and Pioneer Village and its Main Street Historic District. The museum's collections feature mineral and fossil displays, Southwest artifacts, including arrowheads and tools, and numerous household and business items dating from the late nineteenth and early twentieth centuries. The Pioneer Village features such preserved and restored structures as Hamblett Cabin (the scene of a Stockton gang shoot-out on Christmas Eve in 1880), the sheriff's office, the first town jail, and early town businesses. Also on-site is a comprehensive oil field exhibit, which documents through machinery and other items the 1911 discovery of oil in northwest New Mexico and its impact on the area. The museum's garden area accommodates up to 200 for stand-up receptions, and Miss Gail's Inn, a bed and breakfast built in 1907 that is also on the National Register of Historic Places, can accommodate small meetings. In addition to Aztec's Main Street Historic District, a number of historic sites are located nearby, and just a mile and a half away is the remarkable Aztec Ruins National Monument, with its fully restored Great Kiva.

Aztec Multiple Resource Area listed in the National Register of Historic Places

Location: Aztec, county seat of San Juan County, is located on Highway 550, 10 miles east of Farmington, New Mexico, and 35 miles south of Durango, Colorado. Albuquerque is three hours south on Routes 544 and 44. The nearest airports are the Four Corners Regional Airport and La Plata County Airport, within 15 and 25 minutes of Aztec, respectively. Car rental services available.

Aztec Museum and Pioneer Village

Function Space: Garden area
Capacity—200 accommodated for stand-up reception
Food Service: Local catering available
Limitations/Restrictions: No smoking; no food or beverages inside museum; no alcohol
Access: Handicapped accessible; on-site parking; open year-round
Payment: Cash

Miss Gail's Inn

(Phone: 505/334-3452)
Function Space: 420 square feet; 1 room
Capacity—Conference: 25
Food Service: Breakfast with room
Overnight Accommodations: 10 rooms
Limitations/Restrictions: No smoking
Access: Open year-round
Payment: Cash, check, credit card (AmEx, Discover, MC, Visa)

Hamblett Cabin, Aztec Museum and Pioneer Village *(Pam Kirkham. © Atztec Museum, 1996)*

LAS VEGAS

PLAZA HOTEL

230 Old Town Plaza, Las Vegas, NM 87701
Phone: 505/425-3591 or 800-328-1882
(reservations)   Fax: 505/425-9659

A vibrant vestige of the Old West on the Santa Fe Trail, the Plaza Hotel was once known as the "Belle of the Southwest." Today the hotel is again the social center of historic Las Vegas, its architectural and cultural integrity preserved following a $2 million award-winning restoration in 1982. Exactly 100 years before, Romero and Jean Pendaries built the Plaza Hotel, and by the late nineteenth century, not only was it the center of commerce in the New Mexico territory, but it drew some of the West's most infamous outlaws and villains, including Doc Holiday and his companion Big Nose Kate. Cowboy film star Tom Mix was a guest, and the Plaza Hotel appeared in several of his movies. The hotel's Landmark Grill, with a menu of favorite Southwestern dishes, serves breakfast, lunch, and dinner, and visitors will enjoy relaxing in Byron T's Saloon, named for a past owner; legend says that he suddenly disappeared and that his ghost still visits. Meetings, parties, weddings, and other functions are held in the Plaza's Conservatory. Located on the Santa Fe Trail and part of the Las Vegas Historic District, the hotel is within walking distance of a number of historic buildings and attractions.

Listed in the National Register of Historic Places

Location: The Plaza Hotel is located on the historic Plaza in Las Vegas, just off I-25. Albuquerque International Airport is two hours away.
Function Space: 870 square feet; 1 room

Capacity—Conference: 50; Reception: 100; Banquet: 50; Theater: 50
Equipment On-site: TV, VCR, slide projector and screen, copier, and fax
Food Service: Full-service restaurant and saloon
Overnight Accommodations: 36 rooms
Access: Handicapped accessible; off-street parking one block away; open year-round
Payment: Deposit, balance paid at check-out

SANTA FE

THE BISHOP'S LODGE

(Mailing address)
P.O. Box 2367
(Street address)
Bishop's Lodge Road, Santa Fe, NM 87504
Phone: 505/983-6377   Fax: 505/989-8739

INDIANS, Spanish conquistadors, a French cleric, and, later, the Pulitzers of St. Louis all once occupied the site in the foothills of the Sangre de Cristos that would become the Bishop's Lodge. The cleric was Jean Baptiste Lamy, the first bishop of Santa Fe, who arrived in 1851 and later built a private retreat and a chapel, which is still used today. Lamy's adventures and well-known hospitality were recounted in Willa Cather's 1927 classic, *Death Comes for the Archbishop.* In 1918 the Thorpes of Denver acquired the property from the Pulitzers and built a lovely Pueblo Revival-style resort. Colorful Southwestern decor graces the lodge and its conference facilities that provide a retreat setting for board meetings and business sessions as well as family reunions and conferences. The Bishop's Lodge Restaurant serves "New American" cuisine, and box lunches and seasonal cookouts are available to fit meeting plans. A full destination resort, the lodge offers a number of on-site recreational activities, and historic sites such as the Taos Pueblo, the Anasazi ruins at Bandalier, and the once-secret Los Alamos National Laboratory are just a short drive away.

Listed in the National Register of Historic Places (Bishop Lamy's chapel); member of Historic Hotels of America (Bishop's Lodge)

Location: The Bishop's Lodge is at the edge of the Santa Fe city limits, and 3 miles from the Plaza and downtown. The lodge is one hour north of Albuquerque International Airport via I-25; airport to downtown shuttle bus service is available; hotel courtesy shuttle to downtown is also available.
Function Space: 6,000 square feet; 6 rooms
Capacity—Conference: 100; Reception: 200; Banquet: 150; Theater: 150
Equipment On-site: Audiovisual equipment available through local contractor; fax, computer, voice mail available
Food Service: Catering/food service available; restaurant, bar, room service
Overnight Accommodations: 88 rooms
Access: Limited handicapped accessibility; on-site parking; open year-round
Payment: Check for groups; check or credit card for individuals

HOTEL ST. FRANCIS

210 Don Gaspar Avenue, Santa Fe, NM 87501
Phone: 505/992-6354 (sales office) or
800-529-5700   Fax: 505/989-7690

COMBINING the distinctive style of the 1920s with the charming flair of the Southwest, the restored Hotel St. Francis dates back to 1923, when it replaced its nineteenth-century predecessor. As one of the city's most luxurious hotels, it was noted for its large public rooms with high ceilings, clay tile floors, wrought-iron chandeliers, and beautiful decorative features. During the 1930s and 1940s, when the state capitol was across the street, the Hotel St. Francis was also a popular gathering spot for politicians. Today the renovated hotel hosts meetings, banquets, parties, and other gatherings in the De Vargas Room, whose large floor-to-ceiling windows allow plenty of natural light. Receptions are also held at the Artist's Pub and on the garden patio. Each guest room is equipped with a refrigerator and a personal safe, and many rooms enjoy beautiful mountain views. Santa Fe's famous plaza is just a block away, and as the oldest capital in the United States, the city has numerous historic sites—and is second only to New York City for the greatest number of art galleries—many of which are within walking distance of the hotel.

Listed in the National Register of Historic Places; member of Historic Hotels of America

Location: The Hotel St. Francis is one block from the Plaza in downtown Santa Fe, which is just north of I-25 and one hour north of I-40. Albuquerque International Airport is minutes away, and Santa Fe Municipal Airport is 10 miles away; shuttle and local bus service available.
Function Space: 1,090 square feet; 2 rooms
Capacity—Conference: 32; Reception: 50; Banquet: 64; Theater: 75
Equipment On-site: Audiovisual equipment available
Food Service: Catering/food service available; restaurant and pub
Overnight Accommodations: 83 rooms
Limitations/Restrictions: No pets
Access: Handicapped accessible; on-site parking; open year-round

Payment: Cash, check, credit card (AmEx, DC, Discover, MC, Visa)

La Fonda Hotel

(Mailing address)
P.O. Box 1209, Santa Fe, NM 87504-1209
(Street address)
100 E. San Francisco, Santa Fe, NM 87501
Phone: 505/982-5511 or 800-523-5002
Fax: 505/982-6367

AMONG the first businesses established when Santa Fe was founded in 1610 was an inn, or *fonda*. Thus, Captain William Becknell and his company likely found a hotel available when they arrived in 1821 following their trading expedition from Missouri—a journey that established the historic Santa Fe Trail. The old adobe hotel was demolished in 1919, and the present-day adobe-style La Fonda was built in 1920. From 1926 until 1969 it was one of Fred Harvey's acclaimed hotels on the Atchison, Topeka & Santa Fe. Now La Fonda combines historical charm and elegance with today's modern amenities, and the brightly painted guest rooms are furnished with hand-carved Spanish-style furnishings. La Fonda offers a full-service covered patio restaurant, a lounge with nightly live entertainment, and an outdoor bell tower bar on the fifth floor with beautiful mountain and sunset views. Meeting facilities feature a rich Southwestern-style decor, from the wood beam ceilings to the tile floors. Located on Santa Fe's historic Plaza, La Fonda is between the St. Francis Cathedral and the Palace of the Governors, and museums, restaurants, shops, and galleries are all within walking distance; Indian pueblos are just a short drive away.

Member of Historic Hotels of America

Location: Santa Fe is just north of I-25 and one hour north of I-40. Albuquerque International Airport is an easy 75-minute drive on I-25, and Santa Fe Municipal Airport is 10 miles away; shuttle and local bus service available.
Function Space: 13,000 square feet; 7 rooms
Capacity—Conference: 80; Reception: 750; Banquet: 550; Theater: 600
Equipment On-site: Podium, microphone, chairs, tables, and easels are complimentary; audiovisual equipment available for rental; modems on each room phone; photocopier, word processor available
Food Service: Full food service; restaurant, lounge
Overnight Accommodations: 153 rooms
Limitations/Restrictions: Main dining room is nonsmoking; food and beverage service must be catered through hotel
Access: Handicapped accessible; on-site parking; open year-round
Payment: All major credit cards; direct billing with prior approval

La Fonda Hotel

NEW YORK

AMENIA

TROUTBECK

Leedsville Road, Amenia, NY 12501
Phone: 914/373-9681   Fax: 914/373-7080

THIS beautiful old country estate was founded in 1765 when the Benton family settled here, naming the area Troutbeck after their village in England's Lake District. In 1902, Troutbeck was purchased by a remarkable American family, the Spingarns, who hosted some of the country's brightest literary figures and liberal thinkers. Guests included Lewis Mumford and Sinclair Lewis, and it was here that W. E. B. Du Bois and Joel Elias Spingarn created the NAACP. Today Troutbeck is an executive retreat complex offering complete conference facilities set on 442 wooded acres. The elegant and spacious Great Room, built in 1995, accommodates large corporate gatherings and wedding receptions, and the adjacent outdoor patio is the setting for predinner cocktail parties. The paneled library seats up to 30 conference-style, and smaller breakout rooms are available. Guest rooms are in the main house, farmhouse, and garden house. Swimming is a year-round option, as there are both indoor and outdoor pools, and tennis courts are on-site. Videos and a collection of 12,000 books are on hand, and golf, riding stables, and vineyards are nearby.

Location: Troutbeck is two hours north of midtown Manhattan and 90 minutes from Hartford, Connecticut, and is accessible via Route 22 and Route 343. Airport service is available at Westchester/White Plains, Stewart/Newburgh, and Bradley Field 75, 85, and 90 minutes away respectively. LaGuardia Airport is two hours away.
Function Space: 4,000 square feet; 2 rooms
Capacity—Conference: 80; Reception: 230; Banquet: 260; Theater: 325
Equipment On-Site: VCRs, overhead and slide projectors, easels, notepads
Food Service: Rates include 3 meals daily; with advance notice most (special) dietary needs can be met; open bar is included in rates
Overnight Accommodations: 42 rooms
Limitations/Restrictions: No smoking in the dining rooms; no children between ages 1 and 12, except at wedding weekends and family reunions
Access: Limited handicapped accessibility; on-site parking; open year-round
Payment: Corporate or personal check for large functions; lunch and dinner guests and weekenders may pay with credit card (AmEx, MC, Visa)

BOLTON LANDING

THE SAGAMORE

110 Sagamore Road
Bolton Landing, New York, NY 12814
Phone: 800-358-3585   Fax: 518/644-2626

IN 1883 the first Sagamore opened as one of the poshest hotels in the Adirondacks, located on a private island surrounded by picturesque Lake George. Fires in 1893 and 1914 destroyed the hotel, but in 1930 a new Sagamore opened. The white clapboard Victorian landmark closed 50 years later, reopening in 1985 following a $75 million restoration. Donald Ross's 1930 18-hole championship golf course was restored to its original Scottish character, and new facilities were added at the edge of Lake George, including a tennis and fitness center, a conference center, and the Hermitage, a former carriage house and now an executive retreat. A full-service resort, the Sagamore offers its guests luxurious accommodations in the main hotel or in lakeside lodges. Among the hotel's many features are sunlit terraces, fine and casual dining, dinner cruises, a marina, a spa, and an array of recreational activities. The hotel's conference managers ensure smooth planning for everything from small executive meetings to dinner for 700, and the Sagamore's many meeting rooms can accommodate a wide variety of events and requirements.

National Historic Landmark; listed in the National Register of Historic Places; member of Historic Hotels of America

Location: Bolton Landing is one hour north of Albany County Airport, four hours from New York City and Boston, and is accessible via I-87.

Function Space: 17,000 square feet; 19 rooms
Capacity—Reception: 1,050; Banquet: 720; Theater: 1,050
Equipment On-Site: On-site audiovisual company and business center available
Food Service: Catering/food service available; six on-site restaurants; catering manager works with meeting planner
Overnight Accommodations: 350 rooms
Access: Handicapped accessible; on-site parking; open year-round
Payment: All major credit cards

COOPERSTOWN

THE INN AT COOPERSTOWN

16 Chestnut Street, Cooperstown, NY 13326
Phone: 607/547-5756   Fax: 607/547-8779

WILLIAM Cooper, father of author James Fenimore Cooper, founded Cooperstown in 1786. But this charming historic village is perhaps best

The Sagamore

The Inn at Cooperstown
(Milo V. Stewart)

known for its links to the American national pastime. Located in the heart of this nostalgic setting is the creamy-yellow Inn at Cooperstown. An excellent example of Second Empire architecture, the inn was originally built in 1874 as an annex to the posh Fenimore Hotel and was home to the Cooke family until 1974. After extensive renovations, the Inn at Cooperstown opened in 1985 and has since received recognition for achievement in historic preservation. Meeting facilities include a conference room, and an adjacent dining room and front porch (with rocking chairs) are available for group use. Sitting rooms accommodating up to 10 guests may be used for informal discussions. Overnight guests stay in comfortable, cheery rooms and enjoy a continental breakfast featuring fresh-baked muffins. A block and a half from the inn is the impressive

National Baseball Hall of Fame, but this is not the only game in town. The Farmer's Museum, the Fenimore House Museum, and the famed Glimmerglass Opera are also popular, and outdoor recreation, art galleries, antique shops, and craft festivals abound.

Listed in the National Register of Historic Places

Location: Cooperstown is located in central New York State, 70 miles west of Albany and 30 miles south of the New York Thruway (I-90); the Inn at Cooperstown is on Route 80 (Chestnut Street), just three buildings north of the town's only traffic light. Albany/Schenectady County Airport is 70 miles away.
Function Space: 195 square feet; 1 room
Capacity—Conference: 15

Equipment On-Site: Tables, chairs, easel, and paper provided; fax available; other equipment available for rent from outside source
Food Service: Breakfast with room; list of preferred caterers available; coffee/snack breaks, catered deli lunch available
Overnight Accommodations: 18 rooms
Limitations/Restrictions: Smoking restricted to some guest rooms and porch; no pets
Access: Handicapped accessible; on-site parking; open year-round
Payment: Cash, business check, credit card

THE OTESAGA HOTEL

(Mailing address)
P.O. Box 311
(Street address)
60 Lake Street, Cooperstown, NY 13326
Phone: 607/547-9931   Fax: 607/547-9675

ON the southern shore of Lake Otsego in baseball's hometown, this grand resort has been welcoming guests to the Leatherstocking Region since 1909. Built for the Clark family, the neo-Georgian hotel, with its striking classical portico and splendid dome-capped cupola, occupies a stunning parklike setting adjacent to its championship Leatherstocking Golf Course. From the flower-filled lobby to the elegant muraled ballroom, the Otesaga offers a luxurious and relaxing atmosphere. Guests may dine on the terrace overlooking Lake Otsego, the "Glimmerglass" of James Fenimore Cooper's *Leatherstocking Tales,* or enjoy a meal highlighting regional fare in either the candle-lit main dining room or the Hawkeye Bar & Grill. In the evenings visitors can unwind in the Templeton Lounge, and kids will enjoy the hotel Game Room. The Otesaga offers a number of meeting rooms to accommodate a variety of social and business functions, from small corporate meetings to large receptions, which is only fitting since this area was once called "the meeting place" by American Indians. In addition to golf, swimming, boating, tennis, and other recreational options on hand, quaint village shops and the sparkling Doubleday Field are also close by.

Member of Historic Hotels of America

Location: Cooperstown is located in central New York State, 70 miles west of Albany; the Otesaga Hotel is at the southern end of Lake Otsego and is accessible via Route 20, Route 80, and Route 28.
Function Space: 11,000 square feet; 11 rooms
Capacity—Conference: 60; Reception: 400; Banquet: 350; Theater: 300
Equipment On-Site: Overhead and 35mm projectors, TV/VCRs, copier, fax
Food Service: Breakfast and dinner with room; catering/food service available; two restaurants, lounge
Overnight Accommodations: 136 rooms
Limitations/Restrictions: Food and beverages must be purchased at hotel
Access: Handicapped accessible; on-site parking; open end of April to end of October
Payment: Credit card (VISA, MC, AmEx), check, cash

EAST AURORA

THE ROYCROFT INN

40 S. Grove Street, East Aurora, NY 14052
Phone: 716/652-5552   Fax: 716/655-5345

RESTORED in 1995, the Roycroft Inn is part of the historic Roycroft Campus established in 1895. It was here that a colony of artisans known as

Roycrofters developed their mission-style furniture and produced bookbinding, copperware, and leather goods. Modern guest rooms preserve the spirit of the Roycroft Movement with their simple decor and finely crafted furnishings, and guest suites feature Stickley furniture and Roycroft lamps and wall sconces. The inn's distinctive appearance is accented with inn-founder Elbert Hubbard's epigrams carved on the Roycroft's oak doors. The inn hosts meetings, seminars, retreats, banquets, and other special occasions, and menus can be customized exclusively for group events. Guest rates include a complimentary breakfast, and the Roycroft Inn Restaurant serves lunch, dinner, and Sunday brunch, offering both an established menu and seasonal changes. The inn is within walking distance of antique shops, museums, and parks; golf and skiing are just a short drive away, and Niagra Falls makes for an easy day trip.

National Historic Landmark; listed in the National Register of Historic Places

Location: East Aurora is 20 miles east of Buffalo and is accessible via I-90 to Highway 400 south.
Function Space: 4,518 square feet; 5 rooms
Capacity—Conference: 30; Reception: 150; Banquet: 120; Theater: 200
Equipment On-Site: Projectors, screens, flip charts, microphone, podium; modem and fax access in each suite
Food Service: Breakfast with room; catering/food service available; restaurant
Overnight Accommodations: 22 rooms
Limitations/Restrictions: No smoking
Access: Handicapped accessible; on-site parking; open year-round
Payment: Cash, check

GENEVA

BELHURST CASTLE

(Mailing address)
P.O. Box 609
(Street address)
Route 14 South, Geneva, NY 14456
Phone: 315/781-0201
Fax: 315/781-0201 (Same as phone)

BUILT in 1885 in the Richardsonian Romanesque style, Belhurst Castle (the name means "beautiful forest"), with its ivy-covered turrets and red Medina stone walls, certainly lives up to its appellation. Surveys have confirmed Belhurst's reputation as one of the most romantic places in New York State, given its fairy-tale setting and tales of treasure hidden within its walls. From the castle, visitors enjoy a view of sweeping lawns, towering trees, and Seneca Lake. Guests stay in spacious rooms furnished with antiques and oriental rugs, and breakfast is complimentary. On Sundays the largest brunch in the area is served here, complete with complimentary Bloody Marys and Mimosas. Guests can even draw their own glasses of wine from the spigot on the second-floor landing of the inn. Conference facilities and a banquet room are available for wedding receptions, tour groups, holiday celebrations, and other gatherings. Seneca Lake offers opportunities for fishing, swimming, and boating, and there are numerous wineries in the area.

National Historic Landmark; listed in the National Register of Historic Places

Location: Belhurst is at the northern end of Seneca Lake, an hour's drive from Syracuse and Rochester airports and 8.5 miles south of the New York State Thruway.

Function Space: 6,900 square feet; 4 rooms
Capacity—Conference: 40; Reception: 300;
Banquet: 300; Theater: 200
Equipment On-Site: Overhead projector, screen
Food Service: Breakfast with room; restaurant
Overnight Accommodations: 13 rooms
Access: Handicapped accessible; on-site parking;
open year-round
Payment: Cash or credit card (MC, Visa)

HARRIMAN

ARDEN HOUSE

(Mailing address)
P.O. Box 1083
(Street address)
Arden House Road, Harriman, NY 10926
Phone: 914/351-2171   Fax: 914/351-4561

FROM its hilltop setting, Arden House, the
country estate of Edward Henry Harriman, overlooks New York's Ramapo Mountain range and
spectacular woodland valleys. In 1950, during
Dwight D. Eisenhower's tenure as president of
Columbia University, W. Averell and E. Roland
Harriman donated the house to the university for
use by the American Assembly, a domestic and
foreign policy study group. Built in 1909, the
large, magnificent house today functions as part of
the Arden Conference Center and can host up to
three separate groups simultaneously. As the
country's first educational conference center,
Arden House has welcomed foundations, associations, government groups, and other organizations. Meeting facilities include conference rooms,
an amphitheater-style auditorium, a dining room
and adjacent terrace, and a variety of indoor and
outdoor recreational facilities, including a gym
and exercise room, tennis courts, an outdoor pool,

and miles of jogging trails. The house has a pleasant, stylish decor, and the Music Room, with its
choir stalls and Gothic flair, is used for theme dinners, cocktail receptions, and meetings. American
cuisine is served in the dining room, which overlooks the estate's formal lawns, and in summer
guests often dine on the terrace lawn.

National Historic Landmark; listed in the National
Register of Historic Places

Location: Arden House is approximately one hour
from midtown Manhattan and the New York area
airports, and a half-hour from Stewart Airport in
Newburgh. The area is also served by Short Line
and MetroNorth Commuter Rail.
Function Space: 8,500 square feet; 12 rooms
Capacity—Conference: 60; Reception: 160;
Banquet: 144; Theater: 125
Equipment On-Site: Overhead and slide projectors, screen, VCRs, monitors, audio/videotaping,
flip charts, computer lab, LCD display, copier,
fax; in-house graphics service available
Food Service: Conference dining on premises;
coffee breaks with snack options
Overnight Accommodations: 80 rooms
Limitations/Restrictions: No smoking in
meeting rooms; no off-site caterers; all alcoholic
beverages must be served under Arden
Conference Center direction; corkage fees
Access: Handicapped accessible; on-site parking;
open year-round (330 days per year)
Payment: Cash, check, credit card (VISA, MC,
Diners Club, AmEx, Discover)

HYDE PARK

ELEANOR ROOSEVELT'S VAL-KILL

(Mailing address)
P.O. Box 255
(Street address)
Route 9G, Hyde Park, NY 12538
Phone: 914/229-5302 Fax: 914/229-0742

THE only site dedicated to an American First Lady, Val-Kill is Eleanor Roosevelt's former retreat at Hyde Park. Built in 1926 and set on 179 grassy, wooded acres in the Hudson River Valley, Val-Kill comprises Stone Cottage, Mrs. Roosevelt's original retreat, and Val-Kill Cottage, which was first a small furniture factory but converted into a cottage in 1936. This cottage was Mrs. Roosevelt's permanent home after her husband, President Franklin Roosevelt, died in 1945, and it was here that she welcomed visitors from around the country and the world, including John F. Kennedy, who came seeking her support for his presidential campaign in 1960. Today Val-Kill Cottage is a museum exhibiting Mrs. Roosevelt's belongings and household furnishings, and Stone Cottage serves as headquarters and program area for the Eleanor Roosevelt Center. In keeping with Mrs. Roosevelt's tireless humanitarian endeavors, meeting facilities are for the use of educational, public service, and humanitarian organizations. Tourists may visit Stone Cottage during limited weekend hours; Val-Kill Cottage is part of the National Park Service site tour and is open to the public.

Listed in the National Register of Historic Places

Location: Hyde Park is 6 miles north of Poughkeepsie, 61 miles north of New York City, and 65 miles south of Albany.
Function Space: 1,000 square feet; 3 rooms

Capacity—Conference: 20; Reception: 60; Banquet: 40; Theater: 60
Equipment On-Site: VCR
Food Service: Center arranges catering and food service
Limitations/Restrictions: Restrictions on smoking; groups using facilities must be educational, public service, humanitarian, or related organizations
Access: On-site parking; open April through December (can vary)
Payment: Check

ITHACA

ROSE INN

(Mailing address)
P.O. Box 6576
(Street address)
Route 34 North, Ithaca, NY 14851-6576
Phone: 607/533-7905 Fax: 607/533-7908
E-mail: roseinn@clarityconnect.com

FOR years known to its neighbors as "the House with the Circular Staircase," the Rose Inn is a lovely Italianate mansion built in 1850. According to a contemporary press report, in 1922 a master craftsman arrived at the house to find an unfinished staircase and, in the hog shed, hundreds of feet of Honduras mahogany that had been saved for a half century. Two years later, the craftsman quietly disappeared, leaving behind a stunning triple-curved staircase that rose two and a half stories from the main hall to the cupola. Impressive woodwork abounds throughout the house, from large hand-carved oak doors to parquet floors. The large guest rooms feature charming period furniture, and four suites come with a jacuzzi bath. Set on 20 landscaped acres of lawns and gardens at the southern tip of Lake Cayuga, the Rose Inn is a local land-mark offering its guests luxurious accommodations and a full country breakfast. Surrounded by peace-ful, rural countryside, the inn is just minutes from Cornell University and Ithaca College.

Location: The Rose Inn is halfway between New York City and Niagra Falls and is accessible via Routes 13 and 96.
Function Space: 2,000 square feet; 1 room
Capacity—Conference: 60; Reception: 80; Banquet: 60; Theater: 70
Equipment On-Site: Screen, overhead projector, easel, lectern; secretarial and copying service available
Food Service: Breakfast with room; full food service with liquor license available
Overnight Accommodations: 17 rooms
Limitations/Restrictions: No smoking
Access: Handicapped accessible (meeting room only); on-site parking; open year-round
Payment: Personal or company check, direct bill (no credit cards)

KEENE

THE BARK EATER INN

(Mailing address)
P.O. Box 139
(Street address)
Alstead Mill Road, Keene, NY 12942
Phone: 518/576-2221   Fax: 518/576-2071

THE Iroquois Nation, which once occupied the lands surrounding the southern half of Lake Champlain, at times referred to their northern neighbors, the Algonquins, as "Ratirontak," roughly meaning "bark eater." From this term comes the area's geographic name, "Adirondack,"

and its English translation is the source of the inn's own appellation. Originally a stagecoach stop, the Bark Eater Inn is a country hostelry located in the scenic wilderness of the Adirondack High Peaks, and the inn's main building is a cozy 1830 farmhouse with stone fireplaces and antique furnishings. Other lodg-ings are available in the next-door Carriage House and the Log Cottage up the hill, and rates include a hearty country breakfast. Dinner is served family-style in the candlelit dining room. Conference facilities are available for small groups in the farmhouse and in the cottage, which is located in a wooded setting and ideal for retreats. A variety of recreational activities are available, from horseback riding operated through the inn's stables to its 20 kilometers of groomed cross-country ski trails. Twenty minutes away are Lake Placid's Olympic facilities for win-ter sports, and there is also excellent hiking, bik-ing, and canoeing in the area.

Listed in the National Register of Historic Places

Location: Keene is located in the Adirondacks, approximately two hours from Albany, New York, and Burlington, Vermont. The Bark Eater Inn is accessible via I-87 and Routes 73 and 9N. Lake Clear Airport is 45 minutes away, and Amtrak service is available in Westport, 35 minutes away.
Function Space: 900 square feet; 4 rooms
Capacity—Conference: 20–40; Reception: 50; Banquet: 36–40
Equipment On-Site: Phone, fax
Food Service: Breakfast with room; dinner reservations required, trail lunches available
Overnight Accommodations: 19 rooms
Limitations/Restrictions: No smoking
Access: On-site parking; open year-round
Payment: Cash, check

LAKE PLACID

LAKE PLACID LODGE

(Mailing address)

P.O. Box 550

(Street address)

Whiteface Inn Road, Lake Placid, NY 12946

Phone: 518/523-2700   Fax: 518/523-1124

THE Adirondacks are the oldest mountain range on the continent, its forests covering more than six million acres, and among its 2,300 lakes is Lake Placid, site of the 1932 and 1980 Winter Olympics. Although Lake Placid is known for its winter sports venues and recreational activities, its pleasant short summers and spectacular autumns offer visitors much to enjoy. Located on the southwest shore of the lake, the rustic Lake Placid Lodge was built in 1882 and remained a private residence until 1946, when it opened to the public as Placid Manor. Today the renovated lodge reflects its vibrant Adirondack heritage, from the Main Lodge's Moose Sitting Room to the guest rooms furnished with twig and birch-bark furniture; many rooms have large granite fireplaces, and some boast views of the lake and Whiteface Mountain. This luxurious mountain retreat hosts meetings, seminars, receptions, and other gatherings and offers a number of recreational pursuits, including sightseeing cruises, golf, tennis, hiking, and biking. The area abounds in winter sports activities, of course, and the picturesque village of Lake Placid, with its charming alpine architecture, and the Olympic Museum are nearby as well.

Listed in the National Register of Historic Places; member of Historic Hotels of America

Location: Lake Placid Lodge is two hours from Burlington, Vermont, and Albany, New York; Adirondack Airport in Saranac Lake is 16 miles away.

Function Space: 2,655 square feet; 4 rooms

Capacity—Conference: 150; Reception: 200; Banquet: 150; Theater: 250

Equipment On-Site: Slide and overhead projectors, flip charts; fax, photocopier, computer available

Food Service: Breakfast with room; catering/food service available; dining room

Overnight Accommodations: 22 rooms

Limitations/Restrictions: Restrictions on smoking

Access: Handicapped accessible; on-site parking; open year-round

Payment: Check or major credit card

NEW PALTZ

MOHONK MOUNTAIN HOUSE

Lake Mohonk, New Paltz, NY 12561

Phone: 914/255-1000   Fax: 914/256-2161

THE Smiley Family has owned and operated the Mohonk Mountain House ever since twins Alfred and Albert Smiley built the grand hotel in 1869. Originally a small guest house, it has evolved into a Victorian castle with fanciful turrets and towers and is perched on a rocky cliff overlooking Lake Mohonk. The hotel, situated on 2,200 acres of wilderness, is immediately surrounded by formal gardens, offering visitors a scenic and secluded respite just 90 miles from New York City. Since the nineteenth century Mohonk has been hosting important gatherings, including the 1895 Conference on International Arbitration, and the tradition continues. A full-service destination resort, Mohonk provides comfortable, flexible meeting facilities for groups of 10 to 350, and on-site meeting planners can arrange all conference, dining, hospitality, and recreation requirements. In addition, Mohonk offers team-building and challenge courses, using adventure-based skills development programs. The resort's natural setting ensures a variety of year-round and seasonal activities, including golf, tennis, skiing, skating, carriage rides, and hiking the 135 miles of woodland trails. Also on-site are stables, a greenhouse, a museum, and the Sky Top observation tower, which offers splendid views.

Listed in the National Register of Historic Places; member of Historic Hotels of America

Location: Mohonk Mountain House is 6 miles west of the New York State Thruway, 25 miles from Stewart International Airport in Newburgh, New York, and 90 miles from New York City.
Function Space: 8,000 square feet; 10 rooms
Capacity—Conference: 64; Reception: 350; Banquet: 350; Theater: 350

Equipment On-Site: Complete audiovisual services available; fax, photocopy, and secretarial services available
Food Service: Full American plan, room service
Overnight Accommodations: 266 rooms
Limitations/Restrictions: Restrictions on smoking; no alcohol in public areas; no bar on premises but alcoholic beverages available in the dining room
Access: Handicapped accessible; on-site parking, valet parking; open year-round
Payment: Cash, check, credit card (AmEx, DC, Discover MC, Visa)

NEW YORK CITY

ALGONQUIN HOTEL
59 West 44th Street, New York, NY 10036
Phone: 212/840-6800 Fax: 212/768-0244

OPENING in 1902, the Algonquin Hotel was made famous as a meeting place for the literati during the 1920s, and it has continued to be a popular

Algonquin Hotel

NEW YORK ●

gathering spot. It was in the hotel's Rose Room that the authors, critics, and artists of the legendary Algonquin Round Table met almost daily for lunch, swapping witticisms and memorable quips. Memories of that lively and irreverent bunch are still preserved at the Algonquin, where suites named for the *New Yorker*, Dorothy Parker, James Thurber, and others feature Round Table memorabilia. Guest rooms and suites are furnished in the style of an English country house, and the elegant meeting rooms accommodate small conferences and exhibitions, board meetings, receptions, and other social events. Groups may meet in the library, the Helen Hayes Room, and the bright, cheerful Gallery. Set amid the business, shopping, and theater districts, the Algonquin is just a short walk or cab ride away from Central Park, the Empire State Building, and an endless list of other attractions.

New York City Landmark; Literary Landmark (Friends of Libraries USA)

Location: The Algonquin is located on West 44th Street, between Fifth Avenue and the Avenue of the Americas; JFK International Airport, Newark Airport, and LaGuardia Airport are 40, 40, and 35 minutes away, respectively; Penn Station is 15 minutes away; one block from subway and bus service.
Function Space: 1,634 square feet; 4 rooms (2 rooms may be combined; maximum occupancy shown here is for combined rooms)
Capacity—Conference: 65; Reception: 200; Banquet: 120; Theater: 110
Equipment On-Site: Audiovisual equipment and business services available
Food Service: Catering and food service available
Overnight Accommodations: 165 rooms

Limitations/Restrictions: Smoking limited to designated floors and the Blue Bar; outside food and beverages not allowed on premises; no pets, but an Algonquin cat is in residence
Access: Handicapped accessible; parking available across the street; open year-round
Payment: Check or credit card; advance deposit required upon signing contract

ESSEX HOUSE

160 Central Park South, New York, NY 10019
Phone: 212/247-0300 Fax: 212/315-1839

ON Halloween in 1931, the city of New York celebrated the grand opening of its largest hotel to date, the elegant Seville Towers. Renowned for its Art Deco architecture and sophisticated interior design, the hotel quickly became home to the internationally elite and famous, although its name soon changed to the Essex House. The famous sign on the roof, overlooking Central Park, has been a landmark for decades, and the hotel's interior still testifies to a sleek 1930s elegance. In 1991 the Essex House reopened following a two-year refurbishment and restoration, and intricate woodwork and plasterwork rediscovered during the restoration was carefully recreated. Guest rooms enjoy splendid views of the city and Central Park; each is furnished with custom antique reproductions and designed in the style of Chippendale or Louis XVI. Other room amenities include two-line speaker phones with dataport, voice mail, fax, a safe, a minibar and a VCR; rates include complimentary shoe shine and newspaper. A variety of meeting rooms are available for receptions, banquets, business meetings, and other gatherings, and dining options include Les Célébrités, long a Manhattan favorite, and Café Botanica, home of the Sunday Stroller's Brunch.

220 ● ● ● ●

Location: The Essex House is located in the heart of midtown Manhattan on Central Park South between Sixth and Seventh Avenues and is approximately 10 miles from LaGuardia Airport, 15 miles from JFK International Airport, and 20 miles from Newark Airport. Cab, bus, limousine, and helicopter service are all available to and from airport service. Grand Central Terminal and Penn Station are within a mile of the hotel.

Function Space: 11,200 square feet; 8 rooms
Capacity—Conference: 35; Reception: 600; Banquet: 350; Theater: 450
Equipment On-Site: Audiovisual equipment available; secretarial, business equipment, and office space available
Food Service: Catering/food service available; two restaurants, bar, 24-hour room service
Overnight Accommodations: 597 rooms
Access: Handicapped accessible; open year-round
Payment: Cash, check, credit card

HÔTEL PLAZA ATHÉNÉE
37 East 64th Street, New York, NY 10021
Phone: 212/734-9100   Fax: 212/772-0958

SINCE it opened in 1927, the Hôtel Plaza Athénée building has been a landmark in one of the upper East Side's most elegant and quiet neighborhoods. It was built as a luxury residential building known as the Hotel Alrae, but was purchased in 1981 specifically for the purpose of creating a second Plaza Athénée to complement the original in Paris. Meetings and banquets are accommodated in Le Trianon, a beautifully appointed room overlooking 64th Street, equipped with built-in audiovisual equipment. A private dining room, decorated in Louis XV-style, is also available for special functions and is part of Le Régence, the hotel's acclaimed restaurant. Old-fashioned Parisian grandeur permeates the rest of the hotel as well, from the lobby with its marble floors, French antique furniture, and tapestries depicting classical and pastoral scenes, to the guest rooms, which are equipped with both modern conveniences and furnishings in the Directoire style. Guest services and amenities include 24-hour concierge services, complimentary morning newspapers, and a state-of-the-art health lounge. The award-winning hotel is situated between fashionable Park Avenue and the boutiques and galleries of Madison Avenue, convenient to Manhattan's cultural, financial, and business centers.

Location: The Hôtel Plaza Athénée is located at 37 East 64th Street, between Park and Madison Avenues, one block from Central Park. LaGuardia and John F. Kennedy Airports are a 20- and 45-minute cab ride away, respectively.

Function Space: 1,080 square feet; 2 rooms
Capacity—Conference: 32; Reception: 75; Banquet: 56; Theater: 64
Equipment On-Site: Audiovisual equipment and business services available
Food Service: Catering/food service; restaurant, lounge, 24-hour room service
Overnight Accommodations: 117 rooms
Access: Handicapped accessible; open year-round
Payment: Check or credit card

THE PENINSULA NEW YORK

700 Fifth Avenue at 55th Street
New York, NY 10019
Phone: 212/247-2200 or 800-262-9467
Fax: 212/903-3949

KNOWN as the Gotham Hotel, a fashionable apartment hotel when it opened in 1905, this local landmark on Fifth Avenue today is named after its famous sister hotel in Hong Kong. The Beaux Arts building, with its Italian Renaissance detailing, was recognized at the time of its construction as one of the first buildings to harmonize with its surroundings, having been designed to respect the Italianate architecture of its University Club neighbor. A rich array of Art Nouveau furnishings, antiques, and period reproductions grace the Peninsula's interior, and the sweeping grand staircase is constructed of Bianco Classico marble imported from Italy. Meeting space is available for business and social occasions, and state-of-the-art audiovisual equipment is available in all function rooms. Guests have complimentary use of the hotel's remarkable trilevel rooftop health and fitness facilities, which include an enclosed pool and spa. Other guest amenities include concierge service, daily newspaper delivery, and valet parking, and a variety of dining options, including the award-winning Adrienne restaurant, are available on-site. The hotel is within walking distance of numerous attractions, including the Museum of Modern Art, Carnegie Hall, Central Park, Radio City Music Hall, and the theater district.

New York City Landmark

Location: The Peninsula is located in the center of midtown Manhattan, within easy access of Grand Central and Penn Stations. LaGuardia Airport is 40 minutes away; JFK and Newark International Airports are an hour away.
Function Space: 3,300 square feet; 6 rooms
Capacity—Conference: 25; Reception: 200; Banquet: 100; Theater: 90
Equipment On-Site: Audiovisual equipment available
Food Service: Catering/food service (including kosher) available; four restaurants and bars; 24-hour room service
Overnight Accommodations: 242 rooms
Access: Open year-round
Payment: Cash, major credit card, direct billing with preapproval

THE PLAZA

Fifth Avenue at Central Park South
New York, NY 10019
Phone: 212/546-5493 or 800-759-3000 or
800-228-3000   Fax: 212/546-5324

BUILT in 1907 at the staggering cost of $12 million, the Plaza on fashionable Fifth Avenue was in its early days a residence primarily for wealthy New Yorkers who wanted in-town apartments. Architect Henry Jane Hardenbergh designed the hotel as a 19-story French Renaissance "château," whose opulent interiors boast 1,650 crystal chandeliers, marble lobbies, and solid mahogany doors. Kings, presidents, business VIPs, literary greats, and numerous celebrities have all stayed at the Plaza ever since Mr. and Mrs. Alfred Gwynne Vanderbilt were the first to sign the hotel register. In the beautifully restored guest rooms, original crystal chandeliers hang from the 14-foot-high ceilings, and many rooms have their original carved marble fireplaces. The Plaza's spectacular meeting rooms feature eighteenth-century Louis XV and XVI decors and accommodate everything from small business meetings to lavish receptions and galas. Each room has a full complement of state-of-the-art electronic and audiovisual equipment, and the palatial Grand Ballroom, the scene of many a historic social event, has a generous stage for panel or group presentations. The Plaza's renowned restaurants include the Palm Court, a European cafe, and the famed Oak Room, a favorite haunt of George M. Cohan, F. Scott Fitzgerald, and Ernest Hemingway.

National Historic Landmark; listed in the National Register of Historic Places; member of Historic Hotels of America; New York City Landmark

Location: The Plaza is located at Fifth Avenue at Central Park South in Manhattan. Taxi service is available at either lobby entrance.
Function Space: 25,000 square feet; 19 rooms
Capacity—Conference: 150; Reception: 600; Banquet: 600; Theater: 750
Equipment On-Site: Complete audiovisual equipment and business services
Food Service: Catering/food service available; five restaurants, 24-hour room service
Overnight Accommodations: 805 rooms
Access: Handicapped accessible; valet parking, open year-round
Payment: Cash, check, credit card, master bill with approved credit

RHINEBECK

BEEKMAN ARMS

4 Mill Street, Rhinebeck, NY 12572
Phone: 914/876-7077
Fax: 914/876-7077 (Same as phone)

ONE of the oldest continuously operated inns in America, the Beekman Arms was established in 1766, and its tradition of colonial hospitality continues to this day. Over the years a number of notable persons have been guests at the inn, including Thomas Edison, Franklin Roosevelt, and George Washington, who, from the second floor, addressed his troops drilling on the lawn. The inn was completely remodeled and refurbished in 1995 and now showcases country decor. Just as they have for more than two centuries, travelers can visit the 1766 Tavern and its Colonial Tap Room for spirits and a warm welcome. The tavern's Colonial-style banquet room is available for parties and special

Delamater House

gatherings. A few doors down from the Beekman Arms is the inn's guest house, the 1844 Delamater House, considered one of the finest remaining examples of American Carpenter Gothic. A conference center in the courtyard adjoining the house is available for corporate and business meetings. The Beekman Arms, in the center of historic Rhinebeck Village, is convenient to a number of historic sites, including Franklin Roosevelt's home and library at Hyde Park and many of the grand Hudson River estates.

Listed in the National Register of Historic Places;
New York state landmark

Location: Rhinebeck is 95 miles north of New York City and is accessible via Highway 9.
Function Space: 1,350 square feet; 2 rooms
Capacity—Conference: 50/20; Reception: 125; Banquet: 100/20; Theater: 120/30
Equipment On-Site: Overhead projector
Food Service: Food service available
Overnight Accommodations: 59 rooms
Access: Handicapped accessible; on-site parking; open year-round
Payment: Check

SYRACUSE

RADISSON PLAZA, HOTEL SYRACUSE
500 S. Warren Street, Syracuse, NY 13202
Phone: 315/422-5121   Fax: 315/422-3440

A full-service luxury hotel, the Radisson Plaza, Hotel Syracuse has been a central New York landmark since it opened in 1924. Designed by George B. Post & Sons, specialists in hotel design, the red brick structure's exterior features tall arched windows and classical pediments, while inside visitors will find the area's most elegant ballrooms. In addition to the 3 ballrooms, 19 other function rooms are available for meetings, conventions, conferences, and smaller gatherings; next door is the War Memorial Auditorium, which offers additional exhibit space. The guest rooms are handsomely furnished, and several on-site dining options are available, including the Cavalier Room, for formal dining; Coach Mac's Sports Bar & Grill, named for former Syracuse University football coach Dick MacPherson; and a coffee shop and lounge. Entertainment is found in the Rainbow Room and the Wise Guys Comedy Club. Located downtown, the hotel is convenient to the OnCenter convention center, the Civic Center, museums, shops, eateries, and historic Armory Square. Syracuse University and the Carrier Dome are both within a mile of the hotel.

Member of Historic Hotels of America

Location: The Hotel Syracuse is in downtown Syracuse, 15 to 20 minutes from Hancock International Airport, and is easily accessible to I-90, I-81, and Route 490.
Function Space: 35,000 square feet; 22 rooms
Capacity—Classroom: 550; Banquet: 800; Theater: 1,200
Equipment On-Site: Complete audiovisual equipment and business services available
Food Service: Catering/food service available; four restaurants, lounge
Overnight Accommodations: 416 rooms
Access: Handicapped accessible; on-site parking; open year-round
Payment: Credit card

TARRYTOWN

THE CASTLE AT TARRYTOWN

400 Benedict Avenue, Tarrytown, NY 10591
Phone: 914/631-1980   Fax: 914/631-4612

SET on 10 hilltop acres overlooking the Hudson River, the Castle at Tarrytown draws its inspiration from the Norman fortifications found in Wales, Scotland, and Ireland. Now a local historic landmark, the Castle was built between 1897 and 1910 by General Howard Carroll and his wife, Caroline, and was designed for fine living and elaborate entertaining. Restored and refurbished, the Castle opened in 1996 as a luxury inn with a gourmet restaurant and banquet and meeting facilities. The Castle accommodates meetings of varying size, from small, intimate gatherings to lavish receptions for as many as 200. Facilities include the baronial Great Hall, with its 40-foot Gothic ceiling, stained glass windows, musicians' balcony, and heraldic motifs, as well as a formal ballroom and a neoclassical library. Visitors should also note the richly paneled Oak Room, once located in a house outside Paris belonging to James II and brought intact to the Castle during its construction. The room is thought to be where Prince Charles Edward, the Young Pretender, and Angus MacDonald plotted the Jacobite Rebellion of 1745.

Location: The Castle is in Westchester County in the historic Hudson Valley, 60 minutes from both John F. Kennedy and Newark Airports and 20 minutes from Westchester County Airport.
Function Space: 3,500 square feet; 3 rooms
Capacity—Conference: 60; Reception: 200; Banquet: 150; Theater: 200
Equipment On-Site: Podium/microphone/ sound system; use of all other equipment can be arranged

Food Service: On-site catering and restaurant
Overnight Accommodations: 24 rooms; 5 suites
Limitations/Restrictions: No smoking; no pets allowed
Access: Handicapped accessible; on-site parking; open year-round
Payment: Cash or credit card

LYNDHURST

635 South Broadway, Tarrytown, NY 10591
Phone: 914/631-4481;
Lyndhurst caterer: 914/524-7900
Fax: 914/631-5634

SURROUNDED by formal gardens, sweeping lawns, and towering evergreens, this Gothic Revival mansion designed by Alexander Jackson Davis epitomized Romanticism's ideals of architecture and landscape. The compact, castlelike structure was built in 1838, but Davis doubled its sized in 1865 for the addition of the second crenellated tower. Lyndhurst, situated on 67 acres overlooking the Hudson River Valley, remains one of America's finest examples of the Gothic Revival style. Also on the grounds are 13 historic buildings, including a carriage house (1865) and a bowling alley (c. 1894), as well as an award-winning rose garden containing more than 100 varieties of roses, some more than a century old. Three prominent families resided here—the Pauldings, the Merritts, and the Goulds—before Lyndhurst passed into the stewardship of the National Trust for Historic Preservation in 1961. The estate's carriage house has been carefully restored as a conference center for as many as 150 people; in addition, two large paneled rooms lit with elegant carriage lamps are available for board meetings, parties, banquets, or receptions. The courtyard can be tented for large gatherings, and horses and carriage may also be rented.

National Historic Landmark; listed in the National Register of Historic Places; National Trust for Historic Preservation Historic Site

Location: Lyndhurst is approximately one-half mile south of the New York State Thruway (I-87) at the Tappan Zee Bridge on US 9 and is accessible from Manhattan via Metro-North Commuter Railroad.

Function Space: 5,000 square feet; 3 rooms; tented seating adds 300 auditorium style, 200 at round tables

Capacity—Conference: 100; Reception: 200

Equipment On-Site: Equipment available through caterer

Food Service: Exclusive caterer

Limitations/Restrictions: Restrictions on smoking; food not permitted in the house, but allowed in the carriage house

Access: Handicapped accessible; on-site parking; open mid-April through October, and weekends only November through mid-April

Payment: Cash, check

Lyndhurst *(Jim Frank. Courtesy of the National Trust for Historic Preservation)*

TARRYTOWN HOUSE EXECUTIVE CONFERENCE CENTER

East Sunnyside Lane, Tarrytown, NY 10591
Phone: 914/591-8200   Fax: 914/591-4014

SET on a 26-acre estate in the Hudson River Valley, Tarrytown House comprises two magnificent mansions and comprehensive conference facilities that accommodate a variety of meetings, from executive retreats to lavish social events. The focal points of the center's comprehensive facilities are the 1896 crenellated stone castle, Biddle Mansion, home of tobacco heiress Mary Duke Biddle, and the impressive 1840s Greek Revival mansion that belonged to B&O Railroad executive Thomas King. The traditionally furnished guest rooms come with work/study areas, TVs with videotape players, and other upscale amenities. With 30 meeting rooms available, Tarrytown House can easily handle large groups and multiple requirements. The Winter Palace provides breakfast, lunch, and dinner throughout meetings, and menus and food service are designed to accommodate work schedules. Casual fare is available at the Sleepy Hollow Pub, and guests may dine in private dining rooms or on the terraces overlooking the Hudson River. Extensive recreational facilities are available for both indoor and outdoor activities, including weight training, racquetball, swimming, and tennis.

Member of Historic Hotels of America

Location: Tarrytown House is 24 miles north of midtown Manhattan, 1 mile south of the Tappan Zee Bridge, and is accessible via I-87, Route 119, and Route 9.

Function Space: 30,000 square feet; 30 rooms
Capacity—Conference: 250; Reception: 500; Banquet: 450; Theater: 500
Equipment On-Site: Audiovisual equipment and two business centers available
Food Service: Catering/food service available, restaurant, private dining rooms
Overnight Accommodations: 148 rooms
Access: Handicapped accessible; on-site parking; open year-round
Payment: Cash, check, credit card

TICONDEROGA

FORT TICONDEROGA

(Mailing address)
P.O. Box 390
(Street address)
Route 74, Ticonderoga, NY 12883
Phone: 518/585-2821   Fax: 518/585-2210

AS the French and British struggled for control of New World territory during the eighteenth century, the French constructed fortifications along the waterways used in their prosperous fur trade. In 1755 they built Fort Carillon, a star-shaped fortress strategically located between Lake Champlain and Lake George, to block British invasion routes. Three years later the French successfully repelled a massive British attack, but in 1759 the British obtained control of the fort, rebuilding it and renaming it "Ticonderoga." Although Ethan Allen and Benedict Arnold led a daring raid on the fort, gaining both the fort and America's first victory in its war for independence in 1775, the British reclaimed Ticonderoga in 1777. The ruined fort was restored in 1908, and today summer visitors can watch special military demonstrations and Fife and Drum Corps performances. The fort's museum

maintains an excellent display of eighteenth-century military memorabilia, including the hollow silver bullet that contained a spy's message from General Clinton to General Burgoyne. A conference room and the grounds are available for meetings and receptions.

National Historic Landmark; listed in the National Register of Historic Places

Location: Fort Ticonderoga is two hours north of Albany and is accessible via I-87 and Route 74.
Function Space: 1 room
Capacity—Conference: 20; Reception: 250 (outdoor/tented site); Banquet: 250 (outdoor/tented site)
Food Service: Catering arranged
Limitations/Restrictions: No smoking; case-by-case restrictions for using fragile areas of site
Access: On-site parking; Thomson Pell Research Center open year-round, Fort Ticonderoga and the King's Garden open early May to late October
Payment: Check, credit card

NORTH CAROLINA

HILLSBOROUGH

THE COLONIAL INN

153 W. King Street, Hillsborough, NC 27278
Phone: 919/732-2461

MORE than 100 eighteenth- and nineteenth-century buildings still remain in historic Hillsborough, among them the Colonial Inn, built in 1759 and one of the country's oldest inns in continuous operation. Both the inn and the town have witnessed a considerable amount of national history; Lord Cornwallis used Hillsborough as a staging area for his British troops and often dined at the inn. The town hosted the North Carolina state convention in 1788 to ratify the Constitution, and Confederate General Joseph Johnston headquartered in Hillsborough late in the Civil War before signing the final surrender. Over the years the inn has expanded, while retaining much of its colonial atmosphere. Guests enter through the original lobby and may dine in the corner Lord Cornwallis used to favor. The restaurant specializes in Southern cooking, and country ham, Southern fried chicken, and prime rib are among the dishes on the menu. Guest rooms are furnished with antiques, and rates include a full Southern-style breakfast. The Orange County Historical Museum and walking tours of the historic district offer a look at Hillsborough's interesting past, and many antique shops are also within walking distance of the inn.

Listed in the National Register of Historic Places

Location: Hillsborough is just off I-40 and I-85, 12 miles north of Chapel Hill.
Function Space: 900 square feet; 1 room
Capacity—Conference: 30; Reception: 100; Banquet: 60
Food Service: Breakfast with room; catering/food service, restaurant
Overnight Accommodations: 8 rooms
Limitations/Restrictions: Alcohol limited to beer and wine only
Access: Limited handicapped accessibility; street parking; open year-round (closed Mondays except to groups of 45 or more)
Payment: Cash, check, credit card (MC, Visa)

LAKE LURE

LAKE LURE INN

(Mailing address)
P.O. Box 10
(Street address)
Highway 64/74, Lake Lure, NC 28746
Phone: 704/625-2525 or 800-277-5873
Fax: 704/625-9655

THE Lake Lure resort area was developed in 1901, the result of Dr. Lucius B. Morse's dream to create a mountain lake resort in a unique setting. In 1927 the Lake Lure Inn was built, a Mediterranean-style hostelry on the west shore of the lake. During World War II the inn was designated as an "R and R" facility for military personnel, many of whom were veterans of combat missions in the South Pacific. Today the peaceful and relaxing surroundings of the Blue Ridge Mountains continue to attract visitors to Lake Lure, which boasts excellent fishing, abundant wildlife, and lush scenery. A

Lake Lure Inn

1990 restoration enhanced the inn's fine interiors, from its Greek columned lobbies to its comfortable guest rooms. Rates include a complimentary continental breakfast, and the inn's restaurant is known for its fine wines and exotic and traditional cuisine. The various meeting rooms and banquet facilities accommodate conferences, business meetings, receptions, and other gatherings. Golf, tennis, horseback riding, hiking at Chimney Rock Park, and a variety of water sports are just minutes away, and the Biltmore Estate and the homes of Carl Sandburg and Thomas Wolfe are nearby as well.

Member of Historic Hotels of America

Location: Lake Lure is 25 miles east of Asheville in eastern North Carolina; Charlotte is 2 hours away. Nearest airports are at Asheville and Greenville-Spartanburg, South Carolina, 1.5 hours away. Lake Lure is between I-40 and I-26.
Function Space: 5,493 square feet; 5 rooms
Capacity—Classroom: 75; Reception: 200; Banquet: 100; Theater: 100

Equipment On-site: Audiovisual equipment, fax, photocopy machine available
Food Service: Breakfast with room; catering/food service available; restaurant
Overnight Accommodations: 50 rooms
Access: Handicapped accessible (limited); on-site parking; open year-round
Payment: Company check or major credit card

OCRACOKE

THE BERKLEY CENTER

(Mailing address)
P.O. Box 220
(Street address)
Route 12, Ocracoke, NC 27960
Phone: 919/928-5911

SAID to be the headquarters of Edward Teach, the notorious early-eighteenth-century pirate better known as Blackbeard, Ocracoke is a preserved island adjacent to Cape Hatteras National Seashore at the southern tip of North Carolina's Outer

The Berkley Center
(© MCMXCV North Carolina Estates, Inc.)

Banks. Today the island is home to a quieter band of residents, as well as numerous historic buildings and quaint specialty shops. The Berkley Center is part of the Ocracoke Historic District and serves as both a country inn and a conference center, hosting business meetings, seminars, receptions, and other gatherings. At the heart of the center is Berkley Manor, which Samuel S. Jones, a charismatic entrepreneur and philanthropist from Norfolk, Virginia, constructed in the early 1950s around a nineteenth-century structure. The handsome shingle-style two-story building boasts a four-story tower, and the interiors feature juniper paneling, country antiques, and comfortable, spacious rooms. Two guest rooms are available in this facility, and seven others in the adjacent Ranch House. Set on three acres of tree-shaded grounds, the Berkley Center offers relaxed island living, while Ocracoke itself provides a number of leisure activities, including trolley tours, boat trips, and fishing.

Listed in the National Register of Historic Places

Location: Ocracoke is located 60 miles south of Whalebone Junction at Nag's Head and is accessible via Highway 12. Ferry service available from Hatteras Island, Swan Quarter, and Cedar Island. A 3,300-foot paved airstrip is available on the island, and Norfolk International Aiport is 3.5 hours away.
Function Space: 1,000 square feet; 2 rooms
Capacity—Conference: 30 ; Reception: 100; Banquet: 30
Equipment On-site: Audiovisual equipment available
Food Service: Catering/food service available
Overnight Accommodations: 9 rooms
Access: Handicapped accessible; on-site parking; open March 15 to November 30
Payment: Cash or check

VILLAGE OF PINEHURST

PINEHURST RESORT AND COUNTRY CLUB

(Mailing address)
P.O. Box 4000
(Street address)
Carolina Vista, Village of Pinehurst, NC 28374
Phone: 800-487-4653 or 800-659-4653 (meetings)
Fax: 910/295-8503

SITUATED on 5,000 pine-shaded acres in central North Carolina, the Pinehurst Resort and Country Club was known for its croquet and tennis when it opened in 1895. The sparkling white, cupola-topped hotel dominates the resort town designed as a New England-style village by Frederick Law Olmsted. A full-service resort, Pinehurst, dubbed the "St. Andrews of America," has become a golf mecca and the scene of a number of prestigious tournaments, including the 1951 Ryders Cup and the 1999 U.S. Open. Its clubhouse is the only one in the world surrounded by 90 holes of golf, but the resort's other features go well beyond the magnificent greens. A state-of-the-art conference center, an exhibit center, and elegant ballrooms are available to host an array of business and social events, large or small, and outdoor receptions and themed events are easily accommodated as well. Pinehurst also offers gracious overnight accommodations, gourmet dining, and extensive recreational activities, including tennis, swimming, lawn bowling, sailing, and trap and skeet shooting (Annie Oakley gave exhibitions and shooting lessons here after retiring from Buffalo Bill's Wild West Show). Visitors will also enjoy strolling through the historic village, with its fine shopping and beautiful examples of classic Colonial architecture.

National Historic Landmark; listed in the National Register of Historic Places; member of Historic Hotels of America

Location: Pinehurst is located on Highway 5 and is accessible via Highways 1 and 220. Charlotte's Douglas International Airport is two hours away, Raleigh/Durham International Airport three hours, and Southern Pines Airport is 10 minutes from the resort. Amtrak service is also available at Southern Pines.
Function Space: 50,000 square feet; 24 rooms
Capacity—Conference: 30; Reception: 1,200; Banquet: 800; Theater: 1,075
Equipment On-site: In-house audiovisual company available; business center
Food Service: Catering/food service available; four restaurants
Overnight Accommodations: 500 rooms
Limitations/Restrictions: Alcoholic beverages for hospitality must be prepared and served by hotel staff; no pets in guest rooms
Access: Handicapped accessible; on-site parking; open year-round
Payment: Cash, check, major credit card

WASHINGTON

ACADIAN HOUSE BED AND BREAKFAST

129 Van Norden Street, Washington, NC 27889
Phone: 919/975-3967

KNOWN as the "Original Washington," Washington, North Carolina, was the first town in America to be named for the American Revolution general. The town was known as Forks of the Tar as it developed in the 1770s, but in 1776 the name was changed to Washington, and during the war the town served as an important supply port for the Continental army. A fire in 1900 destroyed many of Washington's nineteenth-century structures and paved the way for the late Victorian architecture found downtown, including the Acadian House.

Built in 1902, the house features an unusual ground-level herringbone brick verandah. The house is furnished with antiques and local crafts and enjoys a historic district location just one block from the Pamlico River. Guests are treated to tea in the parlor each afternoon, and a traditional breakfast is complemented with New Orleans and Southern Louisiana specialties. Small meetings, receptions, and other gatherings can be accommodated in the Acadian's living and dining rooms, and the innkeepers can arrange for larger meeting space across the square, as well as additional guest rooms.

Listed in the National Register of Historic Places

Location: Washington is in eastern North Carolina and is accessible via I-95 and Highway 17.
Function Space: 336 square feet; 2 rooms
Capacity—Conference: 24; Reception: 60; Banquet: 24
Food Service: Breakfast with room; lunch and catered meals available

Overnight Accommodations: 4 rooms
Limitations/Restrictions: No smoking; alcohol limited to beer and wine only; no children under age 12 or pets
Access: On-site parking, open February 1 to December 15
Payment: Cash, check, credit card (AmEx, MC, Visa)

WINSTON-SALEM

GRAYLYN INTERNATIONAL CONFERENCE CENTER
1900 Reynolda Road, Winston-Salem, NC 27106
Phone: 800-472-9596   Fax: 910/725-5180

WELL known as an executive conference center, Graylyn has also served several other functions in its past. Completed in 1932, the French-style country mansion on 55 beautifully landscaped acres was built for Bowman Gray Sr., an R. J. Reynolds exec-

Graylyn International Conference Center

utive and later chairman of the board. Gray and his wife, Natalie, filled their home with an amazing and exotic collection of art and antiques from their world travels, including a fifthteenth-century French carved stone doorway and the library's late-seventeenth-century hand-carved paneling from Edward VII's Parisian office. Gray died in 1935, and in 1946 Natalie and their sons donated Graylyn to the Bowman Gray School of Medicine of Wake Forest University. A 1980 fire destroyed the third floor, prompting not only the necessary repair work, but restoration of the mansion as well. As a conference center, Graylyn offers fully equipped meeting and breakout rooms and elegant guest rooms furnished with antiques. Recreational facilities include an indoor Art Deco pool, tennis court, and walking trails.

Listed in the National Register of Historic Places

Location: Graylyn is just minutes from downtown Winston-Salem, and 25 minutes from the Piedmont Triad International Aiport in Greensboro.
Function Space: 17,000 square feet; 21 rooms
Capacity—Conference: 46; Reception: 300; Banquet: 200; Theater: 243
Equipment On-site: VCR, overhead and slide projectors, flip charts, computers, fax, copier
Food Service: Complete in-house food service
Overnight Accommodations: 94 rooms
Limitations/Restrictions: All alcohol must be purchased from Graylyn International Conference Center
Access: Handicapped accessible, on-site parking, open year-round
Payment: Master billing for group, credit card for individual

North Dakota

Fargo

Luigis

613 First Avenue, N, Fargo, ND 58102
Phone: 701/241-4200   Fax: 701/241-4129

HANCOCK Brothers of Fargo designed this classical Revival-style building in 1910 for the Stone Piano Company, where Charles Robert Stone, a former traveling piano salesman, sold musical instruments and established a respected music conservatory on the second floor. The conservatory is now the home of Luigis restaurant, where the fare is Italian and a house speciality is Amaretto Chicken. Luigis is furnished with eclectic antique furniture (no two tables are alike) and 12-foot potted ficus trees, and the Fargo Heritage Society honored the restaurant with its 1992 Historic Interior Award. The restaurant itself boasts 18-foot ceilings and an interior lighted dome, as well as original brass light fixtures. A close look reveals that Stone installed gas cocks with each fixture in the event that electricity proved to be a short-lived trend. The rooms just off the main dining room (once known as fainting rooms, where nervous students waited their turns to perform during music recitals) and facilities on the third floor are available for corporate parties and special dinners. Located in the Downtown Fargo Historic District, Luigis has also been the setting for movie premiere parties and opera performances.

Listed in the National Register of Historic Places; 1992 Historic Interior Award by Fargo Heritage Society

Location: Luigis is located in downtown Fargo, accessible via I-29 and I-94, and is 10 minutes from Hector International Airport, three blocks from the Amtrak station, and just a block and a half from the Metro Area Transit terminal.
Function Space: 5,000 square feet; 9 rooms
Capacity—Conference: 200; Reception: 350; Banquet: 225; Theater: 250
Equipment On-site: TV/VCR available; restaurant can arrange for additional equipment
Food Service: Restaurant; lunch and dinner
Limitations/Restrictions: No outside food service
Access: Handicapped accessible; on-site parking; open year-round
Payment: Cash, local checks, credit card, or direct billing upon credit approval

OHIO

CINCINNATI

THE CINCINNATIAN HOTEL

(Mailing address)
601 Vine Street
(Street address)
Sixth and Vine Streets, Cincinnati, OH 45202
Phone: 513/381-3000   Fax: 513/651-0256
E-mail: info@CincinnatianHotel.com

LOCATED the heart of the Queen City, the Cincinnatian has become a jewel in the city's crown. Built in 1882 and originally known as the Palace Hotel, the Cincinnatian reopened in 1987 following a $23 million renovation that has blended its old-world charm and contemporary flair into a vibrant atmosphere. The hotel's exterior is French Second Empire; the interior boasts a dazzling elegance, including a century-old walnut and marble staircase and an eight-story skylit atrium. Meeting rooms come in all sizes and ambiances, from small intimate settings to a luxurious dining area that accommodates a variety of social and business functions. The stately Maxwell Boardroom provides 12 leather executive chairs around a polished granite table and offers a wet bar, a Bose surround sound speaker system, and a complete audiovisual system. The hotel's renowned Palace Restaurant serves gourmet American cuisine that changes seasonally, and a traditional English tea is held each afternoon in the Cricket Lounge. Pleasantly decorated guest rooms feature Roman-sized tubs. From its downtown location the Cincinnatian is convenient to Riverfront Stadium, museums, theaters, and fine shopping.

Listed in the National Register of Historic Places

Location: The Cincinnatian is located in downtown Cincinnati and is accessible via I-75, I-71, and I-275.
Function Space: 3,100 square feet; 6 rooms
Capacity—Conference: 40; Reception: 150; Banquet: 90; Theater: 50
Equipment On-site: Complete audiovisual equipment and business services available
Food Service: Catering/food service available; restaurant, lounge, 24-hour room service

The Cincinnatian Hotel

OHIO

Overnight Accommodations: 145 rooms
Access: Handicapped accessible; on-site parking; open year-round
Payment: Check

OMNI NETHERLAND PLAZA

35 West Fifth Street, Cincinnati, OH 45202
Phone: 513/421-9100   Fax: 513/421-4291

IN their search for words to describe the new Netherland Plaza in 1931, critics compared the hotel's spectacular decorative finishes to the "splendor of Solomon's Temple." The dazzling French Art Deco structure also claimed a number of cutting-edge features, including indirect lighting, an internal broadcast system, ultramodern baths, and high-speed elevators. The interiors highlight Louis XV-style murals, Brazilian rosewood-paneled walls, Rookwood fountains, marble pillars, custom nickel-silver fixtures, and a decor of stylized Egyptian and floral motifs. Comprehensive meeting and function space is available for conferences, conventions, and social events. Facilities include the Hall of Mirrors, inspired by its namesake at Versailles, three ballrooms, and number of breakout rooms and hospitality suites. Fine dining featuring seasonal Midwestern cuisine is found at Orchids in the opulent Palm Court. Among the Netherland Plaza's famous guests have been Sir Winston Churchill, Presidents Truman, Eisenhower, Reagan, and Bush, Guy Lombardo, and Bob Hope. Located in the heart of downtown Cincinnati, the Netherland Plaza is part of the Carew Tower complex and is within walking distance of the convention center, Tower Place Mall, Aronoff Center, and Cinergy Field.

National Historic Landmark; listed in the National Register of Historic Places; member of Historic Hotels of America

Location: The Omni Netherland Plaza is located in downtown Cincinnati and is accessible via I-75, I-71, and I-275.
Function Space: 45,850 square feet; 26 rooms
Capacity—Conference: 250; Reception: 1,150; Banquet: 750; Theater: 1,100
Equipment On-site: In-house audiovisual services company, business center
Food Service: Catering/food service available; two restaurants, bar, 24-hour room service; kosher service available
Overnight Accommodations: 619 rooms
Access: Handicapped accessible; nearby parking; open year-round
Payment: Advance deposit or credit card

CLEVELAND

THE CLEVELAND GRAYS ARMORY

1234 Bolivar Road, Cleveland, OH 44115
Phone: 216/621-5938   Fax: 216/621-5941

WITHIN its castle-like walls, the Cleveland Grays Armory has hosted concerts by John Philip Sousa and welcomed Presidents McKinley, Wilson, Harding, Theodore Roosevelt, and Taft. Built in 1893, the Richardsonian Romanesque Revival-style armory is home to the Cleveland Grays, established in 1837 as the first private militia west of the Alleghenies. The Grays, whose motto is *Semper Paratus* ("always prepared"), have participated in every major American war since the Civil War, and their honorable history is well documented within the armory. Today groups as small as 10 or larger than 1,000 may use the armory's meeting and banqueting facilities for seminars, dinners, receptions, and other functions. And for trade and business shows, the armory's main floor allows direct access for exhibits and equipment. The Main Hall, with

236

its polished maple floor and balcony, and the ball-room, known as the Flag Room, accommodate large groups, while the Club Room is ideal for business meetings. The armory's downtown location is especially convenient to several local attractions, including Jacob's Field and Playhouse Square, both within walking distance.

National Historic Landmark; listed in the National Register of Historic Places

Location: The Armory is located between Playhouse Square and the Gateway Sports Complex; quickly accessible to I-71, I-77, I-90, I-480, and I-490.
Function Space: 16,400 square feet; 3 rooms
Capacity—Conference: 200; Reception: 500; Banquet: 500; Theater: 1,250
Equipment On-site: Audiovisual equipment available
Food Service: List of preferred caterers provided; alcohol ordered through Armory
Overnight Accommodations: Available across the street and within walking distance
Limitations/Restrictions: Restrictions on smoking
Access: Handicapped accessible; on-site parking; open year-round
Payment: Check

RENAISSANCE CLEVELAND HOTEL

24 Public Square, Cleveland, OH 44113
Phone: 216/696-5600   Fax: 216/696-3102

THE Renaissance Cleveland Hotel occupies a site that has welcomed travelers since 1815, when Phinney Mowrey built the city's first hotel. Just over a century later the property was cleared to make way for the ambitious Terminal Tower Complex, which brought together a railway station, a department store, office buildings, and the new Cleveland Hotel under the shadow of the city's landmark tower. During the 1980s the hotel underwent an extensive multimillion-dollar restoration and renovation, and among its many notable features are the skylighted five-story atrium and the magnificent barrel-vaulted marble lobby. Spacious guest rooms come with complimentary morning coffee and newspaper delivery, and recreational facilities include a health club and an indoor pool. The hotel's conference and banquet facilities range from three splendidly appointed ballrooms to large boardrooms complete with executive amenities and adjacent anterooms, and a variety of other meeting rooms accommodate a wide range of social and business events. Many of Cleveland's numerous attractions are within walking distance of the hotel, such as the Rock and Roll Hall of Fame and Museum, the Playhouse Square theater district, Jacob's Field, and the Flats, a waterfront district of restaurants and nightclubs.

Member of Historic Hotels of America

Location: The Renaissance Cleveland Hotel is located in the heart of downtown and is accessible via I-90 and I-77. Hopkins International Airport is 10 miles away.
Function Space: 62,000 square feet; 33 rooms
Capacity—Conference: 80; Reception: 3,000; Banquet: 1,800; Theater: 2,100
Equipment On-site: Audiovisual equipment and business center available
Food Service: Catering/food service; two restaurants, pub, bar, 24-hour room service
Overnight Accommodations: 491 rooms
Access: Handicapped accessible; on-site parking; open year-round
Payment: Cash, major credit card

MARIETTA

LAFAYETTE HOTEL

(Mailing address)
P.O. Box 719
(Street address)
101 Front Street, Marietta, OH 45750
Phone: 614/373-5522, (in Ohio) 800-331-9337 or
(elsewhere in U.S.) 800-331-9336
Fax: 614/373-4684

A grand reminder of America's riverboat era, the Lafayette Hotel is still an official stop on many of today's Ohio riverboat cruises. The hotel was built in 1892 on the site of the Marquis de Lafayette's 1825 celebratory visit at the confluence of the Ohio and Muskingum Rivers. Many of the renovated guest rooms offer river views, and guests also enjoy complimentary airport shuttle service and fitness center privileges. The handsome lobby boasts an 11-foot pilot wheel from the steamboat *J. D. Ayres*, as well as flood benchmarks indicating a series of historic high-water levels. Fine American cuisine is served in the famed Gun Room Restaurant, with its collection of long rifles, while light fare, cocktails, and happy hour are to be found in the Riverview Lounge. A variety of banquet and meeting rooms, from smaller breakout rooms to the Sternwheel Ballroom, which accommodates up to 500, are available for small- to medium-sized conventions and other business or social events. A number of attractions are within walking distance of the hotel, such as the showboat *Becky Thatcher*, Historic Harmar Village, and the Ohio River Museum.

Listed in the National Register of Historic Places; member of Historic Hotels of America

Location: Marietta is 120 miles southeast of Columbus and 1.5 miles off I-77; Wood County Airport is 5 miles away.
Function Space: 7,085 square feet; 8 rooms
Capacity—Classroom: 350; Reception: 500; Banquet: 490; Theater: 500
Equipment On-site: TV/VCR, overhead and slide projectors, cordless microphones, podiums, flip charts, easels, chalkboards
Food Service: Catering/food service available; two restaurants, room service
Overnight Accommodations: 79 rooms
Limitations/Restrictions: Food and beverages provided by hotel only
Access: Handicapped accessible; on-site parking; open year-round
Payment: Cash or credit card

MARIETTA COLLEGE

215 Fifth Street, Marietta, OH 45750
Phone: 614/376-4724   Fax: 614/376-4896

A riverboat town at the confluence of the Ohio and and Muskingum Rivers, Marietta was founded by pioneers in 1788 as the first organized settlement in the Northwest Territory. The city was named for Queen Marie Antoinette in honor of France's assistance to the colonies during the Revolution. Established in 1834, Marietta College has meetings rooms in historic Andrews Hall (1891), the modern Thomas Hall, and the McDonough Center for Leadership and Business, which offers a 300-seat auditorium and a formal dining room for 35. Andrews Hall, completely renovated in 1993, contains a "great room" that seats 230 and can accommodate 160 for dining. The hall also has conference rooms, a private dining area, and a snack bar. Ban Johnson Field House, built in 1929 and named for

B. Bancroft Johnson, Class of 1887 and founder of professional baseball's American League, has permanent seating capacity for 2,100. In addition to visiting the campus, guests can stroll down Marietta's brick streets to the showboat *Becky Thatcher*. Other local attractions of note are the Mound Cemetery, built by the Adena Indians between 800 B.C. and A.D. 100, the Ohio River Museum, and the Campus Martius Museum.

The President's Home (1822) and Erwin Hall (1834) are listed in the National Register of Historic Places

Location: Marietta is 120 miles southeast of Columbus and 1.5 miles off I-77; Wood County Airport is 5 miles away.

Function Space: 27,400 square feet; 3 rooms
Capacity—Conference: 65; Reception: 350; Banquet: 160; Theater: 200
Equipment On-site: TV, VCR, projectors, power point slides; post office, check cashing available
Food Service: Marriott Dining Services
Overnight Accommodations: 900+ rooms available mid-May to third week of August; 4 guest rooms available year-round (closed December 15 to January 15)
Limitations/Restrictions: No smoking; alcohol consumption regulated by local ordinance
Access: Handicapped accessible; on-site parking; open year-round except December 15 to January 15
Payment: Cash, check, credit card

Oklahoma

Tulsa

HARWELDEN MANSION

2210 South Main, Tulsa, OK 74114
Phone: 918/584-3333   Fax: 918/582-2787

COMPLETED in 1926, Harwelden is a 30-room Tudor-style mansion in Tulsa's Maple Ridge Residential Historic District. Carved of Indiana limestone, outfitted with limestone gargoyles, and topped with a slate roof, the house was originally the home of Mr. and Mrs. Earl Palmer Harwell. Mr. Harwell, an oil man, helped to establish the Tulsa Boys Home, and the couple also generously supported the University of Tulsa. Mrs. Harwell bequeathed the mansion to Tulsa's Arts and Humanities Council in 1967 as a base for the city's art organizations. Handsomely decorated with 1920s furnishings, Harwelden boasts seven fireplaces, and the main floor and stairway feature hand-carved wood coat-of-arms motifs. The house sits on two acres that gently rise above Riverside Drive, and the grounds include the carriage house, where servants lived, and a goldfish pond that was formerly the swimming pool. Hardwelden is available for meetings, seminars, weddings, dances, concerts, dinners, luncheons, and other gatherings.

Listed in the National Register of Historic Places and the Oklahoma State Register of Historic Places

The Philbrook Museum of Art

Location: Harwelden Mansion is 5 minutes from downtown Tulsa and is accessible via Highway 51, I-44, and I-244. Tulsa International Airport is 15 minutes away.
Function Space: 3,000 square feet; 6 rooms (+ foyer)
Capacity—Conference: 50; Reception: 150; Banquet: 60; Theater: 90
Equipment On-site: Slide projector and screen
Food Service: Kitchen available; renter selects caterer
Limitations/Restrictions: No smoking or handguns
Access: On-site parking
Payment: Check

THE PHILBROOK MUSEUM OF ART

(Mailing address)
P.O. Box 52510
Tulsa, OK 74152
(Street address)
2727 S. Rockford Road, Tulsa, OK 74114
Phone: 918/749-7941   Fax: 918/743-4230

OILMAN Waite Phillips and his wife, Genevieve, built their spectacular Italianate villa in 1927 and lived there until 1938, when they donated the mansion to the city of Tulsa for use as an art museum. Surrounded by glorious grounds, including a formal Italian garden and an English landscape garden, the villa houses a fine collection of European, American, Native American, Asian, and African art, including the Samuel H. Cress Collection of Italian paintings and sculpture from the fourteenth to the eighteenth centuries. A magnificent classical rotunda entrance links the villa to the Philbrook's 1990 addition, whose architecture reflects the style of the villa. The Great Hall in the villa is furnished with original oriental furniture and offers a splendid view of the terrace. La Villa Restaurant, overlooking the patio and sculpture garden, the Rotunda Gallery, and large meeting rooms are available for a variety of corporate and social events, from business meetings to cocktail receptions and formal, seated dinners. A group's access to Philbrook's galleries, one hour before or after an event, can also be arranged.

Listed in the National Register of Historic Places

Location: The Philbrook Museum of Art is one block east of Peoria at 27th Place in downtown Tulsa, 5 minutes from Utica Square. The museum is within 5 miles of I-244, I-44, and Highway 51, and is 1.5 hours from Oklahoma City and 20 minutes from the Tulsa International Airport.
Function Space: 2,000 square feet; 4 rooms
Capacity—Conference: 200; Reception: 800; Banquet: 200; Theater: 300
Equipment On-site: Audiovisual equipment and business services available
Food Service: Catering and food service available
Limitations/Restrictions: No smoking; no food or drink in galleries; use of museum facilities is a benefit of membership for patron donors; facilities may also be leased to nonprofit organizations
Access: Handicapped accessible; on-site parking; open year-round
Payment: Check

OREGON

ASTORIA

HERITAGE MUSEUM

1618 Exchange, Astoria, OR 97103
Phone: 503/325-2203

THIS handsome neoclassical structure built in 1904 was originally Astoria's city hall, and from 1941 through 1956 it saw duty as a USO club. But since 1982 the building has been home to the Heritage Museum, which features rotating and permanent exhibits on natural history, geology, Native Americans, early pioneers and immigrants, and the area's past as a center for logging and fishing on the Columbia River. Lewis and Clark's expedition camped in the area during the winter of 1805–1806, and five years later John Jacob Astor's fur trading company established Fort Astoria, the first permanent American settlement west of the Mississippi River. The museum's second-floor gallery is used for special events, and tables, tableware, dishes, and linen for 100 are available, as well as chairs for 150. The museum, located at the east end of Astoria's downtown commercial district, is just two blocks from the Columbia riverfront. Astoria is also an excellent base for exploring the north Oregon coast with its fine beaches, fishing, and sailing, and local attractions include walking tours through old Victorian neighborhoods, the Uppertown Firefighters Museum, and Flavel House, the home of entrepreneurial bar pilot Captain George Flavel.

Heritage Museum
(Courtesy of Clatsop County Historical Society)

Listed in the National Register of Historic Places

Location: Astoria is in the northwest corner of Oregon, where US 101 meets US 30. The museum is 4 miles south of the Port of Astoria Airport, and Portland International Airport is 100 miles southeast.
Function Space: 2,500 square feet; 1 room
Capacity—Banquet: 146; Theater: 312
Food Service: Catering/food service available; kitchen available
Limitations/Restrictions: No smoking; only nonstaining beverages allowed; no fresh flowers; no open flames
Access: Open year-round
Payment: Cash in advance

BAKER CITY

GEISER GRAND HOTEL
1996 Main Street, Baker City, OR 97814
Phone: 541/523-1889   Fax: 541/523-7723

THIS handsome Italian Renaissance Revival hotel was built in 1889 as a remarkable testament to the area's newfound wealth derived from the famed Bonanza gold mine. Restored in 1996, the Geiser is once again one of the finest hotels between Portland and Salt Lake City and is the focal point of Baker City's downtown historic district. All of the hotel's guest rooms have large windows and mountain views of the year-round snow-capped peaks that surround the city. A variety of social and business events are accommodated in the Geiser's various meeting facilities. Large groups can use the lovely Palm Court, with its stained glass ceiling, and the adjacent dining room, which features 12-foot-tall windows, a coffered ceiling, crystal chandeliers, and extensive mahogany woodwork.

Groups of up to 50 may use the wine cellar, constructed of locally quarried rock, and smaller meetings are held in the handsome library. The gold-mine-themed Bonanza Room offers poker, keno, blackjack, and other games of chance, and guests also have use of a lending library and exercise center. Nearby activities include rafting the Snake River and touring the BLM Oregon Trail Interpretive Center.

Listed in the National Register of Historic Places

Location: Baker City is located just off I-84 in eastern Oregon and is two hours from Boise International Airport.
Function Space: 2,500 square feet; 3 rooms; 1,100 square feet available for special events
Capacity—Conference: 36; Reception: 250; Banquet: 250; Theater: 125
Equipment On-site: Audiovisual equipment, fax, photocopying, telephone conferencing available
Food Service: Catering/food service available
Overnight Accommodations: 30 rooms
Limitations/Restrictions: Restrictions on smoking
Access: Handicapped accessible; on-site parking; open year-round
Payment: Check, credit card (MC, Visa)

PORTLAND

THE HEATHMAN HOTEL
1001 SW Broadway at Salmon
Portland, OR 97205
Phone: 503/241-4100   Fax: 503/790-7110

BUILT in 1927, the Italian Renaissance-style Heathman Hotel reopened in 1984 following a two year, $16 million renovation. Noted for its dramatic public spaces of marble, granite, and teak, the hotel's elegance is also evident in its original artwork, which ranges from French eighteenth-century canvases to Andy Warhol's *Endangered Species* silkscreen series, and is displayed in guest rooms and throughout the hotel. The mezzanine level, now private meeting rooms and the setting for curated exhibits, was called "the finest broadcasting facility in the country" when it housed KOIN radio from 1933 to 1953. The award-winning Heathman Restaurant and Bar serves contemporary regional and international cuisine, and in the eucalyptus-paneled Lobby Lounge/Tea Court, afternoon tea is served daily and jazz artists perform nightly. Other amenities include full concierge service, a lending library, and fitness suite. The luxury hotel, located next to the Performing Arts Center in the Portland Cultural District, is also in the heart of the city's financial and shopping districts.

Listed in the National Register of Historic Places; member of Historic Hotels of America

Location: The Heathman Hotel is located in downtown Portland and is accessible via I-5, I-84, I-205, and Highway 26; shuttle service is available to and from Portland International Airport.
Function Space: 3,470 square feet; 7 rooms
Capacity—Conference: 40; Reception: 140; Banquet: 104; Theater: 125; Classroom: 125; U-shape: 40
Equipment On-site: VCR, monitor, flip chart, 35mm slide projector, overhead projector, screen; photocopier, fax, computers available through concierge
Food Service: On-site catering and banqueting department; restaurant, lounge, bistro, 24-hour room service
Overnight Accommodations: 150 rooms

Limitations/Restrictions: Alcohol brought in must be approved, corkage fee applies; no outside food in meeting rooms
Access: Handicapped accessible; on-site valet parking; open year-round
Payment: Cash, credit card, direct billing with approval of credit application

TROUTDALE

McMENAMINS EDGEFIELD
2126 SW Halsey, Troutdale, OR 97060
Phone: 503/669-8610 or 800-669-8610 ext. 233 (group sales)   Fax: 503/665-4209
E-mail: edge@mcmenamin.com

EDGEFIELD Manor, built in 1911, was for many years the Multnomah County Poor Farm. The residents raised hogs and poultry, grew fruits and vegetables, operated a dairy, a cannery, and a meat packing plant, and worked in the laundry, kitchen, and hospital. In the late 1950s the farm operation was eliminated, and the facility later became a retirement home. The McMenamins purchased the property in 1990 and renovated the buildings and grounds, which may be toured daily. This unique village setting features bed-and-breakfast lodging, both fine dining and pubs, meeting facilities, gardens, and an outdoor amphitheater on 25 acres. Room rates include a full breakfast in the Black Rabbit Restaurant, a full-service establishment featuring Northwest cuisine and traditional fare. The Power Station Theater shows full-length feature films nightly, and on-site artisans at work can be observed at the Corcoran Glassworks and Earth Art Clayworks. Also on the grounds are the Edgefield Brewery and the Edgefield Winery, with a distillery in development. McMenamins Edgefield offers a casual and relaxed atmosphere in a rural setting for

McMenamins Edgefield
(Courtesty of Ackroyd Photography)

board retreats, conferences, banquets, family reunions, weddings, and other gatherings.

Listed in the National Register of Historic Places

Location: McMenamins Edgefield is located off I-84, 20 minutes east of downtown Portland and 15 minutes from Portland International Airport.
Function Space: 12,000 square feet; 12 rooms
Capacity—Conference: 100; Reception: 200; Banquet: 200; Theater: 225
Equipment On-site: Microphones, amplifiers, podiums, flip charts, projectors, and screens; other audiovisual equipment available with notice, includes delivery charge; modem, fax, photocopier available
Food Service: In-house catering; three restaurants, two pubs, bar
Overnight Accommodations: 103 rooms plus 24 hostel beds
Limitations/Restrictions: No smoking in guest rooms, meeting rooms, restaurants and bars; no outside food or beverages permitted
Access: Handicapped accessible; on-site parking; open year-round
Payment: Deposit in advance, balance upon departure

PENNSYLVANIA

ANDALUSIA

ANDALUSIA
(Mailing address)
P.O. Box 158
(Street address)
1237 State Road, Andalusia, PA 19020
Phone: 215/639-2077   Fax: 215/639-2078

CONSIDERED the finest example of Greek Revival domestic architecture in the country, Andalusia appears as a majestic temple overlooking expansive lawns and the Delaware River. Benjamin Latrobe built this masterpiece in 1806 for the Craig family; in 1814 the prominent Biddle family bought the property, remodeling and enlarging the house in 1835. As director of the Bank of the United States, Nicholas Biddle was a powerful financial figure, and his visitors included President John Quincy Adams, Daniel Webster, and the Marquis de Lafayette. The home's grand interiors are enhanced by the rich American Empire-style furnishings, many of which once belonged to Biddle as well. The spectacular grounds include a grotto, built as a Gothic "ruin" in 1836, the Graperies (where hothouse grapes were raised), a two-story Billiard Room, and other outbuildings surrounded by natural woodland. The house and porch overlooking the river accommodate up to 120 at a standing reception, while 60 people can be seated at a formal dinner indoors. An area next to the house may be tented to accommodate larger groups.

National Historic Landmark; listed in the National Register of Historic Places

Location: Andalusia is 25 minutes north of Philadelphia on I-95, and less than two hours from New York City.
Function Space: 1,000 square feet; 4 rooms
Capacity—Reception: 120; Banquet: 60; tent required for more than 120 people
Food Service: Outside catering service
Limitations/Restrictions: Restrictions on smoking
Access: On-site parking; open year-round
Payment: Check

BETHLEHEM

THE SAYRE MANSION INN
250 Wyandotte Street, Bethlehem, PA 18015
Phone: 610/882-2100   Fax: 610/882-1223

MORAVIAN missionaries settled Bethlehem in 1741, giving the town its name during their Christmas Eve vigil. In addition to the town's Moravian heritage and fine pre-Revolutionary German architecture, the steel industry played a prominent role in shaping Bethlehem. One of the leading figures in the town's nineteenth-century development was Robert Heysham Sayre, who built his Greek Revival-style mansion in 1850, the first house in the historic Fountain Hill neighborhood. Sayre founded the Fountain Hill Opera House and was involved in the development of a variety of local organizations and institutions, including the Lehigh Valley Railroad, Lehigh University, and St. Luke's Hospital. He also helped to build Bethlehem Iron Works, which later became Bethlehem Steel, one of the largest steel makers in the country. His antique-filled mansion has been carefully restored and blends the convenience of a modern hotel with nineteenth-century elegance. A handsomely furnished conference room is available for meetings, and corporate and social functions are held in the parlors and in a tented garden setting. Overnight guests enjoy a continental breakfast, and historic downtown Bethlehem is just a few blocks away.

Location: Sayre Mansion Inn is 5 minutes from the Allentown-Bethlehem-Easton Airport and less than 90 minutes from Philadelphia, New York City, and the Pocono Mountains.
Function Space: 900 square feet; 1 room (parlors provide additional meeting space for small groups)
Capacity—Conference: 40; Reception: 200 (April to October, tented garden affairs accommodate up to 200); Banquet: 40
Equipment On-site: Overhead projector, copier, fax, other equipment can be arranged; same-day dry cleaning service available
Food Service: Breakfast with room; daily gourmet catering on premises
Overnight Accommodations: 19 rooms
Limitations/Restrictions: Restrictions on smoking
Access: Handicapped accessible; on-site parking; open year-round
Payment: Billing, credit card (AmEx, MC, VISA, DC), checks

CHADDS FORD

THE PENNSBURY INN
883 Baltimore Pike, Chadds Ford, PA 19317
Phone: 610/388-1435   Fax: 610/388-1436

THE Pennsbury Inn, located in southeastern Pennsylvania on territory organized by William Penn in 1682, dates back to 1714, when its original stone section was built. During the Battle of Brandywine in 1777, American troops waited in ambush behind the house, firing several volleys at the Queen's Rangers before being driven out. The building's status as an inn was established by 1822, and local legend has it that Daniel Webster spent two months recuperating at the inn following a carriage racing accident, though no proof for the tale exists. Since the mid-eighteenth century up to the latter half of the twentieth century, additions have been made to the house, but it has retained much of its early character. Today the

The Pennsbury Inn

Pennsbury Inn is a lovely country house furnished with antiques, and its individually appointed guest rooms—some with fireplaces—come with featherbeds and modern conveniences. Room rates include a full country breakfast. Meeting rooms are available for small business and social gatherings, and receptions and garden parties may also be held on the extensively landscaped grounds. The inn is just minutes away from several notable attractions, including Longwood Gardens, Winterthur, and the Brandywine River Museum.

Listed in the National Register of Historic Places

Location: The Pennsbury Inn is located 5 miles north of Wilmington, Delaware, along Route 1, 6 miles south of Route 202, 2 minutes from Chadds Ford and 5 minutes from Kennett Square, Pennsylvania. Philadelphia International Airport is 25 minutes away; Wilmington Airport is 20 minutes away.
Function Space: 2,000 square feet; 5 rooms

Capacity—Conference: 25; Reception: 60; Banquet: 25; Theater: 40
Equipment On-site: VCR, fax, computer available
Food Service: Breakfast with room; catering/food service available
Overnight Accommodations: 6 rooms
Access: On-site parking; open year-round
Payment: Check or credit card

DOYLESTOWN

FONTHILL MUSEUM
(Mailing address)
84 S. Pine Street
(Street address)
Swamp Road (Route 313) and E. Court Street
Doylestown, PA 18901
Phone: 215/348-9461   Fax: 215/348-9462

A leader of the Arts and Crafts Movement of the early twentieth century, tilemaker Henry Chapman Mercer had a little bit of Indiana Jones in him as well, and his resume was nearly as colorful as the thousands of original decorative tiles that adorn the interior of his 44-room castle. Fonthill, built of hand-mixed concrete and completed in 1912, was designed from the inside out, the exterior being considered after the interior was planned. Interior surfaces display a variety of Mercer's tiles, as well as numerous artifacts he collected in his world travels. Curator of American and Prehistoric Archaeology at the Museum of the University of Pennsylvania from 1894 to 1897, Mercer performed site investi-

Fonthill Museum
(© 1993 Barry Halkin)

Mercer Museum
(Courtesy of Bucks County Historical Society)

gations in the Delaware, Ohio, and Tennesse River Valleys, as well as in the Yucatan Peninsula, and he later began collecting pre-1850 tools of early American trades. Meeting space is available at Fonthill, though after touring the castle visitors may want to drop by two other landmarks included in Mercer's legacy: the nearby Mercer Museum (see the next entry) and the Moravian Pottery and Tile Works, where Mercer produced tiles and mosaics that are seen today in buildings around the world, including the rotunda and halls of the Pennsylvania State Capitol.

National Historic Landmark; listed in the National Register of Historic Places

Location: Fonthill Museum is located at E. Court Street and Route 313, one hour northwest of Philadelphia, and is accessible via the Pennsylvania Turnpike, 9 miles south, and I-95, 20 miles east. SEPTA train and bus service available.
Function Space: 800 square feet; 2 rooms
Capacity—Reception: 52; Banquet: 52

Food Service: Food service provided by Fonthill's exclusive caterer
Limitations/Restrictions: No smoking
Access: Limited handicapped accessibility; on-site parking; open year-round
Payment: Check, credit card (MC, Visa)

MERCER MUSEUM (ELKINS GALLERY)
84 S. Pine Street, Doylestown, PA 18901
Phone: 215/345-0210   Fax: 215/230-0823

ONE of three landmark buildings built by Henry Chapman Mercer in Doylestown, the Mercer Museum is a monumental, seven-story structure of hand-mixed reinforced concrete. Amazingly, the Gothic-style building, with its gabled roof, parapets, and towers, was constructed by only nine people, including Mercer, with assistance from a horse. Completed in 1916, the museum houses the collections of archeologist-historian-collector-ceramist Mercer. Artifacts range from Native American tools and implements dating from 6000 B.C. to tools used in more than 60 early American trades. Mercer called his collection of pre-1850 American tools "The Tools of the Nation Maker," recognizing their value in documenting American life before the Industrial Revolution. The museum also displays furnishings, folk art, and everyday objects of early America and historic Bucks County. In addition, the museum houses the Spruance Library, a research facility that maintains local primary source material, including Mercer's papers. Meetings may be held in the Elkins Gallery, a brick structure built in 1907 and now attached to the museum. When booking their events, groups can arrange for a museum tour, which is included in the rental fee.

National Historic Landmark; listed in the National Register of Historic Places

Location: Mercer Museum is approximately 45 minutes from Philadelphia, one hour from Princeton, New Jersey, and two hours from New York City, in the downtown Doylestown Cultural District, 9 miles north of the Pennsylvania Turnpike. R5 SEPTA train service is available one block from museum.
Function Space: 1,584 square feet; 1 room
Capacity—Conference: 80; Reception: 175; Banquet: 100; Theater: 150
Equipment On-site: Slide projector, screen, podium, public address system, piano
Food Service: Food service provided by Mercer Museum's exclusive caterer
Limitations/Restrictions: No smoking; catering only by museum's caterer; no decorations attached to walls, floors, ceilings
Access: Handicapped accessible; on-site parking; open year-round
Payment: Cash, check, credit card (MC, Visa)

EASTON

THE LAFAYETTE INN
525 W. Monroe Street, Easton, PA 18042
Phone: 610/253-4500   Fax: 610/253-4635

ELIZABETH Wagner Leary, whose family had helped settle Easton in the mid-eighteenth century, built this graceful mansion in 1895 as an investment property. Two flights of steps lead to a long verandah overlooking landscaped grounds and an expansive lawn. The first known resident was George Elder, superintendent of Ingersoll Iron Works, and over the years the house had several owners, including a Lafayette University fraternity. After a year-long renovation, the refurbished mansion reopened in 1986, offering guests pleasant lodging in its antique-filled rooms and a complimentary continental breakfast. Conference facilities include the beautifully decorated George Taylor Room, named for an Easton resident and signer of the Declaration of Independence, and indoor/outdoor catered parties and weddings are also elegantly accommodated. One block from Lafayette College, the inn is just a short walk away from the Easton Historic District and the historic canal adjacent to the Delaware River.

Location: The Lafayette Inn, accessible via I-78 and Highway 22, is one block from the Lafayette College campus, 15 minutes from the Allentown-Bethlehem-Easton Airport, and less than 90 minutes from Philadelphia, New York City, and the Pocono Mountains.
Function Space: 700 square feet; 2 rooms
Capacity—Conference: 12; Reception: 75; Banquet: 100
Equipment On-site: Flip chart, screen, copier, fax (overhead projector may be rented)

Food Service: Breakfast with room; caterer available
Overnight Accommodations: 17 rooms
Limitations/Restrictions: No smoking; no pets
Access: On-site parking, open year-round
Payment: Cash, check, credit card

HARRISBURG

HISTORIC HARRISBURG RESOURCE CENTER

1230 N. Third Street, Harrisburg, PA 17102
Phone: 717/233-4646   Fax: 717/233-0635

VIEWED as both a document of American banking history and an achievement in historic preservation, the Historic Harrisburg Association (HHA) headquarters today also serves as a resource center for the capital city's ongoing efforts to preserve and enhance its heritage. Beginning in 1893 and lasting for a full century, this venerable structure operated as a bank, at first housing two corporations that eventually merged and were known as "National Central." Shortly after World War II an adjacent building burned down, leaving a vacant lot, and the bank became the first in central Pennsylvania to offer drive-through services. From 1970 until 1993 the building was home to Pennsylvania National Bank, which donated the structure to the HHA. With its Hummelstown brownstone over Indiana limestone exterior and mix of Romanesque and Queen Anne design elements, the building has long been a local landmark at its corner site opposite the historic Broad Street Farmer's Market. Meeting space is available for lectures, receptions, classes, and special events, and visitors may tour the building. Other site features include a community information center, an exhibition gallery, a vault gift shop, and an architectural preservation library vault; both vaults still have their original 20-ton doors.

Listed in the National Register of Historic Places

Location: Harrisburg is 2 hours from Philadelphia and Washington, D.C, 1.5 hours from Baltimore, and 3.5 hours from New York City and is accessible via the Pennsylvania Turnpike, I-81, and I-83. Harrisburg International Airport, Amtrak, and Capitol Area Transit service available.
Function Space: 2,700 square feet; 5 rooms
Capacity—Conference: 40; Reception: 150; Banquet: 100; Theater: 100
Food Service: Catering kitchen on-site, catering available
Limitations/Restrictions: No smoking
Access: Handicapped accessible; on-site parking; open year-round
Payment: Check

HERSHEY

THE HOTEL HERSHEY

(Mailing address)
P.O. Box 400
(Street address)
Hotel Road, Hershey, PA 17033-0400
Phone: 717/534-8600 or 800-533-3131 (reservations)
Fax: 717/534-8666
http://www.800hershey.com

ITS design inspired by nineteenth-century Mediterranean palaces, the Hotel Hershey overlooks gracious formal gardens and tranquil reflecting pools on 300 acres of countryside in central Pennsylvania. Milton S. Hershey built his grand hotel in 1933, not far from the sweetest-smelling downtown in America, with its world-famous chocolate factory and avenues distin-guished by their Hershey's Kiss®-shaped street lights. The hotel's rich interiors feature mosaic floors, carved woodwork, hand-sculpted foun-tains, and antique furnishings. Its renowned restaurants include the Circular Dining Room, with garden views and original stained glass win-dows, and the more casual Fountain Cafe, which overlooks the town of Hershey. Extensive and flex-ible meeting facilities—three ballrooms, a board-room, and everything in between—are available for business and social events. Championship golf, swimming, tennis, cross-country skiing, and tobogganing are among the recreational activities available, and other attractions include Hershey's Chocolate World® visitor center, the Hershey Museum, and Hersheypark®, a nearly century-old amusement park complex.

Member of Historic Hotels of America

Location: Hershey is 12 miles from Harrisburg and 1.5 hours from Baltimore, 2 hours from Philadelphia, and 2.5 hours from Washington, D.C., and is accessible via I-76, I-78, and I-83. Complimentary transportation is available from Harrisburg International Airport and the Amtrak Harrisburg train station.
Function Space: 19,000 square feet; 18 rooms
Capacity—Conference: 50; Reception: 400; Banquet: 400; Theater: 600
Equipment On-site: Audiovisual equipment and business services available
Food Service: Catering/food service available; two restaurants, lounge, 24-hour room service
Overnight Accommodations: 241 rooms; guest house
Limitations/Restrictions: Restrictions on smok-ing; 4-hour limit to open bar
Access: Handicapped accessible; on-site parking; open year-round
Payment: Major credit card

The Hotel Hershey
(Courtesy of Hershey Entertainment & Resort Company)

MECHANICSBURG

SILVER SPRING PRESBYTERIAN CHURCH

444 Silver Spring Road, Mechanicsburg, PA 17055

Phone: 717/766-0204   Fax: 717/796-2189

SCOTCH-IRISH settlers began crossing the Susquehanna and populating Pennsylvania's Cumberland Valley in about 1730. At Silver Spring the present stone Meeting House was constructed in 1783 to replace a 1734 log structure built when the congregation was founded. Nearly a century and a half later, noted architect R. Brognard Okie removed subsequent alterations and restored the handsome Colonial church in 1929. With the use of only hand tools, the original millwork was recreated, featuring box pews, a wineglass pulpit, and a gallery. The church's gracious interior was completed with a brick floor of used, worn pavers and antique glass windows from neighboring farms. Adjacent to the old church is the 1885 English-style chapel, constructed of limestone and trimmed in red sandstone, and meeting space is also available in additional structures completed in 1960 and 1991. A historic cemetery, including the graves of soldiers killed in the Revolutionary War and the War of 1812, is also located on the site, and the original spring, after which the church and the area were named, still flows in a nearby garden. Set on a 17-acre wooded site, Silver Spring Church offers a variety of meeting places, from intimate parlor and library settings to a gymnasium/dining room hall. The Gathering Place, an attractive brick-floored semi-circular room, is ideal for receptions, and offers a wonderful view overlooking the old stone church and cemetery.

Included in the Commonwealth of Pennsylvania Historic Marker Program

Location: The Silver Spring Presbyterian Church is located 15 miles west of Harrisburg, 1 mile south of US Route 11 on Silver Spring Road. It is easily accessible from I-81, US Route 15, and the Pennsylvania Turnpike.

Function Space: 7,500+ square feet; 13 rooms

Capacity—Conference: 35; Reception: 150; Banquet: 200; Theater: 300

Equipment On-site: VCR, overhead projector, sound system, phone, fax

Food Service: Renter selects caterer

Limitations/Restrictions: No smoking or alcoholic beverages

Access: Handicapped accessible; on-site parking; open year-round

Payment: Check

Silver Spring Presbyterian Church
(Jeanne K. Farinelli)

MERCERSBURG

THE MERCERSBURG INN
405 S. Main Street, Mercersburg, PA 17236
Phone: 717/328-5231   Fax: 717/328-3403

ENJOYING panoramic views of the Tuscarora Mountains and the historic town of Mercersburg, the Mercersburg Inn was once the country estate of Ione and Harry Byron. In 1909 the couple built Prospect, their splendid three-story brick Georgian mansion situated on 6.5 tranquil acres in the Cumberland Valley. The inn is available for a variety of social and business functions, including weddings, receptions, bandquets, and retreats, and complete meeting packages are available. Guest room rates include breakfast; a six-course prix fixe meal is served Friday and Saturday nights at 8:00 P.M. by reservation. The small town of Mercersburg, named for American Revolutionary War General Hugh Mercer, claims a number of rich historic associations. Originally known as Smith's Town, Mercersburg began as a trading center for settlers traveling west and was the boyhood home of President James Buchanan. His log cabin birthplace is near the inn on the Mercersburg Academy campus. Easy day trips from the inn, which can provide gourmet picnic baskets for an outing, include Gettysburg and Antietam National Battlefields, and excellent skiing, golf, and other recreational pursuits are close by as well.

Listed in the National Register of Historic Places

Location: The Mercersburg Inn, in the Mercersburg Historic District, is 90 minutes west of Washington, D.C., and Baltimore.
Function Space: 1,848 square feet; 3 rooms
Capacity—Conference: 24; Reception: 150; Banquet: 60; Theater: 70

Equipment On-site: Slide and overhead projectors, screens, easels; fax available
Food Service: Breakfast with room; catering/food service available
Overnight Accommodations: 15 rooms
Limitations/Restrictions: Restrictions on smoking (allowed only on outside porches); no amplified music; outside caterers not permitted; alcoholic beverages must be purchased at the inn
Access: On-site parking; open year-round
Payment: Check

NEW HOPE

WEDGWOOD INN OF NEW HOPE
111 W. Bridge Street, New Hope, PA 18938-1401
Phone: 215/862-2520   Fax: 215/862-2570

FOUNDED in 1681, New Hope is a charming river community and home to a popular artists colony. The New Hope Historic District boasts three centuries' worth of history and architecture, and among its historic buildings are three nineteenth-century structures that make up the Wedgwood Collection of Historic Inns. Set on two acres of landscaped grounds, the Wedgwood (1870), the Umpleby (1833), and the Aaron Burr House (1873) are uniquely designed and decorated, and each has an old-fashioned atmosphere enhanced with antique furnishings. The expansive lawns and pastoral grounds were once the site of an army encampment in December 1776, just prior to George Washington's legendary crossing of the Delaware River. Today those same grounds, with picnic tables, gazebos, and a covered flagstone patio, are shaded by century-old trees and lined with beautiful flower beds. The Wedgwood offers three conference parlors of varying size for corporate meetings, retreats, and other gatherings. Bed-and-

American Swedish Historical Museum
(Pfaft Photography)

breakfast rates include use of the conference rooms, and the inn will host only one meeting at a time to ensure total exclusivity. Guests also receive complimentary carriage rides, as well as swimming pool and tennis club privileges.

Listed in the National Register of Historic Places

Location: New Hope is on the Delaware River, 30 minutes north of Philadelphia and 90 minutes southwest of New York City. Newark and Philadelphia International Airports are each 30 miles away, and Mercer County Airport is 10 miles away.
Function Space: 992 square feet; 3 rooms
Capacity—Conference: 20; Reception: 30; Banquet: 20; Theater: 20
Equipment On-site: Overhead projector, fax
Food Service: Breakfast with room; in-house catering to client specifications
Overnight Accommodations: 20 rooms and suites
Limitations/Restrictions: No smoking; custom food service in advance

Access: Handicapped accessible; on-site parking; open year-round
Payment: Company check, credit card (AmEx, MC, Visa)

PHILADELPHIA

AMERICAN SWEDISH HISTORICAL MUSEUM

1900 Pattison Avenue, Philadelphia, PA 19145
Phone: 215/389-1776   Fax: 215/389-7701

THE oldest Swedish museum in the country, the American Swedish Historical Museum was built in 1926 and modeled after Eriksberg Castle, a seventeenth-century Swedish manor house. In addition to preserving Swedish and Swedish-American culture, the museum chronicles Swedish influence in America from the founding of the New Sweden Colony (1638) to the present. Changing exhibitions feature displays on Swedish and Swedish-American history, culture, and art, and museum collections include a Viking sword, nineteenth-century household tools, beautiful tapestries, modern sculpture, and stunning glasswork. The Golden Map Room showcases a large bronze-leaf map with scenes of seventeenth-century Swedish life, and the interior of a Swedish farmhouse offers a glimpse of traditional nineteenth-century living. Receptions are held in the impressive two-story Grand Hall with its striking ceiling and wall murals, and business meetings are accommodated in the Assembly Room, its pine walls white-washed in the traditional Swedish manner. Whether the gatherings are private or corporate, formal or informal, guests are welcome to explore the museum during their group's event.

Location: The American Swedish Historical Museum is located at the intersection of Broad Street and Pattison Avenue, just off I-95. The Philadelphia International Airport is 5 minutes away by car; Thirtieth Street Station (with Amtrak and public subway service) is 10 minutes away. Subway exit one block from museum; bus stop directly behind museum.
Function space: 2,400 square feet; 1 room
Capacity—Conference: 40; Reception: 175; Banquet: 150; Theater: 100
Equipment On-site: VCR, screen, sound system, podium, tables and chairs
Food Service: Catering/food service available; kitchen adjacent to Assembly Room
Limitations/Restrictions: No smoking; wine and beer only permitted alcoholic beverages; no open flames
Access: On-site parking; open year-round
Payment: Check; no credit cards accepted

THE BELLEVUE HOTEL

Broad and Walnut Streets, Philadelphia, PA 19102
Phone: 215/893-1776   Fax: 215/893-9868

PHILADELPHIA'S only historic luxury hotel, the Bellevue immediately became a popular meeting place for the city's social and business elite when it opened in 1904. Centered in the midst of the city's business and cultural districts, the Bellevue is convenient to all that Philadelphia has to offer. Originally the hotel boasted more than 1,000 guest rooms; today as a mixed-use facility the restored French Renaissance-style building provides its guests and visitors with easy access to fine dining, boutiques, and the 93,000-square-foot Sporting Club, with more than 300 pieces of fitness equipment. The Bellevue is not only one of the country's top spa hotels, but it also offers extensive meeting and banqueting facilities, including the lavish Grand Ballroom, the scene of a century's worth of fashionable parties and debutante balls. Palatial public spaces, large guest rooms, and custom-designed light fixtures by Thomas Edison are among the Bellevue's extraordinary features. From high atop the hotel, guests can enjoy panoramic views of the city and fine dining at the award-winning restaurant, Founders. Also on-site is the Ethel Barrymore Room, which offers traditional afternoon tea and evening entertainment, and the Philadelphia Library Lounge.

Listed in the National Register of Historic Places; member of Historic Hotels of America

Location: The Bellevue Hotel is located in downtown Philadelphia and is 25 minutes from Philadelphia International Airport and 10 minutes from Amtrak's Thirtieth Street Station.
Function Space: 24,000 square feet; 12 rooms

Capacity—Conference: 100; Reception: 1,800; Banquet: 1,100; Theater: 1,200

Equipment On-site: In-house audiovisual department and concierge services

Food Service: Catering/food service available; two restaurants, lounge, room service

Overnight Accommodations: 170 rooms

Limitations/Restrictions: All food and beverages must be purchased from the hotel; client may utilize one of the hotel's kosher caterers

Access: Handicapped accessible; on-site parking; open year-round

Payment: Direct billing

CARPENTERS' HALL

320 Chestnut Street, Philadelphia, PA 19106
Phone: 215/925-0167   Fax: 215/925-3880

Carpenters' Hall
*(Charles Forbes Ward, Jr., The Carpenters' Company
of the City and County of Philadelphia)*

CARPENTERS' Hall has been the site of meetings that have gone on to have historic, national repercussions, and many of the Founding Fathers spent considerable time here conducting revolutionary business. The Carpenters' Company of the City and County of Philadelphia, modeled after London's carpentry guild, built its two-story brick hall in 1774 as a meeting place for the city's master builders. The First Continental Congress convened here that fall, and the following year Benjamin Franklin and two others met with French secret agent Julien Achard De Bonvouloir to begin negotiating for French assistance in the American cause. Disaffected delegates from the Pennsylvania Assembly met here in 1776 to cut their ties to Great Britain, thus making the hall Pennsylvania's birthplace as a commonwealth. The original home of the nation's War Department and numerous other organizations reflecting a variety of interests in Philadelphia, Carpenters' Hall was also the scene of the country's first great bank rob-

bery in 1798. Today members of the Carpenters' Company, who are active in the local construction industry, continue to preserve the hall, which was restored in 1979 and has been open free to the public since 1857.

National Historic Landmark; listed in the National Register of Historic Places

Location: Carpenters' Hall is located in the Independence National Historical Park in

Philadelphia, two blocks east of the Liberty Bell and Independence Hall; one block from subway service connecting to Thirtieth Street Station and Amtrak service; Philadelphia International Airport is 15 minutes away.

Function Space: 1,800 square feet; 1 room
Capacity—Reception: 125; Banquet: 83; 20- by 50-foot brick patio area can be tented and used for cocktails (does not expand capacity cited)
Equipment On-site: Sound system, podium; other equipment available through outside source
Food Service: Approved caterers list provided
Limitations/Restrictions: No smoking, candles, propane, or open flame of any sort; approved caterers only; liquor allowed, no cash bars; corporate and nonprofit use, no private parties; no dancing; no convection ovens
Access: Nearby garage facilities and street parking; open year-round
Payment: Check one week in advance

Cliveden
(John Chew. Courtesy of the National Trust for Historic Preservation)

CLIVEDEN

6401 Germantown Avenue, Philadelphia, PA 19144
Phone: 215/848-1777   Fax: 215/438-2892

BENJAMIN Chew, chief justice of Pennsylvania, probably built his handsome Georgian summer home with the help of amateur architect William Peters beginning in 1763. The house still bears the marks of cannonballs and bullets from the Revolutionary War, when retreating British soldiers sought refuge in Cliveden during the Battle of Germantown in 1777. The barricaded Redcoats and the sturdy stone walls of the mansion withstood the Continental army's all-out assault, but Chew deemed the house an "absolute wreck" and promptly sold it after the war. Eighteen years later, Chew bought the mansion back, and it remained in the family for six more generations. Today Cliveden, which sits on six acres in a parklike setting, is renowned for its outstanding and exceptionally well-documented furniture collection that helps to tell the prominent family's history over the course of two centuries. The late eighteenth-century Carriage House, available for rentals, has been enlarged and renovated, and opens to an outdoor area that groups may also use.

National Historic Landmark; listed in the National Register of Historic Places; National Trust for Historic Preservation Historic Site

Location: Cliveden is approximately 20 minutes from downtown Philadelphia at the northern edge of Historic Germantown.

Function Space: 1,722 square feet; 1 room
Capacity—Conference: 85; Reception: 125;
Banquet: 70; Theater: 85
Equipment On-site: Slide projectors, screens,
speaker's podium with limited amplification,
10 banquet tables, 90 chairs; renters may arrange
for other equipment rentals from outside sources
Food Service: Renter selects caterer; list of local
caterers available; full-service kitchen with double
oven and industrial dishwasher on-site
Limitations/Restrictions: No smoking; time
limit on events, subject to staff availability; extra
charge for events lasting more than eight hours in
a single day
Access: Carriage House is handicapped accessible;
no on-site parking, but an 80-car lot is available
for rent from nearby church; closed January to
March
Payment: Check or credit card (MC, Visa);
nonprofit rate available

FORT MIFFLIN ON THE DELAWARE

Fort Mifflin Road, Philadelphia, PA 19153
Phone: 215/492-1881   Fax: 215/492-1608

IN 1771, Captain John Montrésor of the Royal
Engineers designed fortification plans for the
defense of Pennsylvania, selecting the strategically
placed Mud Island as a site for the fort, a fort he
himself would later attack. With the coming
British threat, General Thomas Mifflin had the
fort completed in 1775, and colonial artillerists
were able to delay British reinforcements to
Philadelphia. In November of 1777, Montrésor led
a bombardment against the fort's weaker side, and
following a five-day siege, the retreating
Americans set fire to the fort, having gained valuable time for their cause. Rebuilding of the irreg-
ular, star-shaped fort began shortly after the battle;

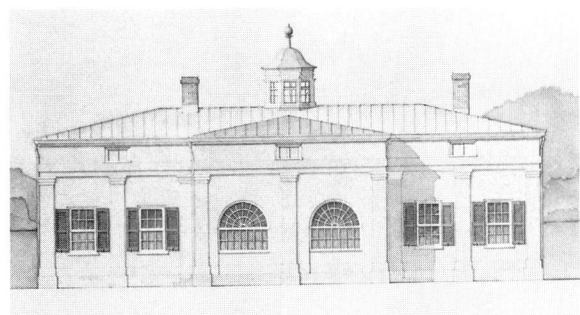

Fort Mifflin on the Delaware
(Atkin, Olshin, Lawson and Bell)

construction continued until 1875, and during the
Civil War prisoners of war were housed here. Fort
Mifflin was deactivated in 1904, but it remains a
remarkable site with 13 restored buildings on 50
acres. A walking tour of the grounds includes the
moat, batteries, arsenal, commandant's house, officers' quarters, soldiers' barracks, and the hospi-
tal/mess hall. Meeting facilities and a picnic area
are available for hosting corporate events, receptions, private parties, and business meetings.

National Historic Landmark; listed in the National
Register of Historic Places, the Pennsylvania Register of
Historic Sites and Landmarks, and the Philadelphia
Register of Historic Places

Location: Fort Mifflin is located on Fort Mifflin
Road off I-95, Exit 13, at Island Avenue, 15 min-
utes from downtown Philadelphia. The Philadel-
phia International Airport is 5 minutes away.
Function Space: 2,500 square feet; 4 rooms
Capacity—Reception: 500; Banquet: 100
Food Service: Full-size, well-equipped
kitchen available
Limitations/Restrictions: No smoking
Access: Handicapped accessible; on-site
parking; open April 1 to November 30
Payment: Check

Chamounix Mansion
(Nancy Khan)

HOSTELLING INTERNATIONAL—CHAMOUNIX MANSION

West Fairmount Park, Philadelphia, PA 19131
Phone: 215/878-3676   Fax: 215/871-4313

HISTORIC Fairmount Park comprises more than 8,500 acres, located on both sides of the Schuylkill River, and within its boundaries are some of the city's most scenic settings and beautiful colonial estates. The park was the scene of the 1876 Centennial celebration, and today visitors enjoy touring the Fairmount Park Historic Houses and the world-class Philadelphia Museum of Art. Among the many country estates that once flourished here is historic Chamounix Mansion, a spacious Georgian house built in 1802 and set on 27 acres. It was first the home of merchant George Plumstead, then book publisher Benjamin Johnson bought the property and named it "Chamounix,"

perhaps for his ancestral links to the Chamounix region in France. The City of Philadelphia acquired the house in 1867 as part of an effort to preserve land along the river, the city's water source. The mansion later housed several businesses before becoming a hostel in 1964. The parlors are furnished with antiques and period furniture, and although the house has been modernized, its early nineteenth-century structure remains intact. Facilities available for conferences, retreats, and other functions include the meeting rooms, kitchen, and dining area.

Location: Chamounix Mansion is located in West Fairmount Park on the west side of the Schuylkill River, 15 minutes from Philadelphia's city center and near the junction of I-76 and Route 1.
Function Space: 993 square feet; 3 rooms
Capacity—Conference: 20; Reception: 30

Equipment On-site: TV/VCR, slide projector and screen, fax, copier
Food Service: Self-serve kitchen and dining area; outside catering permitted
Overnight Accommodations: 12 dormitory-style rooms
Limitations/Restrictions: No smoking; no alcohol
Access: Handicapped accessible; on-site parking; open January 16 to December 14
Payment: Cash, traveler's checks, credit card (MC, VISA)

THE PHILADELPHIA SOCIETY FOR THE PRESERVATION OF LANDMARKS

Administrative Office
321 S. Fourth Street, Philadelphia, PA 19106
Phone: 215/925-2251   Fax: 215/925-7909

ESTABLISHED in 1931, the Philadelphia Society for the Preservation of Landmarks maintains four historic sites available for meetings and receptions. Colonel Henry Hill, a wine merchant and Revolutionary patriot, built *Physick House* in 1786, but it is named for a later occupant, Dr. Philip Syng Physick, who lived there from 1815 to 1837. Samuel Powel, the city's last colonial mayor and its first in the new American nation, purchased the elegant Georgian mansion now known as *Powel House* in 1769, four years after it was built. George Washington was a frequent guest, and the Marquis de Lafayette was among a number of prominent visitors. *Grumblethorpe,* built in 1744 as a country residence for wine importer John Wister, was named by its nineteenth-century occupant, the astronomer and horticulturalist Charles Jones Wister. The house remained in the family until 1910 and today is restored to its original appearance. In addition to the city properties, the society operates *Historic Waynesborough,* a 16-acre eighteenth-century plantation established in 1724 that once covered more than 1,000 acres. The estate's Georgian mansion, where American Revolutionary War General Anthony Wayne was born, has been restored to its appearance at the time when the General's family lived there in the eighteenth century.

Historic Waynesboro is a National Historic Landmark; Grumblethorpe is located in a National Historic Landmark district

Location: Three of the Society's facilities, the Physick House, the Powel House (both in the Philadelphia Historic District), and Grumblethorpe (in Colonial Germantown), are located in Philadelphia; Historic Waynesborough is in Paoli, Pennsylvania, 45 minutes from Philadelphia.

PHYSICK HOUSE
Function Space: 800 square feet; 2 rooms
Capacity—Conference: 50; Reception: 75; Banquet: 50 (garden may also be used for receptions)

POWEL HOUSE
Function Space: 1,400 square feet; 3 rooms
Capacity—Conference: 50; Reception: 75; Banquet: 75; Theater: 50 (garden may also be used for receptions)

GRUMBLETHORPE
Capacity—Outdoor reception: 75

HISTORIC WAYNESBOROUGH

Function Space: 600 square feet; 1 room
Capacity—Conference: 50; Reception: 50;
Outdoor reception: 200

Equipment On-site: Renters may bring their own audiovisual and business equipment
Food Service: List of preferred caterers provided
Limitations/Restrictions: No smoking
Access: Grumblethorpe and Historic Waynesborough are handicapped accessible and have on-site parking; all sites open year-round except Grumblethorpe, which is closed January to February
Payment: Check

THE WOODLANDS

4000 Woodland Avenue, Philadelphia, PA 19104
Phone: 215/386-2181 Fax: 215/386-2431

THOMAS Jefferson called it "the only rival . . . to what may be seen in England," while others knew it as "the Villa Borghese of Philadelphia." In any case, the Woodlands is an outstanding example of eighteenth-century architecture, boasting a classic front portico, classical detailing, and an unusual circular floor plan of nonrectangular spaces. William Hamilton's mansion was built circa 1788, and its first floor was designed for entertaining. Here Philadelphia's elite gathered for some of the city's most elegant social occasions. Hamilton, the first developer of West Philadelphia, planned his own grounds with considerable care. His internationally renowned historic gardens and landscape highlighted the country's largest plant collection during the colonial period. Also on the grounds is a circa 1792 carriage house/stable, and adjacent to the mansion is a section of the Woodlands Cemetery. An active rural cemetery since 1840, the burial grounds feature historic stone monuments and bronze memorials in a pastoral setting, meant also to be a pleasant "resort" for the living. The mansion may be rented for conferences, receptions, retreats, and other gatherings, although renters must be members of Friends of the Woodlands.

National Historic Landmark; listed in the National Register of Historic Places

Location: The Woodlands is located 15 minutes from downtown Philadelphia, at the edge of the University of Pennsylvania, and is accessible via I-76 (exit University Avenue or Spruce Street). The entrance to the grounds is at the 40th Street stop of SEPTA's subway surface trolley lines 11, 13, 34, and 36.

Function Space: 2,260 square feet; 3 rooms
Capacity—Conference: 85; Reception: 80;
Banquet: 70; Theater: 85; tents may be set up on the grounds
Food Service: Approved caterers list provided
Overnight Accommodations: Available nearby
Limitations/Restrictions: No smoking; renters must be members of Friends of the Woodlands
Access: On-site parking; open year-round
Payment: Cash, check

WARREN

STRUTHERS LIBRARY THEATRE

(Mailing address)
P.O. Box 844
(Street address)
302 Third Avenue West, Warren, PA 16365
Phone: 814/723-7231   Fax: 814/723-3856

A unique combination library and opera house, the Struthers Library Theatre was a gift to the town of Warren from local industrialist Thomas Struthers. Built in 1883, the three-story brick structure housed a lower-level theater, above that the public library, and on the top floor a Masonic lodge hall. In 1919 the building was converted from an opera house to a theater better suited for vaudeville and movies. Among the performers to grace the stage were John Philip Sousa and his band, Cecil B. DeMille, Irene Castle, and Duke Ellington. An outpouring of public support and volunteer activity led to the building's restoration in 1983, and the theater was returned to its 1919 appearance. Copper-colored silk brocade wall panels, delicate stenciling, and crystal chandeliers contribute to the elegant atmosphere. In addition to the theater, the original library room, handsomely restored in 1984, is a popular setting for luncheons, dinners, and receptions amid the three-tiered book stacks. The smaller Friends of the Library Room is equipped with brass chandeliers and an antique serving bar, and autographed photos of performers from the 1920s, 1930s, and 1940s adorn the walls.

Listed in the National Register of Historic Places

Location: Warren is located in northwest Pennsylvania, in the Allegheny National Forest, 25 miles from Chautauqua Lake, New York, and 60 miles from Lake Erie, Pennsylvania.
Function Space: 3,700 square feet (+ theater); 3 rooms
Capacity—Conference: 200; Reception: 250; Banquet: 140; Theater: 989
Food Service: Catering/food service available
Limitations/Restrictions: No smoking
Access: On-site parking; open year-round
Payment: Check

Struthers Library Theatre
(Gordan Mahan Photo)

YORK

YORKTOWNE HOTEL

48 E. Market Street, York, PA 17401

Phone: 717/848-1111 or 800-233-9324

Fax: 717/854-7678

DURING the Revolutionary War, York, then known as "Yorktowne," functioned as the nation's capital for a time while Philadelphia was under British occupation, and it was here that the Continental Congress adopted the Articles of Confederation. Despite its name from the city's Revolutionary past, the Yorktowne Hotel reflects the charming history of another nostalgic era, the Roaring Twenties. Built in 1925, the 11-story Renaissance-style hotel features 20-foot-high ceilings, ornate brass and crystal chandeliers, rich, wood paneled rooms, and wall-sized mirrors. Beautifully decorated banquet rooms are available for dinners, receptions, and other functions, and business meetings are easily accommodated in spacious work areas. Over the years the Yorktowne has hosted many famous people, including Eleanor Roosevelt, Glenn Miller, Lucille Ball, and President Bill Clinton. The Commonwealth Room serves American cuisine in an elegant, formal setting, while casual dining is available at Autographs. Located in the historic Center City district, the Yorktowne is within walking distance of the business and financial districts as well as the historic Central Market. A number of museums and historic houses chronicling local history are also nearby.

Listed in the National Register of Historic Places

Location: York is located 25 miles south of Harrisburg, 88 miles west of Philadelphia, and 85 miles north of Washington, D.C.

Function Space: 10,000 square feet; 10 rooms

Capacity—Conference: 64; Reception: 500; Banquet: 425; Theater: 650

Equipment On-site: Audiovisual equipment available; fax, copier, typing also available

Food Service: Full food service available

Overnight Accommodations: 150 rooms

Access: Handicapped accessible; open year-round

Payment: Major credit card

RHODE ISLAND

BRISTOL

BLITHEWOLD MANSION AND GARDENS

(Mailing address)
P.O. Box 716
(Street address)
101 Ferry Road (Route 114), Bristol, RI 02809-0716
Phone: 401/253-2707   Fax: 401/253-0412

SET on a 33-acre estate overlooking Narragansett Bay, Blithewold was built in 1908 as a grand 45-room summer home in the style of a seventeenth-century English manor house. More than a few traditions have been maintained here; when the house was privately owned it was frequently open to visitors during gardening season, and the trees, flowers, and shrubs are still arranged in their original landscaped design. Much of the mansion's furnishings and decor remain from Blithewold's early years as well. In 1976 Marjorie Van Wickle Lyon, daughter of the estate's original owners, bequeathed Blithewold to the Heritage Trust of Rhode Island. Today the stone and stucco mansion welcomes groups meeting for business and social occasions, and visitors never fail to be impressed with Blithewold's stunning gardens. Gardening enthusiasts will note the variety of exotic plants uncommon in New England, and of particular interest is Blithewold's Chinese toon tree and an 85-foot-tall century-old giant sequoia, the largest of its kind east of the Rocky Mountains.

Listed in the National Register of Historic Places

Blithewold Mansion and Gardens
(Mark Zelonis)

Location: Blithewold is located midway between Newport and Providence on Ferry Road (Route 114), about one hour south of Boston; T. F. Green Airport is 40 minutes away.
Function Space: 980 square feet; 4 rooms
Capacity—Conference: 20; Reception: 100; Banquet: 75; Theater: 80
Equipment On-site: Slide projector and screen, lighted lectern; fax available
Food Service: Small kitchen available
Limitations/Restrictions: No smoking
Access: Limited handicapped accessibility; on-site parking; open April to October
Payment: Business check, credit card (MC, Visa)

NEWPORT

THE ASTORS' BEECHWOOD MANSION

580 Bellevue Avenue, Newport, RI 02840
Phone: 401/846-3772   Fax: 401/849-6998

DURING the Gilded Age, Newport emerged as the summer playground for America's wealthy and social elite, and among the spectacular oceanfront mansions on historic Bellevue Avenue is Beechwood, home to the Astor family. Andrew Jackson Downing designed the 1857 Italianate mansion, which is named for the five varieties of beech trees that stood on the site. In 1881, William Backhouse Astor purchased Beechwood, and it became his wife Caroline's favorite home. Caroline Astor, or *The* Mrs. Astor, as she insisted on being called, reigned as the queen of American society and is famous for developing the first American social register, known as the Four Hundred, which conveniently also happened to be the number of guests the ballroom in her New York home could accommodate. At Beechwood The Mrs. Astor added electric light, running water, and water clos-

ets and created a magnificent ballroom. The opulent house is available for weddings and special events as well as business meetings, and Beechwood Theatre Company actors in period costumes can be on hand to mingle with guests and recreate life in the mansion during the Victorian era.

Located in a National Historic Landmark district; listed in the National Register of Historic Places

Location: Newport is 40 minutes from Providence and T. F. Green-Warwick Airport and is accessible via I-95 and I-195.
Function Space: 4,000 square feet; 5 rooms
Capacity—Reception: 300 (500 with outdoor tenting); Banquet: 170 with dance floor, 220 without; 250 with dance floor using additional rooms, 300 without dance floor; Theater: 200
Equipment On-site: Audiovisual equipment and business services available
Food Service: Full catering available
Limitations/Restrictions: Restrictions on smoking
Access: Handicapped accessible; on-site parking; open year-round
Payment: Certified check

THE HOTEL VIKING

One Bellevue Avenue, Newport, RI 20840
Phone: 401/847-3300   Fax: 401/849-0749

MANY of Newport's world-famous mansions are located on fashionable Bellevue Avenue, so it is not surprising that those wealthy residents whose homes were long on entertainment space but short on bedrooms, would build a hotel for their summer guests just up the street. The Hotel Viking opened to great fanfare in 1926; its guests have included Kennedys, Astors, Vanderbilts, international dignitaries, and golf, yachting, and tennis champions. The hotel was named for the Vikings that may have landed in Newport at about the year 1000, but the hotel's Federal-style facade and Queen Anne and Chippendale interiors point to nineteenth-century American sensibilities. Among the hotel's 20 function rooms is the Grand Ballroom—the largest in town, seating 900—the exquisite Bellevue Room, and six distinctive boardrooms. Dining options include the Vanderbilt Restaurant, which serves seafood and New England specialties, the Garden Cafe and outdoor patio, and the seasonal Top of Newport Rooftop Bar, which offers harbor views from the city's highest point. In addition to the gilded marble mansions that line Bellevue Avenue, the hotel is convenient to a number of other attractions, including the International Tennis Hall of Fame, the Touro Synagogue National Historic Site, and the Redwood Library and Athanaeum.

Listed in the National Register of Historic Places; member of Historic Hotels of America

Location: The Hotel Viking is 45 minutes from Providence, 1.5 hours from Boston, and 3.5 hours from New York City; it is accessible via I-95, Route 195, Route 128, and Route 24. The nearest airport is in Providence.

Function Space: 26,000 square feet; 20 rooms

Capacity—Conference: 230; Reception: 1,200; Banquet: 900; Theater: 1,000

Equipment On-site: Audiovisual equipment available

Food Service: Catering/food service available; two restaurants, bar

Overnight Accommodations: 182 rooms

Limitations/Restrictions: No pets

Access: Handicapped accessible; on-site parking; open year-round

Payment: Cash, check, major credit card

The Hotel Viking

PROVIDENCE

PROVIDENCE BILTMORE HOTEL—A GRAND HERITAGE HOTEL

Kennedy Plaza, Providence, RI 02903
Phone: 401/421-0700   Fax: 401/455-3040

SINCE its opening in 1922, when it was hailed as the "Grand Dame of Providence," the Providence Biltmore has been Rhode Island's premier luxury hotel. Lavishly decorated and elegantly furnished, the restored hotel has been returned to its original grand appearance. Built in a unique V-shape, the hotel offers tremendous views of downtown and the waterfront from its rooftop and its outside glass elevator. The historic Garden Room, available for meetings and social functions, was a famous supper club during the Big Band era. At one time its dance floor was converted into an aquarium—with live fish—for an Ester Williams water show, and in another instance the floor was frozen for a Sonja Henie ice skating performance. Complete facilities for social and business occasions are available in settings ranging from the rooftop Grand Ballroom to the muraled Bacchante Room. The hotel also offers a variety of Express Meeting Packages, which can

easily accommodate meetings scheduled at the last minute. The Providence Biltmore borders the city's financial district and is within walking distance of several historic sites, including the magnificent State House.

Listed in the National Register of Historic Places

Location: The Providence Biltmore is located in downtown Providence, 45 minutes from Newport and an hour from Boston. The hotel is accessible via I-95, I-295, and I-195. Bus and Amtrak service available; airport service at Providence's T. F. Green Airport.

Function Space: 19,186 square feet; 16 rooms

Capacity—Conference: 60; Reception: 800; Banquet: 375; Theater: 500; Exhibit booths: 20

Equipment On-site: Available through outside source; business services provided by Pennfield's on lobby level

Food Service: Catering/food service available; restaurant, lounge, room service

Overnight Accommodations: 240 rooms

Access: Handicapped accessible; on-site parking, adjacent garage (daily charge); open year-round

Payment: Credit card

SOUTH CAROLINA

CHARLESTON

DRAYTON HALL

3380 Ashley River Road, Charleston, SC 29414

Phone: 803/766-0188   Fax: 803/766-0878

BUILT between 1738 and 1742, Drayton Hall is regarded as one of the finest examples of colonial architecture in America. The house is located outside Charleston on the Ashley River, where it enjoys panoramic views of the meandering tidal river and surrounding countryside. Through seven generations of Drayton ownership, this historic landmark has stayed in nearly original condition and is the only remaining Ashley River plantation house to survive the Civil War intact. Its design closely matches the architectural concepts fashionable in Britain after 1715, and its two-story portico is believed to have been the first of its kind in America. Its unique state of preservation and rich, hand-crafted details provide a rare and compelling glimpse of a vanished Southern way of life. A visit to Drayton Hall offers a sense of timelessness and continuity from generation to generation, and guests can admire the beautiful grounds and splendid river views on self-guided walks through the garden, along natural scenic trails, and from marsh boardwalks. An administrative conference room is available for meetings, and the grounds may be used for parties and receptions. Groups can also arrange for guided house tours in conjunction with their events.

National Historic Landmark; listed in the National Register of Historic Places; National Trust for Historic Preservation Historic Site

Drayton Hall
(Ron Blunt. Courtesy of the National Trust for Historic Preservation)

Location: Drayton Hall is approximately 9 miles northwest of downtown Charleston on historic Ashley River Road (SC Route 61).

Function Space: 360 square feet; 1 room

Capacity—Conference: 20; Reception: 350 (outdoors); tented use of lawn may be arranged for day or evening functions; picnic tables available

Food Service: Renter selects caterer, preferred caterers list available but outside catering permitted; kitchenette available

Limitations/Restrictions: No smoking; renter must have special event insurance and liquor liability; in case of inclement weather,—tenting, rain date, or alternative location is recommended

Access: Handicapped accessible; on-site parking; open year-round

Payment: Cash, check, credit card (AmEx, MC, Visa)

KING'S COURTYARD INN/FULTON LANE INN

(Mailing Address)

212¹/₂ King Street

(Street Address)

198 King Street (King's Courtyard Inn)

202 King Street (Fulton Lane Inn)

Charleston, SC 29401

Phone: 803/723-7000 or 800-845-6119 (King's Courtyard Inn); 803/720-2600 or 800-720-2688 (Fulton Lane Inn)   Fax: 803/722-8634

THE King's Courtyard Inn and its neighbor, the Fulton Lane Inn, share the tradition of Southern hospitality for which genteel Charleston is known, as well as a charming downtown location not far from the picturesque waterfront. Both inns are in the heart of old Charleston, amid magnificent gardens, splendid churches that trace the city's skyline, and historic houses representing a library of Southern architecture through the centuries. Built

in 1853, the three-story Greek Revival King's Courtyard Inn, with its unusual Egyptian detail, is one of the oldest structures on historic King Street, the main route into old Charles Towne beginning in the seventeenth century. The Fulton Lane Inn, hidden away off King Street on a quiet pedestrian lane, was built by Confederate blockade runner John Rugheimer in 1902. Guests at both inns enjoy a complimentary breakfast and stay in distinctive guest rooms, some with fireplaces, canopied beds, cathedral ceilings, and even whirlpool baths. Meetings, parties, and receptions may be held in the Fulton Lane Inn's Blockade Runner Room, which has been elegantly restored and is noted for its original tin ceiling.

Listed in the National Register of Historic Places; member of Historic Hotels of America (King's Courtyard Inn)

Location: Both inns are located in historic Charleston, 10 miles from Charleston International Airport, and are accessible via I-26.

Function Space: 713 square feet; 1 room

Capacity—Conference: 40; Reception: 85 (standing); Banquet: 50; Theater: 80

Equipment On-site: TV/VCR, overhead projector and screen, flip chart

Food Service: Breakfast with room; full food service available

Overnight Accommodations: 68 rooms (41 at King's Courtyard, 27 at Fulton Lane)

Limitations/Restrictions: No smoking at Fulton Inn; smoking and nonsmoking rooms at King's Courtyard

Access: Handicapped accessible; on-site parking; open year-round

Payment: Cash, check, credit card

SUMTER

CALHOUN STREET BED AND BREAKFAST

302 W. Calhoun Street, Sumter, SC 29150
Phone: 803/775-7035 or 800-355-8119
Fax: 803/775-7035
E-mail: CalhounBB@aol.com

THE Calhoun Street Bed and Breakfast, a Victorian home built in 1890, remains in the family of its builder. Guests stay in rooms furnished with family antiques, ranging from medieval art to a queen-sized Empire poster bed, and enjoy a hearty breakfast in the morning. A charming setting for intimate parties, weddings, receptions, and small meetings, this fine old house offers all the comforts of home, whether one chooses to relax on the verandah, find a book in the library, or enjoy the gardens. Directly behind the house is a park with jogging track and tennis courts available for visitors' use, and as part of Hampton Park

Historic District, the Calhoun Street Bed and Breakfast is easily within reach of many other beautiful homes, antique shops, and galleries. Nearby Swan Lake Iris Gardens is an enchanting place to picnic and explore, and the Sumter County Museum details the area's history.

Location: Sumter is 1 hour from Columbia and 1.5 hours from Charleston, off Highway 378/76.
Function Space: 900 square feet; 3 rooms
Capacity—Conference: 25; Reception: 125; Banquet: 16
Equipment On-site: Fax, copier, computer, e-mail
Food Service: Breakfast with room; special-events food service in-house
Overnight Accommodations: 4 rooms
Limitations/Restrictions: Restrictions on smoking (front porch only); no pets except Seeing Eye dogs
Access: On-site parking
Payment: Check, credit card (MC, VISA)

SOUTH DAKOTA

DEADWOOD

BULLOCK HOTEL

633 Main Street, Deadwood, SD 57732

Phone: 605/578-1745 or 800-336-1876

Fax: 605/578-1382

ONCE the haunt of Wild Bill Hickok, Calamity Jane, and a host of other colorful figures from the days of the Wild West, Deadwood still offers the excitement of a roaring mining town. In 1895, Deadwood's first sheriff, Seth Bullock, built his luxurious hotel, which contrasted sharply with the neighboring flophouses and bordellos. In addition to a Turkish bath and a reading parlor, the hotel boasted a high-ceilinged ballroom that was the scene of gambling and other lively games. Today, in the meticulously restored hotel, visitors can still enjoy round-the-clock gambling, thick cuts of steak, and a turn-of-the-century atmosphere. A unique setting for a meeting or special occasion is Seth's Cellar, situated below the hotel, where banquets, private parties, and dinner shows are held. Guest rooms are furnished in the Victorian style, and Bully's Restaurant and Lounge offers an old-fashioned but relaxed setting. In the heart of historic Deadwood, the hotel is a good starting point for walking tours of the town, including Main Street's old gaming halls. The Mount Moriah Cemetery (Boot Hill), where Hickok and Bullock are buried, is a short walk from town.

Located in a National Historic Landmark district; listed in the National Register of Historic Places

Location: Deadwood is in the Black Hills of western South Dakota, one hour from Rapid City.
Function Space: 1,526 square feet; 2 rooms
Capacity—Conference: 20/50; Reception: 20/95; Banquet: 20/100; Theater: 25/100
Equipment On-site: TV/VCR, overhead and slide projectors, screen, podium, copier, fax, dataports
Food Service: Full food service available; restaurant and lounge
Overnight Accommodations: 35 rooms
Limitations/Restrictions: Alcoholic beverages limited to wine and beer
Access: Handicapped accessible; on-site parking; open year-round
Payment: Credit card, prepay; company check with credit approval

RAPID CITY

HISTORIC HOTEL ALEX JOHNSON

523 Sixth Street, Rapid City, SD 57701

Phone: 605/342-1210 or 800-888-ALEX

Fax: 605/342-7436

ALEX Johnson did more than just build an elegant hotel in 1928; he brought together European architecture and authentic Lakota art, resulting in an aesthetic achievement that continues to honor the Sioux Nation. With its Tudor-style facade on the top floor, the hotel's interior reflects a deep Indian influence, from the rich wood beams and railings to a decor highlighting treasured Native American artifacts. Renovated rooms and suites feature handcrafted replicas of Johnson's original Lakota Sioux furnishings, and the full-service hotel offers complete amenities. Beautifully appointed rooms, including Yesterday's Ballroom, a favorite of Mount

Rushmore sculptor Gutzon Borglum, are available for conventions, conferences, banquets, and receptions. The Landmark Restaurant specializes in regional cuisine, such as choice buffalo steaks and South Dakota pheasant; Paddy O'Neill's Pub & Casino provides a relaxing setting with an Old English atmosphere. Hotel Alex Johnson is located in historic downtown Rapid City, convenient to antique shops, galleries, museums, and the city's business district. The hotel is also a great starting point for touring the Black Hills and some of the region's famous attractions, including Mount Rushmore, Deadwood, Custer State Park, and the Crazy Horse Memorial.

Listed in the National Register of Historic Places

Location: Rapid City, the gateway to the Black Hills, is on I-90 in western South Dakota. The Historic Hotel Alex Johnson is located downtown and is 14 miles from Rapid City Regional Airport.
Function Space: 5,746 square feet; 5 rooms
Capacity—Conference: 50; Reception: 250+; Banquet: 240; Theater: 200
Equipment On-site: Guest corporate office, including fax, computer, modem
Food Service: Catering/food service available; restaurant, pub
Overnight Accommodations: 141 rooms
Limitations/Restrictions: No pets
Access: Handicapped accessible; on-site parking; open year-round
Payment: Cash, check, major credit cards

Hotel Alex Johnson

TENNESSEE

CHATTANOOGA

ADAMS HILBORNE

801 Vine Street, Chattanooga, TN 37403
Phone: 423/265-5000 Fax: 423/265-5555

CALLED the cornerstone of the Fortwood Historic District, the Adams Hilborne is a grand stone Richardsonian-Romanesque mansion in a neighborhood filled with classic examples of late nineteenth-century architecture. The house was built in 1889 as the mayor's mansion, and today as a small European-style hotel it retains its old-fashioned grandeur. Among its notable features are fine hand-carved moldings, Tiffany glass windows, original cherry paneling, and the 16-foot-high coffered ceilings. The Adams Hilborne is available for receptions, business meetings, lectures, private parties, and other events; function space includes private meeting rooms, reception areas, and the grand Fortwood Ballroom. Overnight guests stay in beautifully furnished rooms, some with balconies and views of Lookout Mountain, while the Presidential Suite boasts a fireplace, an Old English armoire, floor-to-ceiling windows, and a 600-gallon marble soaking tub for two. Room rates include a complimentary breakfast, and fine dining is available on weekends; the Porch Cafe offers casual fare from its verandah overlooking the historic district's Victorian neighborhood.

Listed in the National Register of Historic Places

Location: The Adams Hilborne is located near downtown Chattanooga, across the street from the University of Tennessee at Chattanooga, and is accessible via I-75, I-59 and I-24.
Function Space: 2,145 square feet; 4 rooms
Capacity—Conference: 50; Reception: 200; Banquet: 50; Theater: 75–100
Equipment On-site: Computer, fax, copier
Food Service: Breakfast with room; catering/food service available; two restaurants
Overnight Accommodations: 11 rooms
Limitations/Restrictions: Smoking restricted to porch; food and liquor provided by inn
Access: Handicapped accessible; on-site parking; open year-round
Payment: Check, credit card (AmEx, MC, VISA)

Adams Hilborne
(Dan Reynolds)

GREENEVILLE

GENERAL MORGAN INN AND CONFERENCE CENTER—A GRAND HERITAGE HOTEL

111 N. Main Street, Greeneville, TN 37743
Phone: 423/787-1000   Fax: 423/787-1001

FOR its efforts to preserve and revitalize its historic downtown, Greeneville, the second oldest city in the state and named for American Revolutionary War general Nathanael Greene, has earned a designation as a "Main Street" town. Part of this revitalization effort can be seen at the General Morgan Inn, a "new" facility created from four interconnecting railroad hotels that date back to 1889. Located in the heart of Morgan Square, the inn is surrounded by history—for example, the Andrew Johnson National Historic site and the Dickson-Williams Mansion are just a short walk away. The full-service inn offers a variety of banquet/conference facilities, ranging from a garden terrace and a grand ballroom to an executive boardroom. The spacious guest rooms, with high ceilings, restored moldings and woodwork, and marble bathrooms offer an old-fashioned atmosphere with modern amenities. Brumley's, the hotel's fine dining room named for the inn's original restaurant, features continental and Southern cuisines. A wide range of recreational activities are available, including white-water rafting, mountain climbing, and professionally guided fishing expeditions.

Listed in the National Register of Historic Places

Location: The General Morgan Inn is 35 miles southwest of Tri-Cities Regional Airport and 60 miles east of Knoxville International Airport. Greeneville is 12 miles south of I-81; traveling east, take Exit 23; traveling west, take Exit 36.

Function Space: 10,700 square feet; 7 rooms
Capacity—Conference: 100; Reception: 450; Banquet: 400; Theater: 300
Equipment On-site: Complete audiovisual *equipment and video conferencing available; business concierge available
Food Service: Catering/food service available; restaurant and lounge
Overnight Accommodations: 52 rooms
Limitations/Restrictions: No outside food or beverage service
Access: Handicapped accessible; on-site parking; open year-round
Payment: Cash, all major credit cards

MEMPHIS

THE PEABODY HOTEL

149 Union Avenue, Memphis, TN 38103
Phone: 901/529-4000   Fax: 901/529-3677

THE grande dame of Southern hotels, the Peabody is an excellent example of Italian Renaissance Revival architecture. Built in 1925, the 14-story Peabody has long been the social hub of the mid-South, and during the Swing Era its rooftop nightclub featured live big band radio broadcasts. The lavish, two-story Grand Lobby, "where the Mississippi Delta begins," boasts fine furnishings, skylights, and towering *torchères*. Also in the lobby is an elaborately carved travertine marble fountain—home to the famous Peabody Marching Ducks, whose daily red-carpeted parades to and from the fountain began as a Depression-era prank, but the tradition continues to charm visitors. The Peabody offers extensive meeting facilities, from stately meeting rooms to elegant ballrooms, as well as a state-of-the-art Executive Conference Center

The Peabody

designed for smaller VIP groups. Right next door to the hotel is the Tennessee Exhibition Hall, used for trade shows, conventions, and social events. Other hotel features include award-winning restaurants, an athletic club, concierge and business services, a rooftop terrace with river views, and, of course, the penthouse residence of the Peabody Ducks. Beale Street Historic District, with its blues clubs and cabarets, is within walking distance, and Elvis Presley's Graceland is just 20 minutes away.

Listed in the National Register of Historic Places; member of Historic Hotels of America

Location: The Peabody is located in downtown Memphis and is accessible via I-40 and I-55.

Function Space: 62,000 square feet; 32 rooms
Capacity—Conference: 70; Reception: 1,600; Banquet: 1,200; Theater: 1,600
Equipment On-site: Audiovisual equipment available; color photocopiers, computers, word processing, fax available
Food Service: Catering/food service available; four restaurants, 24-hour room service
Overnight Accommodations: 468 rooms
Limitations/Restrictions: Restrictions on smoking
Access: Handicapped accessible; on-site parking; open year-round
Payment: Preapproval for direct billing or deposit 30 days in advance

MONTEAGLE

ADAMS EDGEWORTH INN

Monteagle Assembly, Monteagle, TN 37356
Phone: 615/924-4000   Fax: 615/924-3236

CALLED the Chatauqua of the South, the Monteagle Assembly grounds comprise nearly 100 acres filled with trees, trails, Victorian cottages, and wooden trestle bridges. Also on the grounds is the Adams Edgeworth Inn, a charming Victorian country manor house built in 1896. Space for small banquets, receptions, meetings, and other gatherings is available in the dining room and the library. Original museum-quality artwork, floral chintz fabrics, and antique furnishings highlight the inn's cozy interior. Many guest rooms feature antique furnishings, including footed Victorian tubs and colorful handmade Adams family quilts, and in several rooms French doors open onto the rocker-lined verandah. Rates include a continental-plus breakfast, and fine dining by reservation is available in the candlelit dining room. The nearby South Cumberland State Recreation Area maintains 150 miles of hiking trails, and fishing, canoeing, swimming, and horseback riding are among the local recreational activities. The area also boasts a number of natural and commercial attractions, including Sewanee Natural Bridge, Cathedral Falls, Jack Daniel's home, and the University of the South.

Listed in the National Register of Historic Places

Location: Monteagle Assembly is located off I-24 (Exit 134), midway between Chattanooga and Nashville.
Function Space: 724 square feet; 2 rooms
Capacity—Conference: 30; Reception: 50; Banquet: 30

Equipment On-site: Copier, fax
Food Service: Breakfast with room; catering/food service available; dining room
Overnight Accommodations: 14 rooms
Limitations/Restrictions: Smoking restricted to porches; food provided by inn; wines and liquors must be provided by group
Access: On-site parking; open year-round
Payment: Check, credit card (AmEx, MC, Visa)

NASHVILLE

BELLE MEADE PLANTATION

5025 Harding Road, Nashville, TN 37205
Phone: 615/356-0501   Fax: 615/356-2336

KNOWN as the "Queen of Tennessee Plantations," Belle Meade's history as a stud farm dates back to the early nineteenth century. William Harding, whose father purchased the property in 1805, built the plantation's graceful Greek Revival house in 1853. Although bullets from a skirmish during the Battle of Nashville in 1864 left their mark on the mansion, slaves kept the stud horses hidden during the conflict, allowing the plantation to develop an even greater prominence as a thoroughbred nursery and stud farm after the war. The mansion has been restored to its 1883 appearance, at the height of the family's fortune, and rooms are furnished with many family antiques and decorative period pieces. The beautiful 30-acre estate continues to welcome picnickers, just as it did during the nineteenth century when Belle Meade covered some 5,400 acres. A number of historic buildings remain on the plantation, including a 1790 log cabin, one of the oldest in the state, a smokehouse (1820), a creamery (1884), and the huge Victorian carriage house and stables (1890), which maintains one of the largest antique carriage collections in the South. Groups meeting here may arrange for house tours led by costumed guides.

Location: Belle Meade is 7 miles southwest of downtown Nashville and is accessible via I-65, I-40, and I-24. From I-440 (Exit 1), west on Highway 70 south for 3 miles.
Function Space: 2,000 square feet; 1 room
Capacity—Reception: 250; Banquet: 150; Theater: 200; additional space available by tenting areas of the grounds
Food Service: Preferred caterers list provided
Limitations/Restrictions: No smoking
Access: On-site parking; open year-round
Payment: Cash or check

THE HERMITAGE, HOME OF ANDREW JACKSON

4580 Rachel's Lane, Hermitage, TN 37076
Phone: 615/889-2941 Fax: 615/889-9909

UNTIL he became president of the United States, General Andrew Jackson was best known as the Hero of New Orleans, whose exploits during the War of 1812 won him widespread fame and adulation. In 1821 he built a simple two-story brick house, the Hermitage, in the Federal style, but remodeling and later rebuilding following a fire dramatically altered the home's appearance. By 1836 the expanded house had become an impressive Greek Revival mansion. After his second term as president ended in 1837, Jackson returned to the Hermitage and oversaw his farm and stables until his death in 1845. Although interior traces of Federal-era detailing remain, Greek motifs and classical features predominate,

and large two-story Corinthian columns grace the mansion's front exterior while Doric columns line the back. The attractive grounds range from open fields to a formal garden and include a number of historic structures, including the kitchen, the smokehouse, the spring house, and log cabins. Jackson and his wife, Rachel, are buried in a corner of the garden, their tomb in the style of a circular, domed Greek temple. The Ladies' Hermitage Association has preserved the president's home since 1889.

Location: The Hermitage is 15 minutes northeast of downtown Nashville, off Old Hickory Boulevard.
Function Space: 7,234 square feet; 5 rooms
Capacity—Reception: 200; Banquet: 130; Theater: 140
Equipment On-site: Audiovisual equipment (limited) available
Food Service: Catering/food service available; catering recommendations available
Limitations/Restrictions: Alcohol permitted after 5:00 P.M. only
Access: Limited handicapped accessibility; on-site parking; open year-round
Payment: Cash, check at time of service

THE HERMITAGE SUITE HOTEL

231 Sixth Avenue, North, Nashville, TN 37219

Phone: 615/244-3121   Fax: 615/254-6909

THE Hermitage Suite Hotel is the only historic all-suite hotel in Nashville, but that is only one of its charming distinctions. J. E. R. Carpenter designed the hotel in 1908, and it remains the only commercial Beaux Arts building in Tennessee. Opening to the public in 1910, the hotel served as headquarters for the suffragette movement 10 years later as Tennessee cast the deciding ballot granting women the right to vote. The hotel's elegant interiors display furnishings imported from around the world, and Grecian and Tennessean marble accentuate the lobby, whose beautiful skylight was designed by the Italian artisan Hotojy. The Grand Ballroom features an ornate handcrafted ceiling, and the room is paneled in Circassian walnut imported from Russia. Meeting space is also available in conference rooms and private dining suites. Dining service includes the Capitol Grille, hailed as one of the country's finest new restaurants, and the Oak Bar, where Dinah Shore made her singing debut in 1946. The restored Hermitage Suite Hotel enjoys a convenient downtown location adjacent to the State Capitol, the Performing Arts Center, and the State Museum.

Listed in the National Register of Historic Places; member of Historic Hotels of America

Location: The Hermitage Suite Hotel is located in downtown Nashville, across the street from the Legislative Plaza and State Capitol. Nashville International Airport is 20 minutes away, and I-40, I-440, I-65, and I-24 all lead into the downtown area.

Function Space: 6,800 square feet; 5 rooms

Capacity—Conference: 250; Reception: 300; Banquet: 225; Theater: 300

Equipment On-site: TV, VCR, overhead and slide projectors, screens, sound equipment; fax and typing available

The Hermitage Suite Hotel

Food Service: Catering/food service available; two restaurants, two bars, room service
Overnight Accommodations: 120 rooms
Access: Handicapped accessible; on-site parking; open year-round
Payment: Credit card

RUGBY

HISTORIC RUGBY

(Mailing address)
P.O. Box 8
(Street address)
Highway 52, Rugby, TN 37733
Phone: 423/628-2441   Fax: 423/628-2266
E-mail: hritenn@aol.com

ENGLISHMAN Thomas Hughes, author (*Tom Brown's Schooldays*) and social reformer, founded Rugby in 1880 as a class-free, agricultural community for the younger sons of British gentry, though about half the settlers were Americans from all walks of life. Although the utopian colony did not survive as Hughes had envisioned, today Rugby is one of the most authentically preserved villages in America, its combination of lodgings and facilities ideal for business retreats, workshops, classes, and seminars. Among the 20 historic buildings on-site is the book-filled Newbury House (1880), the colony's first boarding house; accommodations are also available in the village's restored and reconstructed Victorian cottages. Groups receive reduced-rate tours of the village's historic museum buildings, which include Hughes' home, the commissary, the Rugby Printing Works, and other structures. Walking trails laid out by early colonists lead to the Clear Fork River, and nearby parks offer white-water rafting, biking, and horseback rid-

ing. Evening entertainment featuring traditional music, crafts, and storytelling can be arranged. The Harrow Road Cafe, which also hosts lunch and dinner meetings, offers a menu that can be tailored to each group's needs, and lunches for field trips or picnics can be ordered as well.

Listed in the National Register of Historic Places; recipient of Governor's Award in the Arts

Location: Rugby is just south of Big South Fork National Park in eastern Tennessee, 40 miles from both I-40 and I-75 on Highway 52. Rugby is 1.25 hours northwest of Knoxville and 2.5 hours northeast of Nashville. Airport service is available at Tyson-McGee Airport (Knoxville), Metropolitan Nashville Airport, and in Lexington, Kentucky.
Function Space: 980 square feet; 3 rooms
Capacity—Conference: 75; Reception: 100; Banquet: 50
Equipment On-site: Overhead and slide projectors, video with large screen; photocopying and faxing available
Food Service: Full-service restaurant
Overnight Accommodations: 10 private rooms plus three cottages
Limitations/Restrictions: Smoking on verandahs only
Access: Handicapped accessible; on-site parking; open year-round
Payment: Check or credit card (MC, Visa)

SMITHVILLE

EVINS MILL RETREAT

(Mailing address)
P.O. Box 606
(Street address)
1535 Evins Mill Road, Smithville, TN 37166
Phone: 615/597-2088   Fax: 615/597-2090

PIONEER James Lockhart built his successful mill here in 1824, though it was replaced by a number of mills during the nineteenth century. Tennessee State Senator Edgar Evins bought the mill in 1937, and his 1939 mill, which still runs, has been carefully preserved and now functions as a unique conference center. Overlooking Fall Creek is the rustic, cozy lodge Evins built, where three generations of his family enjoyed spending their summers. Guests may stay in the lodge, though most are housed in the adjacent four-bedroom cottages. Business meetings, banquets, receptions, and other events are held in the mill, which offers a large lower-level room and kitchen as well as two spacious meeting rooms upstairs. A full-time chef is on hand to provide country-gourmet meals. The short but challenging walk to Culcarmac Falls is rewarded with the sight of a gorgeous 90-foot cascade. Picnicking and exploring the peaceful natural scenery are also favorite pastimes here, and volleyball, swimming, and horseshoes are available as well.

Location: Evins Mill Retreat is in central Tennessee, 1.25 hours east of Nashville and 2 hours west of Knoxville. From I-40, exit 239A and follow Highway 70E 30 miles to Smithville; turn right onto Evins Mill Road. Smithville Airport is 5 minutes away; Nashville International Airport is 1 hour away.
Function Space: 1,650 square feet; 3 rooms
Capacity—Conference: 40; Reception: 100; Theater: 80
Equipment On-site: TV/VCR, overhead and slide projectors available for rent; phones, faxes, photocopier available; tables, chairs, easels, and podium included in rental
Food Service: Full-service in-house catering
Overnight Accommodations: 14 rooms
Limitations/Restrictions: Restrictions on smoking (allowed in one room); no outside food; renter must provide own wine and liquor
Access: On-site parking; open year-round
Payment: Check, credit card (AmEx, Discover, MC, Visa)

Evins Mill Retreat

SMYRNA

SAM DAVIS HOME CREEK HOUSE

1399 Sam Davis Road, Smyrna, TN 37167
Phone: 615/459-2341

A member of the elite Coleman Scouts, the young Confederate Sam Davis was captured in November 1863 on his way to Chattanooga while carrying papers for General Braxton Bragg. Davis, convicted as a spy and sentenced to hang, was offered his freedom if he would reveal the source of his information; instead he responded, "If I had a thousand lives to live, I would give them all rather than betray a friend." With those words, the 21-year-old Davis slipped into immortality as a gallant Southern gentleman. Today the two-story 1820 plantation home where he was raised operates as a house museum, offering a warm picture of nineteenth-century upper-middle-class Southern living. The Sam Davis Home sits on 168 acres of farmland, along with the original kitchen, smokehouse, and overseer's office. Also on the grounds are authentic Middle Tennessee slave quarters and the Creek House, which is available for meetings. This house was built of bricks that were used in 1867 to construct the Smyrna Presbyterian Church. When the church faced demolition, the bricks were saved by the Sam Davis Memorial Association, and the present meeting house was built in 1942.

Location: The Sam Davis Home Creek House is 35 minutes southeast of Nashville via I-24.
Function Space: 1,053 square feet of meeting space in 2 rooms
Capacity—Conference: 50; Reception: 125; Banquet: 50
Food Service: Renter selects caterer; kitchen available
Limitations/Restrictions: No smoking
Access: Handicapped accessible; on-site parking; open year-round
Payment: Cash, check

TEXAS

AUSTIN

DRISKILL HOTEL

604 Brazos, Austin, TX 78701
Phone: 512/474-5911 Fax: 512/474-2188

WHEN cattle baron Colonel Jesse Lincoln Driskill formally opened the elegant Driskill Hotel in December 1886, his magnificent showpiece quickly became the center of attention in a city that was still a frontier town. Austin architect Jasper N. Preston and his son designed the four-story Richardsonian Romanesque structure that today is a cornerstone of the city's Historic Sixth Street District. Built of brick and native limestone, the hotel is noted for its fine workmanship and the facade's elaborate ornamentation. The hotel boasts three grand entrances with double balconies and the largest arched doorways in Texas. Atop the building are busts of Colonel Driskill and his two sons, above the stylized heads of Texas longhorn steers. Over the years the hotel has hosted a number of dignitaries and heads of state, and President Lyndon Johnson was a frequent visitor. With 14 function rooms, including the impressive Crystal Ballroom and the Maximilian Room, with its eight Austrian gold-leafed mirrors that once belonged to Empress Carlotta, the Driskill easily accommodates a variety of business and social events. Guests can also take advantage of the hotel's self-guided walking tour, which reveals much of Austin's rich history through exhibits and restored rooms.

Listed in the National Register of Historic Places; member of Historic Hotels of America

Location: The Driskill Hotel is 9 miles from Austin International Airport and is 3.5 hours south of Dallas and 2.5 hours northwest of Houston. The hotel is accessible via I-35, Highway 183, and Highway 290.
Function Space: 18,000 square feet; 14 rooms
Capacity—Conference: 70; Reception: 350; Banquet: 230; Theater: 350 Classroom: 180
Equipment On-site: In-house audiovisual services company and business services available
Food Service: Catering/food service available; restaurant, bar
Overnight Accommodations: 178 rooms
Access: Handicapped accessible; on-site parking; open year-round
Payment: Credit card

Driskill Hotel

BRACKETTVILLE

FORT CLARK

Fort Clark Springs Association

(Mailing address)

P.O. Box 345

(Street address)

US Highway 90, Brackettville, TX 78832

Phone: 210/563-2495 or 800-937-1950

Fax: 210/563-2254

SINCE 6000 B.C. people have been drawn to the serene area that is now Fort Clark, an oasis fed by Las Moras Spring and shaded by oak and pecan trees. Comanche, Mescalero, and other American Indians camped here through the centuries, and Spanish explorers and American pioneers spent time here as well. Established in 1852, Fort Clark served as a supply depot and hospital for the Confederacy during the Civil War, and during the late nineteenth century it protected the American frontier from Indian raids across the Mexican border. The Seminole-Negro Indian Scouts, four of whom were awarded the Congressional Medal of Honor, were stationed here, as were units of the "Buffalo Soldiers" and a number of famous officers, including Generals George C. Marshall, Jonathan Wainwright, and George S. Patton. Closed in 1946, the preserved frontier fort operates today as a private recreation community on 2,700 acres. More than 80 historic buildings remain, and visitors can tour the grounds and the museum and enjoy numerous recreational activities. Multipurpose meeting and conference facilities in the fort's historic buildings accommodate groups of 20 to 250. The Las Moras Inn restaurant and lounge, in the fort's original officers club, serves breakfast, lunch, and dinner.

Empty Saddle, Fort Clark
(Courtesy of Fort Clark Springs Association)

Listed in the National Register of Historic Places; Texas Historic Landmark

Location: Fort Clark borders US Highway 90 at Brackettville, 130 miles west of San Antonio.

Function Space: 7,500 square feet; 5 rooms

Capacity—Conference: 250; Reception: 200; Banquet: 150; Theater: 250

Equipment On-site: TV, VCR, overhead and slide projectors

Food Service: Restaurant and lounge

Overnight Accommodations: 38 rooms; other rental properties available

Limitations/Restrictions: No smoking in some facilities; some facilities restricted to member-only use

Access: Handicapped accessible; on-site parking; year-round availability

Payment: Cash, check, credit card (Discover, MC, VISA)

Ant Street Inn

BRENHAM

ANT STREET INN

107 W. Commerce, Brenham, TX 77833
Phone: 409/836-7393 or 800-481-1951
Fax: 409/836-7595

BUILT in 1899, this Romanesque-style red brick building in downtown Brenham once housed a thriving mercantile business. After a three-year renovation, the Ant Street Inn mixes Southern hospitality and Western charm in a town that still has a quaint nineteenth-century atmosphere. Carefully restored guest rooms, furnished with American antiques, have all the modern conveniences as well, and rates include breakfast. The inn hosts corporate meetings, weddings, receptions, banquets, and small conventions in meeting rooms featuring stained glass ceiling domes, 10-foot-tall doors, and Tiffany-style windows. Both large and small groups can easily be accommodated, as the inn offers a variety of function space, ranging from a small, comfortable library to a ballroom. Visitors will enjoy checking out the shops and nightspots in Ant Street and historic Brenham, as well as touring

nearby attractions, including several local museums, the Monastery of St. Clare, renowned for its miniature horses, and the Blue Bell Creamery, which offers tours of its ice cream plant.

Texas Historical Marker Site

Location: Brenham is 1.5 hours from Austin and 1 hour from Houston at Highways 290 and 36.
Function Space: 5,000 square feet; 3 rooms
Capacity—Conference: 220; Reception: 500; Banquet: 250; Theater: 250
Equipment On-site: Overhead projector, screen, TV, VCR, podium, fax
Food Service: Breakfast with room; catering available
Overnight Accommodations: 14 rooms
Limitations/Restrictions: No smoking
Access: Handicapped accessibility to meeting areas, not to overnight accommodations; on-site parking; open year-round
Payment: Cash, check, credit card

CITADEL

(Mailing address)
Drawer C
Chappell Hill, TX 77426
(Street address)
3401 Highway 290 East, Brenham, TX 77833
Phone: 409/836-9463   Fax: 713/686-6140

IN 1924 noted architect Alfred Finn built this remarkable plantation-style structure, which was originally the Brenham Country Club, outside Chappell Hill. During the Great Depression the club members could not sustain the building, and Ms. Johnnie Mae Hackworth, a former clerk in the Texas House of Representatives, bought it on the Washington County courthouse steps for a mere $10,001. She resided here from 1930 until her death in 1980. Now called the Citadel, for its thick walls and hilltop setting, this structure from the Roaring Twenties is once again a magnificent setting for social occasions. An extensive four-and-a-half-year restoration has returned the Citadel to its original grand appearance. The large verandah looks out over acres of vineyards, rolling countryside, and an enormous pool with goldfish. The Confederate Room, used as a dining area, opens onto the North and South Terraces. The third floor provides dressing rooms as well as full bathing facilities and sitting rooms. A grand staircase connects the third floor to the spacious ballroom on the floor below. The Citadel is available for weddings, receptions, private parties, and seminars, and tours for 30 or more are available by reservation.

Citadel
(Edward A. Smith)

Location: The Citadel is accessible via Highway
290 and Highway 36. Brenham Municipal
Airport serves charter flights; the Citadel is
1.5 and 2 hours away from downtown Houston
and Austin, respectively.
Function Space: 2,500 square feet; 3 rooms
Capacity—Conference: 100; Reception: 350;
Banquet: 100
Food Service: Catering/food service available
Limitations/Restrictions: No smoking; no
outside food and beverage service
Access: On-site parking; open year-round
Payment: Cash or check; no credit cards

DALLAS

THE ALDREDGE HOUSE
5500 Swiss Avenue, Dallas, TX 75214
Phone: 214/823-2972 or 214/823-8268

A striking 17-room Italianate structure in Dallas's
Swiss Avenue Historic District, the Aldredge
House was built to be a Southern mansion. The
house was completed in 1917 for William J. Lewis,
a prominent rancher and banker, and his wife,
Willie Newberry Lewis, one of the city's first debu-
tantes. Civic leaders George and Rena Aldredge
bought the house in 1921 and lived there for the
next 50 years. Today the mansion is headquarters of
the Dallas County Medical Society Alliance, and in
addition to hosting philanthropic and educational
programs, the Aldredge House provides a gracious
setting for weddings, receptions, luncheons, teas,
seminars, and business meetings. The home's interiors are noted for their rich walnut and mahogany
paneling, inlaid marble foyer, and a sweeping
mahogany staircase. The beautifully furnished
home includes a dance floor and a sun room with
attached greenhouse. Outside, the mansion is dis-

tinguished by its wraparound terrace and colorful
gardens. Not surprisingly, the stately Aldredge
House has been seen in films, as well as in the television series *Dallas*.

Listed in the National Register of Historic Places; Texas
Historic Landmark

Location: The Aldredge House is 15 minutes
from downtown Dallas and is accessible via I-35E
and Highways 45 and 75 (north and south) and
Highways 30 and 20 (east and west). Dallas/Fort
Worth International Airport is 30 minutes west.
Function Space: 7,000 square feet; 2 rooms
Capacity—Conference: 20; Reception: 200;
Banquet: 50
Equipment On-site: Sound system and screen
Food Service: Exclusive caterer
Limitations/Restrictions: No smoking; no food
upstairs, no kegs; no confetti, birdseed, or berries
on decorations in house; $500 security deposit
required
Access: Handicapped accessible; on-site street
parking; closed one week in August and holidays
Payment: Check

THE ARISTOCRAT HOTEL—HOLIDAY INN
1933 Main Street, Dallas, TX 75201
Phone: 214/741-7700   Fax: 214/939-3639

RISING 14 stories above the Dallas Central
Business District, the Aristocrat Hotel was built
in 1925 and was the first of Conrad Hilton's
hotels to bear his name. Hilton gave up control of
the hotel during the Great Depression, but this
restored landmark continues to offer European-
style luxury accommodations. The hotel's horseshoe design boasts two massive towers with
Beaux Arts elements in its detailing. Rich wood

paneling, etched glass, brass, and period furnishings contribute to the stylish interiors, and the guest accommodations (mostly suites) are beautifully furnished and come with all the modern conveniences. Elegant function space is available for business meetings, receptions, banquets, and other events, and the handsome boardroom offers luxurious armchair seating for 18. Guests can relax in the Aristocrat Club Room, which serves complimentary morning coffee, and the Aristocrat Bar and Grill features mesquite-grilled entrées. Located in downtown Dallas, the hotel is linked to an extensive skywalk and tunnel system that offers access to offices, banks, and shops; nearby attractions include Fair Park, the JFK Memorial, the Dallas Museum of Art, the Convention Center, and the city's entertainment districts.

Listed in the National Register of Historic Places; Texas Historical Marker Site; City of Dallas Landmark

Location: The Aristocrat Hotel is in downtown Dallas at the corner of Main and Harwood Streets, just 5 minutes from I-30 and Highway 75 (Central Expressway). Complimentary transportation is provided to and from Love Field Airport, and Dallas/Fort Worth International Airport is 16 miles away.
Function Space: 3,613 square feet; 6 rooms
Capacity—Conference: 70; Reception: 150; Banquet: 100; Theater: 120 (the hotel also has access to an additional 30,000 square feet at Bank One's Conference Center)
Equipment On-site: Audiovisual equipment available through outside source
Food Service: Catering/food service available; restaurant and bar
Overnight Accommodations: 172 rooms
Limitations/Restrictions: Restrictions on smoking (designated smoking rooms available)

Access: Handicapped accessible; on-site parking; open year-round
Payment: Cash, credit card

MAJESTIC THEATRE
1925 Elm Street, Suite 300, Dallas, TX 75201-4516
Phone: 214/880-0137   Fax: 214/880-0097

THE Interstate Amusement Company, one of the Southwest's largest vaudeville and motion picture chains in the early twentieth century, built its magnificent new Majestic Theatre in Dallas in 1921. Under the company's skillful president, Karl Hoblitzelle, the theater earned a reputation not only for "big vaudeville" shows and, later, A-list films, but also for its humanitarian endeavors during the Great Depression and World War II. Theater architect John Eberson gave the building its Renaissance Baroque exterior, and the auditorium itself—free of obstructing pillars as result of what was hailed as an engineering feat—was based on a Roman Garden theme. The ceiling of painted stars was bordered by a latticework of colored vines and flowers to suggest a garden wall. The lobby was just as impressive, with its enormous mirrors and a marble fountain copied from one at the Vatican gardens. Nearly all of vaudeville's biggest names played the Majestic, including Houdini, Mae West, and Bob Hope. Later a popular movie palace on Dallas's Theater Row, the theater finally closed in 1973. A major restoration of the Majestic led to its reopening in 1983, and today it hosts a number of cultural events and is available for a variety of business and social functions.

Listed in the National Register of Historic Places; Texas and City of Dallas Historic Landmarks

Location: The Majestic Theatre is located in the Harwood Historic District in downtown Dallas and is 5 minutes from I-30 and Highway 75 (Central Expressway). Dallas/Fort Worth International Airport is 16 miles away.
Function Space: 4,500 square feet; 3 rooms + auditorium
Capacity—Conference: 1,500; Reception: 400; Banquet: 200; Theater: 1,648
Equipment On-site: Audiovisual equipment available, business services arranged
Food Service: Catering available
Limitations/Restrictions: No smoking; food and beverage service from approved caterers only; no firearms (even with permit)
Access: Handicapped accessible; open year-round
Payment: Company check

EASTLAND

MAJESTIC THEATRE
(Mailing address)
P.O. Box 705
(Street address)
108 N. Lamar, Eastland, TX 76448
Phone: 817/629-2102   Fax: 817/629-1165

FOLLOWING its opening in 1920, the Connellee Theatre was for years a noted showplace featuring road shows, musicals, plays, and silent films. The theater was built for C. U. Connellee, founder of Eastland, and boasted 1,200 seats. After shutting down for extensive remodeling in 1946, the Connellee reopened as the Majestic Theatre in 1947, and it was considered the finest theater in west Texas, a "showplace of the Oil Belt." Its new look was Art Moderne, and a 50-foot vertical neon sign on the building's

facade announced the theater's new name. Beginning in the mid-1980s local citizens began a restoration of the Majestic, returning it to its stylish 1947 appearance and installing a state-of-the-art sound system. Current films are still screened here, but the theater is also available for performance organizations, civic groups, and business gatherings. An Art Deco mural runs the length of the theater's ceiling, and the handsome wall murals depict images of the Old West. The audience is accommodated in 825 plush opera-style seats.

Texas Historic Landmark

Location: Eastland is located on I-20, approximately 100 miles west of Fort Worth and 55 miles east of Abilene. The Majestic Theatre is located in downtown Eastland, a half-block north of the intersection of Main Street (Highway 6) and Lamar Streets. Eastland Airport can accommodate private planes, and airport service is available in Abilene and Dallas/Fort Worth.
Function Space: 5,000 square feet; 3 rooms
Capacity—Conference: 25; Banquet: 85; Theater: 825
Equipment On-site: 35mm projection, screen, sound, stage lighting
Overnight Accommodations: 8 rooms available next door
Limitations/Restrictions: No smoking or alcohol
Access: Handicapped accessible; open year-round
Payment: Cash, check

FORT WORTH

EDDLEMAN-MCFARLAND HOUSE

1110 Penn Street, Fort Worth, TX 76102
Phone: 817/332-5875   Fax: 817/332-3902

THE elegant and ornate Victorian house overlooking the Trinity River is one of only three remaining examples of cattle baron homes in Fort Worth. English architect Howard Messer designed the three-story house built in 1899, and only two families—the Eddlemans and the McFarlands—ever lived here. The exterior features turrets and gables, and a large covered porch of red sandstone and marble makes for a pleasant luncheon spot. Copper finials accent a slate tile roof on the handsomely preserved structure. House tours offer a view of the home's elaborate interior, which includes mantels of mahogany and other woods, coffered ceilings, and parquet floors. The first floor and the beautifully landscaped grounds (which can be tented) are available for events; meeting spaces include two rooms on the first floor and a modern meeting room in the basement. Nonprofit organizations may use the basement room free of charge during the day; businesses may rent the facilities for daytime or evening use. Groups renting the facilities may arrange for a complimentary tour of the house and grounds.

Listed in the National Register of Historic Places; Texas Historical Marker Site

Location: The Eddleman-McFarland House is located in downtown Fort Worth, 30 minutes from Dallas/Fort Worth International Airport and 45 minutes from Dallas's Love Field. The house is a half-mile west of downtown Fort Worth and is five blocks north of I-30. Bus service is available one block from the house.

Function Space: 2,000 square feet; 3 rooms

Capacity—Conference: 48; Reception: 80 (opening all pocket doors); Banquet: 48; Theater: 50

Equipment On-site: Audiovisual equipment available in basement room only

Food Service: Assistance provided in arranging caterer

Limitations/Restrictions: No smoking; no dancing; no heavy equipment (such as a piano) may be rolled in

Access: On-site parking; open year-round

Payment: Cash, check

Eddleman-McFarland House

GALVESTON

ASHTON VILLA

(Mailing address)
Galveston Historical Foundation
2016 Strand
(Street address)
2328 Broadway, Galveston, Texas 77550
Phone: 409/762-3933 Fax: 409/765-7851

THIS gracious three-story Italianate mansion continues to be favorite gathering place for Galveston society and visitors, just as it was when James Moreau Brown built it in 1859. Brown, a wealthy merchant and banker, designed Ashton Villa and built it using bricks from his own brickyard. His lively daughter, Miss Bettie, presided over the house and its busy social calendar. The first of Galveston's great Broadway homes and the street's only surviving antebellum mansion, Ashton Villa was saved from demolition in the 1960s and has been beautifully restored. Brown family heirlooms, original artwork, and antiques contribute to the nineteenth-century atmosphere. The ornate dining room and opulent Gold Room, which may be rented separately for portrait photography, provide a definition of Gilded Age living, while the family living quarters upstairs reflect a quiet Victorian elegance. The ballroom is available for banquets, luncheons, weddings, parties, receptions, and meetings, and guided house tours may be arranged for an additional fee.

Listed in the National Register of Historic
Places; Texas Historic Landmark

Location: Galveston is approximately 45 minutes south of Houston Hobby Airport and 90 minutes south of Houston Intercontinental Airport via I-45. The Galveston Island Rail Trolley stops one block west of Ashton Villa.
Function Space: 2,500 square feet; 1 room
Capacity—Reception: 300; Banquet: 225; Theater: 250
Equipment On-site: A limited number of tables and chairs (setup included) are provided at no charge with ballroom rentals
Food Service: Caterer's kitchen available
Limitations/Restrictions: No smoking
Access: On-site parking; open year-round
Payment: Cash, check, credit card (AmEx, Discover, MC, Visa)

Ashton Villa
(Jim Cruz)

GARTEN VEREIN DANCING PAVILION

(Mailing address)
Galveston Historical Foundation
2016 Strand
(Street address)
2704 Avenue O, Galveston, TX 77550
Phone: 409/762-3933   Fax: 409/765-7851

GALVESTON'S thriving German community built this eclectic Victorian pavilion in 1876, a centerpiece of the Garten Verein ("Garden Club"). The city's late-nineteenth-century wealth and prosperity as a commercial center and the leading seaport in the southwest led to the construction of grand neighborhoods and social clubs. Designed by architect Nicholas Clayton, the pavilion is a monument to the Victorian era, with its double ballustrading, carved pilaster capitals, narrow cupola, and walls of glass. This club, which soon became popular with non-Germans as well, also featured bowling greens, tennis courts, croquet grounds, and pleasant gardens. Stanley Kempner bought the gardens and pavilion in 1923 as a donation to the city for a public park. The pavilion, located in the Silk Stocking district, continues to be a popular setting for public and private celebrations, and its octagonal design provides unobstructed views and ample floor space.

Listed in the National Register of Historic Places;
Texas Historic Landmark

Location: Galveston is approximately 45 minutes south of Houston Hobby Airport and 90 minutes south of Houston Intercontinental Airport via I-45. An Island Transit bus stop serves the Garten Verein, and the Galveston Island Rail Trolley stop is two blocks away.
Function Space: 6,000 square feet; 1 room

Garten Verein Dancing Pavilion
(Jim Cruz)

The Grand 1894 Opera House

Capacity—Reception: 300; Banquet: 200
Equipment On-site: A limited number of tables and chairs (setup included) are provided at no charge with pavilion rentals
Food Service: Caterer's prep room available
Limitations/Restrictions: No smoking; a $200 security deposit is required
Access: Handicapped accessible; on-site parking; open year-round
Payment: Cash, check, credit card (AmEx, Discovery, MC, Visa)

THE GRAND 1894 OPERA HOUSE

2020 Postoffice Street, Galveston, TX 77550
Phone: 409/765-1894   Fax: 409/763-1068
E-mail: Gugg11b@prodigy.com

DESIGNATED as the official opera house of Texas by the state legislature, the Grand 1894 Opera House on Galveston Island is considered to be among the nation's finest historical commercial restorations. The Grand opened when Galveston was both the largest and wealthiest city in Texas, and over the years numerous big names have graced the stage, including Sarah Bernhardt, John Philip Sousa, William Jennings Bryan, the Marx Brothers, George Burns and Gracie Allen, and Ray Charles. The opera house was threatened with demolition during the 1970s, but a rescue effort and subsequent 12-year, $7 million refurbishment returned the theater to its turn-of-the-century grandeur. The interior features double curved balconies, and no seat is farther than 70 feet from the stage. The opera house is available for private receptions, business meetings, and performances by independent groups. Meeting spaces include three lobbies, auditorium seating, and stage. The Grand is located near Galveston's central business district and the historic Strand district, known for its beautifully restored Victorian neighborhoods.

Listed in the National Register of Historic Places

Location: The Grand 1894 Opera House is 35 minutes from Houston Hobby Airport and 30 minutes from Ellington Field Airport on I-45. Houston Intercontinental Airport is an hour and a half away. The Grand is also accessible by local trolley service.
Function Space: 4,920 square feet; 5 rooms (including lobbies, theater, and stage)
Capacity—Conference: 1,040; Reception: 1,000; Banquet: 400; Theater: 1,040
Equipment On-site: Theater equipment, podium, sound system, tables, chairs
Food Service: Client selects caterer; no kitchen
Limitations/Restrictions: No smoking
Access: Handicapped accessible and barrier free; on-site parking (adjacent and within close proximity); open year-round; hours of availability unrestricted
Payment: Check

HOTEL GALVEZ—A GRAND HERITAGE HOTEL
2024 Seawall Boulevard, Galveston, TX 77550
Phone: 409/765-7721 Fax: 409/765-5780
E-mail: Galvez@phoenix.net

IN the late nineteenth century, Galveston flourished as the leading cotton port in the world and was one of the country's most prosperous cities. Then in 1900 disaster struck. A hurricane known simply as the Great Storm killed thousands and devastated much of Galveston, but it did not destroy the city's desire to come roaring back from adversity. With the 1911 opening of the elegant Hotel Galvez, also called "the Queen of the Gulf," the city was truly back in business. This Spanish Colonial Revival structure quickly became the center of the local social scene. Over the years the hotel has hosted some of Galveston society's most prestigious balls and parties, and Franklin D. Roosevelt, Dwight Eisenhower, and Lyndon Johnson were among it notable visitors. Restoration begun in the 1980s has continued, and the current owners have returned the entrance to its original position at the front of the hotel, which is now approached by a grand circular drive. Located just steps away from the beach, the hotel revels in a tropical atmosphere, featuring poolside palms and a swim-up bar. Extensive meeting space accommodates everything from small board meetings to large receptions.

Listed in the National Register of Historic Places; member of Historic Hotels of America

Location: Galveston is approximately 45 minutes south of Houston Hobby Airport and 90 minutes south of Houston Intercontinental Airport via I-45.

Texas Seaport Museum and the *Elissa*
(Jim Cruz)

Function Space: 10,000 square feet; 6 rooms
Capacity—Conference: 50; Reception: 500;
Banquet: 385; Theater: 600
Equipment On-site: Audiovisual equipment and
business services available
Food Service: Catering/food service available;
two restaurants, lounge, room service
Overnight Accommodations: 228 rooms
Access: Handicapped accessible; on-site parking;
open year-round
Payment: Cash, check, credit card

TEXAS SEAPORT MUSEUM AND THE TALL SHIP *ELISSA*

(Mailing address)
Galveston Historical Foundation
2016 Strand
(Street address)
Pier 21, Galveston, TX 77550
Phone: 409/763-1877   Fax: 409/765-7851

THE *Elissa*, Texas's tall ship moored at the pier
alongside the Texas Seaport Museum, provides a
unique outdoor setting for weddings, receptions,
and business and social functions. Built in
Scotland in 1877, the *Elissa* is a proud reminder
of Galveston's prosperous maritime past, when
the city was the busiest port in Texas. The *Elissa*
first arrived in Galveston in 1883 bearing a ship-

ment of bananas; it returned to the port again in 1886. Rescued from a Greek scrapyard in 1974, the ship has been painstakingly restored and is happily maintained by local volunteers. Today the *Elissa*, a square-rigger whose three masts tower 100 feet overhead, still sets out to sea, her 19 sails billowing in the wind. In addition to sailing excursions, the ship is open for tours in conjunction with a visit to the museum and is available for hosting events. The rental fee includes the *Elissa's* decks, galleries, officers' quarters, and galley, for use as a serving area or bar, as well as the museum's pier and rest rooms, and guests are welcome to tour the museum.

National Historic Landmark; listed in the National Register of Historic Places; Texas Historic Landmark

Location: Galveston is approximately 45 minutes south of Houston Hobby Airport and 90 minutes south of Houston Intercontinental Airport via I-45. The Texas Seaport Museum is served by the Galveston Island Rail Trolley.
Function Space: 4,000 square feet available on ship and adjacent pier
Capacity—Reception: 500; Banquet: 300
Food Service: All functions must be catered, no kitchen facilities available
Limitations/Restrictions: No smoking on board the *Elissa*; rentals available only after museum hours
Access: Handicapped accessible; open year-round
Payment: Cash, check, credit card (AmEx, Discover, MC, Visa)

THE TREMONT HOUSE—A GRAND HERITAGE HOTEL

2300 Ship's Mechanic Row, Galveston, TX 77550
Phone: 409/763-0300   Fax: 409/763-1539
E-mail: Tremont@phoenix.net

LOCATED in Galveston's Strand Historic District, the four-story Renaissance-style Tremont House extends a full city block and provides a blend of European service and Southern hospitality. This architectural landmark was built in 1879 to house the Blum brothers' wholesale dry goods business, one of the largest in the Southwest. The *Galveston Tribune* operated in the building from 1923 to 1963, and in 1985 the renovated building opened as the Tremont House, named for the hotel that was once the center of Galveston society. The four-story atrium lobby is the award-winning hotel's signature feature, and the handsomely appointed meeting rooms range from the private boardroom to large reception areas next door in the 1871 T. Jeff League Building. Guest rooms are furnished in the Victorian style, and the baths feature Italian painted tiles and European towel warmers. Nearly any appetite can be satisfied at the Tremont, which offers fine and casual dining, a bakery, a coffee house, and an ice cream parlor. The rooftop terrace boasts tremendous sunrise and sunset views of Galveston port, and guests also have access to the pool at the Hotel Galvez, the Tremont's nearby sister hotel. The Galveston Island Trolley stops at the hotel's front door, ready to whisk visitors off on a tour of historic neighborhoods.

Located in a National Historic Landmark district; listed in the National Register of Historic Places; member of Historic Hotels of America

Location: Galveston is approximately 45 minutes south of Houston Hobby Airport and 90 minutes south of Houston Intercontinental Airport via I-45.
Function Space: 18,000 square feet; 13 rooms
Capacity—Conference: 50; Reception: 750; Banquet: 700; Theater: 750
Equipment On-site: Audiovisual equipment and business services available
Food Service: Catering/food service available; five restaurants, bar, room service
Overnight Accommodations: 117 rooms
Access: Handicapped accessible; on-site parking; open year-round
Payment: Cash, check, credit card

SALADO

ALLEN HALL AT THE INN AT SALADO

(Mailing address)
P.O. Box 320
(Street address)
307 N. Main Street at Pacepark Drive
Salado, TX 76571
Phone: 800-724-0027   Fax: 817/947-1004

THE Inn at Salado, with its white picket fence and graceful two-story porch, is the town's first bed and breakfast and has been returned to its splendid 1872 appearance. A lovely respite located in Salado's historic district, the inn offers six covered porches, swings and hammocks, and shaded brick terraces for quiet relaxation. Located near the spring-fed Salado Creek, the inn occupies two landscaped acres; also on-site are an original hand-dug well and Allen Hall, a country chapel built in 1901. The hall is available for a variety of social and business functions, including lectures, meetings, weddings, and receptions. A quaint kitchen complex and outdoor patio adjoin the hall, and large gatherings can be accommodated on the grounds as well. Guests at the inn stay in beautifully furnished rooms in either the main house or the carriage house and are treated to a homemade gourmet-style breakfast. Salado's finest shops and eateries are within walking distance of the inn, and golfing, horseshoes, biking, and other activities are also available.

Listed in the National Register of Historic Places; Texas Historical Marker Site

Location: Salado is halfway between Austin and Waco, just off I-35 (Exit 284).
Funtion Space: 1 room
Capacity—Conference: 35; Reception: 150 (indoor/outdoor); Banquet: 50; Theater: 75
Equipment On-site: VCR, monitor, screen, podium, tables, and chairs; fax available
Food Service: Breakfast with room; chef on staff to meet specific meal requirements
Overnight Accommodations: 9 rooms
Limitations/Restrictions: No smoking; in-house catering only; no hard liquor (beer and wine permitted)
Access: Limited handicapped accessibility; on-site parking; open year-round
Payment: Cash, check, credit card (AmEx, Discover, MC, Visa)

Arneson River Theatre

SAN ANTONIO

ARNESON RIVER THEATRE

(Mailing address)
418 Villita Street
(Street address)
503 Villita Street, San Antonio, TX 78205
Phone: 210/207-8610   Fax: 210/207-4390

STRADDLING the San Antonio River in the city's La Villita Historic District, the Arneson River Theatre is an unusual but especially picturesque outdoor theater. The meandering river divides the lawn seating from the stage, which features a Spanish-style arched wall as a backdrop. Rosita's Bridge—also used as a performance area in produc-

tions—connects the audience side to the theater side. Adjacent to the stage are the Spanish-style dressing rooms, and renters may use the concession building on the audience side for food service. In addition to hosting entertainment and receptions, the theater has held small dinner parties on its stage and has been used for events in conjunction with the historic Cos House (described in a subsequent entry). The theater, built in 1939 as a WPA project to beautify the city's River Walk, was named for Edwin Arneson, the project engineer. Today it is the scene of numerous cultural and artistic events and a focal point along the famed Paseo del Rio. Along the River Walk, which at night is beautifully lit, strolling visitors will find galleries, boutiques, and restaurants.

Location: The Arneson River Theatre is in downtown San Antonio between S. Alamo and S. Presa Streets. I-37 is accessible three blocks from S. Alamo Street. Via Metropolitan Transit stops a half-block from the theater entrance.
Capacity—Theater: 800
Food Service: Concession stand available; renter may operate or hire concessionaire
Access: Limited handicapped accessibility; paid parking available nearby
Payment: Check, if event is booked 60 days in advance; cash, if event is booked within 30 days

BECKMANN INN AND CARRIAGE HOUSE BED AND BREAKFAST

222 E. Guenther Street, San Antonio, TX 78204
Phone: 210/229-1449 or 800-945-1449
Fax: 210/229-1061

WHAT is now the King William Historic District began as an affluent German community in the mid-nineteenth century, and at the center of it all was the Pioneer Flour Mill. Carl H. Guenther, founder of the mill, raised his family on the mill grounds and drew others to the area as well. Guenther's daughter, Marie Dorothea, married architect Albert Beckmann, who built a Queen Anne-style house for his new wife on the mill grounds in 1886. After the turn of the century, the house was modified to reflect the Greek Revival style, and in 1913 the porch was extended from the Madison Street side to the Guenther Street side. This gave the house a new street address, which was the desired effect, owing to the infamous brothel also located on Madison Street at that time. The house interiors are furnished with Victorian antiques, and the spacious living room boasts 14-foot-high ceilings and a wood mosaic floor from Paris; meeting space is available in the inn's Victorian dining room. Room rates include a full gourmet breakfast—followed by dessert! The inn enjoys a convenient location for exploring San Antonio, with the famous River Walk entrance just across the street.

City of San Antonio Historic Landmark

Location: The Beckmann Inn is seven blocks from downtown San Antonio, 15 minutes from San Antonio International Airport, 1.5 hours from Austin and 2.5 hours from Houston. One house away from the inn is the Via Transit and trolley stop, allowing easy access to local attractions.
Function Space: 500 square feet; 1 room
Capacity—Conference: 10
Equipment On-site: Inn can arrange for rental equipment from outside source
Food Service: Breakfast with room; inn can arrange for outside caterer
Overnight Accommodations: 5 rooms
Limitations/Restrictions: No smoking except on porches and patios
Access: On-site parking; open year-round
Payment: Check, credit card (AmEx, DC, Discover, MC, Visa)

Cos House

COS HOUSE

(Mailing address)
418 Villita Street
(Street address)
505 Villita Street, San Antonio, TX 78205
Phone: 210/207-8613   Fax: 210/207-4390

A vibrant mix of Spanish, Mexican, German, French, American, and Texan culture, La Villita ("little village") is the city's oldest neighborhood, beautifully preserved and just a block from the winding San Antonio River. The Spaniards founded Mission San Antonio de Valero in 1718, and the church fortress, the legendary Alamo, was built in 1744. La Villita developed into a village for Spanish soldiers and their families, and immigrants from Germany and France arrived in the late nineteenth century, leaving their mark as well. The mixture of architectural styles and historic buildings along La Villita's cobblestone walks speaks of both the diversity and the long history of the community. Within the village are a museum complex, historic houses, galleries, and shops where traditional arts and crafts are still practiced. Among the structures is the Cos House, thought to be the oldest in the village, and where General Perfecto de Cos signed the articles of capitulation after the Texans defeated his Mexican army in 1835. Meeting space is available in the one-story adobe house and outdoor patio area. The Cos House may be rented with the adjacent Arneson River Theatre (see earlier entry).

Texas Historic Landmark

Location: The Cos House in La Villita is in downtown San Antonio on Villita Street between S. Alamo and Presa Streets. I-37 is accessible three blocks from S. Alamo Street. Via Metropolitan Transit stops a half-block from the entrance to Cos House.

Function Space: 614 square feet; 2 rooms; additional space on porch and patio

Capacity—Reception: 100–125 (using patio); Banquet: 50 (indoors at round tables)

Equipment On-site: Audiovisual equipment may be rented from outside source

Food Service: List of approved caterers provided

Access: Handicapped accessible (patio area)

Payment: Check, if event is booked 60 days in advance; cash, if event is booked within 30 days

MARION KOOGLER MCNAY ART MUSEUM

(Mailing address)
P.O. Box 6069
(Street address)
6000 N. New Braunfels, San Antonio, TX 78209-0069
Phone: 210/824-5368   Fax: 210/824-0218
http://www.mcnayart.org

IN 1950, Marion Koogler McNay, a prominent collector of modern art, left her house, her collection of French Post-Impressionist paintings and early twentieth-century European art, and a considerable portion of her fortune for the establishment of Texas's first museum of modern art. Four years later the museum opened to the public, and today the McNay collection numbers more than 10,000 objects and includes works by Cezanne, Gaugin, Piscasso, and O'Keefe. In addition, the museum has developed excellent theater arts and collections of nineteenth- and twentieth-century drawings and prints. The museum is housed in McNay's impressive Spanish Mediterranean-style mansion, which sits on 23 acres of beautifully landscaped grounds with fountains, expansive lawns, and a Japanese garden and fish pond. The museum is available for meetings, weddings, receptions, and other special occasions. Facilities include an auditorium and the adjacent rotunda as well as a lush courtyard. For events other than weddings, groups can arrange to have the front lower-level galleries open. The museum grounds may also be used in conjunction with rented space.

Location: Marion Koogler McNay Art Museum is located north of downtown San Antonio and is accessible via Highway 281, I-35 and I-410.

Function Space: 2,900 square feet; 3 rooms

Capacity—Conference: 50; Reception: 550; Banquet: 300; Theater: 300

Equipment On-site: Equipment available with rental of the auditorium includes podium and microphones, slide projector, 25-inch or 52-inch VHS monitor, audio-cassette recorder connected to sound system

Food Service: Renter selects caterer; list of qualified caterers provided

Limitations/Restrictions: No food or beverages in galleries

Access: Handicapped accessible; on-site parking; open-year round

Payment: Check

UTAH

OGDEN

HISTORIC RADISSON SUITE HOTEL

2510 Washington Boulevard, Ogden, UT 84401

Phone: 801/627-1900   Fax: 801/393-1258

IN 1927 the Reed Hotel, built in 1891, underwent a major renovation, becoming an impressive 15-story Italian Renaissance Revival structure. Located on Ogden's historic Twenty-fifth Street, the hotel was briefly known as the Bigelow Hotel, and later still as the Ben Lomond Hotel. Following its 1985 restoration as an all-suite facility, the building reopened as the elegant Radisson Suite Hotel it is today. The splendid interiors are highlighted by ornate coffered ceilings, inlaid marble floors, and intricately carved stone masonry. The spacious suites are beautifully furnished, and rates include a full buffet breakfast, coffee, and cocktails. From the hotel's top floor guests enjoy a panoramic view of Ogden's city lights and mountain skyline while dining at the Skyline Restaurant. Convention facilities can accommodate groups of 10 to 300 in various-sized rooms for both corporate and social occasions. Set in the foothills of the Wasatch Mountains, the hotel is just minutes away from world-renowned ski slopes, and other nearby attractions include the Browning Arts Museum, the Egyptian Theater, and Dinosaur Park.

Listed in the National Register of Historic Places; member of Historic Hotels of America

Location: The Historic Radisson Suite Hotel is located at Twenty-fifth Street and Washington Boulevard in Ogden, 40 miles north of Salt Lake City International Airport and accessible via Highway 89 and I-15.
Function Space: 10,000 square feet; 9 rooms
Capacity—Conference: 50; Reception: 400; Banquet: 250; Theater: 350
Equipment On-site: Tables and chairs included, additional equipment available; photocopy, fax, and typing services available
Food Service: Breakfast with room; catering/ food service available; restaurant
Overnight Accommodations: 144 rooms
Limitations/Restrictions: Restrictions on smoking; no outside food or beverages permitted
Access: Handicapped accessible; on-site parking; open year-round
Payment: Credit card

SALT LAKE CITY

SALT LAKE CITY AND COUNTY BUILDING

451 S. State Street, Salt Lake City, UT 84111

Phone: 801/535-7280

A majestic Romanesque-Revival landmark, the Salt Lake City and County Building at Washington Square is an impressive sandstone structure featuring a 250-foot bell tower that rises above a panoply of conical-roofed turrets and towers. On this site in 1847, Brigham Young's scouting party set up camp, and the first wave of Mormon pioneers arrived a few days later. As immigrants poured into the area southeast of the Great Salt Lake, the swelling community responded with construction of the massive sandstone building, which was completed in 1894.

The building's exterior boasts elaborately carved column capitals and intricate detail work, while the interior reflects a stately and refined turn-of-the-century elegance. A 16-year restoration of the building began in 1973, and it became the first historic structure in the world to be outfitted with "base isolation," a system of shock absorbers between the foundation and the ground designed to protect against earthquakes. Meeting space is available in several rooms, including the historic Council Chambers.

Listed in the National Register of Historic Places; listed in the Salt Lake City Register of Cultural Resources

Location: The Salt Lake City and County Building is in downtown Salt Lake City at Washington Square, 5 miles from Salt Lake City International Airport and accessible via I-80 and I-15.

Function Space: 4,900 square feet; 3 rooms

Capacity—Conference: 25; Reception: 106

Equipment On-site: TV, VCR, overhead projector available

Food Service: Renter arranges catering

Limitations/Restrictions: No smoking; food and beverages not permitted in some rooms; alcohol is not permitted in the building

Access: Handicapped accessibility; on-site parking; open year-round

Payment: Cash or check

VERMONT

CAVENDISH

GLIMMERSTONE

(Mailing address)
P.O. Box 143
(Street address)
Route 131, Cavendish, VT 05142
Phone: 802/226-7872 Fax: 802/226-7933

CONSIDERED one of the finest early-Victorian stone houses in southern Vermont, historic Glimmerstone was built in 1845 and remains one of the most photographed houses in the state. Decorative barge boards, gingerbread trim, 14 gables, and other traces of neo-Gothic architecture give this country house a fabled appearance. The mansion's facilities are designed to accommodate conferences, parties, retreats, and custom-concept weddings. Glimmerstone welcomes up to 45 conference participants; breakout rooms are available, and spouse programs in conjunction with meetings can be arranged. Complete wedding services, including rehearsal dinner, ceremony, reception, accommodations, and farewell champagne brunch are also available. Receptions of 100 or fewer can be accommodated indoors, while larger gatherings can take advantage of Glimmerstone's historic barn or garden and terrace settings. Numerous recreational activities are available locally, including golf, tennis, clay shooting, fishing, snowmobiling, hiking, and biking, and Okemo Mountain, just five minutes away from Glimmerstone, offers Vermont's most reliable skiing.

Listed in the National Register of Historic Places

Location: Glimmerstone is located on the Black River on Route 13 in Cavendish, less than three hours from Boston.
Function Space: 5,000 square feet; 3 rooms
Capacity—Conference: 40; Reception: 120 (outdoors 200); Banquet: 40
Equipment On-site: Audiovisual equipment, fax and computer hookups available
Food Service: Food service available; chef will customize meal plans
Overnight Accommodations: 10 rooms
Limitations/Restrictions: No smoking in public areas
Access: Handicapped accessible; on-site parking; open year-round
Payment: Prepayment for conference facilities; cash or check

EAST BURKE

INN AT MOUNTAIN VIEW CREAMERY

(Mailing address)
P.O. Box 355
(Street address)
Darling Hill Road, East Burke, VT 05832
Phone: 802/626-9924 or 800-572-5409
Fax: 802/626-9924 (same as phone)

A classic red brick Georgian colonial, the Creamery was built in 1890 as part of Elmer A. Darling's Mountain View Farm. Darling studied architecture at MIT, and his training resulted in a handsome collection of rural buildings. Regarded as the best-preserved gentleman's farm in the area, Mountain View comprises a cow barn, one of the largest ever built in the state, a horse stable, and the Creamery. Surrounded by 440 acres of rolling hills and meadows, the farm also offers spectacular views of Willoughby Gap and Burke Mountain. The Creamery's interior was restored in 1989, and today it welcomes overnight guests and also hosts business and social functions. Guest rooms are gracefully furnished with antiques and handmade quilts, while the parlor is decorated in the style of an English country manor. Rates include a full country breakfast, served in the dining room (which was once the center of butter and cheese production), and gourmet lunches and dinners for groups are also available. On-site activities include hiking, biking, lawn bowling and croquet, and Burke Mountain and Lake Willoughby, a deep glacial lake known for its fishing, are just minutes away.

Listed in the Vermont Historic Register; recipient of Chamber of Commerce Restoration Award

Location: The Inn at Mountain View Creamery is three hours from Boston and is accessible via I-91 and Route 5 to Route 114.
Function Space: 936 square feet; 3 rooms
Capacity—Conference: 50; Reception: 50; Banquet: 50
Equipment On-site: Overhead projector, VCR, easel, fax
Food Service: Breakfast with room; catering/food service available
Overnight Accommodations: 12 rooms
Limitations/Restrictions: No smoking; no pets
Access: On-site parking; open year-round
Payment: Cash, credit card

GRAFTON

THE OLD TAVERN AT GRAFTON

Grafton, VT 05146
Phone: 800-843-1801   Fax: 802/843-2245

ALTHOUGH Grafton is a picture-book New England village, it is far from a "museum town." With a population of 600, the living, working village boasts a cheese factory, a dairy farm, and a blacksmith shop, as well as authentic covered bridges and picturesque steepled churches. Since 1801 the Old Tavern at Grafton has been the centerpiece of the historic village, and it was a popular stop on the Boston-to-Montreal stagecoach runs. Over the years the Old Tavern's guests have included Daniel Webster, Oliver Wendell Holmes, Ulysess S. Grant, and Nathaniel Hawthorne. Exquisite furnishings are found throughout the inn, which also features hand-hewn beams, the rich patinas of wide pine flooring, and pewter and brass appointments. In addition to the Main Tavern building and cottages, accommodations are available in six nineteenth-century guest houses, each with a full kitchen. The restored Old Tavern com-

Inn at Mountain View Creamery

fortably accommodates business gatherings, retreats, weddings, and receptions. The dining room serves breakfast, lunch, and dinner daily with a menu that features traditional New England fare. There is a natural pond for swimming on the grounds, and tennis and biking are also available. The Old Tavern's Ski Center offers 30 kilometers of cross-country trails, ice skating, snowshoeing, and instruction.

Member of Historic Hotels of America

Location: Grafton is in southern Vermont, 12 miles west of Bellows Falls. Bradley International Airport is 2.25 hours away; Logan International Airport, 2.5 hours. From the south, take I-91 north to Route 5 north, left on Route 121, west 12 miles to Grafton.

Function Space: 6,000 square feet; 6 rooms

Capacity—Conference: 30; Reception: 150; Banquet: 65; Theater: 75

Equipment On-site: 35mm slide projector, overhead projector, screen, VCR and monitor

Food Service: Catering/food service available; dining room

Overnight Accommodations: 66 rooms

Limitations/Restrictions: No smoking in dining room; no pets

Access: Handicapped accessible; on-site parking; closed Christmas Eve/Christmas Day and the month of April

Payment: Cash, check, credit card (MC, Visa)

The Old Tavern at Grafton

GREENSBORO

HIGHLAND LODGE

(Mailing address)
RR1 Box 1290
(Street address)
Caspian Lake Road, Greensboro, VT 05841
Phone: 802/533-2647   Fax: 802/533-7494

ON the shores of Lake Caspian sits the lovely white Highland Lodge in the peaceful northern Vermont countryside. Built in 1865, the main lodge and its accompanying cottages accommodate up to 60 guests while offering the comforts of home and a welcome woodland serenity. The lodge is well suited for family gatherings, retreats, and even business meetings, when escape to peaceful, natural surroundings is desired. Comfortable, cozy parlors and a well-stocked library offer a quiet refuge, and guests will find a wide variety of relaxing recreational opportunities no matter what time of year they visit. The lodge boasts 120 acres of fields and wooded hiking paths, as well as tennis, horseshoes, badminton and croquet, and the lakeshore abounds with other activities. The lodge beach house is equipped with a fireplace and grills, and sailboats, rowboats, paddleboats, and canoes are available to guests. Good fishing is an option in June, September, and October, and cross-country skiing through maple groves and evergreen forests and over frozen lakes is a favorite pursuit as well. The Green Mountains and the White Mountains are also just short day trips away.

Location: The Highland Lodge is about 35 miles northeast of Montpelier off VT 16, at the northern end of Lake Caspian.
Function Space: 2,000 square feet; 3 rooms
Capacity—Conference: 30; Reception: 60; Banquet: 80
Equipment On-site: VCR, overhead and slide projectors, screen; fax, photocopying available
Food Service: Full food service
Overnight Accommodations: 22 rooms
Limitations/Restrictions: Restrictions on smoking; beer and wine license only
Access: Handicapped accessible; on-site parking; open late May to mid-October, late December to mid-March
Payment: Cash, check, credit card (Discover, MC, Visa)

Highland Lodge *(Ben Thurber)*

Equinox Hotel

MANCHESTER

EQUINOX HOTEL
(Mailing address)
P.O. Box 46
(Street address)
Historic Route 7-A, Manchester Village, VT 05254
Phone: 802/362-4700   Fax: 802/362-1595

THE history of the Equinox dates back to 1769, when the two-story wooden Marsh Tavern was founded. This tavern was an important meeting place for Vermont's legendary Green Mountain Boys and other American revolutionaries, who seized the Tory property in support of their cause. Over the next two centuries a number of owners added structures, and today the Equinox comprises 17 buildings representing six different architectural styles. The hotel gained fame as a premier summer resort in 1864 when Mrs. Abraham Lincoln and two of her sons visited. Closed during the 1970s, the beautifully restored Equinox reopened in 1985 following years of extensive historical and archeological study. Set on 2,300 acres in the Green Mountains, the hotel boasts a "country grande" decor and cozy New England atmosphere. Accommodations range from pine-furnished guest rooms with antiques, Audubon prints, and richly textured fabrics, to handsome suites and comfortable townhouses. The stately Board Room accommodates 15, and other function rooms hold up to 300 for business and social events. In addition to a fitness spa, tennis, swimming, and golf are available, as well as fly-fishing instruction and the British School of Falconry, the first of its kind in the United States.

Listed in the National Register of Historic Places; member of Historic Hotels of America

Location: The Equinox Hotel in Manchester, located in southwestern Vermont, is accessible via Route 7, Route 7A and Route 313.
Function Space: 8,000+ square feet; 8 rooms
Capacity—Conference: 72; Reception: 350; Banquet: 300; Theater: 280
Equipment On-site: Audiovisual equipment and business services available
Food Service: Catering/food service available; two restaurants
Overnight Accommodations: 181 rooms
Limitations/Restrictions: Restrictions on smoking; some non-smoking guest rooms available

Access: Handicapped accessible; on-site parking; open year-round
Payment: Cash, check, credit card

MIDDLEBURY

THE MIDDLEBURY INN

(Mailing address)
P.O. Box 798
(Street address)
14 Courthouse Square, Middlebury, VT 05753-0798
Phone: 802/388-4961   Fax: 802/388-4563

SINCE 1827 the Middlebury Inn has provided classic Vermont hospitality from its setting above the local village green. Nathan Wood opened the inn as the Vermont Hotel, and it was later known in the nineteenth century as the Addison House. In the year of its centennial it became the Middlebury Inn. The inn's central structure is a

The Middlebury Inn

three-story red brick Georgian, and guest rooms, traditionally furnished and with a simple elegance, are also available in the 1825 Porter Mansion and a contemporary motel; rates include a continental breakfast. Meeting space is available for conferences, banquets, and other events. Plentiful New England fare is served in the Founders Room, and during warmer weather guests enjoy lunch and dinner on the front porch overlooking the green. A quintessential New England town, Middlebury charms visitors with its white-steepled churches, quaint shops, and beautiful foliage. Other local attractions include a walking tour of 155 architectural set pieces, the Vermont Marble Exhibit, the New England Maple Museum, and Middlebury College.

Listed in the National Register of Historic Places; member of Historic Hotels of America

Location: The Middlebury Inn is accessible via Highway 7 and Routes 125 and 30. Burlington Airport is 35 miles north, and Amtrak service is available in nearby Port Henry, New York. Bus service is available a block from the inn.
Function Space: 2,000 square feet; 3 rooms
Capacity—Conference: 50; Reception: 50; Banquet: 35; Theater: 60
Food Service: Breakfast with room; catering/ food service available; restaurant, tavern
Overnight Accommodations: 75 rooms
Limitations/Restrictions: No smoking
Access: Handicapped accessible; on-site parking; open year-round
Payment: Cash, check, credit card

NORTHFIELD

NORTHFIELD INN
27 Highland Avenue, Northfield, VT 05663
Phone: 802/485-8558

OVERLOOKING the historic village of Northfield, the Northfield Inn also enjoys scenic views of the Green Mountains and is surrounded by valleys and wildflower meadows. This restored Victorian home, built in 1901, has been returned to its original grand style and decorated with period furnishings and antiques. Guests sleep in brass or carved-wood beds with European feather bedding and in the morning are treated to a full old-fashioned multicourse breakfast. The inn is available for group dinners, business meetings, retreats, and other special events, and visitors can easily relax indoors or out, whether browsing in the library, playing in the game room, or engaging in a game of croquet or horseshoes on the lawn. Sledding, sleigh rides, horseback riding, and hiking mountain trails also are favorite pursuits, and skiing is just a short drive away. Visitors will also enjoy strolling through Northfield's historic district and Norwich University, the country's first private military college, or touring nearby Barre, the granite capital of the world.

Listed in the Vermont Register of Historic Places

Location: Northfield is just off I-89 (Exit 5); follow signs to Northfield; right on Prospect; right on Highland Avenue. The inn is 9 miles from Montpelier, 40 miles from Burlington; local bus and Amtrak service available.
Function Space: 600 square feet; 1 room
Capacity—Conference: 30; Reception: 35; Banquet: 35 (buffet); Theater: 30
Equipment On-site: TV/VCR, overhead projector, fax, phone

Food Service: Breakfast with room; catering/
food service available
Overnight Accommodations: 12 rooms
Limitations/Restrictions: No smoking; food
and beverage service by arrangement; no pets;
no children under the age of 15
Access: On-site parking; open year-round
Payment: Check

ORWELL

HISTORIC BROOKSIDE FARMS COUNTRY INN
(Mailing address)
P.O. Box 36
(Street address)
Route 22A, Orwell, VT 05760
Phone: 802/948-2727   Fax: 802/948-2015

FROM what had been a farmhouse in 1789, architect James Lamb created a striking Greek Revival
mansion in 1843 that today is the centerpiece of the
300-acre Historic Brookside Farms. Beyond the
restored mansion's bold portico of Ionic columns,
visitors step into large, comfortably furnished
rooms. The grand salon features a Bösendorfer
piano and original 1843 decor, while the library
boasts 10,000 volumes. The inn is available for
weddings, private parties, corporate functions, and
other occasions. Overnight guests enjoy a full complimentary country breakfast—a good opportunity
for sampling the produce of Brookside's working
farm—including maple syrup, fruits, vegetables,
and farm fresh eggs. Lunch, afternoon tea, and a
five-course gourmet dinner are available as well.
Also on the estate is an authentically restored guest
house and antique shop, built at about 1810 as the
original tenant farmhouse. The manicured grounds
and the surrounding meadows and forests offer gorgeous views for quiet walks, and quaint New
England villages are nearby. In addition, museums,

farms, historic tours, and recreational activities are
all close at hand.

Listed in the National Register of Historic Places

Location: Historic Brookside Farms is 45 minutes
south of Burlington on Route 22A. Nearest major
airport is Burlington International.
Function Space: 1,000 square feet; 2 rooms
Capacity—Conference: 50; Reception: 150;
Banquet: 50
Equipment On-site: Audiovisual equipment
and business services can be obtained from
outside source
Food Service: Breakfast with room; catering/
food service available; dining room
Overnight Accommodations: 7 rooms
Limitations/Restrictions: Restrictions on smok-
ing; no pets
Access: Handicapped accessible (all common
rooms and one suite only); on-site parking;
open year-round
Payment: Cash, check, traveler's check

PROCTORSVILLE

BATES MANSION AT BROOK FARM
(Mailing address)
P.O. Box 111
Cavendish, VT 05142
(Street address)
Twenty Mile Stream Road, Proctorsville, VT 05153
Phone: 802/226-7863   Fax: 802/226-7048 (call first)

BUILT in 1894, picturesque Bates Mansion is
now an exclusive retreat and planning center, a
picture postcard come to life. Surrounded by 60
acres of fields, woods, trails, and streams, the 17-
room mansion offers a quiet escape, making it
ideal for a productive corporate meeting or pri-

vate retreat. Brook Farm is also a popular gathering place for family reunions, as guests have unlimited use of the mansion. Visitors, whether sampling the private libraries or relaxing in the parlors, enjoy the cozy, New England charm that permeates the house. A full commercial kitchen, eight fireplaces, and a game room help to make guests feel comfortable and at home. Outdoors, expansive lawns, fields, and stone walls add to the serene setting. Guests at the estate can pursue a variety of recreational activities, including cross-country skiing, hiking, biking, and fishing, and the trout-filled Twenty-Mile Stream runs through Brook Farm.

Listed in the National Register of Historic Places

Location: Bates Mansion is 20 miles west of I-91 and 3 hours from Boston. Nearest airport service is 2.5 hours away in Burlington, Vermont; Hartford, Connecticut; and Albany, New York.
Function Space: 950 square feet; 1 room
Capacity—Conference: 35–40; Banquet: 20
Equipment On-site: Tables, chairs, overhead and slide projector included in rental; copier and fax available
Food Service: Kitchen available; catered meals on request
Overnight Accommodations: 11 rooms
Limitations/Restrictions: Restrictions on smoking
Access: On-site parking; open year-round
Payment: Check

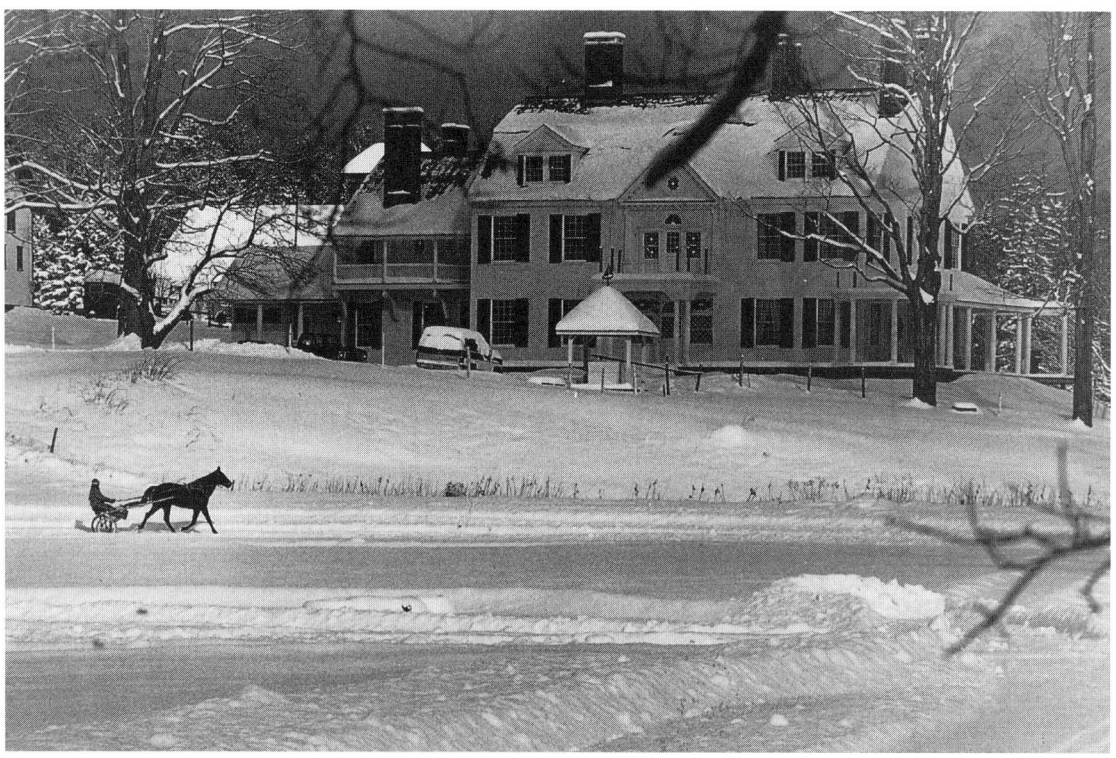

Bates Mansion at Brook Farm

STOWE

GREEN MOUNTAIN INN

(Mailing address)
P.O. Box 60
(Street address)
1 Main Street, Stowe, VT 05672
Phone: 802/253-7301 or 800-253-7302
Fax: 802/253-5096
E-mail: Grnmtinn@aol.com

LOCATED in the heart of a picturesque Vermont village, the Green Mountain Inn was built in 1833 as a private residence for Peter Lovejoy. After he traded the house for a farm, the mansion was converted into a hotel. Over the years the inn has been enlarged, and today it includes the Old Depot built next door by the Mount Mansfield Electric Railroad in 1897. The guest rooms are uniquely appointed with cozy country quilts and period furnishings, and select rooms come with jacuzzis, VCRs, and fireplaces. Meeting and banquet facilities are available for conferences, business meetings, receptions, and private parties. There are also two acclaimed restaurants on-site—the popular Whip Bar and Grill, with its eclectic menu, and the gracious Main Street Dining Room, which offers traditional New England fare. Guests also have use of a fully equipped health club and outdoor pool. The inn is within walking distance of shops, galleries, and the famous 11-mile-round-trip Stowe Recreation Path. Renowned for its winter sports, Stowe also offers extensive recreational activities year round.

Listed in the National Register of Historic Places; member of Historic Hotels of America

Location: The Green Mountain Inn is located on Main Street (Route 100), 10 minutes from I-89

(Exit 10). Burlington International Airport is 40 minutes away, and Amtrak service is available in Waterbury, 10 minutes south.
Function Space: 2,442 square feet; 4 rooms
Capacity—Conference: 36; Reception: 125; Banquet: 100; Theater: 100
Equipment On-site: Overhead and slide projectors, VCR and monitor; fax and photocopying available
Food Service: Catering/food service available; two restaurants
Overnight Accommodations: 64 rooms
Limitations/Restrictions: Food and beverages must be supplied by Green Mountain Inn
Access: Handicapped accessible; on-site parking; open year-round
Payment: Cash, traveler's checks, credit card (AmEx, Discover MC, Visa)

VERGENNES

BASIN HARBOR CLUB

Basin Harbor Road, Vergennes, VT 05491
Phone: 802/475-2311   E-mail: res@bh-on-lc

ON the spectacular eastern shore of Lake Champlain, the Basin Harbor Club occupies a historic site that was once an important maritime center, serving as a shipyard during the War of 1812 and as a commercial wharf well into the 1920s. In 1882 schoolteacher Ardelia Beach acquired the neighboring farm at Basin Harbor and began welcoming guests; by the 1930s, when the original inn was added to the property, the resort was thriving. Today the fourth generation of Beaches welcomes visitors to the club's 700-acre resort. The club offers guests accommodations in the Main Lodge, the Champlain House, the historic homestead, or in a variety of cottages. Seemingly limitless recreational pursuits are available, including water sports, tennis, golf on a world-class course, and bike tours through the countryside. There are several dining options available, from formal dinners to luncheon buffets, and the club's classic American cuisine features the finest produce from local farms. The resort is ideal for executive retreats and gatherings that combine work with recreation, and meeting rooms are available for a variety of business and social functions. Nearby attractions include shops, craft centers, and museums, including the unique Lake Champlain Maritime Museum.

Location: The Basin Harbor Club is located on the eastern shore of Lake Champlain, 30 miles south of Burlington International Airport; a 3,200-foot grass airstrip is on-site. The club is 7 miles from Vergennes, and is accessible via Route 22A to Panton Road to Basin Harbor Road.
Function Space: 4,190 square feet; 9 rooms
Capacity—Conference: 200; Reception: 350; Banquet: 350; Theater: 100
Equipment On-site: Complete audiovisual services available
Food Service: Catering/food service available; three restaurants
Overnight Accommodations: 136 rooms
Limitations/Restrictions: No smoking
Access: Handicapped accessible, on-site parking; open mid-May to mid-October
Payment: Check, credit card (MC, VISA)

WAITSFIELD

THE INN AT ROUND BARN FARM

(Mailing address)
RR1 Box 247
(Street address)
East Warren Road, Waitsfield, VT 05673
Phone: 802/496-2276   Fax: 802/496-8832

IN a rich, gorgeous pastoral setting, the Inn at the Round Barn comprises several historic and architecturally significant structures. The earliest structures, a charming Cape Cod and an icehouse, date back to 1810, and the farmhouse to the 1840s. In 1910 the remarkable 12-sided round barn was added to the 85-acre estate, which until the 1960s was a working dairy farm. Furnished with antiques, the farmhouse welcomes guests into a relaxed but elegant country home. A library, a game room with an antique pool table, and spacious guest rooms, some with whirlpool tubs, are among the amenities, and rates include a full breakfast. Today the restored barn is a focal point of artistic and cultural events in central Vermont and is used for receptions, conferences, exhibitions, and live performances as well. The barn also features a unique 60-foot lap pool, and the inn has its own 30-kilometer groomed, tracked-and-marked cross-country ski course. Hiking, biking, canoeing, and exploring the area's quaint covered bridges and scenic rural landscape are just some of the recreational options available. Popular day trips include visits to the Shelburne Museum and to Ben and Jerry's ice cream factory in Waterbury.

Listed in the National Register of Historic Places

Location: Waitsfield is located 35 miles southeast of Burlington International Airport and is accessible via I-89 and Route 100. Taxi service is available.

Function Space: 2,000 square feet; 3 rooms
Capacity—Conference: 150; Reception: 200;
Banquet: 200; Theater: 150
Equipment On-site: Audiovisual equipment
available for rent; fax, copier
Food Service: Breakfast with room; full food
service available
Overnight Accommodations: 11 rooms
Limitations/Restrictions: No smoking
Access: Handicapped accessibility to conference
facility only; on-site parking; open year-round
Payment: Check, credit card (MC, Visa)

WILMINGTON

THE WHITE HOUSE OF WILMINGTON

(Mailing address)
P.O. Box 757
(Street address)
Route 9 East, Wilmington, VT 05363
Phone: 800-541-2135   Fax: 802/464-5222

THE White House of Wilmington, with its distinctive pair of double-decker porches, is a 1915
Victorian mansion that was converted to a gracious country inn in 1978. Once the summer
home of lumber baron Martin Brown, the elegant
White House is surrounded by Beaver Brook and
the Green Mountains. Considering its setting,
high on a crest among rolling hills overlooking
the Deerfield Valley, it is not surprising that the
White House has been chosen by several newspapers as one of the most romantic inns around; its
interiors are just as appealing, with their beautiful woodwork and their brass and crystal light
fixtures. A variety of rooms are available for business and social functions; guest rooms are furnished with period pieces, and some have fireplaces, balconies or terraces, and large whirlpool
tubs. The inn's dining rooms serve a full breakfast

and dinner daily, and the fare is classic continental cuisine. Recreational opportunities abound,
including the inn's indoor and outdoor pools and
a health spa. Outstanding downhill and cross-
country skiing, sleigh rides, ice skating, and
guided snowmobile tours are available in the area
during the winter, while golf, biking, tennis, and
horseback riding are among the options during
warmer months.

Listed in the National Register of Historic Places

Location: The White House of Wilmington is
located in southern Vermont, 20 minutes west
of Brattleboro and 1.5 hours from both Albany
International and Bradley International Airports;
2 hours from Hartford. From I-91, take Exit 2
to Route 9 west to Wilmington.
Function Space: 2,105 square feet; 8 rooms
Capacity—Conference: 125; Reception: 125;
Banquet: 125
Equipment On-site: Audiovisual equipment
must be obtained through an outside source;
fax available
Food Service: Breakfast with room; restaurant
Overnight Accommodations: 23 rooms
Limitations/Restrictions: Smoking limited to
guest rooms; children over 10 years welcome;
no pets
Access: Handicapped accessible; on-site parking;
open year-round
Payment: Check, money order, credit card

WOODSTOCK

KEDRON VALLEY INN

Route 106, South Woodstock, VT 05071
Phone: 802/457-1473 or 800-836-1193
Fax: 802/457-4469
E-mail: KedronInn@aol.com

SINCE long before it became the Kedron Valley Inn, this handsome 1828 Federal-style brick building in historic South Woodstock has been welcoming visitors for more than a century, whether they were affluent guests attending a cotillion or runaway slaves needing a hiding place during the Civil War. The award-winning inn and its guest rooms are filled with antiques that exude a country charm, and antique quilts from the innkeepers' collection are found throughout the house and in many guest rooms. Guests enjoy a full complimentary breakfast and stay in cozy rooms furnished with canopy beds, antique oak beds, fireplaces, and even Franklin stoves. Meeting space is available for receptions, parties, business meetings, and other gatherings. Functions can also be held on the spacious lawn, which accommodates a large tent and dance floor. Groups are entitled to special rates and may request creative plat-du-jour or buffet menus. A seemingly endless list of activities are available, ranging from skiing and sleigh rides in winter to hiking, canoeing, swimming, golf, and tennis. Beautiful rural scenery and picturesque covered bridges abound, and a number of historic sites are nearby as well, including Calvin Coolidge's birthplace and the summer home and studio of artist Augustus Saint-Gaudens.

Location: The Kedron Valley Inn is 5 miles south of Woodstock; approximately 3 hours from Hartford, Connecticut, and 2.5 hours from Boston. The inn is located on Route 106, 13 miles west of I-89 and I-91. Nearest airport service is in Lebanon, New Hampshire, 30 minutes away.

Function Space: 465 square feet; 1 room
Capacity—Conference: 30; Reception: 135; Banquet: 135
Equipment On-site: Flip chart, projector screen; fax, modem, copier available
Food Service: Breakfast with room; catering/food service available; restaurant
Overnight Accommodations: 27 rooms
Limitations/Restrictions: No smoking (permitted in bar)
Access: Handicapped accessible; on-site parking; open May through March
Payment: Company check

VIRGINIA

ABINGDON

CAMBERLEY'S MARTHA WASHINGTON INN

(Mailing address)
P.O. Box 1037, Abingdon, VA 24212
(Street address)
150 W. Main Street, Abingdon, VA 24210
Phone: 540/628-3161   Fax: 540/628-8885

IN about 1760, frontiersman Daniel Boone camped out in what would become Abingdon, and since the town's establishment in 1778 many more have enjoyed their visits to this historic area. Known as an arts and crafts center, Abingdon boasts an impressive 20-block historic district filled with excellent examples of Early American architecture and buildings dating back to the late eighteenth century. In the heart of the district is the Martha Washington Inn, a lovely Southern mansion built by General Francis Preston for his large family in 1832. Beginning in 1860 the house served as the Mary Washington College campus, and since 1935 it has been a hotel. Beautifully restored, the luxurious inn features elegant parlors, verandahs, and many charming Victorian touches. Antique furnishings grace the comfortable guest rooms, and a continental breakfast as well as afternoon tea are included in the room rates. Receptions, dances, and conventions are among the events held in the Grand Ballroom, and other graciously appointed rooms are available for a variety of functions. Across the street from the inn is the Barter Theatre, the state theater of Virginia, so named

for the early practice of granting admission in exchange for agricultural produce.

Member of Historic Hotels of America

Location: The Martha Washington Inn is 133 miles southwest of Roanoke, Virginia, just off I-81.
Function Space: 6,591 square feet; 5 rooms
Capacity—Conference: 100; Reception: 300; Banquet: 230; Theater: 250
Equipment On-site: Overhead and slide projectors, screens, TV, VCR, microphones, flip charts, copier, fax machine
Food Service: Breakfast with room; on-site banquet food service
Overnight Accommodations: 61 rooms
Limitations/Restrictions: Restrictions on smoking; no outside food or beverage service
Access: Handicapped accessible; on-site parking; open year-round
Payment: Cash, credit card (AmEx, Carte Blanc, Diners, Discover, MC, Visa)

ALEXANDRIA

AMERICAN HORTICULTURAL SOCIETY RIVER FARM

7931 E. Boulevard Drive, Alexandria, VA 22308
Phone: 703/768-5700   Fax: 703/765-6032

THE northernmost of George Washington's five Virginia farms, River Farm occupies 27 acres with splendid views of the Potomac River and beautiful plantings in all seasons. Washington purchased the then-1800-acre farm in 1760 from William Clifton, who had built a brick home on the site. The foundations of that home are still visible today on the site of the existing turn-of-the-century colonial-style mansion. Washington gave his personal secretary, Tobias Lear, a lifetime lease to the property, and later generations of the Washington family lived here as well. The property passed through several other owners before the American Horticultural Society (AHS) purchased it for their headquarters in 1973. Today River Farm's house and gardens are available for weddings, dinner parties, corporate meetings, and other events. Groups renting the house have access to the ballroom, parlor, dining room, and kitchen; the lovely covered porch offers views of the river and several gardens. Not surprisingly, as home to AHS, River Farm is a beautifully landscaped showplace with sweeping lawns, traditional and demonstration gardens, and wooded habitat for wildlife.

Location: River Farm is accessible via the George Washington Memorial Parkway and the Jefferson Davis Highway at the southern end of Alexandria, 4 miles south of Old Town. National Airport is 6 miles north.

Function Space: 5,000 square feet; 3 rooms

Capacity—Reception: 80; Banquet: 80; up to 800 on the grounds

Food Service: List of approved caterers provided

Limitations/Restrictions: No smoking

Access: Handicapped accessible; on-site parking; open year-round

Payment: Check, credit card (AmEx, MC, Visa)

THE LYCEUM, ALEXANDRIA'S HISTORY MUSEUM

201 S. Washington Street, Alexandria, VA 22314

Phone: 703/838-4994   Fax: 703/838-4997

IN the heart of quaint Old Town Alexandria, the Lyceum is once again a center for education and culture. Founded by Quaker schoolmaster Benjamin Hallowell and others, the Lyceum Company organization met for lectures and debates on literary, scientific, and historical topics, later joining forces with the Alexandria Library Company. Together they built the distinctive Greek Revival Lyceum building in 1839, which became the focal point of the city's intellec-

River Farm *(Margaret Alderson)*

tual and cultural life. The building was used as a hospital during the Civil War, later becoming a private residence and then offices. Local preservationists saved the building from demolition, and in 1985 the Lyceum reopened as Alexandria's History Museum. The museum's collections concentrate on city history and culture, beginning with Alexandria's founding in 1749. Items featured in the collection include locally manufactured furniture, silver, and stoneware, as well as prints, documents, photographs, and Civil War memorabilia. The Lyceum's elegant lecture hall is available for weddings, meetings, receptions, concerts, and lectures, and arrangements can be made to have the three exhibition galleries located on the first floor open after 5:00 P.M. for evening events.

Listed in the National Register of Historic Places; a Virginia Historic Landmark

Location: The Lyceum is located in Old Town Alexandria, 15 to 20 minutes south of Washington, D.C., and is accessible via US Route 1, I-95, I-395, I-295, and I-495, and the George Washington Parkway (Washington Street in Old Town). Local bus service is available.
Function Space: 1,624 square feet; 1 room
Capacity—Conference: 150; Reception: 200; Banquet: 150; Theater: 125
Equipment On-site: Slide projectors, screen, amplified lectern, concert grand piano
Food Service: Catering kitchen available
Limitations/Restrictions: No smoking; request guidelines for other restrictions
Access: Handicapped accessible; on-site parking (20 spaces); open-year round
Payment: Check (credit card payment available)

CHAMPLAIN

LINDEN HOUSE BED AND BREAKFAST PLANTATION

(Mailing address)
P.O. Box 23
(Street address)
Route 17 Tidewater Trail, Champlain, VA 22438
Phone: 804/443-1170   Fax: 804/443-0107

LOCATED in rural Essex County, this stately three-story brick house built in 1750 was home to planter Nicholas Faulkner. The house is set on more than 200 acres and surrounded by landscaped grounds, including an English garden, herb garden, and terraced lawn; it was likely named for the large linden tree in the drive. A courtyard joins the main house and the carriage house, and both buildings are furnished with eighteenth-century antiques and reproductions. Groups can meet in the carriage house dining room, and the main house is also available for business meetings, wedding receptions, picnics, reunions, and other gatherings. The comfortable guest rooms have a colonial atmosphere but varied features, ranging from fireplaces to country furnishings to a jacuzzi bath. Rates include a full plantation breakfast, and refreshments are available to guests throughout the day. A number of historic attractions are nearby, including Tappahannock, Stratford Hall, and Wakefield; recreational activities include golfing, fishing, and cruises on the Rappahannock River.

Listed in the National Register of Historic Places

Location: Linden House is 45 minutes from Fredericksburg and one hour from Richmond, and is located on Route 17, 8 miles from Tappahannock. Nearest airport is Richmond International.

Function Space: 800 square feet; 1 room
Capacity—Conference: 30; Reception: 200;
Banquet: 60; Theater: 30
Equipment On-site: Fax available
Food Service: Breakfast with room; food service
available; dinner by reservation only
Overnight Accommodations: 8 rooms
Limitations/Restrictions: No smoking (permitted
on porches); inn supplies mixers, guests supply
own wine, beer, and setups; no high heel shoes
worn on second and third floors
Access: Handicapped accessible; on-site parking;
open year-round
Payment: Cash, check, credit card (AmEx,
MC, Visa)

CHESTERFIELD

WREXHAM HALL

10301 Old Wrexham Road, Chesterfield, VA 23832
Phone: 804/768-8000 Fax: 804/777-9145

THE section of Wrexham Hall originally known as
Goode House when it was built in 1830 is unique
for its symmetrical T-plan design, a style not usually seen in early-nineteenth-century Virginia architecture. The two-story clapboard house served as a
Confederate hospital during the Civil War, and
bloodstains are still visible on portions of the floor.
Dr. Thomas Jefferson Cheatham owned the house
in the late nineteenth century, and it was from here
that the great Chesterfield fox hunts began and the
dogs were turned loose. In 1941, Mr. and Mrs.
Stanley R. Hague purchased the house, naming it
Wrexham Hall for Mrs. Hague's family coat of
arms in Wales' Wrexham Cathedral. The Hagues
renovated the house and added to it part of an older
house, known as Fruit Hill, probably built at about
1750. The two houses share a similar facade, and

their linkage gives the hall its unique dual-portico
entrance. Furnished with antiques and fine period
reproductions, the house maintains all its original
woodwork, mantels, and detailing. Today
Wrexham Hall stands on three acres, about 2,000
feet from its original site, and hosts wedding receptions, corporate parties, and business meetings.

Location: Wrexham Hall is 10 miles from I-95 at
Route 145 and Wrexham Road; 25 minutes
to Richmond, 35 minutes to Richmond
International Airport, and 55 minutes to
Williamsburg.
Function Space: 2,000 square feet; 4 rooms
Capacity—Conference: 40; Reception: 40
Equipment On-site: May be rented from
outside source
Food Service: Catering available
Limitations/Restrictions: Client must supply
any alcohol; bartenders and setup provided as
part of catering fee
Access: Handicapped accessible, on-site
parking; open year-round
Payment: Cash or check

FAIRFAX

THE BAILIWICK INN

4023 Chain Bridge Road, Fairfax, VA 22030
Phone: 703/691-2266 Fax: 703/934-2112

IN about 1810, Joshua Gunnel built his three-
story mansion across the street from the courthouse
where Fairfax County resident George Washington
had filed his will. Years later, Captain John Quincy
Marr became the first Confederate casualty of the
Civil War when he was killed in a skirmish across
the inn's front lawn. Today the Bailiwick Inn, once
at the center of Northern Virginia community life,

is an award-winning inn offering fine dining and accommodations. Filled with antiques, elegant architectural detailing, and nineteenth-century charm, the refurbished and restored Federal-style inn offers facilities for business meetings and special events. Guest rooms are modeled after rooms found in Virginia's great mansions and are furnished to honor some of the state's historic figures, including Thomas Jefferson and Robert E. Lee. Room rates include breakfast and afternoon tea. Located midway between Dulles International Airport and Washington, D.C., the inn serves as a convenient base for business and sightseeing. In addition to the capital's splendid museums and monuments, Mount Vernon, Gunston Hall, and other colonial estates are close by, and the quaint shops and restaurants of Old Town Fairfax are just steps away from the inn.

Listed in the National Register of Historic Places

Location: The Bailiwick Inn is approximately 20 miles west of Washington, D.C. Local shuttle service and the Vienna metrorail station 10 minutes away provide easy access to the capital. The inn is accessible via Route 66, Route 123, and Route 236.
Function Space: 950 square feet; 3 rooms
Capacity—Conference: 12; Reception: 75; Banquet: 26; Theater: 30
Equipment On-site: Inn can arrange for any equipment needed; photcopier and fax available
Food Service: Breakfast with room; catering/food service available; restaurant
Overnight Accommodations: 14 rooms
Limitations/Restrictions: No smoking; no pets; alcoholic beverages limited to wine and beer
Access: Handicapped accessible; on-site parking; open year-round
Payment: Credit card (AmEx, MC, Visa)

FREDERICKSBURG

BELMONT, THE GARI MELCHERS ESTATE AND MEMORIAL GALLERY
224 Washington Street, Fredericksburg, VA 22405
Phone: 540/654-1015   Fax: 540/654-1785

BELMONT is the former home and studio of American artist Gari Melchers (1860–1932), who spent the last 16 years of his life at this country estate located on 27 wooded acres overlooking the Rappahannock River, across from Fredericksburg. A native of Detroit, Melchers studied art in Dusseldorf and Paris as a young man, later setting up studios in Holland, France, Germany, and the United States. Today he is recognized for his society portraits, impressionist-inspired landscapes, and thoughtful depictions of everyday life, and his murals adorn the walls of the Library of Congress. Melchers' 1790s Georgian manor house, which is open for tours, is filled with the furnishings and antiques he and his wife, Corinne, collected during their travels. The 1924 stone Studio Building houses three galleries featuring the artist's paintings, and extensive formal gardens, with their long boxwood promenade, provide a relaxed setting for outdoor receptions. Visitors are welcomed to the museum through a restored 1918 carriage house that features a museum shop, an orientation theater, and a conference room. Belmont, in historic Falmouth in Stafford County, is less than a mile from downtown Fredericksburg and its many museums, antique shops, and fine restaurants.

National Historic Landmark; listed in the National Register of Historic Places; Virginia Historic Landmark

Location: Belmont is located just off Route 17, 1.25 miles east of I-95, Exit 133, and is one hour south of Washington National Airport and one hour north of Richmond. Amtrak and commuter rail service available.

Function Space: 2,275 square feet; 2 rooms

Capacity—Conference: 20; Reception: 80

Equipment On-site: Speaker's podium, tables and chairs, flip chart included in rental; audiovisual equipment must be rented from outside source

Food Service: Renter selects caterer; kitchenette available in Visitor Center conference room

Limitations/Restrictions: No smoking; no red wine; no open flames; Visitor Center Conference Room hours are 9:00 A.M. to 5:00 P.M. weekdays, 10:00 A.M. to 5:00 P.M. Saturday, 1:00 P.M. to 5:00 P.M. Sunday. The Studio and grounds are available 6:00 P.M. to 10:00 P.M. Monday through Saturday

Access: Studio/galleries handicapped accessible, conference room is not wheelchair accessible (no elevator); on-site parking; open year-round

Payment: Check

KENMORE PLANTATION AND GARDENS

1201 Washington Avenue
Fredericksburg, VA 22401
Phone: 540/373-3381   Fax: 540/371-6066
E-mail: Webmaster@kenmore.org

THIS graceful mid-Georgian mansion in the heart of historic Fredericksburg has a colorful history stretching back to the days of the American Revolution. Colonel Fielding Lewis built the house in 1775 for his wife, Betty, whose brother, George Washington, was a frequent visitor to Kenmore. During the War for Independence, Lewis helped establish a gunnery in town to supply arms to American troops. In the Civil War Battle of Fredericksburg, Kenmore was perilously situated between Union and Confederate lines and was struck by cannon fire. During this battle and, later, the Battle of Chancellorsville, the North used Kenmore as a hospital; more than

Belmont
(The Gari Melchers Estate and Memorial Gallery, Mary Washington College)

100 soldiers were buried on the grounds but were later reinterred in national cemeteries. Today the restored mansion revels in colonial elegance, its rooms boasting exquisite eighteenth-century craftsmanship, and its dining room is considered one of the most beautiful rooms in America. Kenmore, whose gardens cover more than a city block, is now a house museum with meeting space available for both business and social events. Groups meeting here may make special arrangements for house tours.

National Historic Landmark; listed in the National Register of Historic Places; listed in the Virginia Landmarks Register

Location: Fredericksburg is approximately one hour south of Washington, D.C., and one hour north of Richmond. From I-95 Exit 130A, follow Route 3 toward Fredericksburg and follow signs to Kenmore.
Function Space: 2,498 square feet; 3 rooms
Capacity—Conference: 18; Reception: 125; Theater: 90
Equipment On-site: TV, VCR, two slide projectors and screen, podium and microphone
Food Service: Approved caterers list provided
Limitations/Restrictions: No smoking
Access: Handicapped accessible; open year-round
Payment: Check

HERNDON

DRANESVILLE TAVERN
(Mailing address)
Historic Properties Rental Services
6332 Barcroft Mews Drive
Falls Church, VA 22041-1237
(Street address)
11919 Leesburg Pike, Herndon, VA 22070
Phone: 703/750-1598
Fax: 703/750-5462

THE original structure on the site was a private home built in 1820, but during the 1840s it was converted into a public tavern and run by the local postmaster. The Dranesville Tavern quickly became a popular stop with travelers, and farmers driving livestock between Leesburg and Alexandria were regular visitors. In 1865 the *Alexandria Gazette* called the tavern "one of the finest roadside inns in the State of Virginia." During the Civil War a stream of military activity flowed past its doors, and in December 1861, Confederate General J. E. B. Stuart clashed with Union forces under General McCall at the Battle of Dranesville, a half mile from the tavern. The two-story tavern has been restored to its mid-nineteenth-century appearance and is available for a variety of social and business functions. There are seven rustic rooms of varying sizes, providing ample space for breakout sessions and conferences, and a shady back porch overlooks a meadow and stream.

Listed in the National Register of Historic Places; Virginia Historic Landmark

Location: The Dranesville Tavern is 45 minutes west of Washington, D.C., and is accessible via I-66 and Route 7.

Function Space: 1,500 square feet; 7 rooms
Capacity—Conference: 60; Reception: 45;
Banquet: 20; Theater: 60; total capacity
indoors: 99; 150 with grounds tented
Equipment On-site: TV, VCR, overhead and
slide projectors, screen, amplified lectern,
tables and chairs
Food Service: Renter selects caterer; kitchen
available
Limitations/Restrictions: No smoking; alcohol
permitted only with Fairfax County permit
Access: On-site parking, open year-round
Payment: Check

HOT SPRINGS

THE HOMESTEAD
(Mailing address)
P.O. Box 2000
(Street address)
Route 220, Hot Springs, VA 24445
Phone: 800-838-1766   Fax: 540/839-7782

THE original Homestead was built in 1766, and
since then visitors—including presidents
Thomas Jefferson and William Howard Taft—
have been drawn to the resort and its natural hot
springs. Throughout the nineteenth century
facilities were added to the resort, and during the
Civil War the Confederates used the Cascades Inn
as a hospital. Located on 16,000 acres in historic
Bath County, the resort offers comprehensive
recreational and meeting facilities in a dramatic,
natural setting. The elegant Georgian-style
Homestead, distinguished by its trademark clock
tower, is the resort's stunning centerpiece. The
Spa, built in 1892, provides traditional mineral
baths in the natural hot springs and a full range
of European-style spa services. Other resort

amenities include three golf courses, a fitness center, a theater, a historical library and museum, a
wine room, and 10 restaurants and lounges. And,
of course, there are the nearby springs pools:
Jefferson is believed to have designed the gentlemen's pool in 1761, and the ladies' pool was built
in 1836. The Homestead's conference center provides state-of-the-art meeting facilities and
breakout rooms; the resort also hosts banquets,
receptions, and other events for groups of 20 to
1,000. Customized programs geared for conference attendees or spouses can also be arranged.

National Historic Landmark; listed in the National
Register of Historic Places; member of Historic Hotels
of America

Location: Hot Springs is in the Allegheny
Mountains off Highway 220, 75 miles north
of Roanoke. Ground transportation to the resort
from regional airports can be arranged.
Function Space: 70,000 square feet; 27 rooms
Capacity—Conference: 85; Reception: 1,000;
Banquet: 900; Theater: 1,000
Equipment On-site: Full range of audiovisual
equipment includes sound systems, TVs,
slide projectors, microphones, and video
production equipment
Food Service: Catering/food service available;
10 restaurants and lounges
Overnight Accommodations: 81 suites,
581 rooms
Access: Handicapped accessible; on-site
parking; open year-round
Payment: Cash, credit card (AmEx, MC, Visa)

LEESBURG

OATLANDS PLANTATION

20850 Oatlands Plantation Lane
Leesburg, VA 20175
Phone: 703/777-3174   Fax: 703/777-4427

GEORGE Carter's plantation home, built in 1803, had been a charming, red brick Georgian house until Carter admired the new design of James Monroe's Oak Hill, which was located nearby. Carter then converted his house into the imposing Greek Revival home it remains today. He also cleverly designed the plantation's gardens and connecting terraces, laid out to shelter the area from the wind and thus extend the growing season. During the Civil War raiding Union troops bypassed Oatlands, but despite this good fortune the estate was still in need of repair when Corcoran and Edith Eustis purchased it in 1903. The Eustises restored the house and formal garden, and during the summer and fox hunting seasons hosted weekend parties that included Franklin D. Roosevelt and other Washington luminaries. In 1965 the Eustises' daughters presented the 261-acre Oatlands estate, house, and furnishings to the National Trust for Historic Preservation. Today the mansion maintains its English-style country house appearance of the 1920s and 1930s, and the large entrance hall and a private meeting room are available for group events. The grounds may also be tented for weddings, receptions, and other gatherings.

National Historic Landmark; listed in the National Register of Historic Places; National Trust for Historic Preservation Historic Site

Oatlands Plantation *(Ron Blunt. Courtesy of the National Trust for Historic Preservation)*

Location: Oatlands Plantation is 6 miles south of Leesburg on US Route 15 and 40 minutes west of Washington, D.C.
Function Space: 800 square feet; 1 room (day or evening use)
Capacity—Conference: 40; Reception: 75; Banquet: 75; Theater: 75
Food Service: Preferred caterers list available; outside caterers also permitted
Limitations/Restrictions: No smoking
Access: Meeting room handicapped accessible; on-site parking; open year-round
Payment: Deposit with balance paid 30 days prior to event

LEXINGTON

WILLSON-WALKER HOUSE RESTAURANT

(Mailing address)
P.O. Box 973
(Street address)
30 North Main Street, Lexington, VA 24450
Phone: 540/463-3020   Fax: 540/463-5377

THE classical revival-style Willson-Walker House, built in 1820, is a handsome fixture in Lexington's downtown historic district. Originally the home of William Willson, postmaster, merchant, and treasurer of Washington College, the building remained a residence until 1911, when it became Harry Walker's meat market and grocery store. Now a restaurant featuring American cuisine using local and regional ingredients, the Willson-Walker House offers a variety of meeting spaces for dinners, seminars, parties, and receptions. First-floor rooms and the lower verandah seat between 20 and 35 and accommodate between 40 and 50 for stand-up receptions. An upstairs conference room seats 12 to

15 and comes with controlled lighting and a private rest room. The spacious upstairs banquet room opens onto a verandah overlooking Lexington's historic downtown. Lexington offers a number of historic attractions, including General Stonewall Jackson's home, the George C. Marshall Museum and Library, and Washington and Lee University (formerly Washington College), where Robert E. Lee served as president after the Civil War.

Listed in the National Register of Historic Places

Location: The Willson-Walker House Restaurant is located in Lexington's downtown historic district, 10 minutes from either I-81 or I-64. Airports at Roanoke and Richmond are within 45 minutes and two hours, respectively. Bus and taxi service available.
Function Space: 4 rooms plus verandah
Capacity—Conference: 15; Reception: 50–120; Banquet: 72; Theater: 40
Food Service: Banquet/restaurant service
Limitations/Restrictions: Restrictions on smoking; wine corkage fee; no outside catering
Access: Handicapped accessible; open year-round
Payment: Check, credit card (AmEx, MC, Visa)

MIDDLEBURG

WELBOURNE
22314 Welbourne Farm Lane
Middleburg, VA 20117
Phone: 540/687-3201

KNOWN as Welbourne since the Dulany family bought it in 1830, this country manor was originally a stone house built in 1755. The Dulanys eventually added a brick and stucco front with six slender two-story columns, as well as extra rooms and a porch. Since then seven generations of the family have lived at Welbourne, a 600-acre farm in Virginia's rolling hunt country. The manor's dependencies, including a greenhouse, a billiards house, and servants' quarters, are now guest cottages that revel in a time-worn elegance. During the Civil War, Confederate soldiers periodically hid out at the mansion, and during one of the area's frequent skirmishes General J. E. B. Stuart is said to have sat calmly on his horse eating breakfast next to the porch as bullets nicked the roof. Both Thomas Wolfe and F. Scott Fitzgerald visited during the 1930s, and each produced a story with Welbourne as a setting. Room rates include a full breakfast and refreshments, and small meetings can be held in the living room, which is furnished with antiques and opens onto the back porch. Nearby attractions include historic downtown Middleburg, Civil War

battlefields, and wineries; the Blue Ridge Mountains and Skyline Drive are just a short drive away.

Listed in the National Register of Historic Places; a Virginia Historic Landmark

Location: Welbourne is 50 miles west of Washington, D.C., 6 miles west of Middleburg, and is accessible via Route 50. Dulles International Airport is 45 minutes away.
Function Space: 300 square feet; 1 room
Capacity—Conference: 15; Reception: 125
Food Service: Breakfast with room; with advance notice other meals are available for meeting groups
Overnight Accommodations: 8 rooms
Access: On-site parking; open year-round
Payment: Check

Welbourne

MIDDLETOWN

WAYSIDE INN

7783 Main Street, Middletown, VA 22645
Phone: 540/869-1797   Fax: 540/869-6038

ORIGINALLY known as Wilkinson's Tavern when it opened as a stagecoach stop in 1797, the Wayside Inn has long been a favorite meeting place, even during the Civil War. Although Union and Confederate forces swapped control of the area more than 70 times, the inn managed to stay in business by catering to whichever side was in command at the moment. Renamed the Wayside Inn at the turn of the century, the hostelry's Valley Pike location and the increase in automobile travel led to its appellation as "America's First Motor Inn." Tradition and history remain strong here, and the restored inn basks in a colonial atmosphere, with its rare antiques, fine art, and individually appointed guest rooms. Authentic regional American cuisine is served in the Wayside's seven intimate dining rooms, and Larrick's Tavern, circa 1720, can accommodate small meetings. Conference and banquet facilities are available for larger groups for a variety of business and social occasions. The Wayside Inn is nestled in the Shenandoah Valley, and historic Skyline Drive, Luray Caverns, Belle Grove Plantation, and Civil War sites are all nearby.

Member of Historic Hotels of America

Location: The Wayside Inn is located at the crossroads of Route 11 and I-81 (Exit 302), 70 miles west of Washington, D.C. Dulles International Airport is approximately 45 minutes away.
Function Space: 2,885 square feet; 5 rooms
Capacity—Conference: 120; Reception: 250; Banquet: 120; Theater: 150

Equipment On-site: Audiovisual equipment available
Food Service: Full service restaurant
Overnight Accommodations: 29 rooms
Limitations/Restrictions: All food and beverage service must be purchased from inn's restaurant and lounge
Access: Limited handicapped accessibility; on-site parking; open year-round
Payment: Cash, check, credit card

MINERAL

LITTLEPAGE INN

15701 Monrovia Road, Mineral, VA 23117
Phone: 540/854-9861 or 800-248-1803
Fax: 540/854-8780

A cedar-lined drive leads to the Littlepage Inn, historically known as Prospect Hill, a handsome Federal-style mansion in the rolling hills of Spotsylvania County. Waller Holladay's inheritance from his half-brother, the colorful General Lewis Littlepage, allowed him to begin acquiring plantation land in 1803. Spotswood Dabney Crenshaw built the main house in 1811 for Waller and his wife, Huldah, where they raised their 13 children. After the Civil War ended their youngest son, James, captured at the Battle of Five Forks, walked home to Prospect Hill from the federal prison at Point Lookout, Maryland. Through James' efforts the farm returned to successful operation. In 1991–1992 the fifth and sixth generations of the Holladay family restored Prospect Hill, and the main house remains essentially as it was in 1811, a beautifully detailed plantation home. The farm's well-preserved outbuildings also offer an excellent look at an early-nineteenth-century Virginia plantation. Guests at the inn stay in spacious rooms, and a full breakfast is included in the rates. Within walking distance is Lake Anna, and four major battlefields surrounding Fredericksburg are just a short drive away.

Listed in the National Register of Historic Places and the Virginia Landmarks Register; recipient of the Great American Home Award presented by the National Trust for Historic Preservation

Location: The Littlepage Inn is 90 minutes southwest of Washington, D.C., 60 minutes northwest of Richmond, and is accessible via Highway 522 to Route 612.

Function Space: 960 square feet; 3 rooms

Capacity—Conference: 20; Reception: 50; Banquet: 20; Theater: 20 inside, 100 on lawn or in nearby meeting hall

Food Service: Breakfast with room; catering/food service available; dinner with reservation

Overnight Accommodations: 8 rooms; other accommodations nearby

Limitations/Restrictions: No smoking (permitted on porches and lawns only); no pets or children near guest activities

Access: Handicapped accessible; on-site parking; open year-round

Payment: Check, credit card

MONTPELIER STATION

MONTPELIER

(Mailing address)
P.O. Box 67
(Street address)
11407 Constitution Highway
Montpelier Station, VA 22957
Phone: 540/672-2728   Fax: 540/672-0411

JAMES Madison grew up at Montpelier, and it remained his life-long home despite the numerous commitments he had elsewhere as a public servant and Founding Father. It was here that James and Dolley returned after Madison left the presidency in 1817, and until his death in 1836 he entertained numerous distinguished visitors, who enjoyed the scenic beauty of the lush Virginia Piedmont and his generous hospitality. Most important, it was here that Madison developed his vision for the young republic that found its expression in one of history's most remarkable documents, the Constitution. The

Montpelier *(Philip Beaurline. Courtesy of the National Trust for Historic Preservation)*

central portion of the mango-tinted Greek Revival house was begun in 1760 when Madison was just a boy, and although succeeding owners later built expansive additions, some of Montpelier's original features remain. Today the estate encompasses the carefully preserved house, the formal gardens, and 2,700 acres of rolling countryside. A monument to the Father of the Constitution, Montpelier is also an active center for architectural, archeological, and archival research. Meeting facilities include a boardroom in the main house that seats 12, and rooms for larger business and social events are available in what was once a pony barn.

National Historic Landmark; listed in the National Register of Historic Places; National Trust for Historic Preservation Historic Site

Location: Montpelier is 4 miles southwest of Orange on Route 20, approximately 25 miles north of Charlottesville, and 90 miles south of Washington, D.C.
Function Space: 4 rooms
Capacity—Conference: 75; Reception: 100; Banquet: 50; Theater: 75
Equipment On-site: Audiovisual equipment (limited) available
Food Service: List of recommended caterers available
Limitations/Restrictions: No smoking; no food or drink permitted in certain areas
Access: Handicapped accessible; on-site parking and shuttle bus service to other parking areas; open daily March to December and weekends only in January and February
Payment: In advance by check (billing is also available)

MOUNT VERNON

THE MOUNT VERNON INN
Mount Vernon, VA 22121
Phone: 703/780-0011   Fax: 703/780-1704

AMONG his numerous distinctions, George Washington was known to be an excellent host, whose guests often remarked on his and Martha's gracious hospitality and the hearty, abundant meals served at their Mount Vernon plantation. A throng of good friends, visitors, and other well-wishers streamed through the mansion over the years, prompting the president to muse, after his retirement, that perhaps he and Mrs. Washington would finally dine alone together. The tradition of Southern hospitality continues at Mount Vernon, for just outside the estate's front gate is the Mount Vernon Inn, established in 1932. Since 1853 the Mount Vernon Ladies' Association has operated the Mount Vernon estate as a monument to America's first president, and since 1992 they have owned the inn as well. The inn features charming eighteenth-century decor and fine dining, and facilities are available for business luncheons, dinners, receptions, and special occasions. Special arrangements can also be made for tour groups visiting the area. The menu offers choices from field and stream—pheasant, duck, lamb, veal, scallops, and seasonal favorites such as soft-shell crabs. Desserts made the old-fashioned way will not disappoint those with a sweet tooth, which would also have included George Washington himself.

Listed in the National Register of Historic Places

Location: The Mount Vernon Inn, adjacent to the Mount Vernon estate, is 16 miles from downtown Washington, D.C., and is accessible via the George Washington Memorial Parkway and

The Mount Vernon Inn

Route 1; local bus service links the inn to the Huntington metrorail station.

Function Space: 3,400 square feet; 6 rooms

Capacity—Conference: 75; Reception: 250; Banquet: 200; Theater: 125

Equipment On-site: Fax and photocopier available

Food Service: Restaurant

Limitations/Restrictions: Restrictions on smoking; inn must provide all food and beverage service

Access: Handicapped accessible; on-site parking; open year-round

Payment: Cash, major credit card

WOODLAWN PLANTATION

(Mailing address)
P.O. Box 37, Mount Vernon, VA 22121
(Street address)
9000 Richmond Highway, Alexandria, VA 22309
Phone: 703/780-4000   Fax: 703/780-8509

IN 1799, George Washington gave his adopted granddaughter, Eleanor Parke Custis, and nephew, Lawrence Lewis, a 2,030-acre portion of his Mount Vernon estate as wedding gift. The impressive brick mansion was designed by William Thornton, the first architect of the U.S. Capitol. Eleanor and

Woodlawn Plantation *(Ron Blunt. Courtesy of the National Trust for Historic Preservation)*

her family lived here until her husband's death in 1839, and Woodlawn was sold in 1846 to a group of Quakers who formed a thriving community in the area. Later owners included playwright Paul Kester and Senator and Mrs. Oscar Underwood of Alabama. The house and remaining 126 acres endure today as an example of the customs and culture of a plantation home between 1800 and 1840. The furnishings date to the Federal period, including pieces once owned by the Lewises and the Washingtons. Space is available for meetings, dinners, and teas in the reception and dining rooms, while very large receptions and other events are accommodated in the garden and landscaped grounds. Also located on Woodlawn's grounds is

the Pope-Leighey House, built in 1940, an early example of Frank Lloyd Wright's "Usonian" houses designed for middle-class Americans. The house was moved to Woodlawn from Falls Church, Virginia, after highway construction prompted its rescue and relocation.

Listed in the National Register of Historic Places; National Trust for Historic Preservation Historic Site

Location: Woodlawn Plantation and Frank Lloyd Wright's Pope-Leighey House are located at the intersection of US Route 1 and VA Route 235 north, 10 miles south of Alexandria.

Function Space: 1,216 square feet; 2 rooms

Capacity—Reception: 100; Banquet: 80; Theater: 60; capacity increases to 1,000 if tents are used in the garden
Equipment On-site: Must be rented from outside source
Food Service: Preferred caterers list available
Limitations/Restrictions: Restrictions on smoking; alcoholic beverages must be purchased through Woodlawn; evenings only for receptions and banquets unless tented in the garden
Access: Handicapped accessible (first floor); on-site parking; open daily 9:30 A.M. to 4:30 P.M. March to December, weekends only in January and February
Payment: Check or credit card

RICHMOND

THE BOLLING HAXALL HOUSE

211 E. Franklin Street, Richmond, VA 23219
Phone: 804/643-2847 Fax: 804/644-6616

CONSIDERED one of the finest remaining examples of Italianate architecture in Richmond, the Bolling Haxall House, an imposing mansion in the heart of downtown, was built in 1858 for Bolling Walker Haxall, president of the Old Dominion Iron and Nail Works, whose fortune was lost in the Civil War. The house survived the war's fiery end, and Dr. Francis Willis, the next owner, embellished the interior with walnut paneling and an elliptical staircase. The Woman's Club of Virginia, whose spirited members founded the organization in 1894 for the serious education of women, purchased the mansion in 1900 for $20,000 from Willis's grandson following a resourceful trip to Baltimore to secure a loan. Fifteen years later the group added an elegant auditorium, which has hosted such notable figures as Amelia Earhart,

Martha Graham, John F. Kennedy, George Bush, and Tom Wolfe. Totally renovated in the 1980s under the direction of Historic Richmond Foundation, the house boasts carved marble mantels, trompe l'eoil architectural effects, and Victorian decor, while the auditorium reflects classical motifs of the later Beaux Arts style. Owned now by the Bolling Haxall House Foundation, the property remains the traditional home of the Woman's Club and is a popular community center. Meeting space is available in the boardroom and the auditorium, which has balcony seating, a curtained, elevated stage, a speaker's podium, and a full size pull-down screen.

The Bolling Haxall House
(Taylor Dabney)

Listed in the National Register of Historic Places;
Virginia Historic Landmark

Location: The Bolling Haxall House is located
in historic downtown Richmond between Second
and Third Streets, within walking distance of
Capitol Square. The house is accessible via I-95
or I-64, and Richmond International Airport
is 15 minutes away.
Function Space: 3,759 square feet; 2 rooms
Capacity—Conference: 200, Theater: 400 (auditorium); Boardroom seats 12
Equipment On-site: Speaker's podium and chairs
included in rental; fax available; audiovisual
equipment may be rented from outside source
Food Service: Full-service kitchen; renter selects
own caterer
Limitations/Restrictions: Restrictions on
smoking; ABC license must be applied for;
contract must be signed and on file prior to event
Access: Handicapped accessible; ample parking
nearby; open year-round; hours of availability
are 8:00 A.M. to midnight, Tuesday to Saturday,
and other times upon request
Payment: Check

THE JEFFERSON HOTEL

Franklin and Adams Streets, Richmond, VA 23220
Phone: 804/788-8000   Fax: 804/225-0334
http://www.jefferson-hotel.com

RECOGNIZED as one of the finest examples of the
Beaux Arts architectural style, the Jefferson Hotel
opened its doors on Halloween 1895. That
evening, the hotel hosted the wedding of Charles
Dana Gibson and Irene Langhorne, better known as
"the Gibson Girl". The famed Palm Court lobby
contains E. V. Valentine's life-size marble statue of
Thomas Jefferson beneath a 35-foot Tiffany stained

glass skylight and side windows. A grand staircase,
thought by some to be the model for the one seen
in *Gone With the Wind*, leads to the Rotunda, with
its monumental faux marble pillars supporting a
soaring 70-foot ceiling. The luxurious guest rooms
all feature high ceilings and rich furnishings, and
guests have complimentary use of the fitness club
and pool located across the street. Dining options
include T. J.'s Bar and Grill, overlooking the
Rotunda, and Lemaire, named for Jefferson's maître
d'. Among its seven dining rooms is the Library,
whose leather-bound volumes from 1895 still line
the shelves. Ever since the Gibson wedding, the
Jefferson has continued to host major events,
including presidential visits and the annual
Fortune 500 Forum, as well as cotillions, conferences, and executive meetings.

Listed in the National Register of Historic Places;
member of Historic Hotels of America

Location: The Jefferson Hotel is located in down-
town Richmond and is accessible via I-64 and
I-95; Richmond International Airport is 20
minutes away.
Function Space: 26,000 square feet; 14 rooms
Capacity—Conference: 300; Reception: 600;
Banquet: 400; Theater: 450
Equipment On-site: On-site audiovisual service
company; computer, fax, photocopying, private
office
Food Service: Catering/food service available;
two restaurants, 24-hour room service
Overnight Accommodations: 275 rooms
Access: Handicapped accessible; on-site
parking; open year-round
Payment: Deposit and payment upon
conclusion of event

LINDEN ROW INN

100 E. Franklin Street, Richmond, VA 23219
Phone: 804/783-7000   Fax: 804/648-7504

THE gardens of historic Linden Row in downtown Richmond were once the childhood playground of Edgar Allen Poe, and served as the inspiration for the enchanted garden in his poem *To Helen*. Today the brick-walled garden forms part of the courtyard of the Linden Row Inn, a series of restored red brick Greek Revival townhouses built in 1847. Decorated with authentic Victorian furnishings and a fine collection of gasoliers and pier mirrors, the inn also offers contemporary conveniences and services suited for business travelers. The Board Room and Parlor Suites are available for conferences, meetings, and small receptions. Guest rooms are handsomely furnished, and many look out onto the manicured grounds, while the garden quarters offer private entrances. Rates include a continental breakfast and an evening wine and cheese reception. Southern cuisine and other American favorites are on the dining room menu, and guests can enjoy light dining and refreshments on the patio. The Linden Row Inn is within walking distance of Richmond's historic, business, government, and shopping districts; guests have free transportation downtown and health club privileges at the nearby YMCA.

Listed in the National Register of Historic Places; member of Historic Hotels of America

Location: The Linden Row Inn is located in downtown Richmond, eight blocks from the state Capitol, and is accessible via I-95 and I-64.
Function Space: 1,247 square feet; 2 rooms
Capacity—Conference: 40; Reception: 75; Banquet: 50; Theater: 60

Equipment On-site: Audiovisual equipment available
Food Service: Breakfast with room; catering/food service available; dining rooms
Overnight Accommodations: 70 rooms
Access: Handicapped accessible; on-site parking; open year-round
Payment: Cash, check, credit card

THE VALENTINE MUSEUM/WICKHAM HOUSE

1015 E. Clay Street, Richmond, VA 23219
Phone: 804/649-0711   Fax: 804/643-3510

FOR more than a century the Valentine Museum, founded in 1892, has been chronicling the rich urban and social history of Richmond, from its colonial prosperity to the ravages of the Civil War through events of the late twentieth century. Among the museum's holdings are the largest costume and textile collection in the South and more than a half million historical photographs. The museum's benefactor, Mann S. Valentine Jr., made his fortune in the dry goods business and by selling his bottled Valentine's Preparation Meat Juice. The museum is connected to the Wickham House next door, a graceful Federal structure built in 1812 for attorney John Wickham, the wealthiest man in town. A house tour contrasts the Wickham family's lavish first-floor public rooms with their simple upstairs living area and the spare basement quarters of the slaves. Meeting space in the museum's conference and gallery rooms is available for business meetings, receptions, and other events. Just two blocks from Capitol Square, the Valentine Museum and Wickham House are located in the historic Court End district.

National Historic Landmark; listed in the National Register of Historic Places; Virginia Historic Landmark

Location: The Valentine Museum is located two blocks from the state Capitol and government offices, 20 minutes from Richmond International Airport, and is accessible via I-95 and I-64. Washington, D.C., is 2 hours north, and Raleigh-Durham, North Carolina, is 2.5 hours south.

Function Space: 2,300 square feet; 2 rooms

Capacity—Conference: 30; Reception: 225; Banquet: 125; Theater: 100

Equipment On-site: TV/VCR, slide projectors, lectern, microphones; museum will arrange with vendors for equipment rental

Food Service: Exclusive caterer

Limitations/Restrictions: No smoking; no food or drink in exhibition galleries

Access: Handicapped accessible; on-site parking (will also arrange for group transportation, overflow parking); open year-round

Payment: Check, purchase order, credit card (AmEx, Discover, MC, Visa)

ROANOKE

HOLLINS COLLEGE

(Mailing address)
Office of College Relations
P.O. Box 9657
(Street address)
8036 Quadrangle Lane, Roanoke, VA 24020
Phone: 540/362-6451   Fax: 540/362-6500

VIRGINIA'S first accredited women's college, Hollins College is a picturesque campus with Jeffersonian colonades and handsome brick buildings dating back to 1856. The campus was originally the site of Botetourt Springs, a mineral spring resort, and the oldest structure on campus is the springhouse, which dates to about 1800. A female seminary was later established here, and in 1855 miller John Hollins made the crucial financial donation that allowed Charles Lewis Cocke's plans for the college to go forward. Construction of the Main Building began on April 17, 1861, the day Virginia seceded from the Union, and the building was finally completed in 1869. The antique-furnished Green Drawing Room in the Main Building is available for receptions, meetings, lectures, and other events. Right outside the room is Main's long front porch—lined with rocking chairs since Cocke's days—which overlooks the campus's historic quadrangle, a classic collegiate landscape graced with ash, elms, and sugar maples. And tucked in the southwest corner of the quadrangle is Botetourt

Hollins College *(Pamela Moize)*

Hall (1890), one of the first octagonal buildings in the state.

Listed in the National Register of Historic Places; Virginia Historic Landmark

Location: Hollins College is 20 minutes from downtown Roanoke, approximately four hours from Washington, D.C., and three hours from Richmond, Virginia. Roanoke Regional Airport is 10 minutes away, and the college is on US Route 11, just off I-81 at Exit 146. Bus service is available.
Function Space: 1,000 square feet; 1 room
Capacity—Reception: 200 (300 using porches); Theater: 100
Equipment On-site: Audiovisual equipment available
Food Service: Catering/food service available
Limitations/Restrictions: No smoking; in-house catering and food service only
Access: Handicapped accessible; on-site parking; open year-round
Payment: Check, 10 days prior to event

SMITH MOUNTAIN LAKE

THE MANOR AT TAYLOR'S STORE, A BED AND BREAKFAST COUNTRY INN

Route 1, Box 533, Smith Mountain Lake, VA 24184
Phone: 540/721-3951   Fax: 540/721-5243

AN enchanting estate in the foothills of the Blue Ridge Mountains, the Manor at Taylor's Store enjoys a picturesque 120-acre setting and warm historical associations. Skelton Taylor, a lieutenant in Virginia's Bedford Militia, established a general merchandise trading post at Smith Mountain Lake in 1799. Taylor's Store served

both the local community and the early settlers heading west on the Old Warwick Road. The restored manor house was built in 1820, and its decor reflects various time periods from the home's past. Two rooms are available for retreats, meetings, and other gatherings. The manor's overnight guests can relax in the formal parlor, library, sun room, and great room, or in the large hot tub on the semienclosed porch. Rates include full, "heart healthy" gourmet breakfasts, and guests can arrange for picnic lunches or a European dinner basket, including wine. Recreational options abound, including hiking, swimming, canoeing, and fishing, or enjoying any of the estate's six spring-fed ponds. Golf, tennis, and fine dining are all available nearby, and the Blue Ridge Parkway is just a 20-minute drive away.

Virginia Historic Landmark

Location: The Manor at Taylor's Store is 45 minutes from Roanoke and is accessible via Route 220 south to 122 north to Burnt Chimney 1.5 miles north. Greensboro, North Carolina, is 1.5 hours south.
Function Space: 1,000 square feet; 4 rooms
Capacity—Conference: 35; Reception: 50; Banquet: 35 Theater: 35
Equipment On-site: TV, VCR
Food Service: Breakfast with room; catering/food service available
Overnight Accommodations: 12 rooms
Limitations/Restrictions: Restrictions on smoking; all food and alcoholic beverages must be provided by the inn; no pets; limited accommodations for children
Access: On-site parking; open year-round
Payment: Cash, check, credit card (MC, Visa)

SPERRYVILLE

THE CONYERS HOUSE INN & STABLE

3131 Slate Mills Road, Sperryville, VA 22740
Phone: 540/987-8025   Fax: 540/987-8709

IN 1810, Bartholomew Conyers built himself a new farmhouse, later moving and attaching an older building to it. Hessian mercenaries who remained in America after the Revolutionary War constructed this second building, which dates back to circa 1790, and the addition was dubbed the Conyers' Old Store. It was later called Fink's General Store, and General A. P. Hill's troops passed by en route to the second battle of Manassas in 1862. Beautifully restored and renovated, the house opened as a country bed and breakfast in 1981. Meeting rooms are available for corporate retreats, seminars, and other gatherings; weddings and receptions are also held here, and the innkeeper is available to officiate. Guest rooms are individually appointed, and the delightful features range from private porches to clawfoot bathtubs to a White House hand basin. Rates include breakfast, and a candlelit seven-course dinner is also served by prior arrangement. Located in the scenic and rural foothills of the Blue Ridge Mountains, Conyers House offers horseback riding trips and serves grand breakfasts to send off the hunt. Excellent recreational opportunities are to be found in the area, including steeplechases, festivals, wineries, hiking, and water sports.

Location: The Conyers House is 8 miles south of Sperryville, 1.5 hours southwest of Washington, D.C. The house is accessible via I-81 (1 hour away) and Route 211 (15 minutes away). Airport service is available at Dulles International, 55 miles north, and in Charlottesville, 45 minutes south.
Function Space: 960 square feet; 2 rooms
Capacity—Conference: 20; Reception: 45; Banquet: 20
Equipment On-site: Fax available

The Conyers House Inn & Stable

Food Service: Breakfast with room; catering/
food service available
Overnight Accommodations: 7 rooms; field
boarding available for horses
Limitations/Restrictions: Smoking outside only;
for alcholic beverages, ABC license, corkage fee
if guests provide own beverages
Access: Handicapped accessible (limited/days
only); on-site parking; open year-round
Payment: Personal or traveler's checks;
credit cards (Discover, MC, Visa)

STAUNTON

FREDERICK HOUSE

28 N. New Street, Staunton, VA 24401
Phone: 540/885-4220 or 800-334-5575 (reservations)

LOCATED in Staunton's Beverly Historic
District, the Frederick House is a small inn comprising five elegant structures built between
1810 and 1910, each with its own architectural
style and decor. With its terraced hillside setting,
small garden plots, and colorful walkways, the
inn is a quiet and relaxing dwelling in a small
town. Guest rooms are furnished with period furniture, and some have their own fireplaces, decks,
and separate entrances. Rates include a full breakfast served in Chumley's Tearoom. The building
next door houses McCormick's, which offers formal and casual dining, and the YMCA, whose
facilities are available to guests at the Frederick
House. Meeting space for business meetings, corporate retreats, and similar functions at the inn is
available daily from 9:00 A.M. to 5:00 P.M. in the
room where Staunton's Chamber of Commerce
used to meet. The Frederick House is within easy
walking distance of many antique shops,
Woodrow Wilson's birthplace and museum, and

numerous examples of fine nineteenth-century
architecture since the town escaped the devasta-
tion of the Civil War. Nestled between the
Allegheny and Blue Ridge Mountains, Staunton
is a good jumping-off point for exploring the
Shenandoah Valley.

Location: Staunton is approximately two hours
west of Richmond and three hours west of
Washington, D.C., and is accessible via I-64
and I-81. Bus and train service available.
Function Space: 480 square feet; 1 room
Capacity—Conference: 20; Reception: 20;
Banquet: 20
Equipment On-site: VCR and overhead
projector, fax, direct dial phones in rooms
Food Service: Breakfast with room; catering
service available
Overnight Accommodations: 14 rooms
Limitations/Restrictions: No smoking in
rooms; no pets
Access: On-site parking; open year-round
Payment: Cash, check, bank card

SWEET BRIAR

SWEET BRIAR COLLEGE

Box F, Sweet Briar College, Sweet Briar, VA 24595
Phone: 804/381-6100   Fax: 804/381-6263

SITUATED on 3,300 acres in the foothills of
Virginia's Blue Ridge Mountains, Sweet Briar
College is a selective, independent liberal arts and
sciences college for women. Founded in 1901, the
school is widely recognized as one of the most
beautiful in the country, with rolling hills, lakes,
and streams surrounding architect Ralph Adam
Cram's handsome Georgian Revival campus
architecture. The Sweet Briar College National

Historic District comprises 16 buildings, and the eighteenth-century home of the college founders is listed in the National Register of Historic Places. Two rooms in the Wailes Student Center accommodate conferences, receptions, and banquets, while the Beemer Room, with a full range of amenities for meetings with as many as 20 participants, is available next door in the Florence Elston Inn. The inn offers a variety of catering options, from box lunches to gourmet dinners. Overnight guests at the inn stay in individually appointed rooms, each of which has a balcony view of the woods, and rates include a continental breakfast. Extensive recreational activities are available, and other leisure options include theater performances, art exhibits, and tours of nearby historic sites.

Location: Sweet Briar College is located just south of the intersection of Route 29 and Route 60, 150 miles southwest of Washington, D.C., 100 miles west of Richmond, and 20 miles from Lynchburg Airport. Amtrak service is available.
Function Space: 2,000 square feet; 3 rooms
Capacity—Conference: 100; Reception: 150; Banquet: 80; Theater: 200
Equipment On-site: Overhead and slide projectors, screens
Food Service: Breakfast with room; full meals, box meals, refreshments available
Overnight Accommodations: 22 rooms
Access: Handicapped accessible; on-site parking; conference and reception room in the Wailes Student Center available daily June 1 to August 15, and from 8:00 A.M. to 5:00 P.M. weekdays during academic year; conference room in the Elston Inn is available year-round
Payment: Check

WARRENTON

AIRLIE CENTER
6809 Airlie Road, Warrenton, VA 20187
Phone: 540/347-1300   Fax: 540/347-5957

The history of Airlie, one of the first dedicated conference centers in the country, reaches back to 1899. Built as a private residence for Harry Groome, a farmer, historian, sportsman, and poet, Airlie was named after a fifteenth-century Scottish castle the Groomes had visited on a golfing trip. This first manor house burned in 1924, and it is the rebuilt Georgian Revival home that remains today. Established in 1959 as a conference center and quiet retreat within easy traveling distance of Washington, D.C., Airlie comprises nine contiguous estates covering more than two square miles and has been the scene of significant international conferences. The house serves as the conference center headquarters, and a variety of restored cottages tucked among the hills house overnight guests. At the turn of the century, Mrs. Groome designed the estate's formal gardens, featuring a pavilion, stone walls, boxwood hedges, and an assortment of annuals and perennials that continue to enchant visitors. Wildflower gardens and orchards abound as well, and Airlie's secluded location and beautiful natural scenery allow visitors to work and relax free of outside distractions. Recreational activities include tennis, swimming, volleyball, and skeet shooting, and there are also walking trails and jogging paths on-site.

Location: Airlie is less than an hour west of Washington, D.C., and is accessible via I-66 and Highways 211 and 29.
Function Space: 13,000 square feet; 16 rooms

The Williamsburg Inn

Capacity—Conference: 200; Reception: 250; Banquet: 200; Theater: 250
Equipment On-site: All audiovisual equipment available in-house; tri-gun projector; 21-computer station learning center
Food Service: Conference dining room, private dining room available, catering and beverages supplied by Airlie
Overnight Accommodations: 150 rooms
Limitations/Restrictions: Restrictions on smoking
Access: Handicapped accessible; on-site parking; open year-round
Payment: Credit card, company account

WILLIAMSBURG

WILLIAMSBURG INN
Colonial Williamsburg Foundation
P.O. Box 1776, Williamsburg, VA 23187-1776
Phone: 757/229-1000   Fax: 757/220-7685

COLONIAL Williamsburg is regarded as one of the finest and most complete community restorations—not to mention the largest living history museum in the world—and much of its preservation is due to the efforts of John D. Rockefeller Jr. The village was established as Middle Plantation, an outpost of Jamestown, in 1633 and served as Virginia's capital from 1699 to 1780. Colonial Williamsburg is the city's 173-acre historic area, which comprises more than 500 reconstructions and 88 original colonial buildings. In 1937, Rockefeller built the whitewashed neoclassical inn that over the years has hosted presidents, prime ministers, and royalty. The individually designed and decorated guest rooms are in the Regency style, and the inn maintains the ambiance of an English country home. Three distinctive function rooms at the inn accommodate meetings and banquets, and numerous additional facilities associated with the inn, including Providence Hall, a restored colonial home, are available for business and social events. As a full-service resort, the inn offers traditional recreational activities and is also within walking distance of the village's remarkable collection of authentic eighteenth-century homes, taverns, and shops and the magnificent Governor's Palace.

Member of Historic Hotels of America

Location: Williamsburg is 1 hour from both Richmond and Virginia Beach, Virginia, and 3.5 hours from Washington, D.C. It is accessible via I-64, Route 199, and Route 143; nearby airports include Williamsburg/Jamestown Airport, Richmond International, Newport News/Williamsburg International, and Norfolk International.
Function Space: 70,000 square feet; 3 rooms[*]
Capacity—Conference: 85; Reception: 1,300; Banquet: 670; Theater: 850
Equipment On-site: Audiovisual services available
Food Service: Catering/food service available; three restaurants
Overnight Accommodations: 102 rooms*
Limitations/Restrictions: No pets
Access: Handicapped accessible; on-site parking; open year-round
Payment: Master bill

WOODSTOCK

THE INN AT NARROW PASSAGE

(Mailing address)
P.O. Box 608
(Street address)
Route 11 and Chapman Landing Road
Woodstock, VA 22664
Phone: 540/459-8000   Fax: 540/459-8001

THE Inn at Narrow Passage, a sturdy log structure built in the 1740s, is a true colonial inn and has been greeting travelers for more than 250 years. It was a welcome refuge from Indian attacks on the Great Wagon Road (now U.S. Route 11) where the road narrowed to one wagon width. During the Civil War the inn served as General Stonewall Jackson's headquarters for the Valley Campaign of 1862. But today such harrowing times have long since vanished, and the inn is a peaceful, relaxing place in the northern Shenandoah Valley, occupying five acres along the Shenandoah River. The oldest guest rooms at the inn feature pine floors and stenciling, while the newer rooms, also decorated in the Colonial style, open onto porches overlooking the river and the Massanutten Mountains. Rates include a full breakfast at fireside in the dining room. The inn also offers a well-equipped conference room available for executive retreats, meetings, and other gatherings. There are ample opportunities for hiking, horseback riding, canoeing, and fishing, and excursions to nearby wineries, antique shops, battlefields, and caverns make for easy day trips.

---

[*]An additional 29 meeting rooms and more than 900 guest rooms are available in facilities affiliated with the Williamsburg Inn.

Location: The Inn at Narrow Passage, 2 miles south of Woodstock, is 30 minutes from Winchester Airport via I-81 and 1.5 hours from Dulles International Airport via I-81 and I-66.
Function Space: 900 square feet; 3 rooms
Capacity—Conference: 25; Reception: 25
Equipment On-site: VCR, slide projector, screen

Food Service: Breakfast with room; catering/food service available
Overnight Accommodations: 14 rooms
Limitations/Restrictions: No smoking (indoors)
Access: Handicapped accessible; on-site parking; open year-round
Payment: Check, credit card (MC, Visa)

The Inn at Narrow Passage

WASHINGTON

COUPEVILLE (WHIDBEY ISLAND)

FORT CASEY INN

Bed and Breakfast
1124 S. Engle Road, Coupeville, WA 98239
Phone: 360/678-8792

CAPTAIN George Vancouver arrived at Whidbey Island, the largest island in Puget Sound, in 1792, and his navigation of Deception Pass clearly demonstrated that Whidbey was not, in fact, a peninsula. Fort Casey was established on the island's western shore in the late nineteenth century, and today the Fort Casey Inn comprises a row of five Colonial Revival-style clapboard homes, decorated with memorabilia of the World War I era and patriotic motifs that recall the fort's role in that conflict. Built in 1909 as officers' quarters, the houses accommodate up to 35 guests in unique two-bedroom suites, each with living area, bath, and farmhouse kitchen, and rates include a continental-plus breakfast. The house known as Garrison Hall is available for retreats, seminars, weddings, and other events, and as part of its military and folk art decor is an unusual "painting within a painting" on the living room wall. The inn overlooks Admiralty Bay on Puget Sound and Crockett Lake—a natural bird sanctuary—and the Fort Casey State Park is right next door. The old fort's bunkers, 10-inch disappearing guns, and lighthouse remain, and the park offers scenic public beaches and trails.

Listed in the National Register of Historic Places

Location: The Fort Casey Inn is on the western shore of Whidbey Island, 2.5 miles west of Coupeville and just under two hours from Seattle.
Function Space: 800 square feet; 1 room
Capacity—Conference: 40; Reception: 95
Equipment On-site: Tables and chairs
Food Service: Breakfast with room; list of approved caterers provided; full kitchen available
Overnight Accommodations: 9 suites
Limitations/Restrictions: Smoking restricted to front porch; alcoholic beverages limited to beer and wine; no pets
Access: On-site parking; open year-round
Payment: Cash, check, credit card (AmEx, Visa)

GOLDENDALE

MARYHILL MUSEUM OF ART

35 Maryhill Museum Drive, Goldendale, WA 98620
Phone: 509/773-3733   Fax: 509/773-6138

PERCHED on a bluff in the Columbia River Gorge, the Maryhill Museum of Art enjoys a setting and a history that are both remarkable. In 1907 entrepreneur Sam Hill purchased 7,000 acres on the Columbia River, where he planned to develop a Quaker agricultural community. When this project did not pan out, he converted his 1914 château-like mansion known as Maryhill into a museum. Hill's generosity to the people of Romania following World War I led to Queen Marie's dedicating the riverside museum in a 1926 ceremony, and Maryhill's Queen Marie Gallery features her gilt furniture, jewelry, and gifts of Russian icons. Other permanent exhibitions include a renowned collection of Auguste Rodin's sculpture and drawings and an extensive

Native American collection of art and artifacts. A meeting room with views of the gorge is available for small groups, and room rental includes admission to the museum. Groups of 10 or more can arrange for guided tours as well. Just three miles from Maryhill, overlooking the Columbia River, is a replica of Britain's Stonehenge, which and was Hill's tribute to local men killed in World War I.

Listed in the National Register of Historic Places

Location: Maryhill Museum of Art is on the Columbia River, 100 miles east of Portland, Oregon, and is accessible via I-84 and Route 14.
Function Space: 325 square feet; 1 room
Capacity—Conference: 30
Equipment On-site: Slide projector, VCR
Food Service: Catering/food service available
Limitations/Restrictions: No smoking
Access: Handicapped accessible; on-site parking; open March 15 to November 15
Payment: Check

PORT TOWNSEND

ANN STARRETT MANSION
744 Clay Street, Port Townsend, WA 98368
Phone: 800-321-0644   Fax: 360/385-2976

REGARDED as an architectural masterpiece, the Ann Starrett Mansion is a three-story Victorian wonder—even the construction methods used in building the free-hung spiral staircase remain unclear. What is certain is that the stairs lead to a remarkable solar calendar in the eight-sided dome ceiling, which is decorated with frescoes depicting the Four Seasons and the Four Virtues. On the first day of each season, the sun shines through the tower roof's small dormer windows, striking a ruby red glass that directs a beam of light toward the appropriate seasonal panel. George Starrett built the mansion in 1889 as a wedding gift to his wife, Ann, and today the inn's antique furnishings and elaborate Victorian decor reflect its splendid past. Guest rooms in the mansion, upper and lower cottages, and carriage house are brightly decorated, and many have spectacular views of Mt. Ranier, the Olympic Mountains, Cascade Mountain, and Puget Sound. Room rates include a full breakfast. Meeting space is available for small business gatherings and social functions, and the inn can arrange package tours and corporate side trips to the San Juan Islands. Visitors will also enjoy strolling through historic Port Townsend's charming nineteenth-century neighborhoods.

Listed in the National Register of Historic Places; recipient of the National Trust for Historic Preservation's Great American Home Award

Location: Port Townsend is a 30-minute ferry ride plus a one-hour drive from Seattle and is accessible via Route 20. Bus and taxi service available.
Function Space: 1,400 square feet; 3 rooms
Capacity—Conference: 28; Reception: 28; Banquet: 28; Theater: 28
Equipment On-site: Audiovisual equipment and business services can be acquired with advance notice
Food Service: Breakfast with room; catering/food service available
Overnight Accommodations: 11 rooms
Limitations/Restrictions: No smoking
Access: On-site parking; open year-round
Payment: Check

SEATTLE

MAYFLOWER PARK HOTEL

405 Olive Way, Seattle, WA 98101
Phone: 206/623-8700   Fax: 206/382-6996

WITH the ambiance of a classic European hotel, the 12-story Mayflower Park Hotel in the heart of downtown Seattle features crystal chandeliers, lofty ceilings, stained glass windows, and period antiques, including a 1776 grandfather's clock. Built in 1927, the hotel has been handsomely restored. Small conventions, weddings, receptions, and other events are hosted in the eight meeting and banquet rooms, including the mezzanine-level Fireside Room that overlooks the beautifully appointed lobby furnished with eighteenth- and nineteenth-century antiques. The Andaluca Restaurant serves seasonal Northwestern cuisine with a Mediterranean flair, and Oliver's, a favorite downtown bar, offers light fare. At the hotel guests can catch a ride on the monorail and head for the Seattle Center and Space Needle, while free bus transportation is available for a trip to historic Pioneer Square and the Kingdome. The Mayflower opens directly into the Westlake Center and its 80 specialty shops, and the historic Pike Place Market and the waterfront are just a short walk away.

Location: The Mayflower Hotel is at the intersection of Fourth and Olive Way in downtown Seattle. The hotel is accessible via I-5, and Seattle-Tacoma International Airport is 20 minutes away.

Mayflower Park Hotel

Function Space: 4,272 square feet; 8 rooms
Capacity—Conference: 54; Reception: 175;
Banquet: 100; Theater: 185
Equipment On-site: In-house audiovisual
company; podiums and screens provided
Food Service: Catering/food service available;
restaurant, bar

Overnight Accommodations: 172 rooms
Limitations/Restrictions: No pets
Access: Handicapped accessible; on-site and
valet parking available; open year-round
Payment: All major credit cards

WEST VIRGINIA

WHITE SULPHUR SPRINGS

THE GREENBRIER
300 W. Main Street
White Sulphur Springs, WV 24986
Phone: 304/536-1110   Fax: 304/536-7834

THE first published mention of the Greenbrier's mineral waters appeared in Thomas Jefferson's *Notes on the State of Virginia* in 1784, and throughout the nineteenth century Southern aristocratic families summered at the resort to avail themselves of its legendary mineral cures. Union troops occupied the buildings during the Civil War, and the hotel was later the summer home of Robert E. Lee. The resort also served as an internment center for German and Japanese diplomats and as a hospital for wounded soldiers in World War II, after which it was dramatically refurbished. Set on 6,500 acres in the Allegheny Mountains, the Greenbrier is a full-service resort, consistently rated among the best in the world. The sprawling classic and colonial buildings include guest houses and guest cottages, and the interiors feature the bright floral motifs of designer Dorothy Draper. The Greenbrier's three-level conference center is equipped to handle the requirements of nearly any group, including high-level meetings, large and small conferences, and social functions. Themed events, casual dinners, and formal white-glove and gold-service dinners are also available. The resort offers children's and spouses' programs and complete recreational facilities, including a spa, championship golf courses, and a falconry academy.

National Historic Landmark; listed in the National Register of Historic Places; member of Historic Hotels of America

Location: White Sulphur Springs is located off I-64 just inside West Virginia's eastern border. Washington, D.C., is 250 miles away. Greenbrier Valley Airport in Lewisberg is 15 minutes away; air service is also available in Beckley and Charleston, West Virginia, and in Roanoke, Virginia.
Function Space: 70,000 square feet; 30 rooms
Capacity—Conference: 50; Reception: 2,000+; Banquet: 1,200; Theater: 1,500
Equipment On-site: Audiovisual equipment, closed-circuit television, business services, in-house cable network for meeting announcements
Food Service: Modified American plan (breakfast and dinner); dining room, four restaurants, lounge
Overnight Accommodations: 672 rooms
Access: Handicapped accessible; on-site parking; open year-round
Payment: Major credit card

WISCONSIN

DE PERE

JAMES STREET INN

201 James Street, De Pere, WI 54115
Phone: 414/337-0111   Fax: 414/337-6135

PORTIONS of the James Street Inn date back to 1858, when Randall Wilcox and Eugene Weber built their stone mill on the site. Later additions to the mill continued through the years before it finally closed in 1982. But in 1995 the mill opened as a luxurious bed and breakfast, with a tranquil riverside location and a pier for guests arriving by boat. The Columbian Room is available for small weddings, business meetings, and special events, and the inn will assist with catering arrangements. Guests stay in rooms and suites, individually furnished in Shaker and traditional styles, with separate working and living areas; most feature a whirlpool, a fireplace, and a view of the Fox River. A continental breakfast is served in the parlor, and wine and cheese are served in the lobby every afternoon. The James Street Inn is within walking distance of a variety of shops and restaurants, and a public walk lined with antique-style outdoor lamps winds past the inn and follows the river to Voyageur Park. Just a short drive from the inn are the National Railroad Museum, Heritage Hill State Park, Lambeau Field, and the Green Bay Packer Hall of Fame.

Location: The James Street Inn is located on the Fox River in downtown De Pere, 5 miles south of Green Bay and 100 miles north of Milwaukee. Austin Straubel International Airport is just a 10-minute drive away. De Pere is accessible via Highways 43, 41, and 29.
Function Space: 600 square feet; 1 room (breakout space available)
Capacity—Conference: 20; Reception: 30; Banquet: 20; Theater: 20
Equipment On-site: TV, VCR, overhead projector, fax, copier, modem ports, (conference calls)
Food Service: Breakfast with room; outside catering available

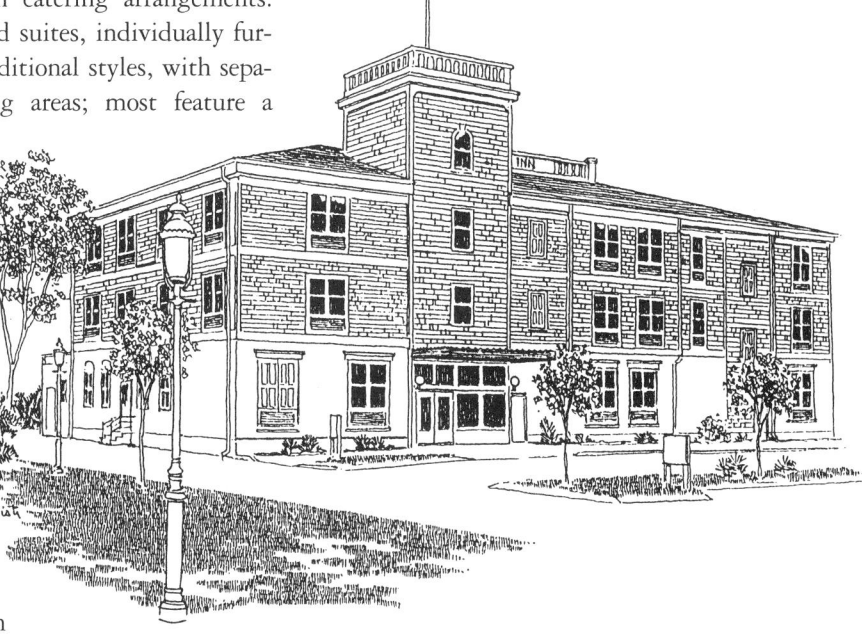

James Street Inn

The American Club
(Courtesy of Kohler Co., Kohler, Wisconsin)

Overnight Accommodations: 27 suites,
30 rooms total
Limitations/Restrictions: Restrictions on smoking
Access: Handicapped accessibility; on-site
parking; open year-round
Payment: Cash, check, credit card (AmEx,
Discover, MC, Visa), traveler's checks, direct bill

KOHLER

THE AMERICAN CLUB
Highland Drive, Kohler, WI 53044
Phone: 800-344-2838   Fax: 414/457-9441

WALTER Kohler, the son of an immigrant,
developed the Village of Kohler in 1917 as one of
the country's first planned communities, where
his company still produces plumbing fixtures and
fine furnishings. The following year, he built a
brick Tudor-style residence hall to house the
Kohler Company's immigrant workers, naming it
the American Club to encourage its early occu-

pants toward a greater appreciation for their new country. The building was refurbished and reopened in 1981 as a premier, year-round destination resort, and it quickly became known for its luxurious accommodations and holiday celebrations. Surrounded by landscaped gardens, the club boasts gracious interiors of hand-crafted woodwork and marble, and each of the elegant guest rooms features a Kohler whirlpool bath. The comprehensive and handsomely appointed meeting facilities comprise a variety of function rooms, including a 78-seat tiered amphitheater. Recreational facilities include a private health and racquet club, a full-service spa, the renowned Blackwolf Run golf course, and a 500-acre wilderness preserve with a rustic cabin retreat. Visitors are also drawn to the Village of Kohler, with its lakeside specialty shops, the Kohler Company factory tour, and the charming Waelderhaus, a replica of the Kohler family's Austrian ancestral home.

Listed in the National Register of Historic Places; member of Historic Hotels of America

Location: Kohler is one hour north of Milwaukee and two hours north of Chicago, and is accessible via I-43 (Exit 126) and Highway 23. Taxi, bus, and American Club van service available.
Function Space: 23,000 square feet; 22 rooms
Capacity—Conference: 160; Reception: 884; Banquet: 600; Theater: 998
Equipment On-site: Audiovisual department; fax, photocopier, computer service available
Food Service: Catering/food service available; nine restaurants, 24-hour room service
Overnight Accommodations: 236 rooms
Access: Handicapped accessible; on-site parking; open year-round
Payment: Billing to master accounts

LAKE GENEVA

T. C. SMITH HISTORIC INN BED AND BREAKFAST

865 Main Street, Lake Geneva, WI 53147
Phone: 414/248-1097 or 800-423-0233
Fax: 414/248-1672

In 1845, Timothy Clark Smith, a successful general merchandise shop owner and eventual Lake Geneva Village president, built his charming home combining Italianate, Greek Revival, and Victorian architectural elements. From its downtown location in this quaint resort town, the house commands a picturesque view overlooking Lake Geneva. Richly furnished with period antiques, the T. C. Smith Inn features hand-painted walls with artist John Bullock's miniature oil paintings and original trompe l'oeil, oriental carpets, and a handsome black walnut staircase. Many of the luxurious guest rooms have fireplaces, and some come with whirlpool baths; guest rates include a full breakfast, refreshments, and a morning newspaper. The courtyard offers a quiet setting amid flower gardens, neoclassic statuettes, and a goldfish pond, and the mansion's rooftop deck is relaxing as well. The parlor and dining room, decorated in the early Victorian style, are available for business and social gatherings. Located in the Lake Geneva Historic District, the T. C. Smith House is within walking distance of shopping, restaurants, museums, and entertainment, as well as the Riviera Bathing Beach, parks, and tennis courts.

Listed in the National Register of Historic Places

Location: T. C. Smith Historic Inn is 45 miles south of Milwaukee and 60 miles north of Chicago and is accessible via Highway 12 and Highway 43.

Function Space: 700 square feet; 2 rooms
Capacity—Conference: 25; Reception: 25;
Banquet: 25
Equipment On-site: TV and VCR;
phone, fax, and computer service available
Food Service: Breakfast with room;
catering/food service available; complimentary
refreshments with meetings
Overnight Accommodations: 8 rooms
Access: Limited handicapped accessibility,
on-site parking; open year-round
Payment: Credit card or call in advance
to arrange for billing

MADISON

MANSION HILL INN

424 N. Pinckney Street, Madison, WI 53703
Phone: 608/255-3999 or 800-798-9070
Fax: 608/255-2217

PERCHED high on the isthmus between Lake
Mendota and Lake Monona, the Mansion Hill Inn
occupies a prominent site in Madison's historic
Mansion Hill district. The 1858 Romanesque
Revival mansion has been restored and is now a
luxurious small hotel in the European tradition.
A four-story spiral staircase winds its way to the
belvedere and rooms above, where a sweeping
view of the capitol, the lakes, and the district's
unique architecture awaits. The carved sandstone
facade, graceful wrought-iron railings, and tall
arched windows all contribute to the inn's opulent exterior and hint of the elegant atmosphere
inside. A function room is available for small
groups for meetings and parties. Overnight
guests stay in richly appointed rooms, some with
whirlpool tubs, marble baths, skylights, and
access to the verandah. A silver-service continen-

tal-plus breakfast is brought to each guest room
in the morning, and in the afternoon complimentary spirits and refreshments are served in the
parlor. Conveniently located downtown, the inn
is just a short walk from the capitol, the university, shopping, and business and cultural centers.

Listed in the National Register of Historic Places

Location: The Mansion Hill Inn is in downtown
Madison, four blocks from the state capitol at
Gilman and Pinckney streets. The inn is accessible
via I-94, I-90 and Highways 12, 18, 51, and 151.
Dane County Regional Airport is 3 miles away.
Bus and taxi service available.
Function Space: 500 square feet; 1 room
Capacity—Conference: 18; Reception: 25;
Banquet: 11; Theater: 18
Equipment On-site: DMX, CD players; fax,
copier, modem jacks, secretarial service available
Food Service: Breakfast with room; catering
available
Overnight Accommodations: 11 rooms
Limitations/Restrictions: No smoking;
children over 12 years welcome
Access: On-site parking; open year-round
Payment: Personal or traveler's check,
credit card (AmEx, MC, Visa)

MAZOMANIE

THE OLD FEED MILL

(Mailing address)
P.O. Box 92
(Street address)
114 Cramer Street, Mazomanie, WI 53560
Phone: 608/795-4909   Fax: 608/795-4942

MAZOMANIE, a small town outside Wisconsin's state capital, was platted as a village in 1857. That year the water-powered Lynch and Walker Flouring Mill opened and began a successful business, with rye and wheat arriving from the Great Plains area and the stone-ground flour shipped by rail to Chicago and Boston. In 1992 the abandoned mill was renamed the Old Feed Mill and was once more doing a brisk business. Today the rustic mill, the oldest structure in Mazomanie's historic district, welcomes visitors to its Flouring Mill Cafe and Bakery and the Old Feed Mill Restaurant in the Rye Room. The bakery offers home-baked breads from freshly ground stone-milled flour, while the restaurant serves up hearty Midwestern meals,

including such favorites as Country Style Ribs. The Granary, the mill's airy upstairs dining room, is available for banquets, parties, receptions, and other special functions. An old-fashioned general store offers a variety of craft and gift items, and visitors will also want to take a look at the operational early-twentieth-century red flour mill on display.

Listed in the National Register of Historic Places; State of Wisconsin Historical Society Certificate of Commendation

Location: Mazomanie is 25 minutes west of Madison, one block off Highway 14. Dane County Regional Airport is 40 minutes away. Milwaukee is 1.5 hours away, and Chicago 3 hours away.
Function Space: 1,200 square feet; 1 room
Capacity—Conference: 49; Reception: 99; Banquet: 99; Theater: 99
Food Service: Lunch and dinner
Limitations/Restrictions: No smoking
Access: Handicapped accessible; on-site parking; open year-round
Payment: Cash, check, credit card (MC, Visa)

The Old Feed Mill

MILWAUKEE

THE PFISTER

424 E. Wisconsin Avenue, Milwaukee, WI 53202
Phone: 414/273-8222   Fax: 414/273-8082

GUIDO Pfister, a successful German-born tanner, never saw the completion of his dream—an opulent hotel that would serve as Milwaukee's grand salon. His son, Charles, brought the dream to fruition, and in 1893 "The Grand Hotel of the West" opened its doors. The Romanesque Revival structure claimed many unique features for its time, including an in-house electrical power plant, and it was America's first hotel with an individual thermostat in each room. Over the years the hotel has hosted numerous dignitaries and celebrities, and its acclaimed English Room has been a popular gathering place since the 1930s. Beautifully restored for its centennial celebration, the Pfister boasts a blend of baroque and rococo flourishes, radiant crystal chandeliers, high sculptured and muraled ceilings, and elegantly appointed guest rooms, while its corridors and galleries showcase the largest collection of nineteenth-century Victorian art on display in any hotel in the world. The seventh-floor state-of-the-art conference center offers a variety of hand-some meeting rooms for business and social events, while the regal Grand and Imperial Ballrooms accommodate large gatherings for special occasions. Other guest amenities include a complimentary shoe shine, a morning paper, concierge service, in-hotel shops, and an indoor rooftop pool.

Listed in the National Register of Historic Places; member of Historic Hotels of America

Location: The Pfister Hotel is located in downtown Milwaukee, 15 minutes from General Mitchell International Airport, and is accessible via I-94 and I-43.
Function Space: 24,000 square feet; 23 rooms
Capacity—Conference: 800; Reception: 1,000; Banquet: 800; Theater: 1,000
Equipment On-site: Audiovisual equipment and business services available
Food Service: Catering/food service available; three restaurants, lounge; 24-hour room service
Overnight Accommodations: 307 rooms
Limitations/Restrictions: Restrictions on smoking; no outside food service; corkage fee; no pets
Access: Handicapped accessible; on-site parking; open year-round
Payment: Cash, check, credit card

WYOMING

SARATOGA

WOLF HOTEL

(Mailing address)
P.O. Box 1298
(Street address)
101 E. Bridge, Saratoga, WY 82331
Phone: 307/326-5525

STILL the tallest building in town, the two-and-a-half-story Wolf Hotel in downtown Saratoga continues to offer "fine food and convivial atmosphere," more than a century after it opened. Built in 1893, the hotel was a stop on the C. M. Scribner–Encampment to Walcott stage line, which connected to the Union Pacific Railroad main line in Walcott. For years known as the Sisson Hotel, in 1977 the inn was remodeled, restored, and given back its original name. Today the Wolf Hotel is a regional favorite, offering quaint and comfortable guest rooms in a historic setting. The Wolf Hotel Restaurant features steak and prime rib, as well as a variety of other dishes, and the old saloon offers beverages and cigars in an atmosphere that evokes Western sporting life. Meeting space is available in the Victorian-style Saratoga Room, and at times the dining room may be used for private group functions as well. Plenty of

outdoor recreation is available in the surrounding area, and Saratoga, which sits on the banks of the North Platte River, is famous for its mineral hot springs pool, which is free and open around the clock, every day of the year.

Listed in the National Register of Historic Places

Location: The Wolf Hotel is in southern Wyoming on the Snowy Range Scenic Byway, Highway 130, 21 miles south of I-80. Shively Field, a half-mile from downtown Saratoga, is available for chartered flights; Laramie Regional Airport is 1.5 hours away, and Denver International Airport is 4 hours south.
Function Space: 700 square feet; 1 room
Capacity—Banquet: 65; Dining room: 80
Equipment On-site: TV
Food Service: On-site dining room
Overnight Accommodations: 8 rooms
Access: Handicapped accessible to main floor, not to guest rooms; open year-round
Payment: Cash, check, credit card, or direct bill

Wolf Hotel

SHERIDAN

SHERIDAN INN

(Mailing address)
P.O. Box 6393
(Street address)
856 Broadway, Sheridan, WY 82801
Phone: 307/674-5440   Fax: 307/672-6313

SOME of the Old West's most famous names, and not a few of its storied legends, are linked to the historic Sheridan Inn. The Burlington & Missouri Railroad built the inn in 1893, just a few months after the railroad came to town. With its long, horizontal facade, the three-story, 64-room hotel modeled after a hunting lodge in Scotland had a distinctive appearance. Colonel William F. "Buffalo Bill" Cody, part owner of the hotel from 1894 to 1902, would sit on the long front porch and supervise auditions for his world-famous Buffalo Bill's Wild West show. Visitors to the inn included Calamity Jane, Will Rogers, western artist Charlie Russell, Ernest Hemingway (who wrote part of *A Farewell to Arms* during his stay), and former president Herbert Hoover. The Sheridan Inn stopped operating as a hotel in 1965, but this historic building, once considered the finest hotel between Chicago and San Francisco, remains a popular gathering place and hosts a variety of events in the Wyoming Room, the Main Dining Room and Ballroom, and the Ladies Parlor. The Buffalo Bill Saloon, featuring a custom-made oak and mahogany bar that was constructed in England for the hotel, is a full-service bar serving lunch, dinner, and catered meals. The inn is open daily and is available for guided tours.

National Historic Landmark; listed in the National Register of Historic Places

Location: The Sheridan Inn is located in north central Wyoming and is accessible via I-90.
Function Space: 4,150 square feet; 3 rooms
Capacity—Conference: 300; Reception: 250; Banquet: 400; Theater: 200
Equipment On-site: Portable sound/stage panel, equipment rental available; photocopy, secretarial, on-line services available
Food Service: Lunch, dinner, and catering available; saloon and service bar
Limitations/Restrictions: Restrictions on smoking; in-house food service only
Access: Handicapped accessible; on-site parking; open year-round
Payment: Cash, check, major credit card

INDEX

SUBJECT INDEX

BOATS & SHIPS
Grand Banks Fishing Schooner, *Adventure*, MA, 154
Texas Seaport Museum/the ship *Elissa*, TX, 295

CHURCHES
Amana Community Church, IA, 110
Old Ship Meetinghouse, The, MA, 155
Silver Spring Presbyterian Church, PA, 253

COLLEGES & UNIVERSITIES
Hollins College, VA, 336
Marietta College, OH, 238
Meadow Brook Hall (Oakland University),
    MI, 173
Ralston Hall (College of Notre Dame), CA, 12
Sweet Briar College, VA, 339

CONFERENCE CENTERS & RETREATS
Airlie Center, VA, 340
Albert G. Brock Conference Center, The, MA, 160
Arden House, NY, 215
Bates Mansion at Brook Farm, VT, 311
Belmont Manor House and Meeting Facility,
    MD, 137
Berkley Center, The, NC, 229
Breckinridge Public Affairs Center of Bowdoin
    College, ME, 129
Evins Mill Retreat, TN, 281
Graylyn International Conference Center, NC, 232
Historic Rugby, TN, 280
Shaker Village of Pleasant Hill, KY, 117
Tarrytown House Executive Conference Center,
    NY, 226
Troutbeck, NY, 210

CULTURAL & CIVIC CENTERS
(Including community centers, public and private halls,
and government and office buildings)
Academy of Medicine, GA, 84
Boca Raton Historical Society, Town Hall, FL, 72
Boston Center for the Arts, MA, 142
Carpenters' Hall, PA, 257
Castle Green, The, CA, 25
Dranesville Tavern, VA, 323
Garten Verein Dancing Pavilion, TX, 292
Gorton Community Center, IL, 104
Historic Harrisburg Resource Center, PA, 251
Historic Thomas Center, FL, 73
Honeywell Center, IN, 109
National Trust for Historic Preservation, DC, 65
Old Government House, The, GA, 86
Old Post Office, The, DC, 67
Old State Capitol, LA, 120
Old State House, CT, 46
Phoenix Room of Newburyport, The, MA, 162
Remembrance Hall, IL, 106
Salt Lake City and County Building, UT, 302
Sky Ballroom, The (Megahertz Building), MT, 187
Southern Cultural Heritage Complex, MS, 181
Struthers Library Theatre, PA, 263
Washington County Historic Courthouse, MN, 177

ESTATES, HISTORIC HOUSES, & HOUSE MUSEUMS
1409 Sutter, CA, 29
Aldredge House, The, TX, 287
American Horticultural Society River Farm,
    VA, 317
Andalusia, PA, 246
Arts Club of Washington, DC, 57

MUSEUMS & GALLERIES